MW01039976

CHARLES CHURCHYARD

NATIONAL
LIES

The Truth About American Values

Axroide Publishing

Axroide Publishing
P. O. Box 390034
Cambridge, MA 02139

www.axroide.com

Cataloging-in-Publication Data

Churchyard, Charles.
National Lies: The Truth About American Values / Charles Churchyard.

p. cm.

Includes bibliographical references and index.

ISBN 978-0-9815716-4-5

1. National characteristics, American. 2. Social Values–United States.
3. United States–Civilization–Philosophy. 4. Individualism–United States.
5. Conformity–United States. I. Title.

E169.1.C454

973–dc22

2008922546

in honor of
Friedrich Nietzsche

"Kein Hirt und eine Herde! Jeder will das Gleiche, jeder ist gleich: wer anders fühlt, geht freiwillig ins Irrenhaus." (*Also Sprach Zarathustra.* Prologue, 5.)

"Sie haben die Tugend jetzt ganz und gar für sich in Pacht genommen, diese Schwachen und Heillos-Krankhaften, daran ist kein Zweifel: wir allein sind die Guten, die Gerechten, so sprechen sie, wir allein sind die homines bonae voluntatis." (*Zur Genealogie der Moral.* III, 14)

"…ihr Psychologen…treibt Vivisektion am 'guten Menschen,' am 'homo bonae voluntatis'—an euch!" (*Jenseits von Gut und Böse.* 218)

CONTENTS

Introduction: Sonny Then and Sonny Now

A good many years ago—it must have been during the late 1950s—I happened to be present at a meeting between a senior executive of a European company and an American company's sales representative. The latter was very much younger than the former, but he was a rising star in his organization. "One of our best men," his divisional manager remarked. "I just wish the others had half his drive."

"Call me Sonny. Everybody does," were the first words out of the American's mouth, and he wasted no time in getting down to business. "Our company is twice the size of our nearest competitor in the States, but we're not satisfied with that, by no means." Saying this, he proceeded to plunge into the details of what he had on offer for a prospective European customer.

His grasp of the material was impressive. Not only did he understand thoroughly and comprehensively the workings of his own company, he was also knowledgeable about the firm whose business he hoped to attract, and he skillfully pointed out the many profitable advantages it could obtain from buying his products.

But this was not all. As he talked on, it became apparent that his interest in the entire transaction went far beyond the ordinary. In his mind, he was involved in something bigger and more important than two businessmen trying to make a deal or two businesses trying to make money.

"It's about the future," he exclaimed at one point. "It's about a better way of life. We are bringing people things they've never had before." He sounded as if he were a missionary of American prosperity to the rest of the world.

The target of his proselytizing was a conservative and somewhat elderly gentleman, who found himself at a loss as to how he should respond. On the one hand, he could perceive the accuracy and persuasiveness of the facts that Sonny was presenting. On the other, he was disconcerted, even repelled, by the brash, insistent manner in which they were being presented. "At moments, I thought I was face-to-face with a religious fanatic," he said later. The best he could do now was to venture a few tentative and ambiguous comments.

Sonny perceived the hesitation and decided that he needed to try even harder. By nature he was what American businessmen approvingly call "aggressive," and he became more so. He played high, describing the benefits, not just for the other company and for the community where it was located, but for the entire nation and even for humanity in general. He played low, offering extras (special bonuses, discounts, guarantees), if only his customer would say yes on the spot. Then he went for broke. With a final barrage of argument and appeal, he produced a written contract, ready to be signed, and pushed it across the table. The European stood up, unable to conceal his disgust, and the meeting was over.

Although this happened long ago, I have never been able to forget Sonny's spectacular performance, topped off at the end by his look of astonished incredulity when he realized that he had failed. He had put forth a tremendous effort, as if he genuinely believed that involved in this one business negotiation were, not only his personal reputation, the success of his company, and the prestige of America, but also the future of a foreign company and its country, as well as the world at large. If the deal had gone through, all these parties would, in his view, have taken a step forward. Since it had not, they had all taken a step backward.

As I grew older, and my experiences in the New World increased, I came to realize that Sonny was not some prodigy of nature but a commonplace American phenomenon in an exaggerated form. His

countrymen regarded as desirable and advantageous the personal characteristics that made him conspicuous, and most of them in fact possessed
these qualities, though in much smaller amounts.

Among the Europeans in the organization where he had suffered
that one unexpected defeat, his name became a byword. They would
speak of "meeting another Sonny" in tones, not just of distaste, but
also of grudging admiration. However much it pained them to do so,
they had to admit that, working together, such people were capable of
astonishing efficiency and accomplishment. One manager even exclaimed
in a moment of exasperation, "What chance does the Old World have
against a nation of Sonnys?"

I shared in the general feeling of uncomfortable bewilderment, but I
was not satisfied merely to shrug or sneer and leave it at that. I wanted
to learn how all this had come about. How had America become the
richest and most powerful country in the world? What made a person
like Sonny tick? These questions remained in my mind, and slowly,
casually, randomly—in the early stages, without even conscious effort
or deliberate intention—I began to look for answers.

Through the years, from personal experience and desultory reading,
I collected information and tried to make sense of it, grouping together
similar phenomena and linking causes with effects. At first, all was
confusing and uncertain, but gradually the contours of a theory began
to emerge. They eventually coalesced into what I have called "the
American formula," the two halves of which form the first two parts
of the present book.

I had just begun to work in earnest on my project, when the 1990s
arrived and along with them the phenomenon known as "political correctness." It apparently started on the campus, but it quickly spread
through public life and invaded the corporate world. In the company
where I worked, all employees, including the executives, were required to
attend special counseling sessions, where they were warned that a casual
derogatory remark about women, black people, or some other "protected
minority" might result in their being fired or at least subjected to a
ritual of humiliating apology and a demeaning program of reeducation,

sensitization, and "consciousness raising." It was no empty threat. During those years, the national or local news would feature from time to time some prominent person who had run into serious trouble on this account, and there were many more victims who were too lowly to attract public attention.

Foreign observers tended to regard the entire business as crazy and inexplicable. Some dismissed it all as nothing more than a passing fad. Adapting Macaulay's famous remark, one cynical Englishman commented that the Yanks were just having another of their periodic fits of moral self-righteousness. But I felt there was more to it than that. Beneath the ludicrous trivialities of political correctness, I sensed larger and more significant forces at work.

It was during those years that I met Sonny once again. I happened to make his acquaintance outside of business, and we struck up a casual friendship. He had changed with the passage of time. Gone was a large part of his buoyant energy and optimism. Although he had enjoyed a prosperous career, he had not risen as high as he had desired and expected. Now he was close to retirement.

One day we ran into each other at a club, and in the course of a meandering conversation I mentioned the research I was doing and the book I hoped to write. "National character?" he asked in a mildly interested but puzzled tone of voice. "National culture? National values? Do you really think such things exist? I mean, aren't we all different? Isn't America a country of diverse peoples?" I had heard this idea many times before. It had settled in as an article of faith with the prevailing climate of opinion in the 1990s, when it received concise expression in the popular dictum, "All we have in common is our diversity."

I was taken aback to find that such a notion had penetrated as far as the consciousness of someone like Sonny, who repeated it as if it were an accepted platitude. But he had another, much bigger surprise in store for me. At that moment, his wife joined us. She had evidently had a drink or two over her limit, for she was unusually voluble. A magazine she happened to have in her hand displayed the title of an article, "One of Every Three Women Sexually Abused as Children." I pointed to it and remarked that it was absurd.

"But I was sexually abused as a child," she retorted. I was too astonished to reply, and she went on, explaining that she had been undergoing "recovered memory" therapy, which revealed to her that the seemingly innocent attentions of an uncle had in fact been a sexual assault and that, as an automatic and subconscious psychological defense against something so terrible, she had suppressed the memory of it. Regaining something of my composure, I ventured to suggest that the source of what she called a recovered memory might in fact have been prompting from her therapist rather than anything she had actually experienced. But this only caused her to become more insistent that it had all been true, unquestionably.

What amazed me was not so much her conviction—airhead that she was—but the reaction of Sonny. He supported everything she said with approving nods. When I expressed my doubts, he countered with an emphatic assertion that his wife was right. "You don't realize how often this kind of thing happens to children," he declared in a tone of characteristic finality.

"Well, what about you?" I asked in a half-embarrassed, half-humorous way. "Did you abuse your nieces or, heaven forbid, your daughters?" My astonishment—already at a high level—rose by perceptible degrees during the seconds that he hesitated. At last, in a voice of troubled doubt, he replied, "I don't know. I hope I didn't."

Once again, I tried to dismiss the idea of recovered memory as a bogus contrivance. "Does it seem likely," I wondered, "that a person could be involved in the violation of one of the most fundamental human taboos and then simply forget about it?" But Sonny rejected this exculpation out of hand. He adamantly maintained his belief in both the certainty of his wife's victimization and the possibility of his own guilt. To have done otherwise, he seemed to think, was to be deficient in realistic perception and moral rectitude. It was to be "in denial," that is, unwilling to confront the sins of the world as well as one's own personal failings.

At this point, I excused myself on some pretext or other and made my exit. Although Sonny and I continued to see each other occasionally, it was no longer with the old ease and nonchalance. Our conversations were awkward, and they became increasingly brief and infrequent. But Sonny, it turned out, had one last surprise in store for me.

Shortly after the terrorist attacks of September 11, we happened to meet for what turned out to be the last time. As I expected, he expressed all the conventional sentiments: revulsion at the carnage and destruction, sympathy for the deceased and their families, insistence that the perpetrators be apprehended and brought to justice. Then he paused. He had something more to say, but he felt uncomfortable saying it. At last he got it out.

"I realize there are millions of people living in miserable poverty all over the world. That must breed fanaticism and hatred. The United States with all its wealth and power is an obvious target for them. Of course, that doesn't excuse what they did. But I can't help feeling that we bear some degree of responsibility. American foreign policy hasn't always done what it should. American corporations abroad haven't always behaved as they ought to." Then, after a moment of hesitation, he added, "We haven't always done the right thing at home, either. Inequality is everywhere. You know this is a deeply racist society."

He fell uncharacteristically silent, and once again I stood amazed. What Sonny had said was a reflection—even if a weak reflection—of what was being said on the political left, particularly in the better colleges and universities. I would have expected him to dismiss such ideas out of hand as irrational and derisory, if he had bothered to take notice of them at all.

After we had parted, I could not help thinking of the contrast between what Sonny had been some forty years ago and what he was now. Where had his tremendous confidence and optimism gone? How had it come about that he could now entertain the most fundamental doubts about himself and his country? It was as if he had become a different person— Sonny Then transformed into Sonny Now.[1] And since Sonny was such an exemplary type, I could ask the same questions about America. Despite a half-century's increase in power and prosperity, why had the nation gone from the self-assurance of the 1950s to the uncertainty and guilt of the 1990s? The last two parts of this book attempt to find the answers, in light of the theory expounded in the first two parts.

THE AMERICAN FORMULA I: MOTIVATIONAL IDEALS

CHAPTER ONE

An Egalitarian People and Their Enigma

—1—

The Founding Fathers of the United States began with great hopes and expectations for the future. They believed the citizens of their new republic could attain a higher level of personal and public behavior, as well as acquire more refined and elevated tastes. Reflecting the prevailing views of their time, they assumed this would come about under the leadership and influence of what they called "a natural aristocracy"—not an aristocracy composed merely of men with high birth and much wealth, but one that contained persons conspicuous for high talent and moral virtue, who would occupy the positions of government, establish the tone of society, and set the standards of conduct both public and private.

One Founding Father who espoused these ideas with notable warmth, pertinacity, and imagination was Thomas Jefferson. He was acutely aware of how far his provincial countrymen fell short. His letters complained about such things as loutish manners displayed at public assemblies or music sunk in a "state of deplorable barbarism." But he was confident of the future. Unlike his more prudent and skeptical contemporaries, he entertained no doubts as to the latent capacities of the common people.

"Under our democratic stimulants," he declared in a typical burst of optimism, "every man" of later generations will be "potentially an athlete in body and an Aristotle in mind."[1]

Such were the notions of Jefferson and the Founders. Ordinary Americans of the time were heading in a much different direction. Far from aspiring to noble pursuits and lofty virtues, they were obsessively involved in a general scramble for money. "Society is full of excitement," one of the panegyrists of the emerging generation later declared. "Some are sinking, others rising, others balancing," some inching toward the top, others plunging toward the bottom. Multitudes were migrating westward in search of better economic opportunities in the recently opened territories. One French visitor marveled at their willingness to endure the privations and dangers of the frontier in their pursuit of wealth and called it nothing less than "heroic."[2]

As roads and turnpikes were constructed in the 1790s, then canals in the 1820s, and finally railroads in the 1830s, the flow of merchandise quickened and spread, and the buying and selling increased. New words were coined to describe the people and their activities: "businessman" (1820s) and "self-made man" (1830s). A German immigrant described the country as "one gigantic workshop" with a sign over its entrance: "No admission here except on business."[3]

As commerce grew in popularity and practice, the moral standards that regulated it became increasingly weak and elastic. Since nearly everyone believed they should be making money, many decided that to do so they could employ whatever means were available. From the egalitarian assumption that any legal occupation was reputable, it was a small step to the conclusion that any enterprise which returned a profit without violating the letter of the law was permissible, if not laudable. Foreign visitors, especially from France, remarked at the nonchalance with which Americans treated bankruptcy. In Europe, a single failure of this kind stained a man's reputation for life. In the United States, it was considered little more than a temporary setback and an occasional misfortune, one of the common hazards of a business career.[4]

The line that separated shrewd and sharp dealing from outright fraud was not one that Americans drew with any precision. Along with the growth of free enterprise came a proliferation of swindling, which was reflected in the simultaneous popularity of two newly invented nouns, "businessman" and "confidence man." "Man...was made to diddle," declared a struggling author in a disquisition on one of several contemporary synonyms for a common practice. This was indeed true of the American, foreign observers agreed, often in tones of indignation and disgust. According to the complaint of one Scotsman, "Quackery and bold pretension in every form meet with extraordinary encouragement and success."[5]

Far from deploring such behavior, Americans regarded it with amusement and even admiration. They enjoyed hearing about the ingenious ways by which some of their more enterprising countrymen managed to separate people from their money. Stories of clever frauds were widely circulated and eagerly repeated. P. T. Barnum, the prince of tricksters, managed to turn the hoax into a form of public entertainment. It was said that after he had humbugged an audience, they willingly paid him to explain how he had done it.[6]

The Founding Fathers who lived long enough to witness these practices were not in the least amused. They were revolted to see what the rising generation of Americans had become, not high-minded and virtuous, but moneygrubbing and often dishonest. Among the voices of complaint, Thomas Jefferson's was prominent. In 1813, he warned of the advance of "commercial avarice and corruption." By 1819, he was speaking of "a general demoralization" in which fraud was "filching from industry its honest earnings."[7]

The young nation paid no more heed to Jefferson and his disillusioned contemporaries than it did to its foreign critics. The passion for profit that it exhibited in the beginning became a settled characteristic of its maturity and has persisted to the present day. According to popular opinion in the 1830s, the first question a Yankee asked himself whenever he made a new acquaintance was whether the two of them could agree to some business deal. A century and a half later, a Swiss banker admitted that he could not meet an American, "even a tourist," without thinking, "What is he going to try to sell me?"[8]

In 1795, a visiting French aristocrat learned that the highest praise one American could bestow upon another was "clever fellow, damned sharp." In 1842, an English novelist reported with some asperity that being considered a "smart man" excused the worst behavior. Then as now, Americans take it for granted that a person will apply whatever brainpower he can muster to the task of acquiring money. Consequently, the more money he has, the more intelligent he must be, and the reverse. This assumption underlies that time-honored retort, "If you're so smart, how come you ain't rich?" as well as the acerbic observation by a modern American economist that "wealth, in even the most improbable cases, manages to convey the aspect of intelligence."[9]

In addition to flexible moral principles, American business from the outset has been characterized by blunt and coarse manners. Since making money was an activity in which so much of the population took so active a part, the accepted tone of behavior settled at a level that was low enough to accommodate most everyone. Businessmen are in a hurry. They want to close a deal and get on to the next one. They have no time for elaborate courtesies, subtle procedures, or lengthy sociable talk. Often they strike the pose and employ the language of rampant lower-class egotism. "Aggressive" selling, for example, is viewed as forthright, virile, and efficacious.

Such behavior is not acceptable in Europe and other traditional societies. There the brash, pushy American is rejected as an ill-bred intruder. He finds, to his great surprise, that even though he has the best product at the lowest price, he may fail to win the contract. He does not realize that who makes an offer and the way in which it is made are fully as important as the substance of the offer itself, if not more so. Things are different in the United States. Not all or even most American businessmen are low and vulgar themselves, but they will tolerate lowness and vulgarity from others in the process of doing business. As a book on international commercial practices remarked, "When there's money to be made, Americans will forgive anyone just about anything." One might call it equality before the dollar.[10]

—◆—

A similar course of development occurred in the world of politics. The Founding Fathers believed most definitely in government "for the people," to some degree in government "by the people," but not at all in government "of the people." They thought that the people should select those of the social elite who would do the governing. This was the idea behind Thomas Jefferson's well-known and apparently puzzling statement that he would rather have "newspapers without a government" than "a government without newspapers." He saw the role of newspapers as that of educating the public, so that they would select the best candidates for office and not be led astray by ignorance and demagogy.[11]

The idea of government by a natural aristocracy did not survive the Founding Fathers. By the time their generation had retired from political life, it had become a widely accepted opinion that every man had the right, not only to vote, but to be a candidate, even for the presidency. A popular platitude asserted that anyone who was able to manage a private household could adequately discharge the duties of office. The general public believed that they would be genuinely represented only by those who were like themselves, not by those who were their superiors.[12]

Andrew Jackson embodied the new traits of political leadership. During his tenure, the White House was open to a stream of uncouth visitors, and the president went out of his way to greet and converse amiably with the most humble of his fellow citizens. His wealthy and socially prominent opponents, the Whigs, saw the way the tide was moving, adopted the tactics of the Democratic Party, and put forward candidates like Davy Crockett and William Henry Harrison as plain men of the people. An English novelist who was visiting America at the time claimed that the slightest display of superiority, from building too grand a house to wearing too luxurious a coat, could lose an election. By 1842, a wealthy Philadelphian asserted that to be successful a politician had to "drink and roar and talk roughly."[13]

Posing as just an ordinary person—"an ordinary Joe"—has become one of the most common techniques employed in contests for public office. Presidents Eisenhower and Reagan were prominent masters of it, but it is something in which every candidate has had to display at least a basic degree of competence. At times the requirements can be quite exacting. Not just revealing cultural sophistication or displaying urbane suavity but merely being too articulate can lose votes. When running for president in 1996, Bob Dole found that he had to make a deliberate effort to curb his brilliant wit because the public disliked someone who was so obviously far above the common standard of clumsy speech.[14]

Not merely the style of leadership but the entire character of political life underwent a fundamental change during the first half of the Nineteenth Century. The Founding Fathers had thought that those who devoted themselves to public service should stand above material gain and partisan rivalry and should promote the highest interests of the entire nation. For the successors of the Founding Fathers, in contrast, politics became simply a job, and not a very elevated one. It centered around the operations of newly developed party machinery, which ran campaigns and divided up the spoils of victory. The issues that dominated most elections were, not high principles of state or the clash of social ideologies, but conflicting financial interests and rival personalities.

This jostling of low people with low manners intent on low purposes naturally depressed the level of political discourse. During the last years of their lives, the Founding Fathers were dismayed at the increasingly loud and numerous voices of petty and dirty squabbling. Thomas Jefferson, the former champion of newspapers, expressed himself in pained and pungent terms as to the sordid practices of the contemporary press and recommended prosecutions for libel as a corrective. A few years later, the French aristocrat Alexis de Tocqueville recoiled in disgust from partisan journalism that shamelessly invaded the private lives of its opponents and broadcast the vilest insults and slanders.[15]

The tenor of public life and the tenure of public office reached their nadir in the second half of the Nineteenth Century, when Mark Twain called Congress the only "distinctly native American criminal class," and an officer of President Grant's cabinet exclaimed, "You can't use tact with a congressman! A congressman is a hog! You must take a stick and hit him on the snout!"[16] Things improved somewhat in the Progressive Era with the appearance of outstanding statesmen like Theodore Roosevelt and Woodrow Wilson. But politics has continued to retain its shabby reputation. Politicians know this, and one of their favorite tactics is to denounce government whenever they are running for government office, to claim that they themselves are not hardened politicos but honest ordinary citizens serving the public interest, and to profess that they are strangers to the insider culture of bureaucratic boondoggles and backroom deals.

Serenity and loftiness characterized the religion of the Founding Fathers. They believed that man's utilization of his higher faculties (such as the exercise of reason and meditation, the practice of science, the contemplation of art, the performance of music) led to a deeper understanding of God and his works, as well as to better conduct in one's personal life and better treatment of one's fellow creatures. In establishing religious freedom for the nation, the Founding Fathers assumed that their own principles and practices would be adopted and advanced by the rest of the citizenry. Thomas Jefferson confidently predicted that "there is not a young man now living in the United States who will not die a Unitarian"—the most cerebral and rarefied of the major contemporary denominations.[17]

The American people, especially the young, seized their religious freedom and began behaving in ways that were not in the least serene and lofty. They had no use for science or art, for subtle argument or rational persuasion. It was raw emotion and wild vision that they desired and exhibited, with anyone who experienced what he took to be divine inspiration claiming the right to interpret the Bible and to preach publicly. A trained theologian asserting a superior understanding of scripture from his knowledge of Greek and Hebrew was as much an anathema in this egalitarian world as the son of a wealthy landowner asserting that his privileged upbringing entitled him to public office.[18]

Inventiveness and ignorance combined to produce a farrago of doctrines (often dubious) and rituals (often bizarre). Sects sprang up, multiplied, and subdivided. Members of one group quarreled with those of another, and at times the rivalry became so intense as to result in physical violence. "All Christendom has been decomposed," exclaimed a contemporary in bewilderment and dismay, "broken in pieces" by the "fiery furnace of democracy."[19]

This new religious tendency had a blatantly social and collective nature. It spread by contagion, and those infected were said to have "got religion," just as one "got" a communicable disease. A customer at a tailor's shop in the 1820s, for example, found his new coat was not ready because "the principal workmen had got religion that morning and could not finish it."[20] People gathered in groups, both indoors ("protracted meetings") and outdoors ("camp meetings"), under the leadership of preachers with a single qualification for the business at hand. They were often poorly educated and occasionally even illiterate, but they knew how to move a crowd and to galvanize its members into uninhibited, physical acts of repentance and ecstasy. At a large camp meeting during its livelier moments, people in various motions (jumping, jerking, whirling, dancing, running, falling, rolling) combined with the noises they made (groaning, sobbing, singing, shouting, screaming, howling, barking) to create a scene of weltering turmoil and uproarious pandemonium.

Foreign visitors, along with many respectable Americans, were appalled. Especially offensive was the sight of women, who often outnumbered men as participants, venting their intimate emotions in public. Jefferson was among those who condemned both the "fanaticism" in general and in particular the unmistakably "amatory and carnal" overtones in the female professions of faith.[21] He had a personal grievance as well. The establishment of the University of Virginia, a project on which he had labored hard and long, nearly came to grief when a key appointment to the faculty, made at his personal urging, was condemned as hostile to religion.

Many of the clergymen in the settled parishes of traditional denominations felt an acute distaste for the new forms of worship. But they realized that these were widely popular and were growing. People wanted an exciting religion, not "corpse-cold Unitarianism," and in this democratic society, where a minister's livelihood depended on the voluntary contributions of the churchgoers rather than a state subsidy for an "established" religion, it was apparent that the people would get their way.[22]

Eventually an informal compromise evolved. Clergymen permitted, encouraged, and even conducted more animated services, while charismatic preachers restrained the more frenzied and grotesque actions of their audiences. People from the higher levels of society began to attend and to promote "revivals," as they had come to be called. Rich and powerful Whigs, in the same way that they adopted the popular style of the common man as a candidate for office, also embraced popular religion as a useful and effective ingredient in their political campaigns. Through the course of the Nineteenth Century, sects that began as bands of enthusiasts slowly grew into organized and orderly denominations. During the Twentieth Century, the excesses of the camp meeting and the hellfire sermon were pushed to the margins of social life.

But religion in the United States has continued to retain some distinct marks of its low origins. Just as American businessmen and politicians have often resorted to underhanded methods of accumulating for themselves the goods of the world, so have American preachers. With the rise of revivalist religion, persons of modest origins who had an aptitude for charismatic persuasion found that they were able to become successful evangelists, and some of them went on to employ their new status and effective talent in the extraction of money and sex from their followers. Sinclair Lewis's novel *Elmer Gantry* is the classic depiction of a familiar type that has persisted to the present day. The sexual and financial scandals that ended the careers of several famous televangelists in the 1980s were a spectacular example of something that often happens, with less publicity, to the shepherds of smaller flocks.

Doctrines, as well as the practices, have reflected demotic tendencies. As one literary critic admitted with a sigh, "Most American religion, of whatever camp…is viciously anti-intellectual." His regret is echoed by that of one rare sophisticate among the devout: "I wish I lived in a world where it was possible to be religious and think at the same time."[23]

The churches of Europe long ago accepted the theory of evolution, since the subtlety of trained theologians has managed to reconcile the discoveries of Darwin with the teachings of faith. Believers in the United States do not follow educated theological leadership, perhaps any more now than in the past. Their ideas of human and cosmic creation express the crudest kind of Biblical literalism, which rejects contrary scientific evidence out of hand. Opinion polls consistently show that about half the national population thinks God created the earth and mankind within the past 10,000 years. One study in Minnesota found that 40 percent of high school biology instructors did not teach evolution, because either the local community rejected it or they did themselves, or both.[24]

The Founding Fathers wanted to elevate all aspects of cultural life and to promote the social education and personal cultivation that would bring this about. Thomas Jefferson was especially active in the effort. He devised a plan for selecting talented poor boys and schooling them at public expense, a process that he described as raking the geniuses "from the rubbish."[25] His chief labor in the years after his presidency was to found the University of Virginia, which he imagined would become the training ground for a natural aristocracy of ability and virtue.

But the egalitarian trend of the nation was moving in a different direction. It had been Jefferson himself who declared that if one presented "a moral case to a ploughman and a professor, the former will decide it as well, and often better than the latter, because he has not been led astray by artificial rules." Jefferson's fellow countrymen simply extended this democratic principle from the sphere of ethics to every other aspect of life. Already in 1771, a clergyman in Philadelphia observed that "the poorest laborer...thinks himself entitled to deliver his sentiments in matters of religion and politics with as much freedom as the gentleman or the scholar." By the first decades of the Nineteenth Century, notions about the worth of the common man and the value of his opinions were well on their way to becoming part of the national ideology.[26]

It was based on the premise that every human being possessed innate, natural faculties which were fully equal, if not superior, to those produced by deliberate nurture and external influence. This meant that on any subject the judgment of an uncultivated and unlearned man was equal to that of a cultivated and learned one, and it followed that on any occasion a majority of ordinary citizens was superior to an elite minority. "The public is wiser than its wisest critic," proclaimed one ardent theoretician of the new democracy. "It is impossible that everybody should be mistaken," asserted a character in a contemporary novel.[27]

These stated principles reflected assumptions that the American people were already putting into practice. Anything above the taste or beyond the comprehension of the common man was denounced as "aristocratic" and dismissed as worthless if not pernicious. The legislature of North Carolina, for example, refused to fund a university on the ground that it would create "an aristocracy of the learned." Education beyond the elementary knowledge of reading, writing, and arithmetic was ridiculed as "obsolete monkish bigotry." Even the professions, like law and medicine, did not escape attack. Restricting their practice to those with degrees and licenses was condemned as an underhanded way of increasing the profits of the practitioners, who were charged with confusing and exploiting the public by a screen of obscurantism and obfuscation.[28]

People with cultivated tastes or professional credentials reacted with indignation and dismay. One college president exclaimed in exasperation that he expected to see the publication of books with titles such as, "Every Man His Own Lawyer," "Every Man His Own Physician," and "Every Man His Own Clergyman and Confessor." Thomas Jefferson, who throughout his life had endeavored to introduce his countrymen to the best of European culture, was taken aback at the younger generation's rejecting "the information of books" and "the knowledge acquired in past ages." They acted as if they "acquire all learning in their mothers' womb and bring it into the world ready-made." He consoled himself with the conviction that they were just passing through a phase of youthful folly.[29]

Jefferson subsequently had the misfortune to encounter the ignorance and intractability of American adolescents in a particularly aggressive form, although it was not at all unusual for college life of those times. A group of students at his University of Virginia put on disguises and publicly expressed xenophobic contempt for those among their professors who happened to be foreigners. The noisy demonstration culminated in the youths exchanging blows with faculty members. When an assembly was held on campus a few days later, it required the intimidating presence of three former presidents of the United States (Jefferson, Madison, and Monroe) to induce the culprits to confess. Jefferson was additionally distressed and embarrassed to find one of his own relatives among the guilty.[30]

Mistrust of anything and everything above the level of ordinary understanding has developed into a distinctive national characteristic. Claims of experts and expertise provoke initial skepticism rather than automatic deference. Even in a highly practical field like agriculture, scientific innovations and educated technicians have had to fight their way to recognition and respect against popular prejudice and suspicion.[31]

In fields that produce no obvious or immediate social benefits, the going has been much rougher. From the beginning, Americans stigmatized the arts as useless, snobbish, and effeminate—the occupation of unproductive "aristocrats" and society women. People with aesthetic tastes learned to conceal them if they wanted to get along in daily life. Conditions have hardly changed with the passage of well over a century and a half. Compared with European nations, the United States government today spends a minute portion of its budget on high culture. The National Endowment for the Arts receives less funding than the marching bands of the armed services.[32]

To counteract the disparagement of their fellow countrymen, many artists have cultivated a pose of aggressive lower-class masculinity. Hemingway was the most prominent example in this line, but others, like Jack London, had preceded him, and many more have followed. A similar, less combative stance might be called Whitmanesque, in which the writer demonstrates that he is no refined connoisseur or exclusive elitist by accepting and celebrating everything low and commonplace. Being able to boast of lower-class origins and experience is a great advantage. Before achieving recognition for his poetry and short stories, one author worked a number of menial jobs, which prompted a critic to comment that "most writers would give a right arm for such authentic redneck credentials," as if the experience of low life were an asset rather than a liability to someone creating high art.[33]

In recent decades, the practitioners of elevated culture have found refuge in colleges and universities. As an increasingly complex techno-logical society demands more specialized knowledge and more trained specialists, the resulting boom in higher education has been so great as to include even those areas of intellect with little or no claim to practical application. It has been said that there are more poets and philosophers at work on American campuses today than there have ever been in the entire world at any other time. This is not the result of an increase in the public appetite for such forms of thought and literature. On the contrary, the audience of poets and philosophers is largely confined to their colleagues and students. Their work attracts as little notice from people outside the field as if it were the product of some esoteric scientific specialty.

While high culture survives in its artificial and isolated situation, American popular culture has gone from triumph to triumph. So pow-erful and pervasive is its appeal, it has penetrated even the higher social levels. People with pretensions of sophistication and superiority used to complain that they were unable to shield their children from its influence. In recent years, they have given up the struggle and embraced the former enemy. The interminable lamentation about "mass culture," which was heard during the 1950s, has ceased long ago. The old snob appeal has faded, if not entirely disappeared. It used to be the customary practice of certain people (upper-middle-class people in particular, who want to distinguish themselves from the rest of the middle class) to affect an interest in the fine arts. Today their new tactic is to applaud the kind of pop art that is low or weird enough to bewilder and repel ordinary middle-class squares.

Among the various forms of popular culture, sports command the most attention, the strongest allegiance, and the most sustained devotion. It is something that almost all Americans—at least almost all American men—at every level in society follow with avid delight. It provides a subject of ready conversation for those, like blacks and whites, who have little else in common. It has enlivened ordinary talk, especially in the business world, with numerous metaphors and similes. Its shared knowledge is taken so confidently for granted that soldiers on the battlefront have used it to distinguish friend from foe.[34]

Since both sports and education are activities of youth, the two have naturally come into contact, and the result has been distinctively American. In the entrance hall of a typical high school, a case of athletic trophies is on display; there are no trophies for academic achievement. The popular author James Michener recalled that the grown-ups of his hometown often praised him for his performance on the school basketball team; no one praised him for his equally outstanding scholastic performance. That was in the 1920s, and after the passage of over half a century, Michener concluded that "across America things are not much different." This was recently confirmed—if confirmation were needed—by a journalist who contrasted the celebration lavished on inner-city boys who become sports stars with the public's indifference to those who succeed academically.[35]

When athletics encountered education at the college level in the late Nineteenth Century, Ambrose Bierce summed up the outcome in his *Devil's Dictionary:* "Academe, an ancient school where morality and philosophy were taught. Academy (from academe), a modern school where football is taught." James Michener pointed out that nowhere else in the world do institutions of higher education provide sports events for the entertainment of the public. Although the scholarly side of universities became increasingly important in the second half of the Twentieth Century as the source of technical knowledge and technicians, sports has continued to hold its own on campus. A top coach often receives a higher salary than the college president. At some public universities, he makes more than the governor of the state.[36]

Even posthumously, the life of the mind is judged inferior to the life of the body. There is a special kind of insurance adjustor who puts a dollar value on the victim in a case of wrongful death, which then may go before a jury. Various characteristics of the victim's former existence can move the estimate up or down. A journalist who interviewed one of these adjustors suggested himself as a hypothetical example and mentioned his "culturally rich" background. "Culture doesn't make a difference," replied the adjustor. Juries have no sympathy for people "who stay home and read." But if he had been "an outdoorsman," his "value would double."[37]

———•———

A gentleman in the Eighteenth Century was supposed to display an unaffected grace of deportment, as well as the poise, dignity, and self-possession that made him "equally at home among lords or gamblers."[38] It was this combination of strength and finesse that Lord Chesterfield recommended repeatedly to his hapless son with the famous phrase *suaviter in modo, fortiter in re.* The Founding Fathers were themselves eighteenth-century gentlemen—or at least their provincial equivalents and imitators. When they talked about improving manners, they had the ideals of the English upper class in mind. In their vision of the new republic, a natural aristocracy would assume the role of social as well as political leadership and by its example would point the way to a more polished standard of etiquette for the rest of their countrymen.

It did not happen. By the 1830s, the word "gentleman" was being applied to everyone, and at best it referred to nothing more than ordinary politeness and civility. Americans liked their manners plain and minimal. They addressed each other by their first names and preferred to reduce those names to words of one syllable. From simplicity it was an easy step to vulgarity. If foreign visitors were occasionally charmed by the former, the latter left them aghast. Travelers' accounts repeatedly exclaimed at repulsive table manners, habitual profanity, copious drinking, and the continuous chewing and spitting of tobacco.

This conduct was understandable. The new democracy was indulging in its new freedom. No longer constrained by deference to their betters, ordinary people were acting as they pleased. One may recall the poor man's response to the fairy's gift of three wishes: all the grog in the world, all the tobacco in the world, and—after some hesitation—a little more grog and tobacco. When a change in the social order releases people who were formerly repressed and deprived, they react by pigging out, as they did in the newly founded Soviet Union and as they had done a century earlier in the newly founded United States. During its first decades, the young American nation consumed more liquor per capita than before or since—"the alcoholic republic," as one historian called it.[39]

Like Dr. Frankenstein, the Founding Fathers were horrified when they saw what their creation has become. They had dreamed of a nation of aristocrats—high-minded, suave, and cultured. Instead, they beheld a population of coarse men who were out to make money by hook or by crook, who elected politicians as low and mercenary as themselves if not more so, who liked their religion noisy and animated, who detested fancy-pants sophisticates of any kind, and who boozed, cussed, chawed, and spat.

Thomas Jefferson shared the disillusion, insofar as a man of his irrepressible optimism was able to do so. He had the misfortune to live long enough to catch an unsavory whiff of the Jackson-for-President movement, which changed the tone of public life from the republican simplicity that Jefferson himself had cultivated during his own presidential administration into the egalitarian vulgarity of the Age of the Common Man. At least he had the good fortune to die before a dirty and disorderly mob actually invaded the White House at the inauguration of Andrew Jackson.

Some foreigners thought that the new nation was only going through a stage of youthful rambunctiousness and that with time it would grow up and behave better, as it developed class distinctions and standards of etiquette like those of Europe. Some Americans agreed. Families that had become rich began to fancy themselves potential aristocrats and to look across the Atlantic for models to imitate. The trend increased in the second half of the Nineteenth Century, as fortunes grew with the rise of industrial capitalism and so did the pretensions of their possessors.

Social aspirations of this kind collided with the social realities of America. In Europe, there was an aristocracy that set the tone for conduct at the upper levels. However wealthy, a coarse and awkward parvenu met with rejection. According to a traditional maxim, it took three generations to make a gentleman, since the son of newly rich parents usually could not avoid bearing some of the offensive marks of their low origin. Only the grandson, with proper upbringing and education, would be accepted as a legitimate member of the upper class. In the United States, there was no aristocracy to bar the way. A parvenu could make a rapid ascent into the world of fashionable society, where "wealth is the grand leveling principle," in the words of a popular antebellum novelist.[40]

The result of this quick mobility was vulgarity in high places. In the 1830s, a German immigrant described what passed for an "aristocracy" in the United States as "a few families who have been more successful in trade than the rest and are now cutting their friends and relations in order to be considered fashionable." Since money excuses almost everything, American parvenus felt then—as they feel now—little need to improve their low habits and poor taste. "You got to be awful rich to dress as bad as you do," remarked a workman to his employer, a highly successful novelist. When the wealthy chose to flaunt their superiority by going on a spending spree, "the result is often as appalling in its hideousness as it is startling in its costliness," shuddered the author of the 1893 Baedeker guide to the United States.[41]

The wives of nineteenth-century American capitalists, assisted by ample leisure as well as ample means, pursued snobbish distinctions with ferocious and untiring energy. But they were struggling against the tenor of the rest of society, including that of their husbands. A life spent in the rough and exhausting world of business did not dispose a person toward acquiring elegant tastes or learning stylish manners. Men "do not take polish readily," warned a contemporary etiquette writer.[42] The pretentious and affected woman, dragging her husband to some high-toned social event when he would rather be playing cards with his pals, became a popular comic stereotype.

In addition to the personal attempts of individuals to rise above the low norm of national manners, there were also efforts to elevate the norm collectively. During the second half of the Nineteenth Century, idealistic Americans proclaimed that the general population could become refined, that everyone, however humble, was capable of acquiring gentility. Various measures for this purpose were tried by government bodies and private charities, but at a certain point they met resistance. Even Americans of humble background do not like other people telling them how to conduct their lives. They might be induced to adopt the most basic forms of courtesy and the most elementary habits of decency as the common practices of civilized humanity everywhere, but they were not going to go much further than that.

The project of elevating the masses, like the practice of imitating a foreign aristocracy, ran contrary to the fundamental character of the nation. America may be characterized as a country with middle-class values and a lower-class tone. The middle-class values (their nature and the process by which they came to achieve dominance among the general population) will be analyzed later (in chapter four). My concern at this point is with the lower-class tone. Far from being a temporary or fortuitous condition, as some would like to think, it is a permanent and essential quality of American social life, being a natural manifestation of the egalitarian ethos.

Just as Americans dislike anything above the level of popular culture, they are also hostile to superior manners. Urbanity and finesse provoke, not admiration and imitation, but suspicion and aversion. A person with a veneer of cosmopolitan suavity is at a disadvantage, rather than an advantage, in the dealings of daily life. Elected officerholders are not the only ones who sense the need to present themselves as just "ordinary Joes" and "regular guys." One model of polished diplomacy in the Federal State Department (Dean Acheson) felt obliged to declare with a straight face that he was "a simple country boy." In such an environment, instead of striving to shine and appear brilliant, a clever person ingratiates himself with others by employing intentionally sloppy speech and making deliberate social fumbles.[43]

The idea of grace being combined with power (the aristocratic *suaviter in modo, fortiter in re*) is incomprehensible to Americans. On those rare occasions when they happen to encounter it in dealing with foreigners, they become perplexed. As one of them remarked in bewilderment after a business meeting with some Japanese, "They're so polite, and yet they're so tough." The civilized machismo of Latin American business executives is likewise beyond the imagination of Americans, who understand machismo only in its coarse, lower-class form.[44]

In the United States, if one is strong, one may show it by acting tough. In some milieus, this is expected; not doing so would be interpreted as a sign of weakness. Politicians occasionally strike crude and belligerent poses to please the electorate, and foreign affairs are often an arena for such posturing. When not in an idealistic mood, Americans tend to regard other countries as they might the dubious and threatening denizens of a bad street. They want to view their own nation as standing up to these characters and not being "pushed around."

Most Americans are not vulgar themselves—at least not grossly vulgar—but they tolerate vulgarity and even approve of it at times. It does not provoke the instant and automatic condemnation that it would in Europe, where it is the stigma and the prerogative of the lower classes. In America, it is neither a taboo nor a rule, but an option. Many people enjoy it now and then, either directly or vicariously, as a refreshing break from the normal restraints of social life. Consequently, it may pop up in the most unusual places. The following are a couple of examples: (1) A man yells obscenities at another man, who yells them back. The exchange rises in a crescendo until both collapse in exhaustion. Is this some backstreet encounter? No, it was a meeting between a professor of classics and the president of a major university (John Silber). (2) "Congratulations! It was…a real street fight…. Nobody will ever call you a wimp again." Is this a lower-class father applauding his son for duking it out with an antagonist? No, it was the head of the Chrysler Corporation (Lee Iacocca) addressing the next president of the United States (George Bush, Sr.).[45]

Some people continue to hope that America will eventually acquire more sophisticated manners, as well as higher cultural tastes, and they have been continually disappointed. In the 1960s, they believed that their dreams were coming true under the leadership and example of President Kennedy. The paeans he inspired, especially posthumously, were wildly unrealistic. Aside from the fact that Kennedy himself was not the social and cultural paragon his idolaters made him out to be, the Sixties were brewing up a stew of low and gross behavior among the young that would lead the country in a direction far from anything elegant or elevated.

Ever since the spring of 1965, when a scruffy kid on the Berkeley campus lifted up a sign with a four-letter word on it, the accepted mode of public expression has descended further toward the bottom with each decade. In the Seventies, the liberties and license already claimed by the young were spreading to the rest of the population. By the Nineties, pundits were commenting on the foul language and vile conduct that had developed during the previous twenty years, with popular culture leading the way. In 2002, a writer at one of the nation's most prestigious and sophisticated magazines was nonchalantly described as reveling in vulgarity, "like everyone else these days."[46]

People at the top have adapted to the trend. Ever intent on differentiating themselves from the rest of the middle class, those in the upper-middle used to imitate the luxuries of the old-money rich. Now they are selecting certain conspicuous practices of the lower classes, such as getting tattooed and riding motorcycles. Newly rich millionaires in Silicon Valley dress like beachcombers, while children of hereditary wealth dress like blacks from the slums.[47]

This represents a remarkable change from tradition. In the past, as a society became richer and more powerful, it tended to become more aristocratic. The people at its higher levels acquired sophistication and refinement, and their culture and institutions exercised an influence on the rest of the population. In eighteenth-century England, for example, a person of low origins who wanted to rise in the world could attend the theater and imitate the upper-class diction and manners that were represented on stage. Anyone who goes to the theater in America today will receive lessons of a much different kind. On one occasion in 1997, President Clinton and his family viewed three of the season's most popular Broadway productions, which exhibited a cloacal farrago of coarseness and obscenity. Clinton himself needed no tutelage in low-life behavior, but perhaps other affluent members of the audience were able to pick up some pointers.[48]

—2—

The preceding section has examined five major aspects of American society: business, politics, religion, culture, and manners. It is clear that all of them, from the past to the present, have been influenced by an egalitarian tendency. This characteristic is so pervasive and enduring that it can be considered a fundamental and distinguishing quality of the entire nation. America is dominated by an ethos of egalitarianism.

Unlike Europeans, for whom certain kinds of work are considered debasing and therefore suited to people of the lower classes, Americans regard all legal occupations as reputable, and those who perform them as deserving respect from everyone else. Much to Tocqueville's surprise, this included even the public employee who executed condemned criminals. Working one's way through college by menial labor is not considered a disgrace, as it would be in Europe. When one son of an American family enters a profession, while another takes a clerical job, and yet another follows a manual trade, it does not cause eyebrows to rise, nor is it all that unusual.[49]

In societies with clearly defined and accepted class structures, a member of a lower class is expected to make certain gestures of subservience to any member of a higher class with whom he comes into contact. This does not happen in the United States, nor has it in the past. In 1906, a German political economist observed that an ordinary citizen and a state governor would receive equal treatment from American waiters, street-car conductors, and policemen—the same kind of people who in England would become obsequious when confronted with any "man of obviously upper-class appearance." Americans admire someone who has made a lot of money, but they do not regard him as a person of a higher and superior order. They would be pleased to meet him and shake his hand, but they would not speak humbly to him or, heaven forbid, bow to him. As one westerner explained to the visiting English author Harriet Martineau, "However great and good another person may be," we feel that fundamentally "we are just as great and good." That is, however successful and prominent he may be, Americans feel they have the potential to become equally successful and prominent.[50]

This spirit of egalitarianism is especially noticeable in the world of work, where positions of superiority and subordination are necessarily present and clearly understood. American workers have always prided themselves on maintaining what they used to call a "manly bearing" toward the boss: they are civil but not servile or deferential. The boss in turn knows that he cannot order them about as if they were his lackeys. They simply would not stand for it. Foreign observers have remarked with surprise at the "respectful tone" that employers and foremen use in dealing with underlings.[51]

No one is "so low as to be beneath dignity." This could stand as a universal American adage, and people at the lower levels of society are especially quick in perceiving slights to their self-esteem, as they are loud in repudiating them. "All I ask is a claim to be considered a fit associate for anybody in this country," declared a lowbred character in a novel published in 1838. Similar demands have echoed through the decades up to the present day, as prickly low-status Americans have asserted that they are "just as good as anyone else" and should be treated accordingly. Around 1900, a United States senator made the mistake of amiably addressing a housepainter as "my man." "I'm not your man!" the fellow growled back. "We are not janitors!" I myself once heard a "custodian" bluntly correct a professor who had used the less honorific term. Europeans would have regarded such outbursts of wounded pride from such people as ludicrously and preposterously pretentious, if not grossly impertinent.[52]

In societies other than America, inequality has traditionally seemed a permanent, inevitable, and natural fact of life. People believe that to prevent chaos and degeneration, there needs to be a distinct and recognized minority who provide leadership for everyone else to follow. Even those who are not part of the elite have tended to accept its legitimacy. Lower-class Englishmen used to speak of "our betters," and one of them admitted, "I like to be set an example and have someone I can look up to."[53] Nothing could be further from the egalitarian ethos that prevails in America. There the very idea of a nationally recognized social elite is unthinkable. In fact, any group of people (for example, policemen or military officers) who have the power to command the behavior of other people are regarded with wariness, at best. And anyone who readily accepts their superiority is viewed as weak and dependent.

Of course, it is a reality of most social arrangements that some people possess more of the desirable things in life than other people. But the spirit of egalitarianism functions as a countervailing force to this tendency. A recognized expert in a particular line of work naturally enjoys more money, prestige, and influence than his less successful colleagues. But Americans are careful to restrict his range of command to the sphere of his occupation and to prevent him from exercising authority beyond its boundaries. The popular pejorative expression "to pull rank" (derived from usage in the military) reflects a consciousness of this danger. It is applied to someone inappropriately or unjustifiably asserting superiority on the basis of his formal position or credentials.

Americans are slow to accept even the limited claims of expertise. In a culture where everyone thinks that his opinion is as good as anyone else's, people do not immediately and automatically give way before a posture of authority. This, after all, is not Germany, where the trappings of high status carry all before them. One of the small but pungent pleasures of life for an American is to catch someone with a claim to superiority making a mistake, however minor, such as an English teacher committing a grammatical error.[54]

Government officials especially are subjected to the discomforting and derogatory assessment of egalitarianism. Their ability to exercise power over their fellow citizens wins them little respect and ordinarily something less than respect. The public regards them as an unfortunate necessity at best, doubts their competence, and questions their motives. Europeans may cherish government as a paternal force, from which they expect guidance and protection. Americans have the opposite feelings, which one sociologist characterized as "egalitarian irreverence"—a phrase that proved quite puzzling to the traditionalist elitism of some Asian translators, who initially surmised that it must be a typographical mistake for "egalitarian reverence." One wonders how they would have coped with the following contemptuous assessment of people in positions of power: "Authority has always attracted the lowest elements in the human race"—that is, those who enjoy bossing other people around.[55]

Americans are willing to recognize and reward superiority in proven performance and actual achievement. What they object to is the individual who goes beyond being superior in a specific context and starts behaving as if he were possessed of superiority in general. The egotistical promptings of human nature may tempt a person to reach for what the ethos of egalitarianism forbids. But Americans are acutely alert to the slightest evidence of such a transgression. They will detect it in someone who puts on airs or even in one who is aloof and unfriendly. Once aroused, they act instantly and in force to bring the culprit to heel, usually by employing some sharply efficacious ridicule.

People lower down the social ladder have rougher ways of expressing their allegiance to the spirit of egalitarianism. In traditional societies, those below often feel a generalized inferiority to those above. The English novelist D. H. Lawrence once drew a comparison between a farmer and a vicar. The former, though far more powerful in body, recognized the superiority of the latter: "Strip them and set them on a desert island, and the vicar was [still] the master." This stands in diametric contrast to the observations of the American novelist Norman Mailer as to the "fear" that "the sons of the middle class" feel in the presence of the muscular and pugnacious "working class." A common American middle-class fantasy of horror imagines a person finding himself in a situation (usually prison) where he is the victim of lower-class assault and degradation. In the sophisticated and generally reputable magazine *New Republic,* one semi-humorous article speculated that "the single greatest hazard in modern offices" results from the contact between "smug yuppies" and "physically stronger blue-collar types."[56]

Living in such a society, people at the higher levels have learned to adapt. One tactic is to isolate themselves in gated communities and other controlled environments. Contrary to appearances, this practice is actually a testimony to the power of American egalitarianism. Only by establishing strong, explicit, and artificial barriers between themselves and others are the privileged able to keep the leveling manners and democratic assumptions of the rest of the population at bay and thereby preserve their distinct position. In contrast, the higher orders in traditional cultures have been able to behave much more freely and still maintain their status, since other people "know their place" and do not "take liberties" (to use the English expression).

The more nimble and savvy among privileged Americans, especially those in the public eye, have adopted a different tactic. They are profuse with the gestures of superficial friendliness and at pains to assure the world that they are just ordinary people, much the same as everybody else. Candidates for political office habitually employ this masquerade. Its features appeared, vividly and pungently depicted, in a novel of 1851: "The judge...went smiling along the street. As is customary with the rich when they aim at the honors of a republic, he apologized, as it were, to the people for his wealth, prosperity, and elevated station by a free and hearty manner toward those who knew him, putting off the more of his dignity in due proportion with the humbleness of the man whom he saluted, and thereby proving a haughty consciousness of his advantages as irrefragably as if he had marched forth preceded by a troop of lackeys to clear the way."[57]

—3—

One prominent and highly problematical manifestation of the egalitarian spirit in America is the prevalence of physical violence. It is similar to the vulgarity of manners, which was discussed above. Like vulgarity, it is characteristic of the lower classes, it has permeated the rest of society, and it has been present since early in the nation's history.

During the antebellum era, there was personal violence, with conspicuous examples among prominent people. Andrew Jackson had been a notorious duelist and frontier brawler, and he became the first president to be the target of an assassination attempt. Congressmen carried weapons, occasionally killed one another, and once or twice did so on the floor of the House while it was in session. Usually they kept their lethal attacks for the off-hours and were satisfied to interrupt working sessions with nothing more than fistfights. The rest of the country was no different. Newspapers recorded numerous assaults and murders for various motives or no motive at all. In 1840, when a professor at Jefferson's University of Virginia attempted to break up a disturbance on campus, one of the students shot him dead.[58]

There was also group violence. Riots, often accompanied by fatalities, might break out for any number of reasons—a contested election, a bank failure, a labor dispute, racial hatred, religious prejudice, even the failure of a balloon launching. During the 1830s, disorders were so frequent that people—including responsible people with considered opinions—began to predict that society would break apart and the union would dissolve into separate, independent, and hostile communities.[59] Foreign observers shared these fears—or hopes, for many of them wanted to see the great experiment in democracy fail.

Both the pessimistic Americans and the resentful Europeans were proved wrong. Not only did the United States remain intact during the first half of the Nineteenth Century, it prospered. Manufacturing flourished, commerce thrived, the population grew, cities sprang up in the western wilderness. The conveniences and comforts of life increased and spread through all levels of society. Visitors from abroad, including those, like Frances Trollope, who were unfavorably inclined, could not help admiring the energy, inventiveness, and material accomplishments of the Americans. In an unaccustomed burst of positive hyperbole, Trollope declared that the very depths of the ocean would prove no obstacle to them, if they decided that something of profit lay on the seafloor.[60]

Both the violence and the progress continued through the rest of the century and into the next. Conflicts between workers and capitalists were far bloodier in the United States than in Europe, but they failed to impede industrial productivity. By 1900, the more discerning and impartial commentators of the Old World had to admit that their young rival was the greatest power on earth—a position which the passage of the next hundred years has only reinforced.[61] High levels of violence likewise persisted through the Twentieth Century. Even in the 1990s, when crime was rising in Europe while declining on the other side of the Atlantic, America still retained its title as the country with the highest murder rate in the Western world.

This is not as stark a paradox or as total a contradiction as it may seem. In America, productivity and disorder spring from a common source. The ethos of egalitarianism encourages people to disregard restrictions imposed from above and to act on their own desires and inclinations. The practical result has been an outburst of activity at all levels of society, including the lower levels, whose members in other cultures would have been intimidated and repressed. Americans, in contrast, go forth in life, driven by personal ambition and the conviction that they can and should attain success. Consequently, they expend tremendous amounts of productive energy, which fuel the nation's collective material progress.

At the same time, egalitarianism also prompts people to disorderly conduct. Convinced as they are that they are as good as anyone else and their opinions are as valid, they have little patience for any rules and regulations that they view as unnecessarily standing in their way and restricting them. The result is the rowdy behavior detailed in the first section of this chapter, as well as outright violence and lawlessness.

The same motives that drive an industrious worker also impel an ambitious criminal. The closeness of the two can be seen by examining the practice of competition. Americans have always been avid competitors. They readily compete with one another, they enjoy watching others compete, they praise competition as bringing out the best qualities in people, and they encourage their children to compete. At times, the language of contention can become quite ferocious. "We'd like to see our competitors dead!" growls the aggressive businessman.[62] Of course, all this rivalry is supposed to be limited by certain guidelines and restraints. The Little Leaguer is supposed to play by the rules of the game. One does not destroy General Motors in the process of trying to become its president.

But the emotions being incited and released are powerful and elemental, and there is always a danger that they may run out of control. This is especially the case at the lower levels of society, where restraints are weak and impulses are strong. Since the ethos of egalitarianism encourages everyone to go out and strive for what he wants, it is not surprising that a number of people, especially those near the bottom, with few choices or resources available, respond to the prompting with the direct and forthright actions of crime.

American criminals display an energy, determination, and self-confidence similar to that of Americans in general. *The Dangerous Classes of New York,* a best-seller of 1880, observed that their misdeeds "have the unrestrained and sanguinary character of a race accustomed to overcome all obstacles.... The murder of an unoffending old man...is nothing to them. They are ready for any offense or crime, however degraded or bloody." This is still true well over a century later. In 1992, London experienced more theft and burglary than New York but far less robbery and homicide. The number of deaths that occurred in the course of burglaries and robberies combined was seven in London and 378 in New York.[63]

Tocqueville observed that a Frenchman fought a duel only because he wanted to tell other people that he had done so, whereas an American fought a duel to kill his opponent. I myself recall hearing an Irishman declare on a radio talk show he would never get into a fight with an American because "he might try to kill me." Yes, indeed, Americans do not engage in violence for honor or recreation; they play for keeps.[64]

In many civilized cultures, after taking another person's life, the perpetrator often commits suicide. Having relieved whatever compulsion it was that prompted him to the act of murder, he is then overwhelmed by the horror of what he has done. Since obedience to social rules is more deeply internalized at the higher levels of society, it is understandable that the higher a murderer's status, the more likely he will be to take his own life. American killers do not behave in this way. Far from remorseful, they are exultant. They regard themselves as competitors who have won. Thirty-three percent of the killers in England commit suicide, and half of them attempt it; only 3 or 4 percent of the killers in the United States do so.[65]

In America, violence, like vulgarity, is not something that has been driven back into the dark and remote corners of social life, but something that is near at hand and may appear at any time. People recognize the possibility of danger and accept it as a matter of course, to a degree that shocks foreign visitors. In 1832, Frances Trollope remarked on the casualness with which the natives treated incidents of assault, robbery, and even murder. Exactly a century and a half later, the *Spectator,* a prominent weekly magazine in England, printed the following as a news item worthy of national attention: "A man was beaten to death after he remonstrated with a group of youths who had disrupted his family barbecue." In the United States, such an episode would have been treated as nothing more than a minor local event. Each year since 1975, a nationwide lifestyle survey has asked Americans, including women, how well they think they would do in a fistfight. To a middle-class European, such a question would be an insult, implying as it does that he might become engaged in such lower-class behavior.[66]

The absence of violence in other countries provokes a reciprocal astonishment in Americans. They could hardly believe that during England's
general strike of 1926 no riots occurred and no lives were lost; in the
United States such a dispute would inevitably have resulted in fighting
and bloodshed. At the 1992 Olympics in Barcelona, an American athlete
complained, "I miss crime and murder.... There hasn't been a brutal
stabbing or anything here the last twenty-four hours."[67]

In view of such attitudes and practices, the widespread ownership of
firearms in the United States is understandable. In the last two decades,
thirty-three states passed laws that permit the carrying of a concealed
weapon. About half of all American households have at least one gun
on the premises. Every year, there are from 65,000 to 80,000 shoot-
ings in self-defense. Efforts have been made to restrict the possession
of handguns, but they encounter adamant opposition from the public.
Some people regard the attempt to deprive them of their weapons as "the
psychological equivalent of government-imposed castration."[68]

For Americans, violence is more than just a danger against which
one needs to take precautions. It exerts a fundamental allure, as its
ubiquitous presence in various kinds of popular entertainment testifies.
Violence in the media is a topic that has been discussed and fretted over
endlessly, but the phenomenon poses no real mystery. A violent person is
simply expressing himself in a dramatic, direct, and elemental way, and
its depiction gives the audience a wicked but safely vicarious thrill. Its
appeal is like that of vulgarity, but it is far stronger and more dangerous,
and its fans usually have sufficient prudence and self-control not to try
it out in their own lives.

Some Europeans, especially the English, after seeing the vulgarity and
violence on the surface of American life, have imagined that Americans
are the lower classes "gone out of control."[69] This is a misperception,
similar to the mistake of concluding from egalitarian manners and
behavior that the United States is a genuinely classless society. One
needs to disregard the lower-class tone and look deeper. Just because
a person in a position of prominence occasionally acts vulgar does not
mean he is a wild low-lifer. Just because an incident of violence occurs

does not mean the public order is seriously threatened. The very reverse is most likely the case. From time to time, Americans have employed collective, informal violence as a means, not of creating disorder, but of suppressing it.

In 1837, Harriet Martineau explained to her European readers that the leaders and participants in some recent American riots were people, not from the lower levels of society, but from the higher levels, and that their purpose had been to stop those who were creating disruption.[70] The same was generally true of lynch mobs. They tended to be organized and headed by the respectable elements of a community, who wanted to eliminate a pernicious and often criminal element. During the labor disputes of the late Nineteenth and early Twentieth Century, it was the capitalists and their allies in government who inflicted most of the violence, to enforce order and repress the workers.

Beneath the occasional noise and fury that make headlines, a profound stability has dominated national existence from its early years. As Tocqueville discovered, an election might be preceded by ferocious rhetoric and rioting at the polls, but once it was over, everyone accepted the results as valid, and tranquility prevailed. In a less secure society, the presidential deadlocks of 1876 (Tilden/Hayes) and 2000 (Bush/Gore) would have resulted in disruption, disorder, civil turmoil, and perhaps even war. The fact that they did not is evidence of the fundamental presence of an inherent and abiding order—so much so that the ship of state does not always require the guiding hand of a chief executive at its helm. According to someone who should have known (that low realist Richard Nixon), the United States needs a president only to handle foreign affairs; domestically the country is able to run itself with nothing more than "a competent Cabinet."[71]

—4—

Why is there such stability in the United States? In view of the liberty and license allowed by this egalitarian nation, the question to ask is not why is there so much violence, but why is there so little? And why is it sufficiently isolated and superficial as not to cause serious social discord? What prevents all the supercharged individual egos—or even a crucially large number of them—from running amok?

An obvious and popular though superficial and inadequate answer is the law and its agent of enforcement, the criminal justice system. Unlike societies that seek to impose order and control on everyone from the outset, the American government gives its citizens extensive freedom and then punishes those who abuse it by injuring others. Harshness and frequency of judicial penalties are a logical consequence of this approach.[72] Alone among developed countries, the United States continues to inflict capital punishment, and its rate of incarceration is the highest in the Western world, by some calculations the highest anywhere.

For a specific example of the connection between breadth of liberty and severity of punishment, one may consider Texas. It is well known as the state where individual egos grow big and range free, producing personalities that are "larger than life" or at least more rambunctious than normal (President Lyndon Johnson, for example). It is also the state that performs over one-third of the executions in the country, that has undertaken the nation's largest program of building prisons, and that boasts laws which are extraordinarily lenient to those who resort to lethal force in the act of defending themselves or their property.[73]

Unquestionably, the legal system performs a necessary function in maintaining a minimal level of social order. But beyond this, the power of the law in the United States has crucial limitations. Americans assume the right to subject any government measure to their own personal judgment, and if they find a law to be unjust or unreasonable, they have few qualms about disobeying it, as long as they think they can escape its penalties. Observers, foreign and domestic alike, have noticed that Americans are ready to pass laws for the remedy of just about any complaint, but they are equally ready to flout laws for just about any excuse. The prohibition act of 1919 and its subsequent widespread violation for more than a decade provided what was probably the most notorious example of this contradictory behavior, but there have been countless other instances, before and since, such as the state laws against gambling that Frances Trollope characterized as made by old women and broken by young men.[74]

A more fundamental objection to the idea of the law as a sufficient source of social stability and an effective curb on dangerous impulses is the fact that it handles only the worst transgressions and disputes. Daily life contains innumerable situations in which people come into conflict. While these are usually too small and too numerous for the law to address, they can be significantly disruptive in their aggregate effect, and they have the potential to grow into more serious forms of disorder.

One solution that has often been suggested is for each person to respect the rights of others, to resolve that he will not pursue his own interests if they injure those of his neighbor. This sounds fine in theory, but it breaks down in practice, under the beguiling and distorting influence of the individual ego. Prompted by personal desires and advantages, people disagree in their evaluation of a transgressive action, depending on whether they are the ones to initiate it or the ones to suffer its consequences. The same harm appears as a tolerable and trivial annoyance to its perpetrator but as a serious wrong and affront to its victim. The subtle persistence with which self-interest warps and clouds the perception of facts and realities to its own advantage is so natural and familiar a part of human behavior as to require no extended demonstration or discussion.

Traditional cultures long ago perceived the injuries that individuals could do to each other and to the social fabric, and they sought to restrain them by imposing authority. This took the obvious form of a ruling elite and the more adroit and pervasive form of inherited customs and mores. America has rejected both these tactics. As indicated above, the spirit of egalitarianism bridles at the very notion of a select minority leading the majority, either formally as government officials or informally as an upper class.

Americans have no use for practices still common elsewhere in the world, where family and kin rather than one's own preference determine the intimate and significant decisions of life, such as those involving marriage and occupation. In the United States, each person is supposed to choose and decide everything pertaining to himself. He does not automatically accept the identity handed to him by the circumstances of birth. He is allowed, even encouraged, to leave parents, siblings, and other relatives behind and go off to assume a new identity, fashioned by his own selection and contrivance.[75]

Europeans have been bemused and occasionally aghast at the ruthless thoroughness with which Americans dismiss the authority of tradition. Religion might seem to be the one thing above all that is routinely transferred from parents to children with each new generation. But even here, the United States recognizes the option of the individual. Foreign visitors have been surprised to be asked on bureaucratic forms to indicate "your religious preference" or "the religion of your choice," which imply that religion may ordinarily be a matter of individual preference and personal choice.[76]

If authority, either governmental or non-governmental, is so weak in the United States, what prevents or resolves conflicts between people? This question becomes all the more baffling when one goes beyond the task of maintaining basic social order and considers the means of promoting economic productivity. It is one thing to keep individuals from attacking and robbing each other; it is something else, something much more difficult and subtle, to induce them to work together harmoniously. The liberties granted and implied by the ethos of egalitarianism have stoked every American with a personal fire of self-esteem and self-interest. What keeps them from running into each other in the resulting scramble? What keeps the competition between individuals from becoming so intense that it damages the collective effort? With everything up for grabs and everyone up grabbing for it, what prevents the entire enterprise from collapsing into chaos?

One answer is at least as old as Tocqueville: the principle of enlightened self-interest (he called it "self-interest correctly understood").[77] It is the realization that by acting collectively and cooperatively, individuals will gain more for their personal selves than if they acted separately and in opposition. It does not eliminate the conflicts and rivalries that naturally arise among people, but it curbs and channels them. Americans generally understand the idea, in concept if not by name, and it is in practice everywhere.

But enlightened self-interest is a description and a rationalization of what already exists, rather than a genuine force that guides or impels human conduct. Like the idea of respecting the rights of others, it is too cold to counteract the burning demands of the ego, and it is too abstract to adjudicate the specific situations where those demands come into play. At what point should two persons stop competing and start cooperating? The principle of enlightened self-interest is incapable of giving a precise answer. In addition, its benefits tend to appear over the long term rather than in the short term, which makes them seem dubious and illusory to the immediate desires of the naturally and spontaneously unenlightened self.

American productivity and prosperity, as well as the stability on which they rest, remain a puzzle, especially to foreigners whose attitudes and assumptions are contrary to the ones that prevail in the United States. When the word "individualism" first appeared in France, before it did in America, it referred to the disintegration of traditional bonds and the resulting altercations of modern life, and it has retained its negative con- notations of egoism and self-seeking to the present day. "Competition" and "competitive" are likewise pejorative in the European mind, to which they imply conflict and insecurity. When Americans employ such words as if they were highly positive, they sound wildly paradoxical, if not positively lunatic, to people on the other side of the Atlantic.[78]

At times, the United States has appeared in foreign eyes as a nation that defies the social equivalent of the laws of nature. In 1803, a French politician attempted to explain to his fellow citizens that, despite the notorious dishonesty of American businessmen, the economy of the country as a whole was prospering. About a century later, a German sociologist tried to correct the popular European notion that the United States was nothing but a heap of unattached individuals, a sandpile of separate human grains. On the contrary, he declared, they formed groups very frequently and effectively. Another century after that, an American journalist living in Europe during the 1990s was repeatedly asked how his country could contain "so much litigation, adversarial confrontation, hype, spin, glibness, and overwrought scandal" and yet at the same time function with such incredible productive efficiency.[79]

Foreigners have not been the only ones to feel bewildered. Any American who attempts to answer their questions usually finds himself as much at a loss for explanations as they. Thomas Jefferson was often wrong in his predictions for the future of the nation which he had helped to create and which caused him so much perplexity and distress in his later years. But he was correct in the dictum he pronounced after the close of his public career: "And so we have gone on, and so we shall go on, puzzled and prospering beyond example in the history of man."[80]

CHAPTER TWO

Individual Freedom as a Beneficial Self-Deception

—1—

The egalitarian ethos is an obvious characteristic of American society that even the most casual visitor cannot help noticing. In an attempt to find answers to the questions posed at the end of the last chapter, it is necessary to go beneath conditions on the surface of life and examine more fundamental aspects of America. One of the most important of these is the national belief in the freedom of the individual (called "individualism" for short).

The following may serve as a succinct catechism of its principles: What is this country's highest ideal and greatest blessing? It is freedom. To what purpose should freedom be employed? That is for each individual to decide; everyone should set his own goals for himself. What will determine his success or failure in attaining them? That should depend on his innate qualities, like talent and temperament; external factors, such as the material or social circumstances of birth and upbringing, should not be decisive.

Those are the basics. To understand the ideal of individualism in its larger and higher dimensions, one may refer to an author who has the best claim to be its philosophical champion, Ralph Waldo Emerson.

In his own day, his emphatic pronouncements won wide applause, and they have remained popular ever since. This was only natural. Emerson took hold of sentiments that most Americans already felt to a greater or lesser degree, consciously or semiconsciously; he worked them into coherent form, pushed them to their logical conclusions, and above all, gave them memorable expression. Despite a somewhat baroque prose style, his writings such as "Address at Divinity College" (1838) and "Self-Reliance" (1841) still ring out with memorable phrases despite a distance of over a century and a half.[1]

The fundamental essence of each individual has been divinely created and inspired, Emerson declared. "The fountain of all good" is in yourself; "obey thyself;" "judge for yourself, reverence thyself."[2] The young nation agreed with him—and so did its posterity. In 1986, for example, a sociologist remarked that "the sanctity of the individual" was a "common American, quasi-creedal phrase."[3]

Emerson was drastic in his conviction that an individual should obey himself and himself alone. "What I must do is all that concerns me, not what the people think.... I shun father and mother and wife and brother when my genius calls me. I would write on the lintels of the door-post, Whim." This very sentiment can be heard from today's lifestyle individualists, who declare, "Next week I might quit my career in banking, leave my wife and children, and join a Buddhist cult."[4]

An individual goes wrong when he follows the dictates or even the example of others, Emerson maintained. "Insist on yourself; never imitate." Each person should act "from himself, tossing the laws, the books, idolatries and customs out of the window.... Let me admonish you...to go alone; to refuse the good models, even those which are sacred in the imagination of men." This has become a pervasive ideal in American culture, high and low alike. In 2000, one journalist and media critic remarked that a single theme dominated nearly all of the award-winning Hollywood movies—contempt for "external moral authority" and glorification of "personally designed morality."[5]

Emerson warned the individual, not only against following others, but also against leading others. "Dominion over myself" should be sufficient. Whenever I "undertake the direction of him also [i.e. my fellow man], I overstep the truth, and come into false relations to him."[6] A man becomes "weaker by every recruit to his banner." The bold novelty of this stance is remarkable. Innumerable proponents of new doctrines have declared: Do not follow others, follow me. Emerson was declaring: Do not follow anyone, do not lead anyone, take charge of yourself alone—an exhortation which Americans then and now have endorsed with verbal enthusiasm and which is reflected in various popular attitudes, ranging from the perennial mistrust of government officials to the maxim of the 1960s New Left, "Don't follow leaders."

Emerson was extremely dubious about people acting in groups. He feared that they beguiled a man into deserting his own individuality and abandoning its superior insight. "They think society wiser than their soul, and know not that one soul, and their soul, is wiser than the whole world." It was the duty of each person to resist collective influences and demands. "Society everywhere is in conspiracy against the manhood of every one of its members.... The virtue in most request is conformity.... Whoso would be a man, must be a nonconformist.... Nothing is at last sacred but the integrity of your own mind." Americans of subsequent times have spoken with similar vehemence at merely the theoretical possibility of a threat to their individual freedom. The following is a synopsis of prevailing opinion, as reported by a sociologist in the 1980s: "Anything that would violate our right to think for ourselves, judge for ourselves, make our own decisions, live our lives as we see fit, is not only morally wrong, it is sacrilegious."[7]

There was, Emerson admitted, a vast distance between ideal and reality, between the free and full development of all individuals and the actual behavior of people living in the world. But again and again, he insisted that everyone contained within himself a splendid treasure and that everyone was capable of possessing it. And Emerson did mean everyone. Different people possessed various talents in varying degrees of ability, of course. But when these were all sorted out and measured up together, it would be apparent that every man was "equal to every other man."[8] Emerson wanted an elite, but he believed that everyone was capable of belonging to it.

Listen to the buzzing stream of articulate American opinion during most any era, and you will hear expressions of optimistic idealism and professions of radical egalitarianism similar to Emerson's. In 1990, for example, a usually realistic and perceptive analyst of society declared that she wanted "a world in which even the lowliest among us—the hash-slinger, the sock-finder, the factory hand—will be recognized as the poet she truly is." In 2001, an educator with many years of practical experience asserted that "genius is as common as air" and that society was utilizing only a "minority of the human talent" available. Back in 1963, when "conformity" was something many people worried about, an article in *Time* magazine pointed out that, after all, few individuals are able to disregard social pressures and act solely on their personal convictions. The very idea that everyone should develop his own independent notions about such things as "politics, ethics, [and] culture" is "to ask the impossible. It is, in fact, to ask for a mass elite." To which a prominent academic commented with approval, "In all its outrageous innocence, this is what America has asked for from the beginning."[9]

So basic and widespread is America's allegiance to the ideal of individualism that its strength is reflected even in the criticism it has sometimes received. Careful analysis reveals that many of the attacks are aimed, not at individualism in its entirety, but at one of its two currently popular forms, by proponents of the other.

"Economic individualism" is the term I would use to indicate what people on the political right tend to favor. In their view, each person should express his individuality by striving to succeed in his chosen line of work (that is, in frankly mercenary terms, by trying to make more money) and so improve his situation in life. This is America's traditional form of individualism. Throughout her history, it has attracted immigrants and motivated natives, and it continues to do so.

"Lifestyle individualism" is what people on the political left favor. They believe that each person should express his individuality by developing or changing any part of his life that he wishes. This is much broader in scope than economic individualism, is a more recent development, and includes an acceptance of the unconventional—everything from selecting an unusual occupation to altering one's sexual preference.

The advocates and practitioners of one form of individualism regard those of the other with suspicion, if not outright hostility. Economic individualists think lifestyle individualists are frivolous and irresponsible, even degenerate, and blame them for high rates of divorce, crime, drug use, juvenile delinquency, and other social ills. Lifestyle individualists regard economic individualists as squares, prudes, and authoritarians and blame them for social inequality, economic exploitation, and national philistinism.

The significant fact—easily overlooked amid the noise of controversy—is that both sides are supporting a form of individualism. The hard-bitten old businessman who growls, "I did it my way," and the dewy-eyed hippie kid who says, "Do your own thing," are both proclaiming the ideal of individual freedom. They are both Emerson's progeny, which can be found everywhere, even in the most unlikely places. On hearing the assertion that the United States should "insure to every child [the] opportunity to develop its natural abilities to their utmost," one might assume this to be a statement from someone on the liberal left. Actually the speaker was the Imperial Wizard and Emperor of the Ku Klux Klan in 1926.[10]

Aside from the squabbling of these two factions (economic versus lifestyle), there is another much more fundamental objection to individualism as a national ideal and practice. Tocqueville first mentioned it when he observed that the American always thinks of himself as "standing alone," which tends to separate him from others and threatens "to confine him entirely within the solitude of his own heart." Following Tocqueville, various social commentators have declared from time to time, in tones of urgency or regret, that their countrymen were excessively devoted to the principle of individualism, that they took too little account of social needs and realities, and that a new balance ought to be struck between the individualistic and the collective. By the 1990s, this complaint had become a platitude among the retailers of intellectual opinion, with an abundance of books and articles applauding the virtues of community and deploring the damage caused by disaffiliated persons. One critic, surveying the literature, exclaimed in exasperation, "Do we need to be told yet again that American individualism is antisocial?"[11]

There has always been, and there continues to be, much frustration among the earnest advocates of more community and less individualism. Despite all their efforts, individualism continues to enjoy the greater popularity by far. That is only natural, for individualism makes a direct, visceral appeal to human self-interest and self-esteem. Every person on earth has an ego, which is normally animated with the desire to think well of and to advance himself.[12] This is a basic instinct, and it is aroused by any evocation of individual freedom, from the most elevated to the most elementary. When Emerson hymns the marvelous potential of all mankind, the reader instantly applies those generalized sentiments to his own specific case and exclaims to himself: Yes! That is me! When an ordinary person declares that America should "let you do what you please," he is expressing an egoistical notion that is shared by most of his fellow citizens, from a war veteran struggling to express what he thinks the flag symbolizes, to something called the Chicago Surreal Group expounding its artistic and anarchistic purposes in the publication *Race Traitor*.[13]

The idea of community inspires no such instinctive sympathy and automatic assent. While individualism promises unalloyed freedom, community offers benefits but also, by its very nature, imposes restrictions. This dual aspect provokes an ambivalent response. A person wants to know what the specific features of a community are, so that he can weigh the restrictions against the benefits before deciding whether to accept or reject the ensemble.

In an argument with individualism, community is consequently at a significant and usually decisive disadvantage. The promises and appeals of "communitarians" (as they have called themselves) tend to arouse skepticism rather than enthusiasm. Their proposals for a better society sound vague and unpersuasive. When they speak about the warmth and care of neighbors, there may be something of a positive response at first, but suspicions quickly arise as to neighborly surveillance and control. The idea of informal collective policing repels Americans, who call it "creepy." "What scares you about community?" an interviewer asked the art critic of the *Nation*, a leftist publication that usually condemns individualism, especially in its economic form. "Other people," was his frank reply. "I'd just as soon not be told what I have to do."[14]

—2—

Economic individualism has at times been contrasted unfavorably with individualism in its more elevated, Emersonian form. During recent decades, these two levels of American values, high and low, have come into acrimonious conflict, which chapter nine will discuss. At the present point in this book, the task at hand is to focus on economic individualism and analyze its enormous historical and cultural importance. The overwhelming majority of Americans in the past, as well as probably most Americans today, have regarded the opportunity for each individual to better his material circumstances as the essence of human freedom. In the words of Woodrow Wilson, when he was campaigning for the presidency, "If America is not to have free enterprise, then she can have freedom of no sort whatever."[15]

A corollary of economic individualism is that each person should earn whatever position he occupies in society. This is a relatively new concept. Throughout history, most societies have considered it right and natural that children should grow up to inherit the occupation and status of their parents. Social mobility has always existed in reality, to a greater or lesser degree, but it was regarded as exceptional and, usually, deplorable. This unfavorable attitude has persisted in much of the world even to the present day, and it stands in revealing contrast to the favorable attitude that has prevailed in the United States since its early years as an independent nation.

The following discussion will often mention Europe and, in particular, England. I realize that in recent years these countries have been undergoing social transformation and that they now present an ambiguous aspect, in some respects resembling the United States but in others remaining traditional. My analysis will refer to them only in their traditional form, as they have existed up to and during most of the Twentieth Century.

In a traditional society, including the societies of Europe, when someone attempts to rise in the world, he encounters opposition both from those on higher levels, who condemn him as an upstart, and from those at his own level, who resent his attempt to get above them. In addition, there is usually a prevailing climate of pessimism as to his chances of success: opportunities are few, the ascent is difficult, and achievement is precarious. Since the number of prizes is assumed to be limited, reality is viewed as being zero-sum: if you go up, someone else must go down.

If a person does manage to make good spectacularly, it tends to provoke rancorous envy and even hatred. When the stock market crashed suddenly in 1987, Americans reacted to it as an unmitigated disaster, but in England there was a public outburst of glee at jumped-up yuppies losing their money. A joke exists with variations around the world (two examples: 1. Why don't you need a secure lid on a bucket of Mexican crabs? 2. Why aren't there any pitchfork devils guarding the pit in hell where the souls of Bangladeshi sinners are tortured?). The punch line is always the same: Because whenever one of them tries to escape, the others pull him back.

Faced with uncertainty, difficulty, and hostility, an individual tends to think and act with caution. The lower-class Englishman doubts that striving to improve his lot is likely to get him anywhere. In Italy, positions in the civil service are highly prized because, while dull and tedious, they are secure. Small businesses abound in Europe because their owners are afraid to expand operations. Avoiding risk is the rule, especially among the French, who have a maxim of life, "Be on your guard."[16]

The attitudes and beliefs that are prevalent in America stand in complete and utter contrast to those of traditional societies. Since at least the 1830s, and probably earlier, individual Americans have been telling themselves that their respective positions in society are determined, not by forces beyond their control, but by their own actions: they could become whatever they chose to be.[17] Personal volition is the crucial factor. Talent and ability are thought to be less important in achieving success than ambition and effort. The highly motivated man with ordinary intelligence can surpass his more brilliant but lazy rival. All you have to do is want something "bad enough" and try hard enough. Accordingly, those who become rich feel free to brag, not that they are smarter than other people, but that they work much harder.

These convictions have shaped the basic outlook and behavior of the American. He faces the world and the future with the self-assurance that his own exertions will get him what he wants. He is determined, not merely to equal the status of his parents, but to exceed it. He knows no rest, always working to advance himself and to surpass others. He is ready to take risks, and he is not crushed by failure. If he happens to lose money in a venture, he is buoyed up by the confidence that he can make more (in contrast to the Frenchman, who feels such a material loss as if it were part of himself).[18] In the midst of all his toil, the American is not infuriated or discouraged by the success of others, for he believes there are plenty of opportunities and rewards to go around. The sight of someone else getting ahead only spurs him on to redouble his own efforts.

Reflections of these national tendencies can be seen even at the lower levels of society. European visitors have remarked with surprise that the poor in America are not passive, inert, and resigned to their situation. Tocqueville in particular noticed that when those on the bottom viewed the affluence of those above them, they always experienced the same emotions, not submission to the hand of fate or indignation at the injustice of the social order, but hope and anticipation that they too would someday enjoy such a life.[19] With the same optimism that animates other

Americans, the poor believe that their own conduct will determine their future and that consequently they will attain prosperity at last.

Foreigners often misunderstand the character of Americans and accuse them of being materialists and loving money. In fact, as Henry Adams and other close observers of the social scene have remarked, Americans actually do not care all that much about material things. If they did, New York would be as beautiful as Paris, and its restaurant cuisine would be greatly improved. After one attains a certain level of comfort, money and the things it buys become important to the American primarily for what they symbolize to himself and to those around him. They are his scorecard in life. They signify that he is a productive member of society, a success. If there is anything that Americans regard as a measure of human competence, it is the ability to make money, as distinguished from its mere possession.[20]

Any American who sets up his own business, however humble, is regarded with approval, and if he succeeds in making it profitable and expanding its size, he wins the highest admiration of his fellow countrymen. Attitudes are different on the other side of the Atlantic. Even up to the present day, Europeans have had a low opinion of the small entrepreneur on the make. In their view, he is no more than a nimble, scheming rogue with little in the way of moral principle or personal integrity, who will change himself like a chameleon at the first glint of money.[21]

A further illustration of these two opposing standards of value can be seen in their treatment of parvenus. In Europe, and probably most everywhere else, such people have traditionally been the object of ridicule and disgust. Their newly acquired wealth has elevated them to high status, but they lack the manners that are supposed to go with it. The literature of comedy has often depicted their pretensions and agonies, as they desperately try to masquerade as members of the upper class, only to have their incorrigible lowness exposed.

America, on the contrary, not merely tolerates parvenus but celebrates them as admirable individuals. Their low origins are evidence of their extraordinary achievement: they started with so little and yet acquired so much. Even their gross vulgarities fail to provoke the visceral aversion that they do in Europe. Ordinary people are pleased to see that the rich are not all that different from themselves, inferring thereby that they might become rich too.

A similar contrast between the two transatlantic cultures appears in their respective ideas about inherited wealth. In Europe, it has a simple and obvious value for its possessors. It provides the foundation for the high position which they have enjoyed and which their descendants will enjoy after them. In America, it is something more problematical. Although it blatantly violates the principle that each individual should earn his place in society, Americans have never made a serious attempt to abolish or even to restrict it. This is partly because, lacking a zero-sum view of the world, they do not feel that one man's good fortune diminishes the chances of everyone else, but also because they regard inherited wealth as a mixed blessing, at times a definite liability.

Since Americans value the ability to make money as a measure of human competence, they long ago came to the conclusion that anyone already born with money is likely to develop into a useless, ineffective person who will eventually lose what he inherited. From the late Nineteenth Century until far into the Twentieth, it was a widely and frequently repeated platitude that the son of a rich man labored under more of a disadvantage in life than the son of a poor man. Even today, from time to time some prominent businessman will announce publicly that he is not going to ruin his children by bequeathing all his wealth to them ("like leaving them a case of psychological cancer").[22] And many of the sons of affluence have doubts about themselves, wondering whether they would be capable of succeeding without assistance from their parents.

The importance Americans place on earning money explains the commercial avidity that exists even at the upper reaches of society. Children of privilege often share the desire of their less fortunate contemporaries to surpass their parents, which is all the more difficult since they are already at such a high level. Lazy rich people feel obliged at least to go through the motions of working. The man who makes a fortune usually does not relax and enjoy it but devotes himself to making more. This last phenomenon has always amazed Europeans—millionaires who continue to slave away at their businesses until age or illness forces them out.[23]

All these striving personal ambitions, at work through the length and breadth of the land, from the top to the bottom of society, have produced a collective culture of overwhelming energy and activity. American society has "the morale of an army on the march," declared a French economist in the 1830s. A century and a half later, another observer remarked that "American cities have the feeling of nomad camps...inhabited, temporarily, by people on the way to somewhere else." In the 1880s, "Go and get it!" was a nationally popular slogan; in the 1980s, people were urging each other to "Go for it!" The rapid pace of life is often disconcerting to visitors from abroad. "They are always in motion...," complained an Italian, "like sharks, who keep swimming even as they eat."[24]

One specific manifestation of this general tendency is geographical mobility. During the first half of the Nineteenth Century, foreigners viewed with astonishment the tremendous and continual flood of people from the East into the West. Each new state had only just become populated when its younger inhabitants began to leave and travel farther west. Even when they were doing well where they were, they abandoned their present locations for what they believed would be better opportunities elsewhere. Since the close of the frontier, Americans have continued to alter their residences at a rate which is probably the highest in the Western world and which, one sociologist claims, is surpassed only by nomadic tribes.[25]

For people in traditional societies, geographical mobility makes little sense. Lacking the confidence that conditions will be better anywhere else, they see no point to giving up the pleasures and advantages of living in a community with an existing network of friends and relatives. It is no surprise that Europeans "move house" far less frequently than Americans. When the English are obliged to do so, they have a special line of self-help books to make the task easier.[26] Americans neither want nor need such assistance.

—3—

Geographical mobility needs to be distinguished from social mobility. The former refers to changing physical location. The latter refers to changing places in the social hierarchy, that is, going up or down in the world (also known as vertical mobility). Economic individualism posits the existence of social mobility. Individual Americans struggling to get ahead in life are encouraged by the belief that countless others have already succeeded in doing so.

But anyone who examines the actual rates of social mobility in America, either upward or downward, will discover that they are much lower than might have been expected. Very few people who have become rich began life at the bottom of the social ladder or anywhere near it. Far from being dissipated by feckless heirs, large fortunes have tended to pass intact through generations. Actual changes in social position tend to occur in small steps, not by going from rags to riches or the reverse. Years ago, two prominent sociologists, Seymour Martin Lipset and Reinhard Bendix, compared the rates of social mobility in several industrialized countries and concluded that those in the United States were not significantly different from those in Europe, either in the present or in the past. Subsequent studies have tended to confirm their findings.[27]

The lack of dramatic social mobility in America is not surprising in view of the realities of social class, specifically the crucial advantages that the offspring of the middle class (especially the upper-middle class) have over those of the lower class (euphemistically called the working class). Superior financial resources are only one factor, and not always the most significant one. Equally important, if not more so, are superior non-financial assets, which have been called "social capital" or "cultural capital." The middle-class child grows up in an environment that encourages and assists him in directions leading to his becoming a middle-class adult. He benefits from such things as the right schools and the right social activities. He has parents who understand how the mechanisms of society work, who employ them to his advantage, and who instruct him in their operation.

This helpful influence is internal as well as external. A middle-class youth naturally and automatically absorbs attitudes and behavior that are suited to the world of middle-class occupations. And he acquires motivation as well. His parents' expectations, his own self-esteem, his taste for the kind of life to which he has become accustomed—all demand that he achieve at least the level where he was born. This is especially true of the upper-middle-class child, who has become addicted to the privileges of his station and will do whatever is necessary to keep enjoying them, thus giving him a ferocious drive which—contrary to popular notions about spoiled lazy kids from affluent homes—surpasses the desire for better things that may prompt someone lower down the social scale.[28]

Lower-class children lack these advantages, which begin to be acquired at an early age. Middle-class parents encourage their sons and daughters to exercise independence within limits. Lower-class parents, in contrast, impose discipline that may be authoritarian or lax or an erratic mixture of the two. Some of their children become so impulsive and headstrong that they have difficulty getting through school or holding down a minimally respectable job. Most learn the lesson of obedience but acquire along with it the detrimental characteristics of fatalism, passivity, and shortsightedness, instead of the middle-class habits of taking the initiative and planning for the long term. They tend just to "let things happen."

When, for example, a middle-class patient learns that he has a serious medical condition, he seeks out information and attempts to educate himself about it; a lower-class patient does what the doctor tells him to do and nothing more. The following statements are from lower-class females: it's foolish to worry about the future, the future takes care of itself, you can't plan everything in life. Such sentiments stand in glaring contrast to the remark by a middle-class woman that having a child is like signing a twenty-year contract.[29]

It is only natural for a person from a lower-class background who enters the world of middle-class work to experience difficulties in adapting to its subtle norms of behavior. At times, he may be too blunt and tactless; at others, he may not be assertive enough. He will probably not know how to promote himself to superiors without acting like an obnoxious braggart or an obvious sycophant. He may refuse to promote himself at all under the mistaken idea that his work will speak for itself. His tendency to separate his job from his private life keeps him from participating in the off-hours socializing that plays an important part in the transmission of business information and the making of deals.[30]

"Antagonistic cooperation" is the term that the sociologist David Riesman used to characterize upper-middle class and professional work. At one moment, people may behave like rivals; at another, they may act like teammates; and sometimes they can be both at once. These shifts and apparent contradictions easily baffle and may even outrage a person whose social upbringing has not made him accustomed to them.[31]

The reality that the social class of parents acts as a decisive factor in determining the future lives of their children would be highly unwelcome news to Americans, not just because it contradicts their own personal hopes but because it is contrary to their notions about the source of national prosperity. They believe that the more social mobility a country has, the more prosperity it will enjoy, as the result of more energetic and talented people occupying higher and more influential positions.

That is a dubious supposition. Too great a concentration of ambition and ability can have undesirable consequences. A team composed of brilliant, original minds is more likely to dissolve into fractious bickering than to perform efficient work—too many chiefs, or would-be chiefs, and too few Indians. In addition, if the ideal of absolute and total mobility were actually attained, and everyone really had an equal chance of rising or falling according to his inborn, natural abilities alone, it would create an intolerable increase in the level of social tension and animosity. Anyone who is familiar with how an upper-middle-class parent views the possibility of his children failing to attain admission into an Ivy League university can imagine his emotions and behavior at the prospect of their descending to a life of menial positions and low occupations.

As a matter of fact, the crucial aspect of social mobility is not its reality but its perception. Americans may very well have no better chance of attaining a level above that of their birth than Europeans have, but they certainly believe that they do, and this is the important thing. As I have explained above, their belief in the principles of economic individualism, specifically their conviction that each individual's fate and future is within his own control, has fueled the enormous energy and productivity which have characterized their nation. What is most remarkable is that they are able to maintain this faith in spite of a contrary reality.

The reality of social class is something which they most emphatically and definitely refuse to accept or even to recognize. Social class, in contrast to social status, includes heredity as a fundamental component. Status is determined by what you do for a living. Class is determined by that but also by what your father did for a living, which is an utterly revolting notion to a people who revere the ideal of individualism. Ever since the early days of their new nation, Americans have been proclaiming that social class is something European, not American. Throughout the Nineteenth Century, they kept reassuring themselves that their population contained neither hereditary paupers nor hereditary criminals. Around the time of World War I, adults were preaching to the young that there was no such thing as the luck of birth or any other kind of luck, that whatever a man received in life came to him only from his own efforts. And even when the young grew up and found reality to be otherwise, they still believed and repeated the credo because it had been inculcated into them with such unhesitating certitude, uncompromising righteousness, and unrelenting persistence.[32]

As the sociologists of the Twentieth Century began to explore American society, they discovered social class, and they also discovered that Americans did not want to hear about it. This aversion has persisted to the present day and shows no sign of abating. Americans are willing to view themselves from almost any other perspective—ethnicity, kinship, or race, for example—but not class. Lower-class people disregard it, despite its overwhelming influence on them, and talk as if life were entirely a matter of free choices made by individuals. Even the intellectual left avoids it: they may profess a trinity of "race, gender, and class" and go on endlessly about the first two, but they have very little to say about the third. On those rare occasions when Americans are obliged to confront the reality of social class, they becomes angry, as if at something utterly reprehensible that has no right to exist. "If you so much as mention it, you're accused of promoting class distinctions," observed an author whose book touched on the sensitive subject.[33]

In such a situation, the appropriate word is taboo, a thing that must not be referred to directly or explicitly. This particular taboo is rigorously observed at all social levels. Although people at the top are more aware of class distinctions than other Americans, they prudently share the reticence of their fellow countrymen. If one of their young offspring—with the innocent indiscretion of children in stating the unmentionable obvious—happens to make some derogatory comment about the inferiority of other people, he is promptly and severely reprimanded with the admonition, "There are no classes in America!" accompanied by an explanation, "Of course there are, but we NEVER talk about it."[34]

The following is a more common example of the taboo, in fact one to which every American who has attended a large public high school can attest. The student body inevitably includes a group of "bad kids"—designated by any number of colorful labels, such as "rogues," "toughs," or "hitters"—who despise the teachers, violate the rules, and get into fights. They are often the subject of conversation among the other students and their parents, but never, through all the length of these vivid and prolonged discussions, is one obvious and elementary fact mentioned. The "bad kids" come from the bottom of society—the poorest homes, the lowest families. Probably every parent perceives this reality, but no one expresses it, at least not in public or in front of the children.

One of the consequences of a taboo is the necessity of resorting to euphemisms. Americans may mention a person's "background," ethnicity, or education to indicate his social class. Accents of speech can serve this purpose. When, for example, a New York newspaper stated that someone revealed his Bronx origins by the way he talked, the implication was that he came from the lower levels. Even the political left avoids the c-word and employs such substitutes as "income groups" or "wage earners."[35]

Not everyone gets the message. When people avoid a subject and speak of it indirectly, if at all, the result is widespread ignorance and misperception, which Americans prefer to the embarrassment of reality. When John or Robert Kennedy pronounced the words Cuba and California as "Cuber" and "Californyer," the general public regarded it as nothing more than a regionalism, even a charming one. It was in fact the perversion of a lower-class Boston Irish accent: the sons of a parvenu trying to talk posh. Kennedy worshippers did not want to know this, just as they did not want to know how close their heroes were—ethnically, politically, and emotionally—to the low-life demagogue Joe McCarthy, and how far they were from the high-minded, sophisticated, upscale liberals who have become their posthumous idolaters.[36]

Go from the United State to Europe and the situation is totally changed. There social class is clearly observed and openly discussed, in England especially. If Americans would rather not even think about the topic, let alone talk about it, the English seem unable to stop doing either. When two strangers meet, each immediately tries to assess the other's place in the social hierarchy. The standard conversational gambit is not that of the United States, "What do you do?" (i.e. what is your status, as determined by your occupation?), but "Where are you from?" (i.e. what are your class origins?).[37] A verbal accent is the most obvious sign of one's position. It used to be said that an Englishman could not open his mouth without arousing the contempt of those who heard him (if he was lower than they) or their hatred (if he was higher). Aside from speech, there are numerous other marks of class identity, most of them easily perceived and universally understood.

While the indicators of social class on that side of the Atlantic are blatantly obvious, on the American side they are quite subtle. During the Nineteenth Century, European travelers in the United States complained that they had difficulty distinguishing people of lower levels from those of higher levels by the clothes they wore. This phenomenon has persisted through the Twentieth Century, as David Riesman observed: "The foreigner who visits America is likely to think that salesgirls, society ladies, and movie actresses all dress alike, as compared with the clear status differences of Europe. But the American knows—has to know if he is to get along in life and love—that this is an error: that one must look for small qualitative differences...." The same is true of other marks of class distinction. Both Europeans and Americans carry them, but the Americans have to pay much closer attention to perceive their own.[38]

Not only are the characteristics of each social class more evident in Europe, they also tend to undergo less of an alteration across space and through time. As a result, a European's knowledge of them tends to be more comprehensive and deep, extending beyond simple recognition of present conditions to an understanding of the entire lives of their possessors. On the basis of the slightest acquaintance, one Englishman can make a reasonable estimate as to another Englishman's parentage, education, income, and future prospects.[39]

This is not the case with an American. Amid the faint and shifting signals of social gradation, he is able to discern enough "to get along in life and love," but strictly speaking his perception extends only as far as status; it does not attain an understanding of class. The ordinary American realizes that there are different levels, where people enjoy greater or lesser amounts of money and power. He does not realize how the occupants of these levels naturally and customarily transmit their respective positions to their children. The specific mechanisms by which this occurs eludes his understanding; he fails to grasp the operational advantages which the progeny of one level have over those of a lower level. The European sees these things, usually down to their most precise details, but not the American.

Such imperception is remarkable and problematical in that it involves an entire people in the denial of fundamental social realities. Americans continue to assert that classes do not exist in their country and that all individuals have more or less the same chance—or at least a good chance—of attaining the better things of life. Europeans wonder how they are able to persist in this delusion.[40] Clearly the next question to consider is the following: What factors have inhibited and obstructed the consciousness of class to such a degree that Americans are able to perform their collective act of self-deception?

—4—

At the outset, it is convenient to mention two phenomena which are of secondary rather than primary importance. First, the animation that characterizes the surface of American society—the constant, roiling change—definitely does help to disguise the stability and continuity underneath. Horizontal mobility (including geographical mobility) is often mistaken for vertical mobility, as people continually change jobs and residences in the belief that they will improve their economic condition. While this is no doubt a contributory factor to the imperception of social class, it does not constitute its fundamental cause. A faith in vertical mobility has to precede the act of horizontal mobility: that is, one must first believe that opportunities are available elsewhere before one is willing to move.

A second phenomenon is likewise no more than a contributory factor. In traditional societies like those of Europe, people who rise to higher levels try to hide their low origins; in America, they often advertise them. As a result, vertical mobility in Europe appears to be less common—whereas in America it appears to be more common—than it actually is.

In addition to these two auxiliary factors, there is a third, which exerts a crucial and decisive influence on the thinking and actions of Americans in dealing with the inequalities of social life. The previous chapter discussed the ethos of egalitarianism that prevails in the United States. As was explained at some length, this dominant mentality induces Americans to disguise and mitigate class differences. Instead of emphasizing their superiority, higher-status people tend to profess their similarity and solidarity with everyone else. Instead of accepting the fact of their inferiority and displaying deference to their betters, lower-status people are alert to detect instantly and to castigate ferociously any signs of snobbery from others. And the entire population joins in agreeing that there are no social classes in America.

Once a person assumes that he is intrinsically the equal of everyone else, it is an easy next step to think that there can be no serious obstacles to his rising in the world. And as he becomes convinced that he will eventually occupy one of society's higher places, he tends to regard the people already in those places as his equals. In this way, egalitarianism and individualism reinforce each other.

The elements of this process were observed as early as the 1770s. The previous chapter quoted a Philadelphia clergyman who observed that "the poorest laborer" expressed his views on "religion or politics" with as much freedom and self-confidence as if they were the opinions of a "gentleman or…scholar." And the clergyman then proceeded to explain the reason for this egalitarian behavior: "Every man expects one day or another to be upon a footing with his wealthiest neighbor—and in this hope, shows him no cringing servility, but treats him with a plain, though respectful familiarity."[41]

These tendencies subsequently developed into fundamental characteristics of the entire national culture. The ethos of egalitarianism flatters each person that he is the equal of every other person, while the ideal of individualism promises him that he can attain whatever he desires, provided he is willing to work hard enough for it. The very opposite incentives have been operating in traditional societies, where consciousness of inferiority produces pessimism as to one's future prospects, which in turn confirms one's sense of subordination.

There is a paradox in the relationship between egalitarianism and individualism in American life. The influence of individualism as a dominant national ideal has produced certain results that are far from egalitarian. Numerous social commentators have pointed out the existence of enormous economic inequalities in the United States. The gap between rich and poor is said to be greater there than in any of the other developed Western countries. The American public has often been informed of this reality, but they do not become indignant or upset, since economic individualism promises them the opportunity of becoming rich themselves. Opinion poll after opinion poll has found that an overwhelming majority opposes any measure aimed at creating a more equal distribution of wealth or income.

The rich can feel secure in America. Although they do not receive the deference and servility that they would elsewhere in the world, they also do not arouse the resentment and hatred. They only get into trouble with the rest of the population when they are perceived as not "playing by the rules," that is, trying to get away with things that the law requires of everyone, such as bouncing checks with impunity, failing to pay Social Security for household help, or being heard to brag, "Only the little people pay taxes." (That remark sent the owner of a chain of hotels to jail.)[42]

As long as the rich avoid such obvious gaffes, the public is content to let them enjoy their wealth and all the huge, entirely legal advantages that it brings to them and their heirs. While the rich in other countries feel the need to conceal their money from the hostility of others, the American rich are able to flaunt it with impunity before people who admire such a lifestyle and, confident in the promises of economic individualism, believe they will someday be able to afford it for themselves. There are a few who think those at the bottom should have more money; almost no one thinks that those at the top should have less. As the philosopher George Santayana explained, "To abolish millionaires would have been to dash one's own hopes."[43]

A striking example of this mentality was the response to the presidential candidate George McGovern's proposal in 1972 for a high tax increase on estates of over half a million dollars. The most vociferous opposition came, not from the rich, but from the poor. One woman explained that she had spent years scrubbing floors to put her son through college. She had no money for him to inherit, but she hoped that he would have some to pass on to his children, and she did not want McGovern to prevent it: "He is against the American Dream!"[44]

While Americans admire and indulge the rich, they treat the poor with severity and contempt. Welfare assistance is far lower in the United States than in other advanced Western countries. Only the decade-long depression of the 1930s induced the government to institute measures like social security pensions, unemployment compensation, and industrial accident insurance, which had already existed in Europe for a generation or more. Even today, there is no national medical coverage. As the director of a cancer clinic remarked, those with insurance or money will receive treatment, the rest will die. The United States is the leading country in the first world, yet many of its people live in conditions like those of the third world. The American public is not indignant or upset over this situation. When an international poll asked if the government should take care of the very poor people who were unable to take care of themselves, the percentages in agreement turned out to be the following: Spain 71%, Britain 62%, France 62%, Germany 50%, United States 23%.[45]

Underlying these transatlantic differences is the presence or absence of economic individualism as a national idea. Since Europeans understand that the influence of social class is the chief factor in determining whether one will be rich or poor, they most certainly do not think that a person's income is a reflection of his personal worth. The very opposite is true of Americans. Since they believe that every individual has the opportunity to improve his financial situation, if anyone fails to do so, it must be the result of laziness or some other personal deficiency, and they consequently feel little sympathy and less obligation toward him. As one homespun humorist remarked, "It's no disgrace t'be poor, but it might as well be."[46]

This outlook on life and economic reality is so crucial and basic for Americans that they adhere to it even in the face of obvious evidence to the contrary. In 1875, during a major national depression, the mayor of Bridgeport, Connecticut—P. T. Barnum, as it happened to be—addressed the unemployed and told them that their own indolence was the cause of their present misfortune. Such a stance in such circumstance was by no means unusual, and it has reappeared subsequently in bad times (including and especially the Great Depression of the 1930s) up to the present day. During the severe recession of the early 1990s, when young people were having difficulty finding jobs, older adults called them "slackers," a term that even some of their parents repeated.[47]

So universally and tenaciously have Americans propagated this conviction, that even the objects of its condemnation (the poor and the unsuccessful) have accepted it. People at the bottom of society recognize that they are at a disadvantage, but to a surprising degree they think that their own actions and not external circumstances have determined their fate.[48] In a similar fashion, when a downturn or some other economic change results in owners losing their businesses and executives losing their jobs, the victims tend to blame themselves. This was true in the 1930s depression, as it was of the corporate layoffs (euphemistically called "downsizing") that went on during the 1980s and 1990s.

—5—

The attitudes just described have characterized American opinion about rich and poor from the beginning to the present, but they have not always gone unchallenged. At certain times, when the national economic situation became so bad that it provoked serious and general unrest, questions began to be raised about basic social assumptions and arrangements. This has happened during three eras: (1) the Age of Jackson (1820s and 1830s), (2) the Age of Industrialization (1870s-1900s), and (3) the Great Depression (1930s).

The Panic of 1819 was followed by a deep and prolonged depression. Banks called in loans, farmers lost their land, businesses failed, unemployment rose. Workers began joining unions and forming their own small political parties, for the first time ever. Some people spoke in angry tones of a conflict between "producers" and "accumulators." The former were the many, who performed the actual labor that produced the wealth of the nation; the latter were the few (capitalists, especially bankers), who by devious means accumulated for themselves the wealth that the others had created.

This sounded like a declaration of class warfare, and it was met by urgent contrary assertions, particularly from prominent politicians like Daniel Webster and Edward Everett. A distinction between social orders was something for Europeans, they declared; it did not apply to America. Here everyone was a worker and a creator of wealth, from the hired laborer to the self-made capitalist. In fact, by steady effort and sober living, "laborers today will be capitalists tomorrow."[49] Workers had no need for their own political party because "a harmony of interests" united them with the rest of society, specifically with businessmen. Large accumulations of wealth by the latter did not operate to other people's disadvantage but, on the contrary, contributed to the prosperity of the entire nation.

In these statements one can discern elements of individualism and egalitarianism, which had already formed a national orthodoxy strong enough to deflect and undermine the contemporary challenge from the left. In spite of all their noise and rhetoric, the two principal popular movements of the time (Jacksonianism and Antimasonry) were not genuinely radical. They did not intend to seize the property of the rich; they only wanted to deprive them of unfair advantages, to make them—in the words of a later era—"play by the rules." The principal fear motivating both the supporters of Andrew Jackson and the opponents of the Masons was that wealthy and powerful men were using their resources to corrupt and control government, so as to secure for themselves more wealth and power. A sinister connection between those with money and those in office seemed especially plausible because it was the government which in this period chartered the hated banks that issued devaluated paper currency and foreclosed on people's property.

After President Jackson was victorious in his war with the national Bank of the United States and after public opinion forced the closure of many Masonic lodges, Americans felt great relief at the thought that the country had escaped from danger, that the integrity of political institutions had been restored, and that the machinations of the few had been foiled. Actually, nothing fundamental had changed. The great inequalities of wealth that had existed in the past persisted into the future, and the rich retained the crucial advantages they have always enjoyed, before and since.

Trade unions and workingmen's political parties, which had sprung up at the beginning of the Age of Jackson, were in decline by its end. The promises of economic individualism, reinforced by egalitarian social manners, affected members of the lower classes in such a way as to prevent them from perceiving their common situation and acting collectively. When workers fell into a dispute with an employer, they viewed him as an individual who was behaving unreasonably or selfishly, not as a member of a social class whose interests were naturally and inevitably opposed to those of their own, as they would have done in Europe. This perspective had the effect of limiting and localizing labor conflicts during the 1820s and 1830s, and ever since. When workers in one trade or in one town went out on strike, the workers of other trades or in other towns did not feel an automatic sense of solidarity with them, as fellow members of the same disadvantaged class. Whenever conditions became seriously bad on the job, a worker, animated by feelings of individualism and optimism, was more likely, not to join with other aggrieved workers in protest, but simply to leave and look for a better situation elsewhere.[50]

Perhaps the most striking evidence of the American worker's lack of class consciousness was his attitude toward small business. Unlike his European counterparts, he did not expect to remain an employee all his life. His chief aspiration in that age and through the decades up to the present day has always been to become an independent proprietor of his own shop. Prompted by this hope, he has tended to view the small businessman with sympathy. Workingmen's political parties of the 1830s actually allowed such persons to join their ranks. So did the Knights of Labor, the first prominent national union in the country and a powerful organization during the 1870s and 1880s, which permitted workers who had become employers to retain their union membership. The contrast with Europe could not be greater. There, anyone who goes from labor to management has joined the enemy, and his former workmates consider him a traitor.[51]

While individualism has weakened labor's position in relation to business, it has strengthened business's position in relation to labor. Ever since the earliest days of unionization, owners of businesses have denounced the very idea of workers acting collectively as a violation of individual freedom—not merely their own but the workers' as well. In a typical statement, the president of one company claimed that he acted against unions "simply to protect the free will of each individual."[52] This stance has been generally popular in America, even among those without obviously self-interested motives. During the Nineteenth Century, courts of law regularly handed down decisions against unions on the grounds that they deprived the individual worker from disposing of his labor as he saw fit (the same rationale that courts invoked when they struck down safety regulations passed by state legislatures).

———

After the Civil War, the conflict between capital and labor became much more serious. With the rise of industrialization, business organizations grew in size and imposed new demands on workers. Unions grew in response and became more militant. Every decade there was a major depression accompanied by strikes, demonstrations, disorder, mayhem, and killings. Lacking the restraint of either traditional upper-class paternalism on one side or traditional lower-class deference on the other, the struggle was more violent and bloody than in Europe, which was going through a similar period of social unrest. From 1872 to 1914, in Great Britain, France, and Germany combined, a total of a little more than fifty people lost their lives during labor disputes; in the United States the figure was between 500 and 800.[53]

The conflict also became more serious on an ideological level. Opponents of capitalism proposed alternative forms of society, the most significant and enduring of which was socialism. In Europe, political parties espousing one form or another of this doctrine have played highly important roles in various countries during both the Nineteenth and Twentieth Centuries. This did not happen in America, to the puzzlement of observers then and since. "Why is there no socialism in the United States?" asked the title of a book published in 1906. Since socialism was a reaction to industrial capitalism, why did it fail to appeal to workers in the most industrialized and capitalistic nation in the world?

Many a proselytizer of socialism has asked this question after being frustrated in his efforts. It was not that he lacked evidence or logic to support the cause he was arguing. He could illustrate the plight of the poor with specific facts. In New York, for example, during the prosperous year of 1903, over 60,000 families (14 percent of the total) were evicted from their homes, and one person of every ten who died in the city was buried with the destitute and forsaken of potter's field.[54] He could demonstrate how the structural arrangements of society had loaded people in the lower class with enormous disadvantages and how the middle class was thereby able to exploit them.

However skilled and persuasive he might be, the socialist repeatedly encountered the same response. A worker who had been listening to him would indicate that he understood the line of argument, would admit that he had to agree with it, and then would declare, with adamant though incongruous conviction, "But there are no classes in America."[55] Socialism had struck the impenetrable shield of egalitarian faith that protects the ideology of individualism.

Throughout the Twentieth Century, people on the left have again and again discussed the reasons for their defeat. They have analyzed various factors that divided American workers against themselves—differences in race and ethnicity being two of the most popular. But these are superficial explanations. Even if the entire workforce of the United States had consisted only of white Anglo-Saxon Protestant males, they still would not have developed class consciousness because the ethos of egalitarianism is so powerful and the ideal of individualism is so attractive.

The undemocratic manners that prevailed in Europe constantly reminded a worker that he was a member of the lower class. He accepted this status and accordingly regarded himself as belonging to a separate order with its own interests, characteristics, and values, which were different from those of the rest of society. "Working men have no country," declared Marx and Engels in their *Communist Manifesto* of 1848. This was not true of the United States, where a worker felt himself to be a member of the entire nation and to share the same attitudes and aspirations as his fellow citizens, high and low alike.

Clear evidence of the difference between America and Europe can be found in a comparison between the career opportunities of their respective trade union officers. In Europe, if a union official had an outstanding talent for leadership and organization, the only direction he could take in public life was to embrace radical politics. No respectable, establishment party wanted such a person of low social origins. If he were in Great Britain at the turn of the century, for example, he would have had to join the Labour Party and accept its socialist principles of class conflict.

This inevitable connection between unionism and radicalism did not occur in America. There, a well-worn path led from the union office to a major party and to the state legislature, where a representative of the workers could join forces with middle-class reformers and associate easily, as a genuine equal, with people who in Europe would have remained his unmistakable and unalterable social superiors. In the process, his thinking became like theirs. He approached a political issue, less as a militant partisan of the left and more as a concerned citizen facing a national problem. Of course, he blamed the greedy bosses who wanted to keep too much of the profits of industry for themselves, but he also blamed the radicals who wanted to destroy the entire system. One labor leader around the turn of the century asserted that, lying beneath the present superficial and transient conflicts, there was a fundamental "harmony between capital and labor."[56]

The social unrest of the Nineteenth Century culminated in the Era of Progressivism. By this time, a consensus had developed—at least among educated and articulate people—that government should intervene and institute reforms to improve social conditions, although exactly what these reforms should be was a matter of much argument and doubt. On a more abstract level, some social critics expressed dissatisfaction with individualism as a national ideal. Since the 1880s, its connection with unrestrained capitalism had brought it into disrepute in intellectual circles. There was much talk about reforming it or finding a balance between it and socialism. "Association" was proclaimed as an alternative to individualism, and it had become a buzzword by the 1890s, much as "community" became a buzzword in the 1990s.[57] Like community, association was a vague and tenuous concept that failed to provoke much of a response from the man on the street or the worker in the factory.

The end of World War I saw a national repudiation of the extravagant hopes and high-flown rhetoric that had characterized the Progressive Era—a "return to normalcy," as promised by the newly elected president, Warren Gamaliel Harding. Talk about such things as association came to an end, and individualism began to be openly and widely approved by journalists and various other retailers of public opinion.

The prominent engineer and administrator Herbert Hoover reflected the transition. In 1917, he had been speaking of the evils that had resulted from "a hundred years of unbridled private initiative," specifically a "lack of responsibility in the American individual to the people as a whole...."[58] In 1922, with a book entitled *American Individualism*, he became a prominent spokesman and advocate of a renewed and reformed individualism, thereby advancing his public career in a direction that led to his being elected president by the end of the decade.

After attaining a high-water mark in 1912 (6 percent of the national electoral vote), the American Socialist Party fell into decline during the 1920s, along with other forms of political and labor radicalism. Laws passed by the Progressives had addressed some of capitalism's worst abuses, such as child labor and workplace sanitation. But nothing fundamental had changed, and the great inequalities of wealth remained.

The third and last significant challenge to America's orthodoxy of individualism occurred during the Great Depression. In some respects, this might seem to have been the most serious of the three. The economic slump was worse than anything that had happened before. It persisted for an entire decade, with the rate of unemployment reaching 25 percent at its lowest point. The public's discontent was more acute and widespread than it had ever been in the past, and the demands for change were consequently more strident and extreme. Half the editors of small-town newspapers—in ordinary times the most blinkered of mossbacks—were calling for the banks to be nationalized. Liberals were referring to America as a "sick society," while radicals were predicting the collapse of the whole "rotten structure" of capitalism. One prominent historian and pundit dismissed individualism as a "myth" and an "old slogan," and he advised his fellow citizens, not to attempt its renovation, but to "get rid of it." In the world of practical politics, the New Deal intervened in the economy to an extent that no American government had ever done before, and unlike any previous president, Franklin D. Roosevelt publicly and repeatedly sympathized with labor and criticized management.[59]

Confronted with the threat of these innovations, some businessmen and other people on the right exclaimed that it all meant socialism, and they cried out that the country was on the road to totalitarian collectivization like that of the Soviet Union. In fact, Roosevelt's attacks on business were almost entirely verbal, and the changes he actually instituted were hardly revolutionary. As a result of his New Deal, the public received some social programs and the unions received basic organizing rights, which were no more radical than similar measures that had existed in Western Europe since the turn of the century or earlier.

Such moderation was entirely in accord with the fundamental and persistent views of most Americans. One must not be led astray by the pronouncements of the sophisticated and the prominent. Among this minority, a climate of opinion prevailed during the Great Depression, as it had during the Progressive Era, that society had become too complex and interdependent for the old-fashioned practices of economic individualism, that the government should staff itself with trained experts, and that it should institute centralized "planning" (a buzzword of the 1930s).

Ordinary people felt differently. They saw the Depression, not as something that demanded a basic alteration of social arrangements, but as an interruption, a long stretch of very bad times, which needed temporary measures of relief, to be sure, but which would eventually end and allow them to return to their old ways. They remained, as a well-known pair of contemporary sociologists reluctantly admitted, "individualists in an individualistic culture." Canny New Dealers, following the lead of President Roosevelt, sensed this and justified their programs as promoting "true individual freedom." Social Security in particular was disguised as a form of individualized insurance, from which each person was supposed to receive benefits according to what he had contributed.[60]

The return of prosperity, which came with World War II and continued into the post-war era, put an end to the revolutionary hopes and radical schemes that had characterized intellectual discourse during the 1930s, and the conservative mood which accompanied the onset of the Cold War buried them under heaps of obloquy and opprobrium.

—6—

By the second half of the Twentieth Century, any threat of serious social disruption had vanished, and the United States was left with a highly motivated and cooperative workforce. Union leadership as well as its rank and file accepted in principle and in practice the idea of a "harmony of interests" between themselves and management. Both sides were intent on increasing productivity, in the conviction that both would benefit from the resulting prosperity.

Visitors from abroad were startled to hear workers' representatives speak with collective pride about facilities where they were in fact only employees: "Did you see OUR plant?" At times, the Europeans had to ask themselves whether they were listening to a spokesman of management or of labor.[61] It was not at all what they would have expected in their own societies, which took for granted a natural and inevitable conflict of interest between owner and worker, with the latter muttering under his breath, "You are not going to get rich on my back."

This cultural contrast has been reflected in day-to-day behavior on the job. American management usually encourages its employees to suggest ways of improving operations and listens seriously to what they have to say. The sight of suggestion boxes in factories prompted an English visitor around the turn of the century to comment that they would be unthinkable in his country. For a worker to claim that he knew a better way of running the business would have been viewed as a gross impertinence and would most likely have resulted in his dismissal. In the 1980s, English unions warned their members against making suggestions for improvement even when they were encouraged to do so, since they were not being paid for it.[62]

In Europe, workers tend to mistrust management, under the assumption that whatever it does will be in its own interest and to their detriment. This is especially the case with the introduction of technical innovations. British workers in particular have resisted new machines that do the job better, because they assume such devices will put them out of work. They automatically oppose change of any sort and want to continue doing things in the old way. American workers, on the contrary, accept and even welcome the new machines because they see them as making their labor easier and more productive. They agree with the idea that, given the threat of competition from technology and from abroad, the only way they can keep their jobs is to work as efficiently as possible.

In the matter of workplace safety, American workers and managers have displayed remarkably similar attitudes. A manager resists safety measures if they reduce productivity. A worker resists them if they reduce his earnings. Since productivity and earnings are linked, their points of view tend to be similar. During the bad old days, foreign visitors were shocked by the lack of safety measures and the high rate of industrial accidents, but they admitted that American workers were not particularly worried about the risks they ran.[63] British workers have behaved differently. For them, safety on the job has often served as a convenient excuse for slowing down the pace of labor or suspending it altogether.

At the bottom of these cultural differences is the perception of social class, or more precisely, its perception on one side of the Atlantic and the lack of perception on the other. Workers in Europe realize with merciless clarity that they have been born into a low level of society and that—barring some extremely unusual stroke of fortune—the normal and natural thing is for them to remain there for the rest of their lives. Their consequent resentment and lack of ambition are understandable. Workers in America have no such understanding and accordingly do not experience the same negative response. Since the ethos of egalitarianism has convinced them that they are the equal of everyone else, and the ideal of individualism has promised them that they can attain anything they desire, they are blissfully unaware of the crucial disadvantages under which they operate, and they are insouciantly indifferent to the enormous advantages enjoyed by their social superiors.

Animated by this mentality, they focus their attention on their own immediate prospects and on people in their circle of peers. Those above them are a source of indifference rather than envy. I remember an account of an American chauffeur. He did not resent the wealth of his employer; it simply did not interest him. But the moment he heard about another chauffeur who was making twenty-five cents an hour more than he did, his attention came to life, and he wanted to know all about it.

This attitude is typical of Americans in general, as the journalist David Brooks discovered when he went out to investigate how much animosity the lower-income people in the hinterland felt toward the higher-income people in the cities. It was a time of economic downturn during the 1990s, and there was much talk among the pundits about a widening income gap separating the rich from everyone else. Brooks found no animosity. The people he interviewed could not even grasp what he was talking about. When he finally resorted to the terms "haves" and "have-nots," he thought they understood, until he realized that they all considered themselves to be "haves," even the ones whose income was well below the median. People compare themselves with their neighbors, he concluded; they do not compare themselves with millionaires they happen to see on television.[64]

Ever since the first appearance of labor discontent in the early Nineteenth Century, radicals on the left have been trying to raise the class consciousness of American workers, so that they might understand the disadvantages of their situation and unite to demand improvements. This effort has made very little progress, which is not surprising, given the mentality of the workers. In 1838, during one of his speeches against class hostility and conflict, Edward Everett told the following story. A man confronted a millionaire and asked him why he did not share his wealth with his fellow citizens. The millionaire made a calculation (the sum of his fortune divided by the total population of the United States) and declared that the man should receive fifty cents as his fair and equal share.[65] In the 1960s, a foreman told me the very same story, as it had been repeated among his crew of carpenters. Unanimously and emphatically they had expressed their sympathy with the millionaire and their contempt for the man who had tried to embarrass him. The futility of trying to preach socialism or any other kind of radical politics to such people goes without saying.

Although the task of class-consciousness raising has become increasingly more difficult and increasingly less likely to attain success, a certain number of people on the left still persist at it. Since the 1970s, they have not been able to pronounce the word "individualism" without disapproval. As they have repeated—so often that the idea has become a platitude in many intellectual circles—individualism works to the benefit of those at the higher levels of society by perpetuating their advantages, while it perpetuates the disadvantages of those at the lower levels. But people simply do not want to hear this message. Books and articles continue to appear, warning that inequalities separating the rich from the rest of the population are large and growing larger, while the possibilities of the poor rising in society are small and growing smaller. The first half of both these assertions is unquestionably true, and the second half may well be. But the public response is nil.

After the stock market collapsed in 2000, and a depression followed, one left-wing journalist and cultural commentator suggested hopefully, "Americans are perhaps finally ready to think…about the ugly realities of social class." It did not happen, and in 2004 he declared in exasperation that his fellow countrymen were failing to make "certain mental connections about the world, connections that until recently were treated as obvious or self-evident everywhere on the planet…. People getting their fundamental interests wrong is what American political life is all about."[66]

But is he correct? Has America's lower class been acting contrary to its interests? Are the workers victims of "false consciousness" (to use the Marxist terminology)? Not precisely. While the lower class is still the lower class in its position relative to the rest of society, it has gained in absolute terms. The conditions in which its members live have been continually improving over what they used to be. This is true of the entire society at all levels. An American today enjoys more comforts, more entertainment, better health, and less degrading work than his grandfather did, and that grandfather enjoyed more and better things than his grandfather, and so on back to the founding of the nation.

America's high standard of living is famous the world over. An Indian from Bombay expressed his desire to move to the United States, because he wanted "to live in a country where the poor people are fat." The Communist revolutionary Leon Trotsky was hardly inclined to applaud life under capitalism, but he could not restrain his admiration in describing the modern conveniences that furnished an ordinary worker's apartment in New York City in 1917. Recently, a lively observer of contemporary trends remarked that if you are unable to reach your electrician or air-conditioning mechanic, he may well be on a Caribbean cruise with his third wife or new girlfriend, enjoying luxuries that used to be limited to the rich.[67]

There is a fundamental problem with these benefits, however. They are not, by themselves alone, a sufficiently strong enough motivation to inspire the effort that is necessary to produce them. Americans invest an enormous amount of time, energy, and attention in their work. They would not behave in this way if they thought that all they were accomplishing was to raise the standard of living for everyone. That would not be enough. They need to believe that they are advancing their own prospects, rising in society, and realizing their personal dreams.

Americans are able to sustain their faith in economic individualism only by being unrealistic in imagining the future prospects of their own personal careers. And this they do grossly and persistently. One poll revealed that over 44 percent of male executives aspired to be CEO. Since each company can have only a single CEO, the odds of all these aspirants becoming one are hardly favorable. Another poll found that

25 percent of all Americans (and 45 percent of those aged 18 to 30) thought it likely that they would someday be rich.[68]

At times, extravagant personal optimism defies, not merely the likelihood of failure, but its mathematical certainty. Twenty percent of voters surveyed in 2000 said that they expected their incomes would eventually reach the category of the top 1 percent, and another 19 percent believed they were already in the top 1 percent.[69] Despite repeated disappointments and unsatisfactory progress, the American does not lose heart but continues to imagine that his main chance may be just around the corner. If advancing age finally wears down his hopes for himself, he can continue to maintain them for his children.

However mistaken these individuals may be, their illusions serve a collective purpose. America's prosperity, in the words of one journalist, "depends on millions of people being motivated to try their best day by day," and nothing can provide the necessary motivation so well as human self-interest, even—or, one might say, especially—when it is unrealistic and exaggerated.[70]

This has been the case throughout American history. The expansion westward in the Nineteenth Century, for example, was littered with failures, with thousands of small farmers and businessmen "who repeatedly overestimated their chances of success," as more than one scholar has pointed out. But their toil, though it seldom resulted in the realization of their private ambitions, did contribute to the general progress and improvement of the country.[71]

The same could probably be said about most any other sector of American society, at any time and place. Even in the depths of the rural countryside, foreign visitors discovered to their astonishment that the inhabitants were not sunk in a culture of backwardness and sloth, characteristic of a traditional peasantry, but were energetic, eager for material innovations and mechanical improvements, and intent on advancing their economic position and income.[72]

Behind this tremendous, massive force of personal exertion and collective achievement stands the ideal of individual freedom. It whispers incessantly to every American that he can be whatever he chooses, that he can attain whatever he wants, that all he needs to do is make the effort and continue making it. I hesitate to call this a lie, even a salutary lie. That would give an ugly name to something which has produced spectacular benefits, which is in fact an essential and fundamental component of national strength and prosperity. Perhaps the most appropriate phrase to describe it would be a "beneficial self-deception."

There is a gap or unbalanced equation between human desires and social realities in America, between the opportunities that people think they have and the conditions that actually exist. The ideal of individualism, assisted by the ethos of egalitarianism, functions as a beneficial self-deception that makes the gap seem to disappear and the two sides of the equation appear to be in balance.

CHAPTER THREE

CHAPTER THREE

The Panglossian Foundation

—1—

T he reader may have noticed that the previous chapter has failed to answer the questions posed at the end of chapter one. While it did go some ways in analyzing the tremendous personal motivation of Americans, it did not explain what prevents all these energetic individuals from running afoul of one another or what keeps their relentless activity channeled in the direction of productive enterprise. This enigma continues to require a solution.

Americans themselves have their own answer. It has never, as far as I know, been expressed as a formal doctrine or articulated as a conscious creed. It consists, instead, of a number of popularly shared attitudes and tacitly accepted assumptions, which, when taken together, constitute a logical and consistent view of fundamental reality that serves as a foundation for the ideal of individualism and the ethos of egalitarianism.

"Panglossianism" is the term I shall employ to refer to this set of beliefs. Perhaps if I had trawled long enough in the vast and dark waters of philosophy—particularly German philosophy—I might have come upon a more appropriate and impressive name, but panglossianism will do. With a lowercase "p," it will refer to certain presuppositions, which are roughly transatlantic cousins, both in their time of origin and in their general substance, to those maintained by the fictional character Pangloss in Voltaire's *Candide*. He asserted that the best of all possible worlds is already in existence; Americans believe they are capable of attaining it in the near future. Underlying their conviction is an implicit metaphysics that assumes reality to be good, harmonious, and simple.

(1.) The first principle of panglossianism is goodness. The belief that things in general and people in particular are fundamentally good permeates the American view of the world. It is reflected in something as commonplace as the popular attitude toward "experience." To Americans, experience in the abstract is not neutral but positive: the more one gets of it, the better. I remember hearing a drug addict on a radio talk show brag that he knew things "that you don't learn at Harvard." Undoubtedly—or hopefully, at least—his claim was accurate, but he did not think to ask whether these things were worth knowing. He had experienced the extraordinary, and that was enough of a justification.

Of course his was an extreme case. Everyone realizes that some experiences are so bad as to be undesirable, and most people would include in that category those of the drug addict. But for Americans, definite negatives are obvious and few; everything else is worth having or at least worth trying. The self thus becomes a voracious consumer of experience, ever in search for the new and exciting.

A panglossian song of indiscriminate celebration has long been heard in American literature. Emerson voiced it incessantly. Walt Whitman, who wanted to embrace the universe and all it contained, became its poet laureate. Almost any articulate American, at some idealistic and elevated moment, will sound its egalitarian note. "Genius is as common as air." "Even the lowliest among us" is a "poet." These are a couple of examples already quoted in the previous chapter.

Panglossianism stands in stark and utter contrast to the prescriptions and restrictions of traditional culture and society. Baldassare Castiglione's courtier, for example, strove to imitate models and raise himself up to an established and recognized standard. America rejects models and standards, at least as a theoretical ideal. Everyone is supposed to sail off on the seas of experience in his own individual quest of self-discovery and self-invention.

Evil (that is, man's innate and persistent tendency to do bad things) does not exist in the panglossian view of reality. There are bad things, of course, but since they are obvious and few, one can easily recognize and avoid them. In addition, whereas good is fundamental, bad is superficial—a mistake that can be corrected, not an inherent and ineradicable flaw. And, to go even further, many of the things that are stigmatized as bad may, with closer experience and clearer perception, turn out not to be bad after all.

Emerson made this last point with the profound optimism characteristic of his nation. Early in his career, when he declared that he would follow nothing but the prompting of his individual self, an orthodox believer suggested that his impulses might come from below rather than from above. Emerson replied with sublime insouciance, "If I am the Devil's child, I will live then from the Devil. No law can be sacred to me but that of my nature. Good and bad are but names very readily transferable to that or this...."[1]

(2.) The second principle of panglossianism is that all the good things of reality operate in harmony. The idea that one of them might conflict with another (such as democracy, with its populist bent, opposing science, with its exacting standards) is alien to Americans. As George Bancroft, an early oracle of American democratic ideology, declared in 1835: "Truth is one. It never contradicts itself. One truth cannot contradict another truth." In 1952, a practical business executive coined a less elevated but far more famous maxim based on the same assumption: What is good for America is good for General Motors and vice versa.[2]

The fundamental force holding society together is a natural and inherent harmony that guides the actions of individuals. Emerson expounded this idea, and it is an article of faith among Americans, though usually implied rather than explicitly stated. They believe that a man who is free to act according to his own genuine interests and inclinations will do what is right and beneficent, and that an entire nation of such men will cooperate spontaneously in its various enterprises of collective productivity.

According to a well-known theory of the social contract, each person must surrender some of his individual liberties in order to receive certain collective benefits. Americans do not accept this idea of necessary sacrifice. They believe that the individual enters society without having to give up anything or to change his behavior significantly. It is not necessary because his natural tendencies lead him to act in ways that are socially acceptable and positive. Of course, disputes, disorders, and injuries occur among people, but the American views these as he views bad things in general—as abnormalities, perversions of the normal, not as an inevitable by-product of human nature.[3]

A presumption of natural harmony pervades American life and thought. It underlies the concept of enlightened self-interest and its extraordinary popularity. It has its manifestations on the right, such as the libertarians, who want government to be reduced to a bare minimum, so as to let spontaneous order, growth, and innovation flourish. It has its manifestations on the left, such as the advocates of civil liberties, who refuse to admit that there is any significant conflict between individual rights and the common good. An avant-garde art critic and prominent leftist once observed that American radicals believe they can advance their cause, not by joining movements or advancing collective principles, but simply by doing something in their private lives that promotes their authentic selves.[4]

(3.) The third principle of panglossianism is simplicity. What is good or bad? What is true or false? How should one conduct oneself? From the very beginning, Americans, along with spokesmen like Emerson and Bancroft, have believed that in practical life finding the answers to such questions requires no extraordinary effort or profound cogitation. Nature has implanted its gifts of reason, conscience, and sociability in the soul of every person. He has only to consult himself; there is no need to seek out wise men or recondite knowledge.

This approbation of the simple and natural at the expense of the complex and contrived is highly congenial to the ethos of egalitarianism. It justifies every American's assumption that he and his opinion are as good as any other man and his opinion. Chapter one described how, at an early stage in American history, the masses of ordinary people rejected elite leadership in various spheres of social life and changed the prevailing norms to suit their own taste, or lack of it. One of their chief demands was for simplicity, and this has continued to the present day, as people seek to make sense of an increasingly complex and bewildering world.

"The future," declared one nineteenth-century historian, "belongs to the masses, or to the men who can explain things simply to them." That, at least, has been the case in practical American politics, with its roll call of famous successful simplifiers, including Teddy Roosevelt, who understood the "psychology of the mutt," and Ronald Reagan, the "great communicator," who could explain public issues in terms that all the mutts could grasp.[5]

The hope, faith, and expectation that Americans have for simple solutions can be found in the most unlikely places, even in the realistic and calculating world of business, as one journalist discovered. Businessmen might "seem dull, selfish, and sober. But inside, they are naive, childlike, and hungry.... These executives believe—desperately want to believe—that the answer to all the mysteries, the secret to market dominance, the key to their glowing transformation and earthshaking success, is just out there, just out of reach, just beyond the next door, if they could only seize it."[6]

The principles of panglossianism arose during the eighteenth-century Enlightenment and formed part of the prevailing climate of opinion. Authors of the time frequently expressed their wonderment at the beneficence and harmony of nature, at the extension of these marvels into the social world of mankind, and at their manifestation in people of diverse locations and circumstances. The Founding Fathers regarded such ideas as self-evident truths, and after the success of their Revolution, they believed that they had a splendid opportunity of creating a new government in accord with them. Although they were ultimately disappointed, as chapter one has shown, the panglossian ideology of their era persisted and became the idealistic bedrock of the American nation.

The generation of the Revolution added two practical corollaries to the three basic principles defined above. First, people could throw off the past and "begin the world over again."[7] They did not have to accept the misfortunes and live with the mistakes of previous ages as an inevitable and inescapable inheritance. They did not have to perpetuate such things as hereditary aristocracy, absolutist monarchy, or uniform religion as institutions necessary for the preservation of social order. On the contrary, they could make a clean break and a fresh start and create new institutions that were in accord with the promptings of nature rather than with the precedents of elders and the legacies of ancestors.

A second corollary followed logically from the first: the size and power of government should be minimal. This would give the forces of panglossian social harmony the opportunity to influence the affairs of men and lead them, without their conscious planning or deliberate action, to a higher level of concord and prosperity. In his first inaugural address as president, Thomas Jefferson declared that the proper role of government was to prevent people from injuring one another but otherwise to leave them alone to conduct their own business. The new republic put theory into practice and refrained from instituting the elaborate and extensive establishments characteristic of European states, including standing armies and national police forces, opulent courts and clerical hierarchies. It has been calculated that, as a percentage of gross national product, government expenses in the United States were five or six times lower than those on the other side of the Atlantic.[8]

——•——

In 1819, as America was proceeding down what it assumed to be the road to democratic utopia, it hit a very large bump. A financial panic led to a national depression that lasted for years. Men lost their jobs, their businesses, and their homes. Cries of anguish and accusations of blame rose in a crescendo. All this distress resulted, not in any repudiation of panglossian principles, but in the very opposite. Popular polemics repeated again and again that the agents responsible for the economic downturn were "complex" and "artificial" and that the remedy was a return to the "simple" and "natural."[9]

Banks were the chief target of the public's anger. They issued paper money that lost its value, they foreclosed on debts, and they were often guilty of reckless and at times illegal practices ("wildcat banking," as it was commonly called). Inflamed prejudice pictured the villains as unscrupulous, sophisticated men who employed the recondite intricacies of finance to cheat ordinary, honest, hard-working people. Voices of protest demanded the institution of simpler banking practices (including the abolition of paper money), which would supposedly prevent such fraud.

The fears and the accusations did not stop at this point but extended further. Since state legislatures chartered banks, and the federal government had established the national Bank of the United States (the BUS), public opinion viewed government as implicated in the cause of the nation's distress and in fact as the principal instrument of wrongdoing. Injury combined with paranoia to produce the belief that conspiracies of wealthy and powerful men were at work in the land. Influencing legislatures to grant them favorable banking charters was only one, though the most blatant, of their underhanded practices. They were said to be corrupting and subverting the very institutions of government, so as to gain for themselves more wealth and power on a permanent basis.

The popular conviction that democracy itself was in danger found a scapegoat in the Masonic lodges. As a secret society of affluent and politically prominent men, Masonry was an obvious suspect. In 1826, the killing of a former Mason who had threatened to reveal secrets and the subsequent failure of the courts to bring the perpetrators to justice sparked public outrage. If such an organization was capable of frustrating the judicial system in a case of murder, it must have been guilty of countless other nefarious schemes and practices. Anti-Masonic groups began to organize and publish newspapers. When they found that the existing political parties avoided them, they formed their own party and held state and later national conventions. They elected

Anti-Masonic governors in Vermont and Pennsylvania and even ran candidates for president.

Although the Anti-Masons were rivals of the Jacksonians, the two parties sprang from the same fears and employed the same panglossian logic and rhetoric. Both believed that affluent and powerful men had contrived by complex and clandestine machinations to use government as a means of securing economic benefits for themselves. If they could be stopped and their artificial advantages destroyed, the natural functioning of economic life would revive. Good times would return, and there would be opportunities for everyone to thrive and get rich.

For many people, Andrew Jackson was the hero who would save the day. A simple man of the people and a son of the natural West, he would ride into town, root out the corruption, and restore government to its proper and salutary form (a sequence of events that has been revived many times in the American imagination, which has often dreamed of sending a Mr. Smith to Washington). As president, Jackson played his assigned role with convincing success. He found a plausible scapegoat in the Bank of the United States, and his destruction of the BUS monster was at least as reassuring to the public as the closing of Masonic lodges—probably even more so.

—2—

The popular agitation of the 1820s and 1830s vindicated one of the most significant and familiar manifestations of panglossianism—the ideology of the free market, which forms the basis of economic individualism and which comprises two basic tenets. First, the market rewards and punishes individuals according to their merits. If a man is an efficient worker, he achieves economic success; if he is not, he fails. Like Americans in general, then and now, the Jacksonians and Anti-Masons believed in equality of opportunity, but not at all in equality of results. In their view, a person who was more productive than his neighbor should and would, under normal circumstances, receive higher economic returns. What they objected to was any attempt to cheat the natural justice of the market by contriving unnatural, artificial, and thus unfair advantages (such as perpetrating financial fraud or obtaining favors from government).

Second, the market, employing Adam Smith's "invisible hand," translates individual ambition into collective benefit by requiring customer satisfaction as a condition of economic success. If one is to make money, he must sell something that others consider worth buying. From this perspective, profit becomes, not a mark of greed, but a measure of service, and American businessmen have always insisted on regarding it as such. Doing well by doing good is the watchword of these sturdy panglossian practitioners of enlightened self-interest. Their loud idealism is something that foreign observers have often noticed, and the more honest and discerning among them have not been able to dismiss it as mere hypocrisy.

As a foundation of economic individualism, the belief in the beneficence of the free market has inspired Americans to great efforts of productivity. The problem with the market, as with individualism, is the distance separating faith from reality. The first principle of free market ideology (rewards according to individual merits) runs up against the same adverse conditions that the previous chapter described as hindering low-born individuals from rising in the world. People do not enter life or the market as equals; the advantages and disadvantages of social class apply in both. All the efforts of the Anti-Masons and the Jacksonians or of various subsequent reformers did not change this fundamental reality.

Prompted by the promises of economic individualism, many persons of humble origin have saved their money until they believed they had enough to start a small business. Most of them then met with disappointment, either losing both their investment and their business or else struggling along, making as little or less in profits compared to their wages as manual employees.[10] The market, they discovered, does not give everyone a scratch start or distribute prizes with a fair and impartial hand. A turn of the business cycle from good times to bad, for example, brings ruin to the entrepreneur of slender means: he will most likely be driven out of business. For the established businessman with deep pockets, however, the same situation can prove highly advantageous: he may pick up some great bargains from the bankruptcies of the vulnerable.

Defenders of the market often employ the second principle of their ideology (the invisible hand) to explain and excuse financial downturns and other such misfortunes as necessary and beneficial for the long-term health of the economy. However true this may be, it is no more satisfactory a justification than the knowledge (analyzed at the end of the previous chapter) that the vain efforts of individuals to better their economic condition nevertheless contribute to the nation's wealth and progress.

At this point, beneficial self-deception, which disguises the realities of life from those who believe in the principles of individualism, steps in to disguise the inequities of the market from its naively devout participants. The unfortunate are told that their unhappy fate is their own fault. During the 1990s, for example, laid-off executives of middle age, who found themselves sinking from the upper-middle to the lower-middle class (and sometimes lower), were blamed for not anticipating and embracing change. Even in their present situation, they could recover from their loss by assuming a positive and flexible attitude. What seemed like a disaster could be an opportunity for occupational and personal growth. If they would only seek out new kinds of work, they could become more efficient and valuable workers, as well as better human beings. The best-seller *Who Moved My Cheese?* (1998) preached this line of panglossian effrontery in the form of a concise and cute parable. Americans have difficulty resisting such arguments because, as explained earlier, they are resolutely certain that they control their own destiny; so when things go wrong, they logically have only themselves to blame.

The cheese rationale is not always entirely convincing, especially in those cases when the economic debacle results from obvious fraud, as in the case of Enron in 2001. Confronted with such embarrassments, apologists of free enterprise respond by pointing to the very fact that business malefaction has been exposed and proclaiming this as evidence that "the market works; it corrects itself." But the fact remains that employees, investors, and consumers have been cheated and that they usually receive nothing like adequate compensation, often no compensation at all. And fraud persists. There is no evidence that the natural tendencies of the free market are reducing it to smaller dimensions. When it is uncovered in one place, it thrives elsewhere. After all, the white-collar crime one hears about is the kind that is gross and flagrant enough to be detected. In its more subtle and nimble forms it flourishes unnoticed.

When confronted with the undeniable failings of the free market, its defenders fall back on lame excuses: Yes, the market isn't perfect, but it works most of the time. Besides, it's the best there is; the alternatives (socialism, a planned economy, or any other collectivist option) would be worse. All this may well be true, but it is not good enough. The prospect of eventual collective benefit is not an adequate source of sufficient motivation for the individual. If Americans are to continue working with their customary energetic enthusiasm, they must not perceive the market as unfair and capricious. They need to believe that its winners deserve their success and its losers deserve their failure, that it rewards, not luck and low cunning, but admirable human qualities. To maintain such a faith, people must possess or acquire a voluntary blindness to the realities of the market. Self-deception is not an easy act to perform, combining as it does the roles of both perpetrator and victim, but in this case the task has been made much easier by the identification of a plausible scapegoat.

When those who were caught in the depression of the 1820s began to voice their complaints, they quickly discovered a villain—the government. Despite the minimal size of the American state in that era, people agreed that it had become too big and too powerful. It accomplished little good and did much evil. Conniving men with wealth and influence were using it to advance their own interests at the expense of the public. If it were reduced, these villains would lose their means of illicit self-aggrandizement. At the same time, by eliminating the artificial and obstructive interference of government in the dealings of men, the natural and beneficent tendencies of human nature would be able to emerge and flourish. This theme was repeated again and again by Jacksonians, Anti-Masons, and other would-be reformers of the age. Some of them speculated that natural harmonies would eventually take control to such a degree as to leave little or no place for government.

Contemporaries responded favorably, even enthusiastically, to such talk. Emerson, who had no affection for the Jacksonians (he called them the "rank rabble party"), applauded the motto of their political newspaper: "The world is governed too much." He himself declared that "the growth of the individual" would counteract the abuses of government, and finally "the appearance of character" would "make the state unnecessary." Presumably, it would "wither away," as the Marxists later predicted. So strong was the current of antigovernment sentiment that even the Whig Party, which in practice favored government-sponsored projects, adopted the Jacksonians' rhetoric and used it to attack "King Andrew" for abusing and enlarging the powers of the presidency.[11]

Since those times, the American people have maintained a remarkable hostility toward government. It is not just that they regard bureaucrats as drones at best and blunderers at worst, or that they think of politicians as low and corrupt. That would account for only contempt and anger, and the public's negative feelings go deeper, reaching the level of hatred and loathing. They believe that government is responsible for inflicting significant harm and real damage on society.

In accord with this conviction, government has become American's all-purpose scapegoat, whipping boy, and devil. Whenever anything goes wrong, the natural, automatic, and immediate reaction is to blame government. Pondering the difficulties that young people at the bottom of society have in growing up, a journalist reached the following conclusion: "I blame the government." When a huge abstract sculpture was removed from Federal Plaza in Manhattan because people objected to it, its creator did not blame the unsophisticated and philistine public; he blamed the government. When challenged as to the accuracy of a movie on the assassination of John F. Kennedy, the filmmaker replied, "Even if I am totally wrong [as to the actual facts].... I am essentially right because I am depicting the Evil, with a capital 'E,' of government."[12]

Antigovernment sentiment is especially strong on the political right. It is the one thing—perhaps the only thing—that the various factions have in common, and it comes in several varieties. There are the practical businessmen, who oppose government regulations as an unjustified interference with their individual freedom to make money. There are the ideologues (the libertarians in particular) for whom the state is the enemy. According to them, it is guilty of causing every major bad thing that has ever happened to the country, including economic depressions. It should be reduced to an absolute minimum, and individuals should be allowed to roam free, guided by the natural harmonies of the free market. Many people find these ideas attractive and idealistic, if impractical and unrealistic.

Finally there are the fringe groups. They do not hate government because it has injured them personally; they begin with hatred and then contrive rationalizations for it. Their paranoia is directed, not so much at the local or the state as at the federal level, with which they have the least contact. Its very remoteness and unfamiliarity stimulates their fantasies. During the Cold War, fanatics claimed that Communism had taken over Washington, D. C. After the Soviet Union collapsed, they found new reasons to justify their terror and loathing of the feds. And they have continued to join rural militias, stockpile guns, and occasionally leave bombs at government offices.

Although such behavior is characteristic of a very small number of people, they enjoy a certain degree of sympathy among ordinary conservatives, similar to that which Communists used to enjoy among ordinary liberals in the 1930s. Fellow travelers of the right, as one might call them, are not difficult to find. The respectable and conventional suburban businessman with an extensive gun collection for sport shooting and for possible defense against robbers and other intruders often fantasizes using the weaponry against the agents of a federal government gone out of control.[13]

The political left is more ambiguous about government than the right. Liberals, radicals, and social reformers of all sorts have used, or tried to use, the powers of government to bring about desired change. And they have often been frustrated when their intended beneficiaries—the workers, the disadvantaged, the ordinary people of America—persist in identifying bureaucrats and politicians, instead of capitalists and bosses, as the villains. But even the left has antigovernment tendencies with very deep roots. It has been opposed to the abuses of power and the powerful for much longer and with much more sincerity than the right. Panglossian notions about the basic goodness of mankind and the underlying harmony of nature are more intimately implanted in the soul of the left than in that of the right. From the Industrial Workers of the World (IWW or Wobblies) in the 1900s to the New Left in the 1960s, American radicalism has favored anarchy and liberation as its immediate and ultimate goal, rather than political discipline and the creation of a workers' state.

People on the left often criticize "big government" while at the same time using it to advance their social programs (tax-and-spend liberals denouncing the Washington bureaucracy). But this kind of contradiction is not to be found entirely or even chiefly on their side of the political fence. With nonchalant fatuity, a conservative columnist averred, "Government should be less intrusive, more modest. Except when it should be the reverse." That is to say: except when it is promoting causes that he and those like him favor (such as suppressing pornography).[14]

Corporations regularly denounce government interference in the market, then run to Washington for help when they get in financial trouble. The head of the U. S. Chamber of Commerce drew a distinction between businesses getting government to protect them from the effects of "their follies and their errors" (which he opposed) and businesses going to government to find "cooperative ways to resolve problems" (which he approved).[15] In actual practice, it would probably be difficult to distinguish between the two situations, unless of course the latter refers to one's own business and the former to the businesses of others.

Such inconsistencies are a result of the antigovernment impulse encountering the reality of government in the modern world. Government is not becoming smaller; in fact, the reverse has been happening. As society becomes increasingly complex, government is increasingly called upon to intervene and sort things out. The same people who condemn government in the abstract have no hesitation in resorting to it when a specific situation arises which they have difficulty handling. Being aware of both the public's need and its aversion, partisans of whatever stripe use government or attack it, depending on whether they think the one tactic or the other will gain them an advantage.

Both right and left have accused each other of "legislating morality" and have declared that "you can't legislate against prejudice." The real objection is not to government exceeding its proper function but to the particular morality or prejudice in question. Neither side has any problem with legislating the kind of morality it supports or banning the kind of prejudices it dislikes. By decrying the government's intrusion into the intimacies of private life, the left has managed to defeat the right's efforts to prohibit abortions. Using the same argument, the right has managed to defeat the left's efforts to fund abortions for the poor.

In the boldest and most blithe instance of self-contradiction, politicians themselves often denounce government. It is in fact one of the oldest electoral tactics in the country. Tocqueville observed that there was no surer way of wooing the voters than by fulminating against the expansion of federal power. Politicians ever since have struck this pose and mouthed its rhetoric. One of the most successful of them was Ronald Reagan, who asserted repeatedly that government was not the solution to problems, it was the source of problems. In 1994, a government officer in Montgomery County, Maryland, proposed dropping the word "government" from official usage because it had become so highly pejorative.[16] Of course, all this verbosity has done nothing to change practical realities and actual tendencies. Under Reagan, as under his predecessors and successors, the federal bureaucracy grew and its regulations multiplied.

Despite its persistent futility and stubborn fatuity, the popular animus against government shows no sign of abating, and that is just as well, for it serves as a stout pillar holding up the public's faith in both the market in particular and panglossianism in general. If one is to believe that nature, mankind, and free enterprise are good, something else must be responsible for the bad things that occur from time to time. Hence the need for a scapegoat, and government has filled this role with notable and repeated success, whatever shortcomings there may have been in the other services it has performed.

—3—

The belief in a salutary free market and a baneful government is only one prominent manifestation of panglossianism. There are many others, such as the idea of progress. Since reality is fundamentally good, the application of human effort can and should succeed in improving the world. Americans are confident that this is in fact what has been going on ever since the founding of their nation. Each successive gen-eration—with one or two possible exceptions—has left the country a better place, with new improvements and more prosperity. There have been occasional setbacks, but these are seen as rare lapses rather than the rule. The overall trend has been forward.

Americans consequently favor change. To say that one opposes change is "practically un-American." The assumption is that something new will always be available to replace the old and that the new will be better. Tocqueville encountered this mentality when he asked why American steamboats were not constructed to last longer and received the answer that the continual progress of steam navigation made older boats obso-lete. Over a century later, a visitor from India saw an engineer sketching plans of an enormous skyscraper in the process of being built, only to be taken aback on learning that the man's purpose was to assist future wreckers, when it came time for the structure to be demolished.[17]

"Optimistic fatalism" is the phrase coined by a prolific inventor of history and science to describe the mentality of Americans in both their individual hopes and their collective aspirations. Its opposite, pessimistic fatalism, is characteristic of traditional societies—the feeling that bad things may occur and that one can do little to avoid them. Americans, in contrast, think that things are going their way, in their personal lives especially. They are always expecting something better to come along. Until the day they die, they are ready for another chance.[18]

This national panglossian creed has developed the following specific tenets: Since reality is positive, all that needs to be done is to approach it with an equally positive frame of mind. If one believes he can overcome an obstacle, he will most likely do so, since no obstacle is insuperable and most are less formidable than they appear. If people think that a desirable objective can be achieved, they will tend to act in such a way that they in fact succeed in achieving it. With these convictions lodged in their heads, Americans have arrived at the unshakable conclusion that an optimistic attitude is the crucial ingredient of success, individual or collective.

That is the reason why they applaud and actively practice what they call "positive thinking" and why they sharply condemn and instinctively avoid pessimism. Taking a negative view may be the result of disinterested consideration and realistic evaluation, but it damages morale, inhibits action, and creates a "self-fulfilling prophecy." When clear certainty in assessing a situation is not possible, Americans choose to err on the side of the positive rather than the negative, in the hope of directing the outcome toward the former rather than the latter. As has often been said in contemplating an attractive but highly unrealistic goal, "It may be impossible, but it will surely be impossible if we decide so beforehand."[19]

In earlier times, when moralistic speakers used to preach to the young about the virtues they should cultivate, the word that kept recurring was "willpower." To achieve anything worthwhile, one had to put forth effort. If one failed initially, he should try harder. In the old view of education, the subject matter could be most anything, as long as it was difficult and thus imposed on the learner "a mental discipline." Latin and Greek often served the purpose, and I recall hearing of a small religious school in the Midwest that required all its students to learn how to ride a unicycle. By mastering that, they would presumably acquire the willpower necessary to overcome any challenge which life might throw in their way.

In recent years, "self-esteem" has replaced willpower as the one thing that young people are supposed to need. If they feel good about themselves and have a positive self-image, their natural abilities will emerge, and they will do well—in education, on the job, in life generally. Just as personal failure and social dysfunction used to be blamed on a lack of willpower, now it is attributed to low self-esteem.

The two qualities may seem to have little in common. Their respective proponents (conservatives for willpower, liberals for self-esteem) usually despise each other. But both of them view the world as fundamentally panglossian—that is, as benevolent and simple. For both, the chief source of difficulties are not external circumstances, about which one may have insufficient knowledge and over which one may exercise inadequate control, but internal attitudes, which one is capable of understanding and altering for the better.

—••—

Of course, bad things exist, but these are superficial, even artificial, and underneath them lie the abundant natural resources of harmonious good. Various popular ideas reflect this assumption, for example, the tendency to view social conflict as the result of misunderstanding. Emerson asserted that if two people in disagreement converse together honestly and openly, they would find that their quarrel was over words rather than substance.[20] Americans agree with him and try to apply his diagnosis to disputes of any kind or dimension. They like to think that the prejudices which impel one group to hate another are the result of ignorance. If members of each group could become personally acquainted with those of the other, their antipathies would vanish. A variation of this hope has been applied to international relations. With their inclination to blame everything on government, Americans often assert that political leaders are responsible for the conflicts that arise all over the world. If ordinary people could meet face-to-face, there would be no wars (hot or cold) and no hostilities (ethnic, religious, or any other kind).

Seen from the perspective of such convictions, the large size of social organizations in modern society provides an all-purpose explanation for almost anything that goes wrong. When there were disorders on campus during the 1960s, people repeated to each other, "The university is too big." When there was a feeling of national frustration during the presidency of Jimmy Carter, people began saying, "This country is too big for any one person to govern it." Americans have always disliked, not just big government, but big business, big labor, or big anything. The presupposition is that the impersonality and hierarchy of such organizations prevent the natural sympathies of human nature from expressing themselves and the natural harmonies of human association from exerting their benign influence.

Given the complexity of contemporary life, Americans have not been able to do much to reduce it back to a state of simple, intimate association. But occasionally they have managed to induce or to force members of hostile groups to become more closely acquainted with each other. The results have not been encouraging. The perceptions of collective antagonism may be exaggerated, but they tend to be basically accurate. The parties know very well why they dislike each other, and proximity only confirms and intensifies their animosity.

The biggest illusions turn out to be those of the people who dismiss social prejudice as the product of illusion. Their conviction may well be "one of the most foolish clichés of our time," according to a conservative journalist, but it is dearly cherished among Americans, including one female bureaucrat in San Francisco. When black residents began attacking the Asians whom a government authority had moved into their public housing project, she declared that the violence could have been prevented by organizing "potlucks or sleep-overs for groups that are not familiar with each other."[21]

One of America's favorite platitudes is that society would benefit from any program which obliges people "of different backgrounds" to associate with each other. This notion was repeatedly cited as an argument in favor of the compulsory military draft, and it can be heard from pundits on the right as well as the left. Although the actual proposals for such social readjustment may seldom get beyond the stage of hopeful intentions, their combination of egalitarian conviction with panglossian faith can produce an attitude of formidable self-righteousness. The advocate of one plan for mixing income levels in neighborhoods condemned those who would refuse to dwell side-by-side with the less affluent as "irredeemable snobs" who "impoverish their lives."[22] In the American view, everyone—old and young, rich and poor, black and white—should live together and like it, for their own good as well as society's.

A few decades ago, there was a deliberate, extensive, and prolonged effort to break through the external crust of human relationships and tap the reservoir of harmonious benevolence presumably lying underneath. The practical means of achieving this objective originated in the business world as a technique for getting corporate managers to communicate better with each other. It was called the "t-group," "encounter group," or "sensitivity training." It developed and spread during the 1950s, then emerged into public notice during the 1960s, when it was hailed as promising a "new era in industry."[23]

The basic procedure was to take a group of people who worked together, remove them to a private setting for several hours or perhaps a day or two, and encourage them to interact verbally without inhibitions. As they proceeded to vent feelings they had previously suppressed, there would initially be much anger and hurt, but gradually these emotions were supposed to give way to sympathetic understanding and appreciation, and when it was all over, the participants would emerge better and happier people, as well as more efficient and effective workers.

For a time, encounter groups and sensitivity training were touted as the cure for practically every social ill, inside or outside the workplace. But gradually their popularity waned, and finally it disappeared altogether. The reason is not difficult to discover. The differences between people proved to be far more recalcitrant and intractable than expected. Some groups that underwent the treatment ended up even more fractious and divided than when they had begun.

The method, in short, simply did not deliver on its promise. Although this particular form of panglossian practice has had its day, one can confidently predict that some other form of the same thing will appear in the future. Despite all experience to the contrary, Americans continue to believe that, deep down, beneath all their suspicions and hostilities, people would like each other and get along, if only they could know each other's real self. "Be not disheartened," proclaimed Walt Whitman; "affection shall solve the problems of freedom yet."[24]

The practical people of the United States have been highly adept at devising things to improve material life, and this success has induced them to assume that they can likewise improve emotional life. It is an old idea. When the savants of eighteenth-century Europe found that science was able to explain the phenomena of the natural world, they concluded that it should also enable them to understand the workings of the human mind and emotions. Americans have inherited their hopes and expectations. If your car or your body fails to function properly, you take it to a person with knowledge of auto mechanics or medicine, who is supposed to restore it to good working order. Why shouldn't you be able to do something similar when you are angry, depressed, frustrated, having troubles with your spouse, or suffering from any of the numerous emotional maladies that afflict mankind, probably more frequently and painfully than a broken-down car or an ailing body?

From early on, Americans have been concocting practical therapies and regimens that were supposed to improve the behavior of their fellow citizens. In 1758, Benjamin Franklin wrote "The Way to Wealth" to explain how someone could change his personal habits so as to become rich. In the 1830s, Tocqueville noticed the presence of temperance societies and remarked on the novelty of such organizations, where people banded together for the purpose of "resisting what is most intimate and personal to each man, his own inclinations."[25] Gradually, from these small beginnings, arose the vast, surging tide of self-help books and therapy groups, which are a familiar feature of life today.

When Freudian psychiatry reached the United States early in the Twentieth Century, it was welcomed and applauded as the fulfillment of a promise made some two centuries earlier. Here at last was a science of human motivation that would allow experts to understand and treat mental problems the way physicians and engineers did physical ones. "Love could be made to work like anything else," like a malfunctioning automobile engine, for instance.[26]

Although the actual effects of this particular mental medicine failed to satisfy the public's large expectations, the underlying hope has remained. Americans are still looking for an auto mechanics of the heart and mind, and they now have an extremely wide spectrum of theories and practices from which to choose. The more prosaic can pick a therapy that promises such specific benefits as ridding them of bad emotions, improving their personal relationships, or helping them to make money. The more imaginative can select one that offers an updated form of Emersonianism: self-fulfillment, self-realization, self-actualization, getting in touch with your inner child, attaining your wonderful congenital potential.

Some of the barkers in the marketplace of emotional rehabilitation and enhancement are rather extravagant in their claims. Without a flicker of hesitation or a blush of modesty, one book admonished its readers that, just as no jet pilot would attempt to fly his airplane without first understanding how it worked, no person should attempt to conduct his life without first mastering this "operator's manual to the psyche."[27] Others boast the impossible. "Stop Aging Now!" declared one title.

Optimism combined with ignorance leads to gullibility. In traditional societies, the ordinary man views the world beyond his sphere of familiar experience as something unknown and potentially dangerous. He does not expect anything good from it, so he avoids it as much as possible. The American, animated by the principles of panglossianism, feels and behaves just the opposite. He ventures forth in hope and confidence—and, if he is not too bright, sometimes into the clutches of those who lie in wait for him. A saying attributed to P. T. Barnum claimed that "there's a sucker born every minute." As if this were not enough of a warning, it later received the addition, "—and two to take him."

During the Jacksonian era, notions of individualism, egalitarianism, and panglossianism combined to make people of modest origins believe that the entire country was their splendid possession and patrimony. Their bright, new, naive confidence created many opportunities for hoaxes, quackery, and fraud. The Age of the Common Man was also the age of the "confidence man," as chapter one has indicated, when some of the sharper citizens in the land of the free exercised the opportunity to fleece some of the duller ones.

And so it has continued. In 1922, the notorious journalist and polymath H. L. Mencken described "the boobus Americanus" as "a bird that knows no closed season...if he won't come down to Texas oil stock, or one-night cancer cures, or building lots in Swampshurst, he will always come down to Inspiration and Optimism, whether political, theological, pedagogical, literary, or economic." In 1996, an author contrasting the mentalities of Britons and Americans remarked, "Scratch an ordinary American, and you find a man with a dream, a scheme, a plan. He will save the world or get filthy rich or, usually, both."[28]

Amid all this deception and self-deception there is a mitigating factor. In addition to the admonitions of basic intelligence and common sense, panglossianism's promise of simplicity tends to keep Americans from becoming seriously ensnared by the fantasies of optimism and improvement. Good things are supposed to be simple as well as abundant—that is, they should be obvious, easy, and quick. They should not require much time, effort, or money. When a person finds that the self-help guide he is studying or the therapy program he is following does not produce immediate results and begins to become difficult or boring, he gives it up. It made him feel good for a little while, and that was sufficient. Later, when he happens to have some spare time and a few spare dollars, he will try something else.

—4—

The role of religion in American society has often been viewed as highly paradoxical. Considered at first glance, it seems, by its very nature, to be incompatible with national tendencies. Its doctrines value tradition and authority. They preserve what was handed down from the past. They demand to be accepted on faith. They disparage the present world and emphasize an afterlife. Since all these things are contrary to the inclinations of Americans, one might suppose that religion in the United States would be of little and diminishing importance, as it is in Europe.

The very opposite is true. Ever since the early Nineteenth Century, one of the first surprises to confront foreign visitors has been the frequency with which God is invoked in the formal ceremonies of public life. Large meetings often begin with a clergyman offering thanks to the deity and requesting divine blessing. This is especially the case with the operations of government, such as the opening of legislative sessions or the inauguration of officials. Politicians from the president on down are expected to make reference to God in their speeches on solemn occasions and to be seen attending church. As one puzzled Canadian was heard to ask, "Why do they [the Americans] have this thing about themselves and God?"[29]

At the same time, it has also been observed that these pious practices are extremely vague in content and highly circumscribed in expression. The references to God are general enough to embrace nearly every variety of believer and almost any sect. Politicians take pains to express the wide latitude of their religious inclusiveness, though seldom with the bluntness of President Eisenhower, who once declared, "Our form of government has no sense unless it is founded in a deeply felt religious faith, and I don't care what it is."[30] Aside from the formal invocation of God as the nation's protector and the abstract profession that one is personally a believer, religion has little place in public discourse. Any politician who might venture to employ the language of faith or the logic of theology in addressing an issue of the day or a question of policy would be considered unsound, unstable, even a dangerous zealot.

Both the popularity and the limitation of religion in public life are also characteristic of religion in private life. On the one hand, the percentages of Americans who say that they believe in God, that they pray, and that they attend services regularly are much higher than those of Europeans. On the other hand, as polls also reveal, Americans are astonishingly ignorant of the most elementary points of their professed faith. They have difficulty reciting the Ten Commandments or identifying the members of the Holy Trinity or explaining the difference between the Old Testament and the New Testament or between Catholics and Protestants.[31] People say that the Bible is the word of God, but they do not read it or have much knowledge of its contents. Anyone who does and makes reference to it in daily life is dismissed as a "Bible nut."

However much Americans may like to think of themselves as religious, their actual practice is very superficial, as foreign observers have consistently reported. In the early Nineteenth Century, an Italian Jesuit remarked that two Americans could live together for years without either becoming aware of the other's religious convictions. At about the same time, Harriet Martineau discovered that whenever her talk about religion became "intimate and earnest," her interlocutor automatically assumed that she must be a convert to some sect.[32] The same is true today, and even more so. Religion has its place (divine service on holy days, ceremonies for birth, marriage, and death), but otherwise it does not intrude into one's life. A person may engage in activities organized by a religious body, but these are usually social, recreational, charitable, or even commercial in substance, and only superficially religious.

Americans agree, and have agreed for the last two centuries, that it does not make much of a difference which particular religion a person belongs to—one is more or less as good as another. Prompted by convenience, personal taste, or social advantage, they have changed from one creed to another with casual ease, and in recent times the practice has increased—"faith-hopping" as it has been called. Clergymen themselves have been able to shift their careers from one denomination to another—an act that is still considered extraordinary and scandalous in other countries.[33]

America's freedom of religion goes beyond a choice among recognized doctrines and formal organizations. In response to a poll, 80 percent agreed to the statement that "an individual should arrive at his or her own religious beliefs independent of any churches or synagogues." A good number of people are not participating members of any religious group, yet they consider themselves to be personally religious. The more inventive mix and match various beliefs and practices and come up with their own unique blends, like the woman who did so and named the new faith after herself—"Sheilaism."[34]

In view of the enormous latitude that Americans tolerate in religious practice, one might expect them to be equally tolerant of those who reject religion entirely, but this is not at all the case. As interpreted by public opinion and expressed by the occasional politician (including one vice president in 1921 and one vice-presidential candidate in 2000), the guarantee of religious freedom in the United States Constitution does not mean freedom from religion.[35] Utter and outright disbelief has always been abhorrent to Americans, and they have persecuted it with a ferocity that has astonished foreign visitors.

In 1837, Harriet Martineau heard people whispering about a suspected atheist in tones of loathing and malice, as if they were referring to someone who was possibly guilty of a vicious crime or afflicted with a hideous disease. Tocqueville encountered similar attitudes. In 1996, one social critic and declared unbeliever averred that atheists were as much abominated as pedophiles—perhaps more so, since they could not claim the excuse of involuntary physical compulsion. Despite the recommendation of his father's name, President Reagan's son admitted that he could never be elected to anything because he had publicly declared his disbelief in God. Back in President Eisenhower's day, and in his very presence, a prominent and respected clergyman pronounced the terse verdict: "An atheistic American is a contradiction in terms."[36]

The nature of American religion, as represented in the preceding paragraphs, may seem puzzling and perplexing, but there is an explanation. One needs to understand that in essence the national faith is a cosmic endorsement of panglossian principles. Americans believe that the power which constitutes and directs the universe has established goodness, harmony, and simplicity as the basic qualities of nature and mankind in general, and of the United States in particular. By thus raising their characteristic idealism and optimism to such a high level of abstraction, they have produced a religion that is vague and amorphous in substance but at the same time commands fervent allegiance.

The popular poem "Each in His Own Tongue" (1908) by W. H. Carruth is a vivid example of American faith. It selects some attractive phenomena from the natural and human worlds and arbitrarily labels them "God." However simpleminded and unreasonable this may be, it reflects the national conviction that religion contains all the good of the universe, especially all the good of mankind—that is, all morality. Ever since their earliest days in what some of them like to call God's country, Americans have been telling each other over and over again that religion is a necessary reinforcement and essential guarantee of moral behavior.

If religion is equated with the good, it follows logically that anyone who is a disbeliever rejects the good. Atheism is therefore unthinkable and intolerable. Since religion is specifically equated with morality, anyone who rejects it rejects morality. Seen from this point of view, an atheist is naturally and automatically a loathsome creature—someone who accepts immorality in the abstract and therefore is most likely to be immoral in his personal conduct.

The reverse side of condemning irreligion is the remarkable favor and indulgence that religion enjoys among Americans. School textbooks mention only the attractive features and positive benefits of various faiths and carefully avoid any of the vicious behavior and benighted ideas they may have engendered and propagated. There is a general feeling that every religion deserves respect and that religious practices, however outlandish and bizarre, are not to be publicly ridiculed.[37]

When a sect of fanatics does something so atrocious that it cannot be excused or ignored (such as the mass suicides at Jonestown, Guyana, in 1978), editorialists, pundits, and public figures unite in declaring that the behavior was entirely exceptional and that its perpetrators in no way represent other people of faith. Even a crime as abhorrent as pedophilia has been mitigated by the fact that the perpetrators were Catholic priests, and so, during recent scandals, they did not have to face the full fury and punishment of the secular law but were left to the indulgent mercies of their own ecclesiastical authorities.[38]

Religion has not always appeared attractive enough to inspire such indiscriminate favor and partiality. During the early years of national growth, America's powerful influence went to work on the dogma of traditional theology and recast it in an acceptably panglossian form. Doctrines of original sin and innate human depravity were discarded, along with the idea that heaven was for the few and that many if not most souls were destined for damnation. The entire orientation of rejecting the world and preparing for an afterlife was turned around.

By the early Nineteenth Century, the task had been completed. Americans could now listen to preachers of religion who told them that sin was superficial and goodness was fundamental, that everyone could attain salvation by a simple act of willpower, and that the efforts of a righteous people would create a millennium of peace and prosperity on earth.

This was indeed an act of putting new wine in old bottles. As foreign visitors have often noticed, there is a lack of sanctity and holiness in American religion. Its sects and denominations do not stand apart from the world; they are active participants in it. They promise their members blessings in the present life, specifically the realization of personal ambitions and desires. "Follow me, and you will get rich," an English essayist paraphrased their appeal. "Follow me, and you will get well. Follow me, and you will be cheerful, prosperous, successful."[39] Instead of man serving the purposes of God, in America God serves the purposes of man.

One should not be surprised at this development. From the beginning of the new nation, with the disestablishment of religion and the consequent loss of automatic state funding, separate denominations have had to compete with each other to attract paying customers. In the process, the men of God resorted to whatever tools and tactics the men of the market managed to devise—business strategies and advertising gimmicks, techniques of mass communication and the allure of popular culture. One or two churches even offered a money-back guarantee: make donations for 90 days, and if you haven't received a blessing in your life, you can get back what you contributed. "I am selling the greatest product in the world," declared one highly successful evangelist. "Why shouldn't it be promoted as well as soap?"[40]

In terms of real, practical assistance, churches have played an enormously important role in American life as the providers of social services that people would not have found elsewhere or could not have afforded to purchase on their own. This was especially the case during the migration westward in the Nineteenth Century, and it has remained so to the present day. The range of activities sponsored and undertaken by religious organizations is so wide as to include many things that have only the most tenuous connection, or no connection at all, with the promotion of piety and faith, which may find themselves dominated and overshadowed. One of Garry Trudeau's Doonesbury cartoons ridiculed this tendency by depicting a fictional denomination that cancelled its church service because of "a conflict with the self-esteem workshop" and obliged its congregation to perform their acts of worship on its web site, so that it could use the church building for other functions.

Americans, as was discussed earlier, have long engaged in the devising of methods and strategies for the improvement of human behavior and the enhancement of human well-being. Religion has been intimately involved in these endeavors. Religious language, techniques, and personnel have appeared in many if not most of them, from the reform movements of the early Nineteenth Century to the therapies of the late Twentieth Century. This is only natural, since practitioners of moral and mental betterment assume that by utilizing religion they are wielding a potent and powerful instrument for accessing the benevolent forces of the universe. Norman Vincent Peale, for example, added religion to optimistic autosuggestion and produced a turbocharged positive thinking. Some innovators, like Mary Baker Eddy (Christian Science) or L. Ron Hubbard (Scientology), threw science—or what they called science—into the mix. From time to time, a new combination of psychology with mysticism produces a brew that is heady and novel enough to attract a notable number of followers.

However vague and exalted the methods, doctrines, or language, the results they promise tend to be very practical and at times grossly tangible. There have been several pious programs aimed at helping women lose weight, from the old-fashioned *Pray Your Weight Away* (1957) to the contemporary dieting as spiritual empowerment ("The diet is within me, I shall not cheat"). Even more popular is the idea that one can make money by being religious. In 1836, Thomas P. Hunt wrote *The Book of Wealth*, in which he declared, "No man can be obedient to God's will as revealed in the Bible without, as the general result, becoming wealthy." The book became a best-seller, and its theme has been repeated in religious exhortations of every subsequent era, such as, "Godliness is in league with riches" (1901) or "Be Christians and you will be successful" (1921). Today, downmarket customers can listen to a Bible-thumping evangelist who tells them that Jesus was not poor and that their faith will bring them money. Upmarket consumers can listen to a New Age guru who tells them that "the more spiritual you are, the more you deserve prosperity."[41]

There have always been a few zealous persons who regard the religion of their fellow countrymen as crass and shallow. They complain that the new wine in the old bottles is nothing but a soft drink.[42] Actually it is a pep tonic. The American's conviction that God is working with him and favoring his enterprises gives him a boost in morale. It makes him more confident and energetic, ready to try harder and put forth more effort.

The beneficial influence of panglossian religiosity extends through the entire population, affecting all groups and persons, from the national majority to single individuals. Americans believe that God directed the founding of their country, has presided over its development, and continues to guarantee its prosperity. The ceremonial oratory of politicians reflects this faith, as does the inscription "in God we trust" on the currency and the phrase "under God" in the Pledge of Allegiance. This has been called a "civil religion," and it contributes to self-confidence and optimism, both collective and personal.

The national body politic is not the only group that invokes supernatural sanction and has its resolve strengthened thereby. Almost any organized effort to induce people to behave better can assume religious overtones. This tendency first appeared in force during the antebellum era, when a swarm of idealistic causes sprang up, ranging from the promotion of temperance in drink to the prevention of cruelty to animals. Their leaders spoke as if they were doing the work of the Lord, they frequently operated with the assistance of church bodies, and they were often clergymen themselves.

Ever since that time, it has been easy and natural for most any attempt at achieving an improvement in human conduct to present itself as appealing to transcendent motives and purposes. This can be illustrated by something as prosaic as a campaign to encourage personal cleanliness. Some years ago, the following printed statement appeared in restaurants all over the country: "Sanitation is a way of life. As a way of life, it must be nourished from within and grow as a spiritual ideal in human relations."[43] Foreign visitors must have found this a rather grandiloquent way of urging people to wash their hands before meals.

Invocations of God and his assistance in human affairs are particularly loud and frequent among businessmen and business groups. They proclaim the beneficence of the free market and the perniciousness of government interference, not merely as economic concepts, but as spiritual convictions. If there is an "invisible hand" regulating the economy, it must be the hand of God, and the politicians and bureaucrats of Washington should not presume to think that they can do a better job than the Almighty.[44]

This commercial faith or pious commercialism was prominent in the Nineteenth Century. At the beginning of the Twenty-first, it is as strong as ever, if not stronger. "I believe in God and I believed in free markets," declared the CEO of Enron just before his company went bankrupt, and he was indicted for fraud. "Competition always works better than state control—I believe that premise as a matter of religious faith," asserted one of the architects of California's electricity deregulation in the face of rolling blackouts.[45]

As explained earlier, businessmen like to think that by making a profit they are contributing to the nation's prosperity (doing good by doing well). Panglossian religious faith reinforces this belief and, in addition, assures them that they are also doing the work of the Almighty. Other cultures may regard serving God and making money as two entirely separate and usually opposite activities. In America the two are seen as closely joined, in a commercial partnership, as it were. Bruce Barton's *The Man Nobody Knows* portrayed Jesus as an aggressive businessman and successful entrepreneur. Since its publication in 1924, it has remained continually in print and has inspired various imitations and updates, such as *Jesus CEO* (1995).

"America is the most moralistic nation on earth and also the most materialistic."[46] The two are in fact intimately connected. The American mind contains a simple, obdurate, and enduring linkage of materialism, morality, and religion: religious practice promotes moral conduct, which in turn results in emotional well-being and material prosperity. The equation works in both directions: if a person is moral and religious, it is assumed that he will prosper; if he prospers, it is assumed that he is most likely moral and religious.

The celebration of this inclusive view (individual self-advancement as collective social progress as well as personal self-improvement) is an incessant theme of business rhetoric. In a milieu that is notorious for cold calculation and ruthless competition, one may hear the most extravagant and gaseous pronouncements of higher aims and larger benefits. Business conferences and conventions exude the aura of revival meetings. Inspirational speakers extol the noble enterprise in which they are engaged, and the ordinary participants are expected to share the enthusiasm.

A certain amount of all this is artificial and simulated, but much is genuine. Many businessmen—probably most of them—sincerely believe the panglossian theology that they repeat, and it motivates them, as it does Americans in general. Instead of the traditional "great chain of being," there is a great chain of service, in which the individual employee, by his efficient performance at work, promotes the interests of himself, of his company, of the consumer, of the nation, of mankind, and ultimately of God. Participation in so grand an alliance bestows blessings and benefits, but it also imposes discipline and responsibilities, as a popular manifesto of commercial uplift entitled "Skyhooks" once emphasized: managers, stockholders, and the Supreme Being are all in agreement, "No one has a right to 'louse up a job.'"[47]

—5—

Stoked with optimism, idealism, and religion, Americans have gone forth to improve the world. Since the early Nineteenth Century, they have been devising causes, advancing movements, and creating organizations to promote good and suppress evil. With ferocious energy and thoroughness, they have taken up and pushed to its limit whatever the spirit, mood, or whim of the times happens to designate as a moral principle.

During the antebellum era, foreign visitors noticed the extreme delicacy of women in avoiding any reference to certain parts of the body. On occasion, they went as far as to fashion trousers to cover the legs of pianos.[48] The case might be made that in Britain itself Victorian prudery never reached the extremes that it did in certain quarters of the United States. There seem to have been no trousers on pianos in England.

In 1862, a mood of discipline and sacrifice prompted the abolition of the liquor ration in the American Navy for the rest of the Civil War and permanently thereafter (just as, a little over half a century later, a similar surge of wartime fervor would impose the abolition of liquor on the entire country). No national emergency, no matter how threatening or severe, ever induced the British Navy to give up its grog—to the envious resentment of dry American sailors.

It is generally true that moralistic reformers have been able to wield a greater influence in America than in other countries. In the 1920s, an Englishwoman recalled, "In every city...I have visited there are clubs, both male and female, to forbid or promote some harmless triviality...." The tendency she observed was confirmed by H. L. Mencken, who expressed his unsympathetic view of it all in terms of a formula: "Whenever A annoys or injures B on the pretense of saving or improving X, A is a scoundrel." During the 1990s, at the height of the vogue for political correctness, the London *Economist* received complaints about its use of the words "niggardly" and "spic-" (a hyphenation of "spicing" at the end of a line referring to Latin Americans). "Why do we get such letters only from America?" asked a bewildered editor.[49]

If moralism can change the petty into the serious, it can transform a national issue into a crusade that enlists the active participation of nearly everyone. Once the whirlwind of public opinion gets going, it spreads through the country with an irresistible force that levels everything in its path. During World War I, the United States managed to work itself up into a frenzy of hatred against the advertised evils of the Kaiser and his Germany that was more fanatical and widespread than anything seen in Europe.[50] Other public passions of the moment have perhaps been more positive in their orientation, but they too have been characterized by an equally remarkable sweep and intensity.

The panglossian assumptions upon which American idealism is based often lead it into naive thinking and unrealistic action. If good is abundant, natural, and obvious, all that needs to be done is to take a decisive step, remove some superficial obstacle, and good will emerge and become predominant. The following are examples of this faith and its practical consequences: (1) Outlaw alcohol; the slums will vanish, and the prisons can be closed. That was the promise. Prohibition tried it, but drinking continued, and crime increased. (2) Institute private enterprise in the Soviet Union; the population will become productive, and prosperity will result. That was the promise. When it happened, the natives grasped only the self-interested half of enlightened self-interest and ignored the enlightened half. Private crime, inefficiency, and dysfunction grew to such an extent that they rivaled traditional state crime, inefficiency, and dysfunction. (3) Overthrow the dictator Saddam Hussein; Iraq will emerge as a model democracy for the Middle East. That was the promise. The disappointing and frustrating events which followed are too recent to need recounting. Although the last two of these three situations may eventually improve and produce a result that is better than what they replaced, all three are object lessons in the folly of easy expectations induced by panglossianism.

Whenever reality frustrates the efforts of idealism, it comes as an unexpected shock to Americans. Sometimes, the reaction is moodiness, depression, and sorrowful complaint. The revelation that the Kennedy brothers had been gorging themselves on callous and casual sex from female admirers aroused much agony among idealistic votaries. One of them composed a long and bitter lamentation, which a major intellectual journal saw fit to print. The author was not some mooning youth or innocent choirboy, but a seasoned reporter and novelist—rather old, one might have thought, to need instruction from a few sharp words (such as Lord Chesterfield's) about women's natural if unfortunate susceptibility to male celebrities.[51]

The tone of puerile self-righteous disillusion can be heard from people of most any age or background, for example, a sophisticated author and journalist like Tom Wicker with his autobiographical protagonist who "wishes he were still eighteen, still loosing thunderbolts against the world's wickedness, still on campaign with Peter Pan." In 1976, a foreign participant in the bicentennial celebration suggested that the United States should be marking its twentieth birthday, instead of its two-hundredth, since it was still "a promising adolescent who is lost among many dreams and disappointments."[52]

Sometimes when reality fails to live up to idealistic expectation, the reaction is much stronger. American Jeremiahs are a numerous and well-known species, being in fact the reverse side of national boasting and bragging that used to be a perennial annoyance to visitors from abroad. The anger and denunciations which these prophets of woe direct at the shortcomings of their country are loud, extravagant, naive, and indiscriminate—much like the pronouncements heard from the nation's boosters and panegyrists. They have a ready and attentive audience, since Americans are, in the words of one historian, "if not the most self-critical, at least the most anxiously self-conscious people in the world."[53] They are willing, even eager, to be told of their faults, in the earnest hope these can be corrected, and they can become even better than they are.

Foreigners in general and Europeans in particular view both the premises and the manifestations of American idealism as incomprehensible and preposterous. They do not believe in panglossianism. While Americans say, "Let people be free and they will be good," Europeans say, "Teach people to be good so that they will not abuse their freedom." Societies outside the United States do not think that there is a natural harmony regulating human affairs, either inside or outside the economic market. Nor do they imagine that there are vast reservoirs of human amity and affinity lying behind superficially forbidding exteriors, like petroleum reserves underneath a desert. "Surely you agree that all men are brothers?" the American president Woodrow Wilson is said to have asked the French premier Georges Clemenceau at an exasperating impasse during the negotiations of the Paris Peace Conference in 1919. "Yes," the Frenchman replied, "Cain and Abel."

The confidence with which Americans believe that a sufficient application of resources and goodwill can solve all the problems of the world arouses among non-Americans a mixture of astonishment and contempt. Their petty moral scruples provoke amusement. In the 1920s, an English author told of how he offered cigars to successive American reporters who came to interview him. The first declined with the stiff coldness of one who had been invited to sin. The second accepted with the shamefaced nervousness of one who was yielding to temptation.[54] Today, the politically correct American may have replaced the clean-living American, but he is fundamentally the same morally fastidious person, and his behavior elicits the same puzzled and patronizing reaction from people of other, less scrupulous and less naive cultures.

Europeans long ago came to a verdict about these panglossians of the New World, and it has been repeated countless times over the decades: Americans are nothing but big children. "The same adolescent features, plump, smug, sentimental, ready for the easy tear and the hearty laugh and the fraternity yell," commented an English novelist in 1937. "Light-hearted, open, good, quick to get passionately involved and quick to forget, with the assurance of a fool that the history of the human race has no relevance to them--friendly and superficial, and with young faces until they are eighty," agreed a Russian novelist in 1989. One could cite any number of corroborating witnesses.[55]

But American idealism also has a dark side, which can turn the smiling superiority of foreigners into alarm. The United States is a land where Kant's categorical imperative prevails. When someone wants to make a case for something, he feels obliged to justify it in terms of the good it will bring to people in general. This is an invitation to hypocrisy, with professions of high aims and broad perspectives disguising the low and narrow views of self- and special interest. When the advocates of American foreign policy proclaim its benefits for other countries, representatives of those countries sometimes have the indiscretion to point out that its chief beneficiary is the United States. This causes the Americans to become extremely indignant that their motives are being questioned. After all, as panglossians, they assume that what is good for their nation should also be good for the rest of the world.[56]

Far more formidable than the hypocrisy that idealism encourages is the fanaticism that it incites. Do not get between a mother lion and her cub, common sense warns. It should also warn, do not get between the Americans and anything they have fixated on as a moral purpose. Once they have applied the designations of good and evil to a situation, they will persist with stubborn and occasionally savage tenacity in an effort to achieve the success of the former and the defeat of the latter.

The outlawing of alcoholic beverages, for example, began in 1919 as a "noble experiment," but it soon became obvious that it was not working, yet the Americans refused to give it up. In 1931, an official commission admitted the utter failure of Prohibition, as well as the crime and corruption it had created, but their report concluded with the recommendation that it should continue. Not until 1933, after twelve years, ten months, and nineteen days (H. L. Mencken's calculation) of continual defeat and frustration, was the "noble experiment" reluctantly abandoned.[57]

Experiencing an initial setback only makes the idealistic American all the more determined to prevail, and this can lead to ferocious behavior. High aims are no guarantee of high practices; the very opposite may be the result. The more elevated and important the objective, the more willing are its proponents to employ any means to attain it. Thomas Jefferson, for example, acknowledged and excused the murders perpetrated by the French Jacobins and declared that he would willingly see "half the earth desolated," if only what he called the cause of freedom could emerge victorious. His was a theoretical fanaticism, but other, more active, and less scrupulous Americans have carried their convictions into real life. An English journalist happened to encounter some of them. "I can deal with gangsters," he later declared, and I can deal "with Boy Scouts." But he confessed that he found himself at a loss when confronted with people who talked like Boy Scouts yet acted like gangsters.[58]

The Vietnam War was recent history's most notorious and extreme example of America resorting to vicious behavior in order to achieve ends that were high-minded and even sentimental (John Wayne in the movie *The Green Berets*, comforting a Vietnamese orphan with the assurance, "You're what this war is all about"). The covers of two separate issues of *Life* magazine illustrated the Janus face of the conflict. One showed a tall, friendly Marine taking a small Vietnamese boy on a fishing trip. The other showed a sky filled with American planes and the bombs they were dropping.

Whenever an American president uses ominous and threatening moral language in a foreign policy statement, such as a reference to an "evil empire" (Ronald Reagan) or an "axis of evil" (George Bush, Jr.), the rest of the world shudders and wonders what these children with nuclear weapons are going to do next. "I never knew a man who had better motives for all the trouble he caused." That was one Englishman's assessment of an idealistic American in a remarkably prophetic novel about Vietnam, and he concluded, "God save us always from the innocent and the good."[59]

—6—

While emotional cant and idealistic postures go swirling around the surface of American public life, there is at the same time a substratum of realistic perceptions and actions operating underneath. International affairs often provide the setting for striking examples of these two forces at work. It occasionally happens that the representatives of a foreign country make a plea for aid that provokes a spontaneous outburst of sympathy from the American people. This is immediately seconded by extravagant promises from public officials. Later, after the emotions of the moment have cooled, politicians in a more sober frame of mind reckon up the actual costs and assess the practical consequences, and the foreign delegation at last departs with far less than it had been led to expect and with many a complaint about American insincerity and hypocrisy.[60]

Other peoples of the world, as well as Americans themselves, are often distracted by the conspicuous idealism and miss the underlying realism, as they did during Watergate. When seen from abroad, the affair appeared ludicrous and inexplicable. What was all the fuss about? Politicians are always spying on each other. It seemed as if the whole thing had been cooked up by America's overheated moral conscience.

The actual facts told a different story. President Nixon's real sin was not a bungled break-in and subsequent cover-up. Well before that happened, his Department of Internal Revenue had been coercing large political donors into changing their contributions from the Democrats to his own party.[61] Earlier administrations (such as Harry Truman's) had used the IRS to favor their friends, but Nixon's employment of its powers for the purpose of outright extortion went beyond the pale. It was tantamount to bringing the low practices of some scummy local district into the running of the federal government. Democratic politicians were outraged at the theft of their party's very blood—cash being the vital nutrient of every political organization—and when the incident at Watergate happened, they saw their opportunity. What might otherwise have been a minor embarrassment, to be huffed at for a moment and then forgotten, became the basis of charges for impeachment, to the accompaniment of a great deal of vapid and pious verbiage about the president not being above the law.

While the average citizen is no doubt ignorant of the realities of Watergate, he has seen similar situations in his own life. Anyone who has worked in an office is familiar with the maneuver of a convenient pretext, in which the nominal charge that is used to fire someone has little or nothing to do with the real reason for getting rid of him. Although Americans are quick to accept and repeat whatever idealistic rhetoric happens to be in the air, they are not gullible fools in matters that count. If they are prone to use the language of hypocrisy, they are just as quick to detect it. When the head of General Motors declared that what was good for America was good for General Motors, the public immediately turned his statement around to read, "What is good for General Motors is good for America." And it has remained in that form ever since, as a byword for the inveterate combination of self-righteousness and self-interest in business practice.

Moralizing on the surface, realism underneath—that duality characterizes much of American life, even when personal matters are involved. In answering questions from pollsters, people speak of their "reverence for life" and disapprove of abortions for anything other than serious medical reasons. But they do so in such a way that allows the procedure to remain a practical option in case of urgent personal need or desire. "What they exhibit," explained a journalist, "is a rock-solid, European-style support for abortions, with American moral posturing plastered on top."[62]

When actions diverge from idealistic talk, it may be tempting to dismiss the latter as inconsequential and nugatory. But that would be wrong, for it is in precisely these situations that American idealism makes its most important contribution. Andrew Jackson's war against the Bank of the United States (the BUS) may serve as an illustration. The historian Bray Hammond examined the facts of the conflict and found that it was essentially a struggle between two groups of capitalists fighting over money and power, and that the victory of one group—admittedly the more numerous and energetic of the two—failed to produce any significant material benefit for ordinary people. As for the pronouncements of Jackson and his partisans about being on the side of the honest working poor against the dishonest idle rich or being in a democratic majority of productive citizens against a manipulative and devious financial elite—all that Hammond dismissed as "the most ignorant but popular clap-trap."[63]

What his cool judgment failed to perceive were the psychological benefits resulting from Jacksonian rhetoric. However far it deviated from reality, it succeeded in articulating an ideal that appealed to the American people in general. Everyone, from the poor man to the capitalist, responded favorably to the idea of abolishing special privileges because it promised to give them more opportunities to make money. Even the wealthy could be included, since popular anger blamed only those few among them who were presumed guilty of unfair and underhanded practices. In this way, Jacksonian moral posturing and its apparent victory enabled Americans to get through a period of economic depression that threatened to create serious class conflicts and social disorders.

Something similar happened during the bad times of the 1930s, when a persuasive president (Franklin D. Roosevelt) gave voice to popular ideals. If his actual policies did more than those of Jackson to relieve economic distress, they were also superficial, incoherent, and at times contradictory. But they made the public feel better, as did his denunciations of simplistic scapegoats ("economic royalists" instead of the BUS monster), and eventually the onset of war got rid of the Depression.

In the 1980s, the phenomenon occurred again, as a milder remedy for milder complaints. The public's frustrations over Vietnam, Watergate, Jimmy Carter, rampant inflation, and various other ills were forgotten during the years of Ronald Reagan with his smiles and optimistic talk. All the chatter about Reaganomics and a revival of entrepreneurialism probably affected economic reality even less than the 1830s attacks on the BUS, but the alleviation of the national malaise was significant and salutary in both cases.

Idealism has done more than just help Americans get through occasional hard times. The previous chapter explained how the belief in the principles of individualism, though contradicted by reality, has motivated an entire population to high levels of productivity. The same is true of the belief in the principles of panglossianism. The conviction that they are serving higher purposes and that higher forces are assisting them bolsters Americans' confidence and causes them to put forth more effort, which translates into greater national strength and collective wealth.

Europeans have long observed their transatlantic rival, and it continues to puzzle them. They preen themselves on their sophistication and realism, which they contrast to the naive moralistic talk of the Americans. Yet they cannot help realizing that it is the United States which has achieved the largest amount of material power and prosperity. Occasionally, they glimpse the truth. Their own accurate perceptions have made them skeptical, pessimistic, and cautious, which puts them at a disadvantage. The beliefs of the Americans, however erroneous, have filled them with optimism and enthusiasm, which work as a motivating force to their advantage. They are, in a word, profiting from self-deception.

THE AMERICAN FORMULA II:
REGULATORY REALITIES

CHAPTER FOUR

National Uniformity

—1—

The questions raised at the end of chapter one and elaborated in chapter two have remained unanswered. What keeps Americans, who are pursuing their own individualistic purposes and interests, from falling into conflict with each other and creating disorder? What coordinates and harmonizes their separate actions, so that the result is collective productivity and prosperity? In short, what keeps America from becoming a nation of rampant, destructive egotists?

These questions are all the more perplexing in view of the analysis in chapter three. Panglossianism fills Americans with notions of pervasive goodness, natural harmony, and easy simplicity which are illusory but which have the real effect of adding to the quantities of energy and self-confidence already generated by the ideal of individualism and the ethos of egalitarianism. This is beneficial in that it increases motivation, but it also increases the danger of people running out of control. What keeps America from becoming a nation, not merely of self-absorbed egotists, but also of fanatical idealists? Why isn't the United States a country filled with Don Quixotes and Madame Bovaries, all obsessively intent on living exciting, extraordinary lives and all leaving trails of chaos and ruin behind them?

So far, this book has described only the first half of what I call the American formula. It has explained the beliefs that motivate Americans. The next task is to present the second half of the American formula, which limits and regulates the forces created by the first half. The second half contains those factors of social reality that prevent Americans from falling into discord and that induce them to work together in the advancement of collective, constructive tasks.

Obvious evidence of the abiding presence and effective influence of the formula's second half is the social and cultural uniformity that prevails in America. It is one of the first things that foreign visitors, from whatever country and in whatever era, have noticed. Wherever they went, they found the same main street, the same stores, and the same products. Even an observer from Stalinist Russia, with all its regimentation, exclaimed at the "perfection in standardization" that Americans had achieved. In 1996, an English historian stated that nowhere else in the world could a person travel one or two thousand miles and still "hear a common language being spoken in an identical form…find people living in identical houses…see the crowd dressed in identical clothes…walk streets built in identical style…find towns served by identical schools, businesses, public utilities." Testimony from natives—at least those who have not been led astray by the recent cant of multiculturalism—concurs. In the words of a sociologist writing in 2004, "From one end of the country to the other, Americans shop at the same stores, listen to the same music, follow the same sports, read about and watch the same celebrities…."[1]

What is true of physical appearances is also true of mental and emotional tendencies. Tocqueville observed that American society provides its members with "ready-made" opinions, which they all readily adopt "on public trust." The subsequent stream of foreign visitors has echoed his remarks with their comments that Americans have the same ideas and even employ the same cliches in expressing them. One English novelist delineated the intimate details of uniformity in his description of a receptionist: "She was the standard product. A man could leave such a girl in a delicatessen shop in New York, fly three thousand miles and find her again in the cigar stall at San Francisco, just as he would find his favorite comic strip in the local paper; and she would croon the same words to him in moments of endearment and express the same views and preferences in moments of social discourse."[2]

Precise and discerning observers, both domestic and foreign, have occasionally drawn a distinction between American individualism and American individuality. There has always been a conspicuously large amount of the former, as each person strives to advance himself and promote his own interests. There has also been a remarkably small amount of the latter, as crowds of animated individuals pursue basically similar goals in fundamentally similar ways and have little inclination or tolerance for idiosyncratic whim and waywardness. The result is a population of individualists who display little individuality.[3]

Though it may seem paradoxical, traditional cultures with their precise and often rigid social demands are able to allow a surprisingly large degree of individual uniqueness and self-expression. Provided that a person obey certain rules and discharge certain obligations, he may otherwise have wide latitude to do what he pleases. As one critic of art and society noted, the "standardized manner" characteristic of a people like the French or the English takes up much less of one's self and permits much more variety of behavior than the "standardized personality" displayed by Americans.[4]

The uniformity of the United States is a remarkable phenomenon, especially in view of its great size. Tocqueville was surprised to find that, although a thousand miles separated the states of Maine and Georgia, there were fewer differences between them than between the neighboring French provinces of Normandy and Brittany. Other Europeans have made similar comparisons. In their countries, short distances and small geographical barriers often mark divisions between dissimilar peoples with distinct customs and mutually incomprehensible dialects; in America, they are all the same people.[5]

Particular groups in the population of the United States have, as a general rule, failed to keep themselves separate and to reinforce their singularity over time. Geographical mobility has prevented that from happening, as Tocqueville discovered: "Those who dwell in isolated places arrived there yesterday," bringing with them all the characteristics of the general culture. In addition to the actual physical movement of individuals, the means of communications, assisted by modern technology, have swept the country with the latest ideas, fads, and trends. The homogenized result would have been remarkable in a country of moderate size; for one of the enormous dimensions of the United States, it is astonishing. In the words of the English historian quoted above, unlike the other large nations of the world (Russia, China, and India), "only the Americans have succeeded in creating a society of complete cultural uniformity."[6]

This achievement is all the more extraordinary considering the diversity of sources from which the United States has drawn its population. Groups of immigrants have arrived from every nation in the world. In the beginning, their separate identities were very apparent, but gradually they were transformed and absorbed. The terms "melting pot" and "assimilation" have recently come to be severely disparaged (for reasons that will be examined in chapter nine), but they refer to a process that has been going on since colonial times and continues today.

Foreign languages were a noticeable feature of the United States during the late Nineteenth Century. Non-English newspapers flourished and multiplied. In the public schools of Cincinnati, St. Louis, and elsewhere, a significant part of the instruction was conducted in German. Within a single county of Nebraska, one could hear a Sunday sermon in Norwegian, Danish, Swedish, French, or Czech. With time, this variety faded and eventually vanished, as the younger generation acquired the ways of the larger society and abandoned their parents' culture. Holland, Michigan, for example, had been originally founded by Dutch immigrants; by the mid-Twentieth Century it was indistinguishable from any other midwestern town, except for the Dutch names on the storefronts.[7]

"American life is a powerful solvent," George Santayana observed. And it has been at work for a long time. In 1782, a French immigrant noticed how intermarriage diluted the differences and distinctions of national origins. In 1787, the Founding Father John Jay, himself French and Dutch without any English parents or progenitors at all, could speak as an American and proclaim his country to be "one united people...descended from the same ancestors, speaking the same language, professing the same religion, attached to the same principles of government, [and] very similar in their manners and customs...."[8]

Since that time, the descendants of each new wave of immigrants have followed a familiar path, mingling with the rest of the population, moving up in society, and at the same time becoming Americanized. This happened with the great influx of eastern and southern Europeans, who arrived before World War I, and it is still happening with the most recent immigrants from Asia and Latin America, as statistical evidence indicates. They are speaking English, becoming educated, and marrying outside their group at rates as high as those of their predecessors, if not higher.[9]

After the first generation, foreign origins play a diminishing role in a person's life. They may retain a sentimental attraction, but they grow ever more shadowy and become less and less a factor in career, marriage, or anything else of real significance. Taking their place are the things that influence all Americans, such as income and status. I recall a work of sociology making the point that a person's occupation as a truck driver, for example, is a far more important factor in his life than the fact that he is of Italian or Polish heritage.[10]

How has this massive transformation of foreigners into natives come about? One obvious and crucial element is the attitude of Americans toward settlers from abroad. When an immigrant evinces a desire to imitate the ways of his new countrymen, he receives their encouragement and assistance. This is exactly the opposite of what would happen most anywhere else in the world, where natives become angry and indignant when a foreigner attempts to act like them. In their view, he is trying to become something he is not and has no right to be. They may tolerate and even welcome him as an alien, but only so long as he understands that he is an alien and will always remain one. In contrast, Americans are ready to adopt suitable and willing foreigners with remarkable rapidity. In 1997, a local newspaper described Jonathan Raban as "a near institution in Seattle, one of our best and best-liked hometown writers." The author in question was an Englishman who had moved to Seattle only seven years before.[11]

Immigrants to the United States have quickly recognized their opportunities. By acting like Americans, they found that they could gain acceptance and were able to make their way in the New World. As they advanced occupationally and socially, they became increasingly indistinguishable from the natives. This is a natural process that has operated through the ordinary relationships of everyday life. It has not owed all that much to deliberate programs of Americanization, such as those promulgated in the public schools of the late Nineteenth and early Twentieth Century. Nor has it been seriously impeded by infrequent outbursts of hostility against foreigners, such as occurred in the 1840s and 1920s. Those were directed at groups rather than individuals, specifically at groups thought to be unwilling or incapable of being absorbed into the larger society.

<hr />

In addition to the favorable attitudes of the natives, the very nature of Americanism makes its genuine membership easier to attain than that of other cultures. To become an Englishman or a Frenchman or almost any other nationality requires passing the impressionable years of one's childhood among that people and in the process unconsciously absorbing a subtle and indelible integument of mannerisms and attitudes that will forever after mark one as a member of that tribe. To become an American requires the learning of mannerisms and attitudes which are fewer, simpler, and more obvious—closer to the level of conscious perception and choice—and which are linked to a particular set of openly professed and commonly shared principles and beliefs. Such a panoply of personality and conviction can be acquired by a person at almost any age. One Indian, who spent his early years in Asia, moved to the United States and, after two decades, declared that he truly felt he had "become an American." He added that it would not be possible for someone to do the reverse. An American might move to India, but after twenty or forty years or a lifetime, he would not have "become Indian."[12]

Just as Americanism can be acquired by a deliberate act of will, it can also be forfeited. The word "un-American" implies this possibility. It was first used in 1818, and it refers to actions or opinions that violate an unwritten ideological consensus. To be a Communist during the Cold War, for example, was called un-American, and those who were Communists were considered unworthy of American citizenship. In other countries, such an expression and such a test of national identity make no sense. One is an Englishman or a Frenchman by birth and for life. He may be a pariah among his countrymen and a traitor to his country, but he cannot be un-English or un-French. In the United States it is different. If one rejects certain values that are considered to be fundamentally American, he loses his Americanness.[13]

"It has been our fate as a nation," declared one historian, "not to have ideologies but to be one." Americans share a single, coherent system of fundamental beliefs: most obviously, the principles of liberal democracy, as reflected in the United States Constitution; below that, individualism and egalitarianism; at the bottom, panglossianism. Other countries lack such a unity. One Indian immigrant recalled that his high school in Bombay contained students who professed to be "monarchists, Fabian socialists, Christian democrats, Hindu advocates of a caste-based society, agrarians, centralized planners, theocrats, liberals, and Communists." European universities contain a similar variety of people, holding distinct and unrelated political and philosophical points of view, and ready to expound and defend them. Such a farrago of ideologies is not to be found on an American campus, nor a fortiori anywhere else in American society. The possibility of its presence in an American high school, that habitat of mindless and banal teenage conformity, is too preposterous even to imagine.[14]

Americans, it has been observed, "behave as though all of the basic questions of life have been settled."[15] Thanks to this unanimity, they have enjoyed profound social stability. Where there is underlying agreement, the disputes that arise are over suitable means rather than fundamental ends and accordingly tend to be superficial and transitory. Without such agreement, disputes may develop into controversies over essential objectives and primary questions, and consequently persist through time, fester, and cause lasting damage.

The contrast between stability in the United States and instability elsewhere can be seen in a comparison of American and European politics. Ever since the early years of the Nineteenth Century, travelers from both sides of the Atlantic have remarked on the differences. In Europe, momentous issues were raised, with rival ideological systems locked in combat and the future direction of entire societies put in question. By contrast, the issues in American politics have been ordinarily pedestrian, if not trivial: the personalities of candidates, local and special interests, the spoils of office (getting "within grabbing distance of the pie counter," as one homely metaphor put it).[16]

Since so much is at stake in European politics, they have attracted wide participation and intense interest among the populations of their respective countries. The opposite is true of Americans. The appearance of some burning controversy may arouse them momentarily, but normally they are indifferent to politics. The percentage of citizens who bother to vote is far below that of Europe, and their declining interest stands in contrast to the rising popularity of consumer products and entertainment. That is no wonder: American politics are mundane—in a word, boring. Aside from a tiny minority of fanatics, ideologues, and idealists, the people who invest significant time and effort in political activity only do so in the hope of gaining special benefits or solving specific problems. The candidates they elect look to find practical solutions and pragmatic compromises that will satisfy as many of their various constituencies as possible.

This slow, steady, undramatic functioning of the political process has been much more difficult to achieve in Europe, owing to the presence of conflicting ideologies. The feeling that one's basic beliefs and fundamental interests are involved inflames the individual participant and transforms him into an intransigent partisan. Practical measures and realistic considerations give way to demands for theoretical rectitude, unquestioned loyalty, and outright victory. In Italy, for example, such a mind-set can turn something as bland and ordinary as a meeting of a Parent Teachers Association into an argumentative battlefield. One American observer predicted as far back as 1947 that the Italians would never achieve domestic tranquility and prosperity until they turned their attention away from politics and acquired the preoccupations of a consumer society.[17]

—2—

How well the forces imposing uniformity have done their work in the political sphere may be seen by examining those Americans who are called and who call themselves conservatives. Traditional conservatism, as it originally appeared in Europe, displayed certain distinctive characteristics: a reverence for what had been inherited from the past and an aversion to changing it; a respect for authority and a reluctance to challenge it; a mood of caution, of wanting to preserve what one had rather than to strive for something new. As might be surmised, these qualities do not agree with the temperament of Americans. In fact, if one listens to those on the right who are prominent in American political life, one will hear something that is much different from conservatism in its traditional form.

Ronald Reagan, their most celebrated recent leader, continually reassured his audiences that America was experiencing constant and unlimited change for the better. One of his favorite quotations came from that grand old radical and revolutionary Thomas Paine, who wanted to discard the past and put something new in its place: "We have it within our power to begin the world over again." Other politicians on the right have taken a similar stance, bragging about improvements and innovations, especially technological ones, and promising the public a future that will give them more choices.[18]

A traditional conservative does not want more choices (in effect, more opportunities for fools and knaves to go astray). He wants what his forefathers had already demonstrated to be good, even the best, and what subsequent generations should accept with gratitude and contentment. This does not suit Americans, including Americans who sport the conservative label, nor has it in the past. In the 1830s, a German immigrant opined that the English must be puzzled by Americans applying the word "conservative" to themselves, since they were not interested in preserving what they had but in acquiring more, and since they ignored the past in preference for hopes of the future.[19]

If such are the attitudes and opinions of Americans on the right, one might ask what distinguishes them from Americans on the left. Both sides share an allegiance to the ideal of individualism and the principles of panglossianism, including an appetite for innovation and optimism, which these values involve. Where the two differ lies chiefly in what each thinks are the proper means for attaining their common objectives. Conservatives champion the free market, with as little government interference as possible. Their doctrine is economic individualism, and their hero is the independent entrepreneur, discovering new and better ways of doing things and inventing new and better products, thereby benefiting his fellow countrymen at the same time as he acquires personal wealth.

This was the dominant ideal of nineteenth-century America, and by European standards of the day it was not conservative at all but liberal, even radical. It was, after all, the ideology behind Jacksonian democracy. More than one social historian has pointed out that what is today called conservatism in the United States used to be liberalism in the world of one-and-a-half centuries ago. As such, it has much more in common with modern American liberalism than it has with traditional European conservatism.[20]

Tocqueville spoke of traditional societies as having forged a chain that linked the people of the present with those of the past. Because things changed slowly and children usually assumed the situations of their parents, the living could feel a continuity between themselves and the dead, extending back even to remote ancestors. The conditions of American life broke this chain and severed every link, and they continue to do so.[21] The entrepreneur, along with his big brother the capitalist, has assisted mightily in the process. He is indifferent toward heritage, rooted communities, or anything from the past. All he cares about is developing new enterprises. If these result in change that damages old ways of living, it does not bother him. In fact, he likes to think of himself as a liberator, freeing people from the restrictions of inherited customs, rules, and hierarchies.

By celebrating capitalism in general and entrepreneurs in particular, the American conservative is promoting something that works against traditional conservatism. And this is not the only instance of such behavior on the right. The elderly would seem to be a natural constituency of conservatives. Having lost the naive idealism of youth, they are the one segment of the population least likely to succumb to the blandishments of the left or specifically to the appeal of liberals in the Democratic Party. Yet the Republican Party does little to attract them. Instead, it tries to reduce their Social Security pensions. The American conservative is not interested in a constituency of slow, sour senior citizens. Like the liberals and everyone else in the country, he wants to ally himself with youth and its dynamism, innovation, and productivity.

The same is true of environmentalism. One might think that this would naturally be a conservative cause—preserving the world as God made it and opposing changes created by modern man. But once again, it is not so. Protecting endangered wildlife and safeguarding the beauties of wilderness are not on the agenda of American conservatives or the Republican Party. They want to develop the wilderness for human use (and make millions for themselves in the process). They strenuously proclaim the cause of progress, in opposition to those whom they regard as perverse cranks and fanatics—people who would bring it all to a halt for the sake of some small and unattractive species and its habitat of sterile desert or fetid swamp.

Heritage from the past is not the only feature of traditional conservatism that fails to appeal to American conservatives. Tocqueville spoke of a chain that linked all the members of society in a line of authority "from the peasant to the king." Each class or order in this hierarchy had its own specific rights, privileges, and duties. Each recognized and, when necessary, defended those of the others above and below it, seeing in their permanence and security the protection and guarantee of its own. Once again, the conditions of American life broke the chain and severed every link. Motivated by the hopes of social mobility and the attitudes of egalitarianism, Americans, including Americans on the right, have no reverence for and little patience with established customs and inherited status.[22]

The conservatives of Europe have long allied themselves with the power, stability, and paternalism of government. American conservatives do not celebrate these things. Government is their archenemy, so much so that one or two social commentators with the temperament of traditional conservatives have spoken against the unrestrained antagonism of their comrades in arms: How can people who call themselves conservatives love their country, if they hate its government?[23]

Like government, large corporations are attractive to the European but not to the American conservative, at least in theory. The former admires their collective strength and solidity, which is just what repels the latter, who applauds the entrepreneur as a lone individualist. In a similar way, American conservatives are suspicious of the professions. In contrast to entrepreneurs, whose success appears to have been won in the open competition of the public marketplace, professionals make their way in a world of select bodies, inscrutable influence, esoteric criteria, and recondite prestige.

Like Americans in general, American conservatives are suspicious of anything that claims to be above the understanding or taste of ordinary people, and they are quick to accuse their enemies of snobbish pretensions. In 2004, one of their advocacy groups stigmatized the supporters of the Democratic presidential candidate Howard Dean as "latte-drinking, sushi-eating, Volvo-driving, New-York-Times-reading." A favorite word of conservative condemnation is "elite." Rush Limbaugh, the most prominent right-wing talk-show host in the United States, regularly decries elites of all kinds, not just "the liberal media elite," but "so-called professionals and experts," such as "the medical elites, the sociology elites, the education elites, the legal elites, the science elites."[24]

This stance of ferocious populism should not be surprising, since the rank and file of American conservatism is filled with parvenus and, far more numerous, would-be parvenus, who bristle with resentment at any hint of social or cultural superiority. I recall the fuss they made, including speeches on the floor of Congress, over the National Endowment for the Arts awarding $750 for a poem that contained just one word ("Lighght" (1969) by Aram Saroyan). Given the ordinary scale of government graft and waste, the mere sum of $750 does not deserve even a passing growl. But the promotion of arts and culture—a proud feature of European conservatism—is a subject that especially arouses the egalitarian ire of American conservatives and brings out their inveterate philistinism.

Far from attempting to imitate the heritage, exclusivity, cautiousness, and sophistication of Europeans, American conservatism has been doing its utmost to appear typically American, celebrating the new, open, energetic, and democratic. George Gilder, a prominent author on the right and an interminable panegyrist of entrepreneurs and the free market, composed a paean to the motley crowd of workers who flocked to the high-tech opportunities of California's Silicon Valley during the 1980s: "Immigrants and outcasts, street toughs and science wonks, nerds and boffins, the bearded and the beer-bellied, the tacky and uptight, and sometimes weird...." It reads like an updated and animated revision of the lines that were written during the 1880s and inscribed on the base of the Statue of Liberty ("Huddled masses yearning to breathe free...the wretched refuse of your teeming shore"). And Gilder topped it off with a sneering description of the *New York Times* reporter who reacted with disdain at the demotic scene.[25]

There is, in sum, very little of the actual conservative (i.e. the preservationist) in all the things currently being called by that name in the United States. A few fastidious writers, I understand, find the phrase "American conservative" to be such a contradiction in terms that they use only the words "right-winger" or "rightist" in referring to the phenomenon. Unquestionably, anyone who goes searching for traditional conservatism in the United States is bound to end in disappointment and frustration.[26]

The important thing to understand and appreciate is the irresistible power of American uniformity. Just as it has taken over and transformed the traditional dogma of religion, so has it taken hold of something as alien and uncongenial as traditional conservatism and shaped it to serve its own purposes, with the result that America's so-called conservatives have emerged thinking, talking, and acting very much like other Americans.

—3—

National uniformity extends far deeper than the realm of politics. Foreign visitors have often noticed that Americans of diverse backgrounds and occupations exhibit the same personal values and attitudes. On the basis of this homogeneity, some observers have declared that the nation contains no social classes but is one enormous middle class. Americans themselves seem to agree, for their pundits speak of "the middle class" as if it included everyone except the desperately poor and the extremely rich.

In some respects, the idea of a single-class society is inaccurate. As chapter two explained at length, there are in fact significant differences of social class in the United States, and it is only their relative subtlety that allows both foreigners and natives to overlook them. But, on the other hand, there is a large amount of truth in the idea of middle-class values dominating America. Not only are the divisions of class that have existed in Europe and in other traditional societies marked by more obvious external signs than those in the United States, their internal substance is also deeper and more fundamental. The basic values of people at one social level can be entirely different from and even opposed to the values of people at another level, so much so that the members of different classes in the same society have difficulty understanding and empathizing with one another. Consequently, it is easy for them to fall into conflict, both individual and collective.[27]

This is not true of the United States. To a remarkable extent, all Americans recognize the same values (particularly those of economic individualism), which are the values of the middle class. So widespread is their acceptance that they are not identified as belonging to or originating in any particular part of society but are viewed as universal—the way in which everyone behaves or ought to behave. What differentiates the various levels or classes of American society is the degree to which their respective members actually possess and exhibit these values, as distinct from merely acknowledging their validity and importance, which everyone does. People at the bottom have much less of this social capital (as it has been called) than people at the top, and that results in their remaining on the bottom, as chapter two explained. But the fact of everyone at least sharing the same standard of values, if not exhibiting the same amount of these values, prevents the creation of the stark barriers of incomprehension and hostility that exist in traditional societies. (It also prevents individual rebels and eccentrics from taking refuge in a thicket of the class differences: the searching eye of America's totalitarian value system seeks out and stigmatizes deviants at any and every social level.)[28]

In the mid-Nineteenth Century, one international traveler found that human solidarity and sympathy, which were confined within each separate social class in Europe, extended to the entire nation in America: "There is no man there whose position every other man does not understand; each has in himself the key to the feelings of his neighbor...." A later and far more famous visitor, James Bryce, enlarged on the observation: "What the employer thinks, his workmen think. What the wholesale merchant feels, the retail storekeeper feels, and the poorer customers feel. Divisions of opinion are vertical and not horizontal." David Riesman, whose perceptive insistence on the reality of class differences in America was quoted in chapter two, also spoke of a substantial uniformity among Americans: "Middle-class values and styles of perception reach into all levels except perhaps the fringes at the very top and the very bottom."[29]

At an early stage in the development of American society, the middle class became dominant over both the upper class and the lower class. This was not what happened in many traditional societies, where hereditary wealth developed an ethos of aristocracy that exerted its influence on the rest of the population. Middle-class people tried to mimic it, and even rogues on the street could be heard disputing points of honor and repeating what they believed to be courtly figures of speech. Something entirely different occurred in the United States. The egalitarian spirit of the new nation swept away the remnants and imitations of old-world aristocracy, and it has continued to frustrate the pretensions of would-be aristocrats and incipient aristocracies ever since. There are many people of hereditary wealth in the United States today, but they do not set the tone or the standards for the rest of society. If anything, they try to act like those on the level just below them, "the credentialed upper-middle class."[30]

The extension of middle-class values to the lower class was more difficult and required a more prolonged effort. From the 1820s onward, society after society and organization after organization was founded to improve some aspect or other of lower-class life. Although many of these groups (such as those of the temperance movement) sought to reform undesirable behavior wherever it occurred, among high and low alike, the reality was that middle-class people usually directed the operations, while lower-class people were most often the object of their attentions.

From the outset, individuals perceived the connection between adopting the self-discipline of middle-class life and attaining the rewards of economic productivity. By becoming more sober, punctual, and industrious, a person became a more efficient, more valuable, and more highly paid worker. This was also the route into the business world. As Tocqueville explained, the desire for wealth led Americans to commerce and manufacturing, where a person needed "strictly regular habits and a long routine of petty uniform acts" in order to prosper.[31] Throughout the Nineteenth Century and most of the Twentieth, moralistic speeches and tracts repeated an incessant message: clean, regular living makes for success in life.

This insistence on middle-class virtues has been much ridiculed in recent times, at least in certain intellectual milieus. Past efforts to reform the lower classes have been condemned as attempts to control them and make them susceptible to the exploitation of capitalism. Such criticism would appear to be a repudiation of middle-class values by the middle class itself, or more precisely by elements of it. The nature and significance of this apparently paradoxical development require further analysis, which they will receive in chapters nine and ten. For the present, two points can be made.

First, lower-class Americans did not generally resist middle-class values. Many, especially those at the higher end of their class, actively sought to acquire them, as a way to better their condition. It is the poor, after all, who are most likely to be the victims of drink, violence, and other lower-class vices. It was the poor who accordingly responded in greatest number to the various temperance movements of the Nineteenth Century and who were the firmest and most enduring supporters of Prohibition in the Twentieth. Just as immigrants have become Americanized far more by their own actions than by any formal program of Americanization, people of the lower class—often the immigrants themselves—have acquired middle-class self-discipline by their own volition, rather than having it imposed upon them from above.[32]

Second, the extension of middle-class values to the lower class has been a great success. It resulted in the rural and urban poor acquiring the essential and necessary behavior that made them capable of participating in and deriving benefits from the developing industrial economy. Like the assimilation of immigrants, it has continued to the present day, counteracting the threat of class conflict and contributing to the strength of a unified people.[33]

The triumph of middle-class values is especially evident in one particular facet of social behavior—the control of sexuality. A comparison with English society is illuminating. Puritan attitudes arose in both countries, but in England only the middle class accepted them as an iron standard of respectable behavior; in America they dominated the entire society.[34]

Folk music vividly reflects the contrast between the lower classes of the two peoples. The lyrics of numerous English folk songs, like love ballads everywhere, present a variety of emotions, ranging from joy to sorrow and including much tenderness and melancholy, but they also deal openly and naturally with the realities of sex. Such songs did not survive on the other side of the Atlantic. Americans either scrubbed them clean of anything explicitly erotic or banished them to the shadows of social life, where they degenerated into crude obscenity.[35]

The power of sexual restrictions in the United States was equally impressive at the higher levels of society. Affairs and seductions had long been a source of interest and amusement among the fashionable circles of Europe, where a successful Don Juan could become an alluring celebrity. This was not the case in America, where both the formal provisions of the law and the informal sanctions of public opinion imposed heavy penalties on anyone, no matter how prominent, who strayed into adultery. So effective were these prohibitions that in the 1830s a visiting Frenchman declared, with mixed feelings of frustration and admiration, this country "is the paradise of husbands."[36]

Tocqueville noticed the contrast between the severe treatment of sexual offenses and the lenient treatment of bankruptcies, and he pointed out that both practices had the effect of promoting a single objective—material productivity. One kept a man from dissipating his energies in an unremunerative enterprise and from disturbing his neighbors' emotional tranquility, which was an important foundation of their steady efforts on the job. The other permitted him to be bold and venturesome in his commercial career. Discourage sex and encourage business, impose restraints on the former and give freedom to the latter—that used to be a classic if unstated rule of society, which had the effect of diverting effort and attention from the one activity to the other. As a character in an Edith Wharton novel remarked, the real crime of passion in America is a "big steal."[37]

In the 1960s, all this began to change, and today people have difficulty understanding the sexual repression of the past and realizing what an achievement it was. American society succeeded in controlling an unruly and restive force that every orderly culture has found to be problematical and dangerously disruptive to some degree. The most conspicuous sign of success is the fact that many, if not most, Americans no longer view sex as a threat. So strong, embedded, and innate have middle-class habits of productivity become in the population at large, that casual sex can now function as a reward for personal achievement and a recreation from work, without arousing the fear that it might get out of control and cause significant social damage.[38]

The transition from puritan morality to superficial hedonism will be examined at greater length in chapter eight. For the present, it may be noted that the change has created much confusion. So tenacious are the old attitudes toward sex that the new attitudes have left many people troubled and uncertain. Conservatives, provincials, and various other nervous individuals think they are witnessing the rise of decadence and degeneration.

Critics in other countries are similarly puzzled and ambiguous. One moment, they call Americans puritans and the next moment pornographers. The confusion has been going on for some time. Many a foreigner has been deceived by the flagrantly erotic content of American movies and other products of popular culture, only to find on his arrival in the land of the free, not a sink of profligacy and self-indulgence, but a people industriously going about their work and preoccupied with making money, as they always have been for the last two hundred years at least.[39]

—4—

Standing on a solid foundation of national uniformity gives Americans great stability and confidence. From time to time, they may toy with this or that bit of trivial diversity, but underneath lies a bedrock consensus that is universally shared though seldom expressed. Since its fundamental beliefs face no serious challenge from any rival ideology, no one needs to define and defend them, or even to think much about them.

Americans proceed on the implicit assumption that, regardless of individual variations, people are basically the same everywhere. This idea does not stop at their national borders. With thoughtless nonchalance, they apply it to the rest of the world. In their view, the differences that exist between cultures are superficial; fundamentally, everyone has the same attitudes and desires, which are common to humanity.

The citizens of other nations do not see reality from this universalist perspective. They regard the things that distinguish themselves from foreigners as innate, permanent, and crucially important. They see themselves as the members of one particular culture, which has imparted to them its own special qualities, and they are confident that other people, since they were born into other cultures, do not have and could not possibly acquire these qualities.

Americans, in contrast, lack an awareness of non-physical barriers and boundaries that might set them apart from the rest of mankind. Instead of having a sense of exclusive uniqueness, they have a sense of being generic and consequently inclusive. They assume that their ways of thinking, acting, and feeling are those of the human race in general rather than those of one particular people.

There is a certain degree of sociological truth that might justify this frame of mind. American individualism, egalitarianism, and panglossianism tend to reduce things to the simple and elementary, so that they are comprehensible to the most commonplace mind and palatable to the most ordinary taste. This is especially the case in popular culture, which, ever since the 1920s, has had a remarkable and notorious appeal all over the globe. The products of the American entertainment industry present characters, situations, and ideas at a basic level, which most anyone, living in however remote a place or in however marginal a situation, can understand and enjoy.

National pride exists everywhere in the world, and it usually takes the following form: the natives of a country feel superior from the conviction that their ways are uniquely their own, not shared by their neighbors or anyone else on earth. American national pride is different: it reflects a sense of common humanity and international bonds. Americans feel superior from the conviction that their country has advanced the furthest in a direction that all countries are taking, are trying to take, or should try to take. As such, the United States sees itself, not as an alien and domineering power, but as a strong and benevolent older brother, who can serve as a source of inspiration and assistance to the less mature children of the world.

This idea of the United States as international leader and model has often provoked much resentment. Foreign leaders and spokesmen make sarcastic remarks about Americans wanting all countries to be free, as long as they imitate American ways and become like the United States. Such complaints puzzle Americans, who see their way of life, not as peculiarly and exclusively American, but as something that people everywhere naturally desire and would freely choose: "Don't you want democratic government, health care, education, full employment, recreation, et cetera, et cetera?" Seen from this point of view, the spread of American popular entertainment and consumer goods all over the earth is not the imposition of an alien and undesirable culture but the extension of progress and modernity. International uniformity in a globalized world is thus nothing more than a natural result of panglossian harmony and simplicity at work.

Such a justification provides a ready though specious answer to questions that arise from the contrast between the promise of freedom and the reality of uniformity. If there is so much freedom in the United States, why are things there so much the same? The American apologist can resort to his panglossian convictions and declare that uniformity is simply the result of free choice. People choose what they consider best, which tends to be the same everywhere. There are alternatives to high literacy and effective sanitation, for example, but surely everyone would choose these things over any other options.

That is the defensive argument in its general form, and it can be employed whenever the presence of control (the second half of the American formula) becomes too embarrassingly evident to be ignored. Asked if journalists were guilty of a bias in favor of liberalism, one of their august and eminent spokesmen replied that they were not: "they merely tended 'to side with humanity rather than with authorities.'"[40] Bias in favor of humanity can hardly be considered a blameworthy bias, just as uniformity that results from the common and natural desires of mankind can hardly be viewed as a reprehensible uniformity.

Panglossian assumptions of this kind (including Kant's categorical imperative) are widely accepted and promulgated throughout the land of the self-proclaimed free, and it is good that they are. There is a need for contrived excuses, high-minded rationalizations, and various other forms of self-deception to disguise, not just uniformity, but additional realities of social control. As the next chapter will demonstrate, actual life in the United States often curbs, abridges, stifles, and represses human liberties. This too, like uniformity, is a necessary, essential, and indispensable part of the formula's second half.

CHAPTER FIVE

Group Control

—1—

I nstant friendliness is one of the first things that strikes the foreign visitor to the United States. From the moment of introduction, an American proceeds to address his new acquaintance by his first name or his nickname, and he expects to receive the same treatment in return (a practice that has disconcerted Englishmen since at least the 1830s).[1] This happens even when an obvious difference in status separates the interlocutors. Employees and supervisors speak that way to each other, so do salesmen and customers, students and professors, children and adults.

After being initially taken aback by this atmosphere of friendliness, a foreigner is further confused when he realizes that it is quite indiscriminate and very superficial. The existence of friendly relations between two people does not necessarily mean that there is any significant or lasting affection between them. The coworker who chats with you amicably may run you down behind your back without the slightest feeling that he is being treacherous. The boss who amiably inquires after your well-being and that of your family in the morning may give you a bad performance review in the afternoon—or he may do both during the same encounter—without imagining that his actions are at all contradictory.

The fact is that in America friendliness serves the function that formal politeness serves in other cultures. It facilitates relations between people in the world at large, outside the limited circle of one's intimates in blood and personal attachment, but it does so by applying the language and gestures of personal intimacy to all relationships. This requires a certain balancing act. On the one hand, a person who behaves with cool formality and aloof courtesy is resented as snobbish and "undemocratic." On the other hand, there is the danger of going too far in the other direction and lapsing into gross and inappropriate familiarity. "Be impersonal but friendly." That advice is often given, and Americans do not regard it as a contradiction in terms by any means.[2]

All this can be very confusing to visitors from abroad. They most likely come from traditional cultures that draw a strict line between friendliness and formality, with the former being employed among genuine intimates and the latter among everyone else. It is a disorienting transition to go from an apartment building in Paris, with not a single name on any door, to a midwestern American suburb, where a sign on a house may proclaim to every passerby, "The Joneses Welcome You." If the bewildered foreigner happens to be lucky, a kindly American will take him in hand and explain that when people he has just met tell him to "drop in at our home anytime," they do not really mean it, and he should not act on the invitation.[3]

It would be wrong to conclude that American friendliness is nothing but a hypocritical facade. In contrast to the manners of the traditional European, which are often a polished surface with indifference and egoism underneath, the American is animated by genuine goodwill. He feels an authentic desire to please, a real sympathy for the other person, an actual willingness to perform some minor favor for him. Although these impulses are shallow and momentary as far as they pertain to any particular individual or situation, in the aggregate they are pervasive and persistent, and as such they create an environment that makes ordinary social relations in the United States much easier than elsewhere in the world.

In other cultures, when two strangers meet, their dealings with each other tend to be stiff and awkward and to remain so for a long time as they slowly and carefully feel each other out, since they both realize that they are just as likely to discover incompatibility and aversion as mutuality and attraction. American encounters proceed in a different way. The spirit of friendliness puts both strangers at ease, and within ten minutes they "are communicating with each other in truly cordial terms."[4] It is not genuine friendship, but rather an effective social grease, which smooths the interaction between people. It makes them more tolerant, more willing to accommodate one another, and less apt to assert themselves or take offense.

This is especially useful in the workplace, where people need to interact harmoniously in order to be optimally efficient and productive. An atmosphere of friendliness cushions the conflicts and personal incompatibilities that naturally result when individuals of diverse experience, temperament, and background are obliged to deal with each other. While animosity—often a great deal of it—may persist underneath, amicable norms prevail on the surface and create a milieu of pleasant or at least tolerable association.

American friendliness springs from American social conditions. First and most obvious, in this land of apparent freedom and perceived opportunity with its constant movement and change, the bonds between people are usually weak and often broken. People become friends, not so much from a compatibility of mind or emotion, as from their participation in a common activity. They have a job at the same office, their children attend the same school, or they are involved in the same sport. When they no longer share the activity, as eventually tends to happen, the friendship lapses. Even ties of blood and marriage can be tenuous and transitory. Children move away, relatives are remote, couples get divorced. Friendship follows functionality and also dissolves with it.[5]

The consequence of all this instability and mutability is reflected in the familiar comment that Americans are "the loneliest people in the world." They seem to be on a continual search for "community," which has become a buzzword among pundits diagnosing social ills. Friendliness alleviates the need but does not satisfy it; in fact, the very ubiquity of friendliness is a symptom of the complaint. "So much cordiality, so little intimacy," remarked a visiting Englishman. Half a century later, a native of the country agreed, "Americans are the most gregarious people on earth. They have to be: they have no friends."[6]

A second condition in national life that gives rise to friendliness is the lack of fixed and certain values. As earlier chapters have explained, America rejected the ways of the past, along with the figures of leadership and bodies of authority that once transmitted them. It is now all up to the individual, who is supposed to discover and fashion his own values, which will guide and justify his life. This leaves him isolated and insecure. He is not sure that he is what he should be. Often he is not even sure what he should be. The uncertainty naturally leads to fears of inadequacy, to the question, how can I tell whether or not I am any good?[7]

Driven by these emotions, the individual seeks relief in the smiling company of other people. Their friendliness reassures him of his personal worth. Because other people like him, he must be all right. And the more people there are who like him, the better he thinks he is. Conversely, if fewer people like him, he feels less worthy. To be alone is intolerable; that means he is worthless.[8]

The result is a compulsive, indiscriminate, and insatiable need to receive the signs and expressions of affection. It even has a name (attributed to the novelist F. Scott Fitzgerald): "the American disease," wanting to be loved or at least well liked. The country is filled with people who are ready to express their friendliness to everyone they happen to meet and who both desire and expect to receive the same in return.

Children acquire this distinctively national tendency at an early age. In France, a young person who has a large number of friends is dismissed as superficial. Not in America. When a girl says she wants her entire first-grade class to be invited to her birthday party "because they're all my friends," her mother feels a glow of pride. Her daughter is popular. She is headed for success in the social relationships of her native land.[9]

Mere physical proximity is sufficient to trigger friendliness, and even the most extreme differences in social status fail to inhibit it. When the Queen of England visited an American housing project, one of the residents embraced her with a big, friendly hug. In a less dramatic and more commonplace incident, a rich man greeted the porter at his apartment building in the following way: "Hi, Tom." (His name's really Jack.) "How are the kids, Tom?" (He has no children.) Despite its slipshod shallowness, the friendly intention of the inquiry made both parties feel good.[10]

Just as Americans are pleased and reassured to receive the overt signs of friendliness, they become disconcerted and upset when they fail to receive them. It is as if their self-worth were being put in question. Tocqueville encountered this kind of behavior when he found it was very difficult to make an American realize that his presence was not wanted and that he should go away. The fellow simply refused to take any number of hints, because he could not admit to himself that another person did not like him, and Tocqueville realized that if he expressed his aversion so openly that it could not fail to be perceived, he would create an enemy for life.[11]

The result of this pervasive need for emotional reassurance is a society where, as one sociologist explained, "all relationships" are supposed to "bear some resemblance to those of love and friendship." Or, as I once heard a businessman remark, "Everyone is everyone else's good friend." That is, everyone is supposed to act as if he were. The practices of commerce and advertising play on and contribute to a dominant atmosphere of amiability with their ceaseless professions and enticements to the potential customer: "You're not just a number here, you've got a friend in the business," et cetera, et cetera, in a thousand variations.[12]

The literature of self-help and personal advice recognizes the social demands for friendliness as a reality which the reader is supposed to accept and to which he should adapt himself. Dr. Spock's famous baby book recommends that a mother lay the groundwork for teaching her child manners by first encouraging him to like people. A universal how-to manual outlines the specific steps you can follow to establish friendly relations with a neighbor at the outset, so that later he will be more inclined to heed any complaints you may have about his behavior. A business career guidebook warns that your colleagues at work are not really your friends, but you must act as if they were, or else you will not get ahead on the job.[13]

Some of the works in this genre are even more emphatic. They urge everyone to go out and "sell yourself," and they accompany the exhortation with a stern warning that "if you are not saleable, you will starve."[14] The general message has been delivered many times already. In 1952, Norman Vincent Peale's best-seller, *The Power of Positive Thinking*, was advertised under the slogan, "Make people like you—increase your earnings." And before that, there was Dale Carnegie's highly popular *How to Win Friends and Influence People* (1936).

One should not think that these books advise people to prostitute themselves emotionally by feigning sentiments they do not feel. The authors inevitably stress that one must be "sincere." In this they differ from the tutors of social poise and manipulation in traditional societies, like Lord Chesterfield, but they are on firm ground with their fellow countrymen. Americans want to express sincere if superficial friendliness for others, just as they desire others to be sincerely if superficially friendly to themselves.

American sensitivity is not limited to the opinions of other Americans. The visitor from abroad is met with an inevitable question, how do you like us? And it is not an empty form of conversation or merely a polite courtesy. Americans really do want to know what other people think of them. This differs from the practice almost everywhere else in the world. Ordinarily the natives simply do not care about a foreigner's reactions. The very fact that he is a foreigner, a transient and ignorant outsider, causes them, as insiders, to regard with indifference any opinion he might have of their society and to dismiss any criticism he might make as uninformed, inconsequential, and impertinent.[15]

Americans lack such impervious unconcern. In the estimation of an English political scientist with wide international experience, no other people, with the possible exception of the Japanese, are more elated by praise or more distressed by blame.[16] This has always been the case. During the Nineteenth Century, when Americans were notorious the world over for loudly and incessantly boasting about their country, discerning observers perceived the nervousness and insecurity underneath their bravado.

Whenever the news reports a demonstration against the United States in some remote corner of the globe, Americans feel a quiver of dismay. "Why don't they like us?" they wonder. And they conclude, "If only they could meet us personally, they wouldn't feel the way they do." Given this mentality, Americans are inevitably enthusiastic about any program, like foreign exchange students or the Peace Corps, which promotes contact between people of the United States and those in the rest of the world. By this means, others will presumably learn that Americans are not rich and arrogant, but down-to-earth, friendly people.[17]

Closely related to friendliness is openness. The latter has impressed foreign visitors as much as the former, especially in its contrast to their own modes of social discourse, which may employ an elaborate panoply of irony, persiflage, posing, and posturing. As one international reporter complained, "The hardest thing to get in Europe is simplicity, people saying what they think and feel, openly and directly. It never happens." It certainly does happen in America, so much so that non-Americans find the revelation of personal matters disconcerting, at times even obscene. One British traveler remarked that people you have just met will tell you things that an Englishman would not utter on his deathbed. Another noticed that Americans exchange such intimacies between each other as if they were a common courtesy of ordinary social conversation.[18]

Self-disclosure, like friendliness, is more than a desirable option; it is a mutual obligation, which people expect to receive as well as to give. In the past, Americans were notorious for subjecting others, especially strangers, to scrutiny and interrogation. F. Scott Fitzgerald referred to the towns of the Midwest "with their interminable inquisitions which spared only the children and the very old." While the grosser and more blatant forms of these practices may have disappeared, at least in most parts of the country, the emotional needs and social demands that produced them have remained very much alive.[19]

In the Age of Jackson and ever thereafter, anyone seeking public office has been considered fair game for the most egregious prying and the most personal inquiries. In recent years, politicians have themselves taken the initiative and added to their campaign repertoire accounts of personal agonies—the loss of parents, siblings, or offspring being especially prized and popular. Celebrities in the world of entertainment have long traded on the scabrous details of their private lives, and today they do so all the more, under the increasing license granted to freedom of expression. Since the mere confession of something intimate tends to win the applause of an audience, numerous amateurs seek to join the scene on television talk shows, with each participant trying to surpass the others in disclosing something outrageous and bizarre about himself.[20]

"The right to privacy" is a phrase that has often been heard in the last few decades. It might seem to contradict the tendency toward openness, until one realizes that it is directed against intrusions by government agencies, corporate bodies, and investigative businesses—the powerful snooping on the people. It does not refer to the people, in the form of nosy neighbors or journalists, snooping on dubious individuals. That—if it could be said to involve rights at all—would fall under the category of "the public's right to know," in practice if not in theory. The English notion of privacy, of turning one's home into a castle by means of garden walls or shrubbery, has never taken hold in America, as is apparent in suburban properties, which are usually separated from each other by transparent fences and sometimes by no demarcation at all.[21]

Chapter one mentioned Americans' enthusiasm for competition. At first glance, this kind of behavior might seem unrelated to their desire for friendliness and self-disclosure. But competition arises from the same source as the other two phenomena—from an absence of stability and certainty. Things are in flux, and everyone is engaged in an effort to win prestige, power, and money. Americans make sense of the ongoing melee by viewing it in terms of specific contests, deciding who or what has won or lost, then calculating the overall results to determine the superiority or inferiority of the competitors in relation to each other. As one longtime observer, writer, and researcher has remarked, "There are few activities Americans enjoy more than rating things." Sports by their very nature lend themselves to this treatment, and they accordingly enjoy great national popularity and attention. The annual ranking of colleges and universities in *U.S. News* provokes intense interest in certain quarters. Most every sphere of activity has its own ratings tabulation, formal or informal, which are closely scrutinized and endlessly discussed by participants and other interested parties.[22]

Competition does more than provide a lively scene for Americans as spectators; it also engages them in an intensely personal way. Being a member of a society where status and position are perceived as insecure and changeable, each individual senses that he must struggle to seize what he can: "Get yours, I got mine!" "Grab a piece of the action!" "The real American is a competitor!" Internally, he experiences a relentless, gnawing doubt: how do I know whether or not I am any good unless I compete and win?

America is a country filled with people who go through life troubled by the impulse that they need to prove something, to the world and especially to themselves. Examples range from the boy who feels compelled to engage in a successful fistfight to the businessman who feels compelled to make a fortune. Back in the 1960s, an army recruiting advertisement exploited this emotional vulnerability: "Vietnam. Hot. Wet. Muddy. Perilous. To prove yourself here is to prove yourself to the world. No test is harder. No trial more demanding. But when a man serves here, he proves himself a man. To his country. To himself." Usually self-vindication assumes a less dangerous form, as in the case of the executive who, getting on in years, chose to seek less demanding work and justified his decision with the defensive statement: "I've been successful; I don't have to prove anything."[23]

The same insecurity that drives a person to friendliness also drives him to competition. As early as the 1930s, a prominent psychologist perceived a connection between the two and analyzed them together: "neurotic competitiveness" and "the neurotic need for affection."[24] Both answer a demand for external validation. It is other people who decide whether or not one is popular. Likewise, it is other people who define whether or not one is a success. Achievement by itself is not sufficient. There must be rivals whom one has surpassed and spectators who recognize one's victory. The intrinsic value of the prize is only part of the reason for competing, and usually not the main reason. Remove the rivals and the spectators, and many—perhaps most—would not make the effort, or at least would make far less of an effort.

These peculiarly national compulsions add a special urgency and edge to the natural human inclination of gravitating toward the winning side and shunning the losing one. Through the course of the Twentieth Century, from their high point—such as it was—at its beginning to their final eclipse at its end, socialists have complained of their inability to attract or retain recruits, because Americans did not want to be members of a political party that kept suffering defeat at the polls. To attach oneself to a persistently losing cause, however noble, is to cast doubt on one's own personal worth, whereas the reverse is true if one is on the side of the winners. "It's difficult to be an American and not worship success," admitted one sadly discouraged socialist at the century's end. Over a hundred years earlier, James Bryce agreed: nowhere else in the world is it so true that "nothing succeeds like success."[25]

The opposite, however, is also true, though less recognized and not at all celebrated. Success in its initial flush of victory may look as if it will drive everything before it and attain every objective. But a single check, a single reverse, can bring the triumphal parade to a halt. Questions begin to be raised, and doubts begin to be expressed. Unless the champion is able to silence them with a quick, new, and resounding achievement, his laurels will wither, his adulators fall silent, and his followers disappear. If nothing succeeds like success, it is also the case that you're only as good as your last performance. The momentum created by victory is ephemeral; it must be continually renewed by a succession of new victories. And so, in America, competition never ends.

The collective and conformist nature of competition is especially apparent in what is probably its most popular arena—the purchase and exhibition of luxury goods. This is the conventionally accepted way in which a person can indicate to everyone else that he is successful: he has made enough money to afford something beyond the merely necessary or practical. Although similar behavior has probably gone on in every society that has enjoyed a material surplus, among Americans the crucial element is not the actual possession or enjoyment of the goods but the perception of other people. It is not enough that one has something which should boost his self-esteem. It will not do so unless he knows that others are aware of it and value it as he does.

The moment an American attains a level of income above subsistence, he feels the urge to buy and display. Near the end of the Nineteenth Century, when new and larger amounts of affluence were moving down the social ladder, a Catholic archbishop in the Midwest reported that American workingmen "spend their money as fast as they earn it. They want their daughters to be ladies. Go into their houses: you will find car-pets, pianos." And he added that they did not really care for these things; they just wanted "to make a show." Around the same time, a German psychologist observed that the chief purpose of opulent expenditure in the United States was the opportunity it gave a person to demonstrate that he could afford the best. If he could not, he preferred to renounce a luxury entirely rather than be seen to possess an obviously inferior version of it.[26]

During the Nineteenth Century, the most conspicuous status symbol in American homes was the piano. It did not need to be played (often no one in the family knew how); its mere presence signified genteel prosperity. In the early Twentieth Century, the piano gave way to a more conspicuous and expensive possession, the automobile, which soon began to undergo an "annual model change." The manufacturers in Detroit had discovered that the public wanted the cars of the current year to look distinctly different from those of previous years, so that whenever a person was able to buy a new one, it would be instantly obvious to all who saw it.[27]

The consumption of luxuries may have become less grossly conspicuous by the end of the Twentieth Century, at least at the higher levels of society, as a comparison of Thorstein Veblen's *Theory of the Leisure Class* (1899) with David Brooks' *Bobos in Paradise* (2000) suggests. But the old uncertainties and the visceral doubts that have perturbed every generation of Americans still remain, played upon by the seductive arts of commercial advertising, which insinuate the conviction that the products they proffer will make the purchaser esteemed and beloved among his fellows.

—2—

The emotional needs that promote friendliness, openness, and competition promote social association in general. Americans have a strong and impulsive herd instinct: they form groups with readiness and facility. As a British diplomat remarked in 1859, "They must congregate and combine, for the smallest as well as the most important objects." In 1928, an English journalist agreed that they have the habit of "doing everything in common." Around the turn of the century, a Russian political scientist spoke of their "morbid need of friendly contact" and found "something pathetic" in the fact that sharing a superficial characteristic or minor interest could form the basis of a social group. In the mid-Nineteenth Century, a Swedish novelist summed up the national trait: "These people associate as easily as they breathe."[28]

The result has been a proliferation of voluntary organizations. Tocqueville was surprised by their number and declared that no other society in the world could equal it. The trend has persisted since his time. In 1944, one historian dubbed the United States a "nation of joiners," and statistics have continued to confirm that sobriquet. During the last years of the Twentieth Century, a book entitled *Bowling Alone* raised fears that the tendency might be diminishing, but there is no cause for worry. If Americans have been participating less in the activities of the community, it is because they have become more involved in the activities of the workplace, as will be explained in chapter eight. Their social appetites remain as keen as ever.[29]

Most associations in the United States are not founded or maintained for the pleasures of sociability alone; they serve definite and highly practical purposes. Foreign observers have marveled, not at the mere presence of groups in America, but at the work they have succeeded in carrying out. Their achievements have been so great and so numerous that they have extorted praise even from unsympathetic witnesses. The individual Yankee was "not a very elevated specimen of human nature," said the British diplomat quoted above, but when he joined with others of his kind, they became "the most...enterprising people in the world." An American clergyman who viewed antebellum behavior with a critical eye agreed: "Everything is done now by societies," whose members "act together with the uniformity of a disciplined army."[30]

Closer inspection, by authors like Tocqueville and James Bryce, revealed the process by which Americans were able to operate collectively with such success. When a problem arose, those affected did not petition some higher authority to intervene, as they would have done in Europe. Instead, they met together, set up a committee of directors, and went to work themselves. Spontaneous coordination characterized their actions. Some persons assumed the role of leaders, others filled the ranks as followers, and everyone cooperated. An obstacle had to be formidable indeed to withstand so concerted an effort.[31]

The ability to work together is a characteristic of Americans in all their activities. Whether they are on the job or off it, dealing with the formal rules and positions of profit-making organizations or with informal gatherings on random occasions, they exhibit the same facility and ease of collective action. The aggregate result is the tremendous productivity that distinguishes the nation as a whole.

To function effectively and efficiently, a group must exercise control over its members, directing their separate exertions toward a common goal and preventing their individual differences from hindering the united effort. This is something that Americans have been able to do remarkably well. The very weakness that impels people into association makes them naturally subordinate to the body they have joined, as well as zealous enforcers of its corporate spirit and consensus. They will not stand to see their unanimity weakened or their friendly embrace slighted by a member's personal aversion or willfulness. "Be my brother or I'll bash your skull in!" was the informal slogan of Nazi youth.[32] Americans, when engaged in acting together, share a similar emotion, though they usually express it with somewhat more subtlety.

As a result, groups of all sizes are able to exert internal discipline. In 1898, a social critic spoke of the "moral terrorism" that just two people were able to impose on a third. Although that may be an exaggeration, the general principle is accurate. An American is socially and psychologically conditioned to obey the collective will of any group to which he happens to belong, just as he has learned to resist the individual will of each single person he happens to encounter. Groups are consequently able to wield decisive power over their members, and the larger the group, the more power it has. When its dimensions reach a point where it represents what is commonly called "public opinion," its strength becomes formidable indeed.[33]

Tocqueville's famous phrase "the tyranny of the majority" has often been misinterpreted as referring only to a national majority in the arena of politics. Along with his somewhat abstract discussion of the subject, one should also read the more concrete and detailed analysis by his Scottish contemporary, George Combe (1788–1858), whose role as an advocate for the young and controversial science of phrenology evidently induced him to pay close attention to the social factors that influenced people for or against new ideas. As he discovered, the "tyranny of the majority" goes deeper than politics. It is a social phenomenon that may appear wherever there is a group of any size. An individual can encounter it in his dealings with his neighbors or his coworkers, and its force and presence are a recurring theme in the various accounts and depictions of American life through the entire course of its history.[34]

Soon after the founding of the United States, enthusiastic Frenchmen began arriving on its shores to behold and experience the new land of freedom. They were quickly disillusioned. Along with formal political and legal liberties, they encountered informal social restrictions, which prevailed in public and especially in private life. Most of them came to the realization that France, despite its oppression, poverty, and conflict, offered more latitude for a person to behave as he wished. One even declared that the United States was "the least free country on earth."[35]

The contrast between liberty on the statute books and regulation in social practice was confirmed by Tocqueville, who marveled that public opinion in America could command a far wider and more profound obedience than "the most absolute monarchs in Europe": "As long as the majority is still undecided, discussion is carried on; but as soon as its decision is irrevocably pronounced, everyone is silent, and the friends as well as the opponents of the measure unite in assenting to its propriety." He went on to describe the miserable ostracism inflicted on any who dared to dissent openly, and he concluded that he knew of "no country in which there is so little independence of mind and real freedom of discussion as in America." One of the more honest and perceptive of his American informants agreed: "Public opinion does with us what the Inquisition could never do."[36]

Contemporary travelers from Great Britain and other countries made similar reports. "Politically," Americans are "the most free people on earth," declared a visiting actress, "socially the least so." One popular novelist and former sea captain spoke of "that fear, so universal in the United States, of expressing an opinion contrary to the majority." Harriet Martineau agreed, "The worship of opinion is...the established religion" of this nation. Citing the greater independence that prevailed among Europeans, they stigmatized the Americans' behavior as contemptible and disgusting. George Combe accused them of "moral cowardice" for remaining silent even on those occasions when public opinion was "unquestionably wrong."[37]

As some of the more perceptive observers have recognized, then and later, Americans had good reason for their timidity and fear, since they faced a different social reality than their transatlantic visitors. In Europe, the distinctions of class favored a diversity of opinion. If a man offended the high and mighty, he could take refuge among the people; if he offended the people, his superior status would shield him from their wrath. In America there was no such protection; the dissenter stood alone. Public opinion was overwhelming in force and universal in application. Its "Argus eyes" saw everything and spared no one, remarked a German immigrant. It could cause even the rich and powerful—everyone from the president on down—to tremble. It intruded its gaze into the most minute matters and might pronounce on something as trivial as the wearing of a certain kind of coat.[38]

Americans themselves occasionally confirmed the assessment of foreigners. James Fenimore Cooper was a persistent critic of the tyranny of public opinion. His fellow novelist Nathaniel Hawthorne added a word of complaint, which was seconded by the contemporary poet Henry Wadsworth Longfellow. But Americans in general were silent on the subject. They were certainly aware of the reality, and Harriet Martineau found that they would admit its existence "when the plain case is set down before them," but they had "worn their chains so long" that they took them for granted as a simple condition of life.[39]

The foregoing testimony is from the antebellum period of American history, and it has been confirmed by similar evidence from every subsequent era. In the late Nineteenth Century, James Bryce, often regarded as second only to Tocqueville in the depth and breadth of his analysis of America, spoke of the power of public opinion much as Tocqueville had done some fifty years earlier. To Americans, "the voice of the multitude" was "the voice of fate," and, whatever their personal feelings, they submitted to it automatically and voluntarily, even before it applied any actual coercion.[40]

An even more striking and emphatic witness was the newspaper magnate, Lord Northcliffe. He was a prominent and vocal friend of the United States, a boundless admirer of its material progress, and a frequent visitor.

But the uniformity of the natives and the conformity that produced it revolted him. "I tell you," he exclaimed, "the American people are the most docile, the most easily led, the least individualistic people in the world." When an interviewer from the *New York Times* asked him, "What is our very greatest fault?" he replied without hesitation, "Your servile fear of the majority." And he illustrated the point in detail, citing, among other instances, the wearing of straw hats and the refusal to wear wristwatches, in careful obedience to the general practice.[41]

As before, other foreign visitors expressed similar complaints, and so did a few isolated Americans. In 1898, an essay referred to "the world-famous 'timidity' of Americans in matters of opinion" and their "deference to reigning convention." A few years later, a magazine article appeared with the title "Our Lost Individuality."[42] But it was Mark Twain who provided the most spectacular illustration. In 1906, he, along with other American dignitaries and celebrities, welcomed the author Maxim Gorky as a refugee from czarist oppression. In the subsequent stream of banquet speeches and newspaper pieces, the contrast was often pointed out between American liberty and Russian tyranny. Then, it transpired that the woman who was traveling with Gorky was not his wife, and in an instant his status changed from hero to pariah. Mark Twain, the champion of human freedom and the satirist of American social foibles, was highly embarrassed and, like everyone else, assumed the stance of disapproving respectability.

Twain had already, some years earlier, coined the aphorism that explained, excused, and justified the conduct of himself and his fellow citizens: "It is by the goodness of God that in our country we have those three unspeakably precious things: freedom of speech, freedom of conscience, and the prudence never to practice either of them."[43] A more precise statement of the third item would have been "the prudence not to practice either of them whenever public opinion thus dictates."

In the years following World War I, various Frenchmen crossed the Atlantic to view the new world power firsthand. Their reaction was rather like that of their predecessors a century earlier. One of the more prominent among them spoke of the illusions Americans entertained as to their personal independence, the reality of their submission to prevailing standards of behavior, and the persecution they faced if they resisted. The feelings of visiting Englishmen were similar. One of them expressed himself in memorably emphatic terms: "This the land of the free! Why, if I say anything that displeases them, the free mob will lynch me.... I have never been in any country where the individual has such an abject fear of his fellow countrymen."[44]

More Americans than ever before agreed with these assessments. During the 1920s, the idea became fashionable among many young people that Europe offered a more independent and civilized life. Voices condemning the provincialism, philistinism, and conformity of the United States were heard with increasing frequency. One of the most famous novels of the day, Sinclair Lewis's *Babbitt*, contained a section (chapters 32–33) that deserves to stand as the classic depiction of an ordinary American who happens to run afoul of his peer group of friends and colleagues and the emotional agonies he suffers as a consequence.

In the wake of World War II, more foreign visitors arrived, and they found the same conditions as before. A French philosopher remarked that "public opinion...plays the role of the policeman," and people felt themselves natural and free when they were "acting like everyone else." A German philosopher stated that American society "conditions each of its members so perfectly to its exigencies that no one knows that he is conditioned." The editor of the eminent intellectual journal *Esprit* pronounced the following verdict: "The American state is liberal, but American society is totalitarian. It is perhaps the most totalitarian in the world."[45]

British visitors agreed. One of them spoke of the "morbid dread of being thought in any way peculiar" and the "marked intolerance of eccentrics." It was the time when the Cold War was at its hottest. Whereas in Britain the privileges of social class protected eccentrics in general and leftists in particular from persecution by the public, in the United States the tidal wave of McCarthyism was sweeping through the land, and the popular mood was ready to brand as "Communist" anything out of the ordinary that made it feel uncomfortable.[46]

After a few years, there was a reaction, and by the second half of the 1950s "conformity" was being discussed everywhere as a national problem. This produced the ludicrous spectacle of Americans deploring conformity in unison. Parents blamed teenagers for servile conformity to the dictates of their peers; teenagers retorted that parents were attempting to make them conform to the rules of adults. A sociologist surmised that many individuals were trying to figure out what would be "an acceptable norm of nonconformity" to which they could conform.[47]

The preoccupations of that era faded with the passage of time, and the aversion of Europeans diminished as American ways have become more familiar in their own countries. But one can still hear the occasional growl from abroad or grumble at home. In 1994, a London columnist asserted, "When a notion takes hold in America, virtually every person suddenly agrees with it as if afraid of being left out. The biggest crock of all is American rugged individualism." In the same year, an American sociologist declared, "This is not a nation of rugged individualists, but of timid joiners, petulant victims, and self-denigrating conformists." The attitude in the United States, whenever anyone bothers to address the subject, tends to be one of weary recognition rather than indignant surprise, for example the following from a literary critic and social commentator: "It is a condition which Tocqueville was one of the first to notice: the United States is a country in which people, permitted to say whatever they like, all somehow end up saying the same thing."[48]

At a very young age Americans begin to absorb the attitudes that underlie what their culture regards as normal social relationships. One of the most frequent complaints of visitors from abroad has been that children in the United States are spoiled, overindulged, under-disciplined little egotists. "The small American boy" is an evil "for which there is no remedy" was a typical comment (from the author of the 1893 Baedeker guide to the United States). Foreigners also noticed that this state of affairs went on with the passive compliance if not the active encouragement of parents, who allowed their children a large degree of independence and tolerated a certain amount of misbehavior.[49]

At the same time that American children are learning to take adult authority and supervision lightly, they are also engaged in the serious business of interacting with others of their age. This too happens with the assistance of parents, who encourage their offspring not to come automatically to them for guidance or assistance but first to try working out matters on their own. "Even our children never turn to their masters," one of Tocqueville's informants told him. "They manage everything among themselves."[50] A schoolchild soon learns that he risks serious disapproval from his classmates if he is too subservient to adults or too dependent on them. Seeking a teacher's intervention in a dispute is considered cowardly and a betrayal of the group. Reporting other children's misbehavior to an adult is regarded as outright treason.

Sensitivity and obedience to peers is the reverse of the coin whose more obvious side is disregard and disrespect for authority. In the 1830s, Harriet Martineau was startled to hear American children expressing caution about "the opinions of others" and talking "about the effect of actions upon people's minds." Over a century later, the same kind of children were still in evidence, and probably more so. When a twelve-year-old girl was asked if she would like to be able to fly, as her comic-book hero did, she replied that she would "if everybody else did, but otherwise it would be kind of conspicuous."[51]

In adolescence, these tendencies develop further. The flouting of adult rules has been a persistent source of parental and public worry ever since the term "juvenile delinquency" came into use, and long before that. At the same time, in his slavish conformity to the sometimes obnoxious and often bizarre fads that prevail among teenagers, an American youth is reinforcing the lesson that society has been inculcating into him ever since he left the playpen, if not the cradle: peers are important, peers are those who must be obeyed.

As has often been observed (as early as Tocqueville), the pattern of adolescence in America is unlike that in Europe, where young people find it necessary to stage an actual rebellion against their parents in

order to assert their personal independence. For the American teenager, the process is usually much less explosive, as he gradually leaves
his parents behind and becomes increasingly involved in the activities
of his peers.[52]

Then the seemingly miraculous transformation occurs. The adolescent graduates from school and assumes the responsibilities of an adult.
His peers are no longer restless, moody, dependent (or semidependent)
teenagers but people who are holding down jobs and raising families,
and he adapts to their norms, since he has been socialized to adapt to
whatever the norms may be of those around him. Many onlookers, both
foreigners and natives, have been astonished by the change, and find it
inexplicable. They include the author who was quoted above, condemning
the American boy as an evil without remedy, but who also admitted that
the same boy grew up to be a courteous, considerate adult.[53]

Higher education prolongs the period of adolescence and reinforces its
social lessons. A standard of superficial friendliness is enforced in college
dormitories as well as in high school corridors. Campus demonstrations
of youthful antagonism towards adults in authority appear under the
familiar colors of youthful conformity with their peers.[54]

Since the end of the 1960s, teachers of liberal education have occasionally complained about the docility of their students. Instead of being
the bold and free spirits of Emersonian individualism, they are cautious
and timid. According to the account of one disapproving professor, they
desperately desire to blend in with the group and fear being embarrassed.[55] Such behavior is understandable. Students are neophytes, and
in their nervous inexperience they exaggerate the social norms they have
acquired. They hardly deserve reproach, especially from their academic
instructors, who, being themselves properly conditioned Americans, only
strike bold and defiant postures when they have the collective support
of like-minded peers.

The conformity that American society imposes on individuals differs fundamentally from that which traditional societies impose. They

enforce obedience to long established mores and generally accepted customs. An American, in contrast, is supposed to adapt himself to the norms of whatever group he happens to be in, and he is supposed to change whenever they change. Since peers set the standard, they can alter it as well.

Having been equipped with a mental facility for what may be termed flexible (or ad hoc) conformity, Americans are able to take change in stride, even when it produces a complete reversal of previously existing rules. In the early years of the 1960s, marihuana was generally regarded as a dangerous and hence justifiably prohibited drug. If a student smoked it, his fellow students asked each other what psychological problems might be troubling him. By the end of the 1960s, marihuana had become highly popular on many campuses, and students asked each other what psychological problems might be troubling anyone who refused to smoke it.[56]

Young people are particularly adept at adjusting to new circumstances. When they arrive at a highly selective and expensive liberal arts college where an atmosphere of theoretical left-wing radicalism pervades the faculty, they quickly sense the dominant spirit and perceive the accepted norms. They accordingly proceed with energy and flair to learn the principles and apply the techniques of such things as postmodern critical thinking and advanced deconstructionism. On graduation, they will most likely go off to the business and corporate world, where they will find a different environment with its own principles and techniques, which they will acquire with similar rapidity and success, having shed the old ones.[57]

Social adaptability is a characteristic of Americans of all ages. I recall the case of a prominent segregationist politician in the South. He may even have been the one who had vowed to stand in the schoolhouse door shouting "Never!" to the forces of racial integration. A decade or two later, he was noticed performing the typical and familiar ritual of crowning a local high school's homecoming queen. The distinctive thing was that she happened to be black. When a reporter confronted the politician with the contradiction between his past actions and his present behavior, he replied, without the slightest embarrassment or confusion, "Times change." The shrug was almost audible; no further explanation was necessary.

Popular feeling in the United States can alter with startling rapidity, and the American has learned to stay attentively poised, ready to discern its movement and to change himself accordingly. As George Santayana noted, "He can conceive of no more decisive way of recommending an opinion or a practice than to say that it is what everybody is coming to adopt." Ambitious and contriving persons have at times tried to turn this instability and uncertainty to their advantage. They seek to persuade others to support something they want by cunningly insinuating and propagating the notion that it already enjoys growing popularity. This is an old trick, and an author as early as John Fenimore Cooper indignantly condemned it more than once.[58]

For all Americans, the successful strategy in the conduct of their lives is to change with the times, not after them or before them. There will probably always be a number of unfortunately stubborn people who think that they should receive applause and congratulations for adopting an unpopular cause that later became popular. Instead, they are more likely to be treated as an annoying embarrassment. This happened with the early opponents of the Vietnam War, and before that with the 1930s opponents of Hitler and Mussolini, whom government agents, in their postwar hunt for Communists, stigmatized as "premature antifascists."

With such mentalities and emotions at work, it should be no wonder that the United States is a country of fads. *The Contrast* (1789), the first comic drama written by an American and commercially produced on the American stage, laughed at the fanaticism with which women followed fashions, even to their personal disadvantage. Accounts by foreign visitors, including one also entitled *The Contrast* (1924), have recorded their surprise at the way popular crazes spring up unexpectedly, spread ferociously, then disappear suddenly. Other peoples also adopt and discard favorites, but Americans do so, in the words of an English author, with an "astonishing unanimity." Their herd instinct makes everyone want to join in, and no one wants to be left out. Advertising and modern communications media have often been blamed for fads, but they are only a facilitating means, not the primary cause, which was present long before they arrived on the scene.[59]

If Americans are able to turn a trivial whim into a national practice, whenever a serious issue gets hold of them they are capable of attaining a collective unity and power that is truly awesome. They demand from every citizen an expression of sympathy and solidarity, if not active participation. In the trumpeting words of Justice of the Supreme Court Oliver Wendell Holmes, Jr., "It is required of a man that he should share the passion and action of his time at peril of being judged not to have lived." George Santayana agreed: "Even what is best in American life is compulsory—the idealism, the zeal, the beautiful happy unison of its great movements. You must wave, you must cheer, you must push with the irresistible crowd; otherwise you will feel like a traitor, a soulless outcast, a deserted ship high and dry on the shore."[60]

The result can be an overwhelming surge of social action that astonishes and terrifies onlookers from other countries. "The same impulse seems to possess everyone at the same moment," observed James Bryce, and it goes sweeping across the land with an overwhelming strength like that of a force of nature. One witness (G. K. Chesterton) compared it to a prairie fire, another (George Santayana) to a tornado. Anything standing in its way is demolished—torn to bits or flattened to the ground. In such circumstances, obedience is automatic. Opposition is not merely futile; it is self-destructive. Bryce noted that a dissenter provokes, not merely disapproval and condemnation, but astonishment: he must be insane to act as he does.[61]

When President Woodrow Wilson led the United States into World War I, the men he appointed to manage the effort on the domestic front took pride in their minimal use of the tools of formal legal coercion. Police arrests, judicial trials, prison sentences—those were clumsy and offensively obvious measures that foreign governments needed to employ. America had its own way of doing things, which produced much better results. Whenever some manufacturer tried to resist the demands of

Wilson's War Industries Board, he received a hint that his behavior might be brought "to the attention of public opinion, particularly the public opinion of his home community." That did the trick; nothing more needed to be said. In fact, it was "only rarely" that "the gentle insinuation" of a resort to informal pressure had to be expressed in actual words; its abiding presence and savage potentiality were obvious to everyone.[62]

Ready and easy collective coercion is practiced throughout America in the most mundane circumstances on a day-to-day basis. The implied threat is not nearly so enormous as it was in those instances of national consensus just described, but it is sufficient to obtain the desired results. An ordinary group does not need to be promoting the entire country's agenda in order to feel itself animated by a spirit of potent unanimity. That arises naturally and automatically from the social characteristics and vulnerabilities of Americans. An ordinary group does not need to represent national opinion for its commands to be obeyed. It has sufficient force and will to impose them—whatever they may be—on an offending member in its ranks. The individual is sufficiently weak and fearful in the face of collective disapproval that he will get back in line and toe the mark, perhaps as promptly as Wilson's initially uncooperative manufacturer must have done.

Everywhere at every moment in the United States, its citizens are engaged in playing the roles of collective domination and individual submission. "It is an urgent, terrible force which reaches out of the most banal phenomena," including the "warmth in the manners of shop assistants," exclaimed the American expatriate author Herb Greer. "All this says, softy but inexorably, *join or die*. It is...the gregariousness of the species raised to a ferocious intensity. One feels it like the force of gravity on a planet larger than one's own...."[63]

Greer himself fled abroad to escape being dissolved "in the acid of other people's social demands." His case is, of course, highly unusual. For every American who feels oppressed by the conditions that Greer describes, millions have been sufficiently acculturated to accept them as normal, in fact, not even to take conscious notice of them.

—3—

Foreign visitors have often observed what seems to be a paradox in the behavior of Americans. On the one hand, they enjoy great freedoms, which they exercise to a degree that has shocked people in more sedate and constrained societies. On the other hand, they display a fearful caution and a quick obedience to the collective feelings of their fellow citizens, to an extent which goes far beyond the prudent deportment of those in more traditional cultures and which has frequently provoked their contempt. American children are supposed to be independent and "stand on their own two feet"; yet they are also supposed to "get along with others." Americans adults want to be free and self-assertive; yet they also want to be well-liked and popular. The apparent contradiction is so striking that it found its way into two sayings which became popular among the French: "Americans are individualists" and "Americans are conformists."[64]

Both generalizations are accurate, and George Combe analyzed their precise relationship. "An American will pursue his pleasure and his [self-]interest as if no other being existed in the world," but the moment his behavior arouses collective disapproval, he shrinks back and obeys the dictates of the group. He realizes that the penalty for resistance is ostracism or expulsion, if not worse. In this way, the consensus of those with whom an individual has significant dealings—his coworkers especially, but also the neighbors or any other important peer group—is able to regulate his conduct.[65]

Such control is crucially important for the promotion of national strength and welfare. To achieve and maintain the high level of goods and services that have made the United States the richest and most powerful nation in the world, it is necessary to have workers who are both individually motivated and collectively coordinated, both personally ambitious and gregariously cooperative. The first half of the American formula fills individuals with large amounts of energy and ambition. It is the task of the second half to ride herd on all these separate, striving egos, to point them in the right direction, and to keep them from falling afoul of one another.

In a typical American office, certain norms of behavior prevail. One of the most obvious of these is the suppression of open conflict. This is a characteristic of American society in general, but at work it is especially conspicuous. People shy away from controversial topics of discussion. The expression of strong emotion, especially negative emotion, makes them uncomfortable. If someone has a particular sore spot or pet peeve, it is respected and avoided. Individuals repress personal quirks that annoy—or that they think might annoy—their fellow workers. The social grease of friendliness (discussed above) is not optional but required, and it is spread with a generous hand. In business, when two deadly rivals or bitter enemies happen to meet, they may greet each other, not with a snarl or even with frigid courtesy, but with such a convincing display of amiability that no outsider could guess their real relationship.[66]

This is not how people in other cultures behave on the job. Europeans in particular refuse to disguise their real feelings. That would be hypocrisy, dishonesty, a compromising of one's personal integrity. Instead they freely air their likes and dislikes. "It's important to show yourself as you are," declared one Frenchman, "with the authenticity of your failings, with your own little zany side, and with your contradictions.... Nothing is worse than to have to wear a mask." Quarrels and feuds spring up that no one attempts to settle or even to paper over. In fact, they provide an opportunity for the display of skill in argument, which both participants and spectators enjoy.[67]

Beneath the avoidance of open conflict lies another, more profound rule of the workplace: productive performance should trump all other considerations. It is "that obsession, common to all Americans, for getting a specific job done." The declaration "I'm just doing my job" serves as a definitive justification and explanation, and is heard everywhere. The worker—clerk and executive alike—is not supposed to allow his entire personality to intrude into the workplace; he is supposed to perform only the function assigned to him or assume the role that his position dictates. The friendliness and sociability of coworkers may be pleasant in themselves, but they are very superficial and entirely subordinate to the accomplishment of the business at hand.[68]

This fragmentation of the self and predominance of the demands of work facilitate certain kinds of behavior that greatly assist productivity. People are able to interact easily even though they do not know one another and often would dislike each other if they did. So long as a person performs his job adequately and gets along with his colleagues, no one cares what else he may be or what he may do after hours. Members of traditionally hostile religious and ethnic groups, who would have been at daggers drawn in the Old World, can be seen working together efficiently and even amicably in American offices.[69]

Just as Americans are able to relate to and judge other people in purely functional terms, so they are able to consider and evaluate situations from a purely business perspective, with the minimal interference of extraneous considerations. Arguments in meetings behind closed doors may become heated and even ferocious, but they tend to focus on the merits of the issues at hand rather than irrelevant personal denigration or display. The egos of the participants are involved—they cannot help being so—but they are far less involved than those in other cultures, where an attack on one's ideas is considered an attack on one's self, and where verbal virtuosity carries the day. In America, "it's just business."[70]

In traditional cultures, businessmen who do not know each other often engage in lengthy preliminaries before getting down to the actual negotiation of a deal. Each wants first to understand the other as a person: Is he a civilized human being? Is he worthy of my trust? Then, once a personal bond is established, they can begin their commercial transaction. American businessmen do not feel a need for this kind of procedure. They see themselves, not as entire and unique personalities, but as the performers of a specific task, that of conducting business. Anything else is inconsequential and a waste of time. Strangers or not, they are ready to begin negotiating the instant they meet.[71]

Amid an ambiance of such detached and depersonalized utilitarianism, the American worker is able to change and move about with ease. Though intent on adjusting to and performing well whatever job he happens to have at the moment, he feels little attachment to the job over the long term. If something better comes up, he will take it and leave his old place with no regret.[72]

This attitude is characteristic of an American's relationship with the groups he joins: willing engagement and conformity but shallow allegiance. Today the booster of a local community is the sincere, enthusiastic, and diligent promoter of its welfare; tomorrow he may relocate to a community in another state and become the equally sincere, enthusiastic, and diligent promoter of its welfare.[73] Continual mobility and ready adaptation are the result. By frequently altering one's residence and employment, a person becomes adept at adjusting himself to new groups of people and to the norms that prevail among them. "Go along to get along" is his maxim. "I get along with everyone" is his cheerful claim, and he regards this to be a highly desirable and useful virtue, not a loss of individual integrity or evidence of emotional shallowness, as persons of other cultures might view it.

The protean personality that flexible conformity favors and nurtures has its negative side. One may feel rootless, without a center, unstable, and, in extreme cases, liable to go spinning out of control. According to one novelist and social critic, "this ungrounded quality reflects the oldest and deepest strain in actual American life." The very opposite is true of people in traditional societies. They tend to stay put, to live out their existence in the locality where they were born. Their habits, their values, and everything about them are consequently ingrained and indelible.[74]

Whatever else may be said about the advantages or disadvantages of Europeans as compared to Americans, the latter are unquestionably more suited to meet the demands for flexibility and change in the modern world and particularly in modern work. In 1900, an author with much international experience presented a hypothetical contrast: if by some chance one British aristocrat married an English shop girl and another one married an American shop girl, the odds would be overwhelmingly in favor of the American girl, rather than the English girl, successfully adapting to a social environment that was utterly unfamiliar to her.[75]

This case is a specific instance of a general rule: Americans are remarkably willing and able to adjust themselves to new situations.

A businessman in a traditional culture is usually upset, or at least disconcerted, when the person in another company with whom he has become used to dealing is replaced by someone whom he does not know. To an American, such a change hardly makes a difference. It is the position that matters, not the person who happens to fill it. He is a replaceable part, and one is reassuringly like another, having learned to fashion himself as such.[76]

The essence of the American achievement is the delicate and dynamic balance that it has struck between individualism (in the first half of the formula) and conformity (in the second half). If there were too much individualism, the result would be disorder, with egotism and capriciousness running wild. If there were too much conformity, the result would be stultification, with initiative and innovation being suppressed. But when the two are harnessed together and synchronized, the result is a productive synergy that can be seen in the groups at work throughout the United States.

An individual is permitted, even encouraged, to be ambitious and to assume responsibilities, but he is not allowed to go too far. The moment his actions start to interfere with those of his coworkers, the group steps in and calls him to order. This balance is present in the mode of work known as "antagonistic cooperation" (mentioned in chapter two), where people behave sometimes as teammates and sometimes as rivals. A collective consensus, unspoken and unnoticed, constantly presides over the entire operation, keeping it in motion and in tune.

The American formula is rarely found elsewhere in the world. Groups in traditional societies demand a strict obedience to established customs and ways of doing things. In such an environment, the individual reacts with resigned indifference and sullen passivity, interrupted by the occasional impulse to vaunt himself and defy the group. The social results are the very opposite of harmonious productivity. "The Mexican is not a team player," declared a journalist. Nor is the Frenchman or for that matter a citizen of most any country, at least when judged by American standards. One official from the U. S. State Department complained, "We often found it harder to get Latins [i.e. Latin Americans] to agree with each other than it was to get them to agree with us."[77]

The superiority of the American model is especially obvious in the interaction of superiors and subordinates on the job. Each worker is quick to perceive and ready to accept his position, not just in relation to those on the same level as himself, but also in relation to those up and down the hierarchy. In the same spirit of impersonal industriousness with which he efficiently performs a task without needing to understand its final product, he also dutifully carries out orders even when he disagrees with them.[78] As was mentioned in chapter two, there is a minimum of resentment felt by subordinates toward their superiors. There is also a minimum of mistrust felt by superiors toward their subordinates. Managers are therefore able to delegate authority to levels below them without the fear that their power will be usurped or that their juniors will disrupt the orderly functioning of operations.

These conditions enable American enterprises to utilize the talents and capabilities of their personnel to a greater extent than is possible in other cultures. European businesses are notorious for ignoring and discouraging the contributions of younger staff members and for making seniority an essential requirement for higher positions. Keeping subordinates on a tight rein is normal in the organizations of traditional societies. If you want anything done, you need to see the boss; his underlings are only allowed to perform routine tasks.[79]

Resorting to authority is a common practice in a country like France. When a dispute arises among coworkers, instead of handling it among themselves, they appeal to a higher level. When a community wants to initiate some public improvement, instead of forming an ad hoc group and mobilizing its own resources as Americans tend to do, it petitions a governmental agency. As a consequence, formal and defined structures of power play a much more significant role among the people of such a society than in the United States, and their actions are more cumbersome and less efficient than the informal and spontaneous behavior of Americans.[80]

Back in the days of the Cold War, right-wing pundits occasionally worried that their fellow countrymen might not have the internal qualities necessary to achieve victory. After all, theirs was a society that promised freedom for all persons to pursue their own desires. How could the resulting agglomeration of self-interested and self-indulgent individuals attain the unity of purpose and the spirit of self-sacrifice that the Soviet Union or Communist China could demand from its citizens?

They need not have worried. The most absolute powers of the most fanatical and totalitarian regimes in the world proved to be no match for the profound and pervasive influence of the American formula. Its second half labors incessantly to regulate the actions of people in the most conspicuous events as well as in the most commonplace tasks. It stirs the public up into a tidal wave of unified and selfless effort whenever a major threat is perceived. At all times, normal and abnormal alike, it is busy prompting the everyday working group to swat any of its members who create disruption or annoyance. Such behavior springs spontaneously from the inclinations of ordinary people. It is not something that commissars could contrive or secret police could enforce.

The contrast between American and Soviet cultures may be seen in something as specific as the psychological approach to social discipline. The heavy-handed methods of the Russian authorities won them international notoriety. They would declare dissenters insane, stick them in so-called psychiatric wards, and subject them to abusive treatment. This created much bad publicity, it was not especially effective (at least no more than other forms of state punishment), and it could be applied only to a limited number of people.

The American practice is incomparably superior, being more informal, extensive, and efficacious. As has been emphasized and illustrated repeatedly above, whenever public opinion decides upon something, everyone submits to it. Anyone who resists is regarded as crazy. Faced with such unanimity, an opponent naturally breaks down. There is no need for the brutal and clumsy actions of the police, secret or otherwise; the entire people act as a police force. "Everyone wants the same thing, everyone is the same, anyone who feels otherwise commits himself voluntarily to a mental institution."[81] That was an early prediction; today it would be updated to read, "voluntarily seeks psychological counseling."

In the years when Communist Russia was attempting to advance to economic power and primacy, there were those perceptive enough to discern its fundamental inferiority to the United States. An English author declared in 1937 that Americans were able to act collectively "with an ease, force, and natural cohesion beyond Lenin's dreams." His judgment was subsequently confirmed, especially by people who had the opportunity to see both systems at work. A sociologist and former refugee judged that, whereas Russia had deliberately tried to "functionalize" personal relationships in the service of economic productivity and had failed, the United States had succeeded at the same task without even intending to do so. A Soviet pilot arrived at the same conclusion after viewing the efficient operations of a working crew on board an American aircraft carrier: "They were all one team.... You couldn't terrify, intimidate, threaten, or coerce men into doing what they were doing. They had to want to do it...." The last word belongs to a group of Eastern European teachers, recently freed from the blundering oppression of a Communist regime and eager to embrace a more attractive alternative: "Only Americans know how to make things work."[82]

CHAPTER SIX

A Necessary Secret

—1—

American strength and affluence are the result of the two halves of a formula operating in tandem, but the two are not equally esteemed or even equally recognized. Americans loudly and incessantly tell themselves and everyone else that they are independent individualists, that their country is great because it gives people the freedom to do as they please. They would be far more justified in bragging about their facility for collective action, and they would be far more accurate in asserting that their country is great because its people know how to work together.

This bias in favor of the first half of the formula seems all the more puzzling because the second half is the more difficult to achieve. Energetic personal ambition can be found anywhere in the world; cooperative, coordinated behavior is much rarer. The great number of voluntary organizations in the United States, which has impressed so many visitors from abroad, is not a characteristic of other countries. Nor are the social attitudes that underlie these organizations. Outside their immediate families, people in traditional societies have great difficulty forming and maintaining efficient, productive groups.[1] They lack both the internal inclinations and the external pressures created by the second half of the American formula.

The consequences of this deficiency become apparent whenever Americans attempt to export their way of doing things. The natives of other cultures can grasp the idea of individual initiative and effort readily enough, but what they and their American tutors usually overlook are the collective restraints. Self-interest comes easy; enlightened self-interest is far more difficult. Americans can preach the virtues of competition and urge everyone to turn out and compete energetically because they take for granted the social mechanisms that keep competition from going too far and becoming divisive and counterproductive. Prudent people in other cultures are nonplussed by these American exhortations. For them competition is not a positive quality. In their experience, it entails rivalry, hostility, conflict, and disorder.

Commentators, both foreign and domestic, have occasionally remarked on the blindness of Americans to the significance and prevalence of their superlative performance as members of groups. Although they call themselves "rugged individualists," they are in fact "cloyingly gregarious, profoundly communitarian, boringly conformist," in the words of an Oxford professor, who went on to declare, "It was never self-help that made the United States great; it was mutual support. In the formative era of the modern American identity, for every gunslinger in the street or maverick in the corral, there were thousands of solid citizens in stockades and wagon trains."[2]

Despite this social reality, extraordinary deeds associated with the first half of the formula are able to move and inspire Americans to a depth that those of the second half cannot. A comparison of Lindberg's solo flight from New York to Paris (1927) with the landing on the moon (1969) illustrates the contrast. As a feat of aviation, the former was not all that outstanding; other pilots had already crossed the Atlantic. But the public response was overwhelming. It repeated over and over that Lindberg had flown alone, that he was the "Lone Eagle." It made him a national idol, and he remained so for years.

The landing of a man on the moon was, objectively considered, an incomparably greater achievement. But there was no way in which it could be celebrated as the triumph of an individual hero. Its collective nature was obvious and overwhelming. The astronauts were human automatons. Their actions were precisely scripted and rigorously controlled, and they were backed by an army of support staff. The public applause that greeted this tremendous achievement of teamwork was perfunctory. Its memory only added a new phrase to the rhetoric of complaint: "If we can put a man on the moon, why can't we...[do whatever]?"

Early in chapter two, I discussed how individualism enjoys an advantage over community in appealing to the fundamental self-interest and self-esteem of human nature. The word "compete," for example, provokes a stronger and more positive response than the word "cooperate" because it touches each person's ego in a direct and immediate way. This difference is certainly a significant factor in the popularity of the first half of the formula and the neglect of the second half. But something much more crucial and profound is involved, something pertaining to the fundamental way in which the two halves function together.

At the end of chapter two, I referred to an unbalanced equation between human desires and social realities, between the opportunities that people want and the conditions that actually exist. At the same time, I explained the necessity of concealing the latter by an act of beneficial self-deception, so that illusions about the former could persist and continue to exert their motivating influence. A similar relationship exists between the two halves of the American formula.

The ideals of the first half stand in utter, complete, and irreconcilable opposition to the realities of the second. If Americans were ever to perceive this contradiction, if they were ever to comprehend and admit to themselves how much collective coercion and control direct their lives, the result would be a psychological, moral, social, and economic disaster. They would no longer be able to believe that the freedom of individualism and the beneficent harmonies of panglossianism were alive and flourishing in their nation. As their faith drained away, so would the animation and optimism it had sustained. At the same time, in an effort to obtain genuine individual freedom, they would reject and assail the regulating practices of groups, thereby nullifying the forces that had prevented disorder and had directed their undisciplined energies into productive channels.

To prevent such ruin and chaos from happening and to keep the two halves of the formula operating synergistically together, it is necessary that the second half stay hidden. People must believe that only the first half exists. They must remain ignorant of the second half, even while they submit to its demands and enjoy the bounties it bestows upon them. They must absorb its restraints and discipline at so profound and intimate a level that they do not even notice them. When it speaks, they must obey without realizing that they are obeying. This is a beneficial self-deception—the greatest, the most profound, and the most essential of all those which Americans have imposed upon themselves.

The bargain that Faust struck with the Devil was no more stupendous than the one that America has accepted in return for the dominion of the world. It stipulates that her people must make enormous exertions in curbing their immediate self-interest and their spontaneous inclinations, that they must endure incessant collective regulation and supervision in things large and small. And it further stipulates that they must do all this without realizing what they are doing, without perceiving the burdens they have undertaken, as they proclaim themselves to be free, entirely free, the freest people on the face of the earth.

Other nations, in submitting to the demands of a modern economy, have understood very well that they were undergoing an ordeal, and they have been very loud in their complaints. The following is a frank admission from an English poet in 1911:

> To get the whole world out of bed
> And washed, and dressed, and warmed, and fed,
> To work, and back to bed again,
> Believe me, Saul, costs worlds of pain.[3]

Such regularity and punctuality are, of course, only the most basic requirements of industrial labor. Americans, in their climb to world supremacy and their achievement of leadership in technology and the global marketplace, have gone far beyond these rudiments. And they have done so while persisting in the childish panglossian faith that their success has come to them as the easy and automatic result of human beings acting freely and naturally.

If Americans were to perceive reality clearly and embrace it fully, they would proclaim the following: We are the myrmidons of modernity. We have succeeded in subordinating the unruly and conflicting impulses of individuals to collective regulation. We have surpassed other peoples because our self-discipline and self-sacrifice are greater than theirs, because we obey the dictates of our peers rather than those of our own egos, because we are more attentive and responsive to the demands of the working groups of which we are members rather than to our selfish personal desires and immediate self-interest. If other nations wish to attain power and prosperity like ours, let them institute and endure a regimen like ours, if they can.

That is what Americans do not and cannot say. Instead, they declare in all innocence: We are a free people. Every one of us can do whatever he wants. If we have become strong and wealthy it is because we have been free. We would like the rest of the world to be free like ourselves, so that they may enjoy blessings like ours.

Self-deception of this magnitude is a mighty achievement indeed, yet it can be seen in the most trivial and mundane circumstances of daily life. If you make the mistake of telling an American that you are deliberately going to do something or refrain from doing something because you do not want to arouse the disapproval of other people, he will reproach you with a remark along the lines of, "I think everyone should make his own choices." It will not be a stern or severe reproach, as it would be if you were altering your behavior in fear of a single person, but it will be a reproach nonetheless.

Your error was that you confessed to acting in a way in which everyone acts, but they do not want to admit it, even—or rather, especially—to themselves. They dare not, they cannot, they must not, they will not. That includes the person who criticized your behavior. You may be sure this confident champion of personal independence would himself become acutely uneasy the moment he sensed that he was out of step with his group of peers. Of course, it never happens because, as a typical American, he has been properly conditioned to perceive the subtle shifts and alternations in the people around him and to adjust himself accordingly before he receives an explicit warning from them. When the occasion arises, he will no doubt join the group in expressing its consensus and imposing it on any recalcitrant member. Most likely he is also a person who feels a vicarious thrill of excitement when he sees a lone cowboy on the screen or an unruly athlete on the field or some other contrivance of popular entertainment, which panders numerous simulacra of the rugged individualist.

—2—

The presence and power of the second half of the American formula are so enormous and pervasive that they can be difficult to ignore, and at times Americans have had to resort to some tricky mental maneuvers in an ongoing though largely subconscious struggle to make sure that the necessary secret remains a secret. Probably the most common tactic is simply to deny that forces of collective coercion and control exist. As one anthropologist discovered, Americans resolutely and consistently reject the idea of a social culture that influences and directs their behavior. They insist that they are independent individuals, each acting according to his unique personal circumstances and wishes.[4]

The widespread faith in panglossian harmony has proved useful in soothing and reassuring uneasy minds and putting to rest disturbing questions. If an individual is supposed to seek truth and guidance only in himself, as Emerson proclaimed, what will prevent him from running into conflict with other people? Emerson had the answer. The same "divine soul" that inspires one man inspires all. "Speak your latent conviction, and it shall be the universal sense.... If the single man plant himself indomitably on his instincts, and there abide, the huge world will come round to him." This fantasy is the basis of a primal American myth which has been repeated many times. One of its more fanciful versions features a bird (Jonathan Livingston Seagull) as its main character; in another it is a deer (Rudolph the Red-Nosed Reindeer). They are both versions of the old and perennially popular story of a rebellious innovator or initial outcast who at last wins the acceptance and applause of his fellow creatures by bestowing on them some special gift derived from his individuality.[5]

Since only a limited number of persons can assume the roles of teachers and leaders, what about the masses of ordinary people who form the rank and file of groups and organizations? Are they too independent individuals? Indeed they are, asserts the American apologist. They are not supine imitators and submissive followers, led by the example of their peers, molded and remolded by the changing climate of opinion, acutely alive and responsive to the approval or disapproval of those around them. Not at all. Each of them, directed by his personal interests and desires, has freely and deliberately chosen to join with others in a common enterprise. This, Americans believe, is the genuine and legitimate basis of all society: autonomous individuals making free choices. They do not have to do anything more to achieve collective productivity; panglossian harmony takes care of the rest.[6]

From time to time, some pundit in a reflective and mildly troubled mood will entertain the idea that American society is perhaps not entirely a nation of free and independent individuals. He may suspect that there is a great deal of coercion, control, intimidation, and influence going on. And at last he ends up making a general appeal for more freedom, for more individuals acting in accord with their own desires rather than those of others. This would be a recipe for disaster if it were actually put into practice, but fortunately it never is. The mood passes, and the pundit turns to more obvious and pressing concerns.

The minds of Americans have been so cunningly warped and clouded in the process of their unique socialization, that even when they do occasionally feel that they are not as free as they should be, they do not recognize the true source or nature of their bondage. Inevitably they blame—not the democratic majority, not their peers and equals, who are the real agents and enforcers of the formula's second half—but the minority of superiors, the figures of authority, in particular the government.

This misperception appears early in life. High school students are quick to gripe about bossy teachers and administrators; they say nothing against the real tyrants of the school, the other teenagers. They have already been sufficiently socialized, not just to accept the commands of their peers, but even to welcome them. Far from trying to resist adolescent group culture, they want to join it and become fully accepted members.

Adults manifest the same purblind perspective. If something is curtailing or threatening their freedom, they think that it must be something from above—bureaucrats from Washington or agents from a gigantic corporation. As true and faithful believers in egalitarian democracy, they cannot possibly entertain the notion that those responsible might be their fellow citizens, ordinary people like themselves.

This bias is apparent even in something as minor and peripheral as the popular view of prisons. What makes these misnamed "institutions of correction" hellish places of bestial viciousness is the conduct, not of the guards, but of the inmates. Life there is a nightmare version of American's rule by peers. But one would never realize that from watching Hollywood prison movies, which consistently portray the guards as sadistic bullies and the inmates as blameless victims and resourceful resisters.[7] It is just another version of the old American morality fable of ordinary citizens struggling against those in formal positions of power.

Popular culture in general helps to perpetuate the unreality by plying its audiences with tales of personal liberation, which inevitably pit an individual protagonist against obnoxious authority figures—overbearing parents, arrogant cops, dictatorial bosses, corrupt politicians. Movies and television would never and could never portray the real, insidious, everyday workings of the tyranny of the majority.

Advertising adds to the confusion. It understands that Americans like to think of themselves as independent individualists, and it cynically proceeds to flatter them as such, so as to sell its products.[8] There is even a subdivision of this strategy aimed at children and teens, the most fanatical of conformists, whom commercial broadcasting depicts as sophisticated and free, in contrast to their ignorant and inhibited elders.

——————

Despite all the ignorance, denial, and obfuscation, a few people at times cannot help encountering the truth. These tend to be scholars in the social sciences, whose work brings them face-to-face with the actual functioning of American society and requires them to give an account of it. They have developed some special tricks to achieve their own self-deception.

One of these is to recognize the larger and more obvious manifestations of Americans' herd instinct, but not to perceive that a less conspicuous version of the same thing is going on everywhere at all times. Yes, they admit, people have occasionally been swept away by collective passions, but these mass movements are infrequent and thus not particularly dangerous or significant.[9]

An opposite tactic is to acknowledge that Americans act as conformists in their daily existence but to maintain that this behavior affects only the superficial aspects of their lives. In listing the major values of American society, one major textbook of sociology cites "conformity" but takes care to label it "external conformity." Underneath it all, a person is able to retain an "inner autonomy."[10]

A more desperate refuge from reality might be termed "weekend individualism." Society significantly restricts one's conduct on the job, but he is free to express himself in private life. This dodge has often been proposed, and its inadequacy is obvious. Unless a person is a schizophrenic, he cannot behave one way during part of the day or week and then behave in a completely opposite way the rest of the time. His behavior during the more dominant and demanding hours (those of work) will inevitably pervade and color his behavior during the other hours (those of non-work).[11]

Finally, when all else fails, there is a last ditch: freedom for me and those like me but not for everyone else. As a professor of American cultural history once put it, Emerson's "radical individualism" is a superlative "tonic formula" for "aspiring writers, artists, theoretical scientists, philosophers, intellectuals—anyone indeed whose work depends on original insights." But it is not suitable "as a general social philosophy." That is to say, it should not be espoused for and practiced by all those other people—the conformist drones who produce the goods and services that the professor and other creative thinkers depend upon, as does everyone else.[12]

Higher education has endeavored to create a protective environment for the independence of the minds that it certifies and employs. Its tenured professors receive employment for life; their writings, however controversial, are safeguarded by the doctrine of academic freedom; and they can make a convincing noise of indignant fury at anything they regard as an imposition of external influence or interference. Despite all these privileges, they are nonetheless susceptible to discipline exerted by their peers, as are other Americans. An individual academic may enjoy posing as a daring radical, with sneers and denunciations directed at religious fundamentalists or fat-cat capitalists, who are safely distant from his world. But the moment contention approaches his doorstep, and he catches a whiff of disfavor from colleagues in his profession, he will scamper back to their comfortable and secure ranks in an instant.[13]

This is not surprising. However much academics like to think of themselves as bold thinkers and brave innovators, they are also properly conditioned Americans. Their illusions of being rugged individualists are, after all, much like the illusions of their fellow citizens in other lines of work—corporate executives imagining themselves to be Promethean entrepreneurs and wage slaves dreaming of starting their own businesses. On the campus or off, such fantasies serve equally well to keep up morale and are equally remote from reality.

—3—

Ordinarily, there is little need for the awkward mental contortions of self-deception just described. They may be helpful in specific, personal cases, but for most people at most times, the second half of the formula has remained comfortably below the level of their conscious perception.

They have been able to go happily along, celebrating "mavericks," saying things like "feisty people…made this country special," and believing that they are as free as the ideal of individualism in the first half of the formula tells them they should be.[14]

Americans may catch an occasional glimpse of the social controls that prevail in their society and direct their lives, but their usual reaction is to become all the more adamant in affirming the importance and validity of the first half of the formula and, as described above, to call for more freedom and more individualism. It is very seldom that the opposite happens. On very rare occasions, however, one may hear Americans praising the values of the second half and, on even rarer ones, actually denigrating those of the first.

During the antebellum era, some authors applauded public opinion as a force for moral good, an ever-vigilant and all-seeing censor, "before which the most exalted tremble for their future as well as present fame," as Thomas Jefferson proclaimed with warm approval. In a treatise entitled *Democracy* (1841), George Sidney Camp went further than the rest of his contemporaries in this direction. He positively exulted in the fact that public opinion would ruthlessly crush anyone who dared to advocate bad ideas—like atheism, monarchy, or aristocracy. Such thinking deserved to be suppressed, he declared, and in doing so, Americans were acting, not as a tyrannous majority, but as a free and enlightened people giving expression to "the nature of man."[15]

However accurate it may have been as a description of reality, Camp's enthusiastic if inchoate proclamation of a panglossian dictatorship of the masses failed to win enduring popular support or to inspire imitators. As Emersonian individualism increasingly took hold and became the dominant ideology of the new nation, praise for restrictions imposed by collective opinion was expressed with increasingly less frequency and less conviction.

It is only in times of national distress and doubt, when freedom seems to have allowed large numbers of individuals to go astray, that voices in favor of the second half of the American formula begin to be heard. This happened after the excesses of personal liberation in the 1960s and

1970s. During the last decades of the Twentieth Century, various authors and pundits called in effect for a new balance to be struck between the values of the first half of the formula and those of the second. In chapter two, I discussed the efforts, as well as the failure and frustration, of those who have advocated more community and less individualism.

A similar phenomenon arose in the 1930s, when the Great Depression called into question the freedom and license of the 1920s. Among the diverse sages and prophets who responded to the national disaster, one in particular stands out, Henry C. Link (1889–1952). Born the son of a pious but ambitious carpenter, he graduated with a Ph.D. in philosophy from Yale University, entered the world of private enterprise, and made his way in the new field of industrial psychology, where he devised and supervised tests to determine the suitability of applicants for jobs. One invention in which he took particular pride was the "personality quotient" (PQ), which he claimed could measure emotional maturity as the "intelligence quotient" (IQ) measured mental capacity. He published extensively, and by the end of the 1920s he was a nationally recognized expert.

The Great Depression prompted Link to consider larger issues. In 1936, he published the first in a series of books addressed to the general public, which expressed a point of view that was as radical in its ideas as it was emphatic in its tone. He advocated, not merely a readjustment in the balance of the American formula, but its complete inversion. Far from disregarding, dismissing, or deploring group coercion and control, he praised and exalted them. Instead of celebrating individual freedom, he denigrated it and recommended its subordination to the dictates of the majority.

Anti-Emersonianism might be an appropriate term to describe this doctrine. The individual must not look into himself and follow his own promptings for guidance in life, Link warned. That was "introversion" and led to self-absorption, isolation, personal unhappiness, and failure. The business of life was "extroversion," associating with other people, and to be successful at this, one needed to engage in activities that they considered desirable, thereby developing "the habits and skills which interest and please" them—in a word, "personality."[16]

The proper conditioning should begin in childhood, Link advised. He rejected the idea that "children are individuals and must be treated as such." Instead, he declared, "Children are individualists, but must be taught to become social beings." They need to acquire "hundreds of specific habits" that "represent activities and standards which parents or society consider desirable," and they can do so "only under discipline," which has to be enforced "regardless of the child's desires, impulses, or arguments."[17]

Such behavior, learned at an early age, would serve well later in life. "The child who often pays compliments or says things which he knows will please other people, who tries to be friendly with all people whether he likes them or not" is developing highly valuable "personality traits." The pupil who knows "how to please the teacher" will, in the future, be able to "please the bosses." The youth who "learns to take his place in the group or on the team" will find that "teamwork...is the very foundation of personal and social happiness."[18]

Things went best, Link believed, when society imposed its demands early and heavily on potentially wayward individuals. Hard work produced "habits conducive to self-forgetfulness and happiness." But in recent (pre-Depression) years, conditions had become lax. Affluence and leisure time had increased, families had become smaller, and people had begun to indulge in new and harmful liberties. "Where every person insists on thinking for himself...the thinking of one person contradicts that of another," and social disorder is the result. Especially dangerous was "the philosophy of self-expression," which encouraged each marriage partner to pursue his or her "selfish desires," with a rising number of divorces as the consequence.[19]

Young people in particular were at risk. Many of them went to college and came out with no marketable skills. In addition, Link asserted, "there is a growing body of evidence...that the prolongation of formal education results in a deterioration of personality." In fact, "statistics show that the higher the education, the higher the divorce rate." One psychological study found that "'the divorced, both men and women, have more intellectual interests than either of the married groups.'" The source of the problem was clear: "Intellect and imagination often become the chief enemies of personality.... Psychic surgery proves that certain people would be better off with less brains."[20]

Faced with these threats, Link proposed stern measures (falling short of lobotomies, however beneficial those might be in individual cases). In 1933, President Roosevelt had established the Civilian Conservation Corps (CCC), which provided work in rural localities for young, unmarried men. The volunteers lived in camps under semimilitary supervision. Being a staunch political conservative, Link opposed and deplored other programs of the New Deal, but he was enthusiastic about this one. The CCC operated "on the principle of enforced work and group discipline," he noted with approval; it provided "a situation…where other people do the thinking and give the orders, and you do the work." In the process, the CCC participants, having been thrown together with individuals of various kinds and backgrounds, "learned to respect and like people whom they would never voluntarily have chosen as friends.... If I could make only one recommendation in regard to the American educational system," Link concluded, "it would be that all boys between the ages of eighteen and twenty-one be compelled to spend a full year in the Civilian Conservation Corps camps…rich and poor alike, and especially college students."[21]

In three books (*The Return to Religion*, *The Rediscovery of Man*, and *The Way to Security*), Link did something that no other author has done before or since, so far as I am aware. He openly recognized the existence of the second half of the American formula, he proclaimed its overwhelming power and importance, and he championed its preeminence over the first half.

His first book, *The Return to Religion* (1936), was a best-seller, thanks to the mood of the times and the theme of religion. The Great Depression had initiated an era of fear. Americans temporarily ceased to be the incessant and irrepressible advocates of individual freedom that they normally are. They began to speak about the need to "adjust" a child to society, rather than to encourage him to cultivate and pursue his own personal desires. People in this state of mind were receptive to Link's message.

In addition, though religion was in fact a minor and incidental part of the book, its presence in the title provided a strong enticement. Americans, as explained in chapter three, are attracted to religion in the abstract as a purveyor of generalized good. Other, even more unlikely works (such as Evelyn Waugh's snobbish and remote *Brideshead Revisited* and Arnold Toynbee's ponderous and esoteric *Study of History*) have enjoyed unexpected success in the United States for the same reason.

Link's subsequent writings lacked an obvious religious hook, and they enjoyed far less popularity than the first. During the 1950s, the climate of opinion began to change, as economic prosperity persisted and public confidence gradually returned. Americans, having regained their normal view of individual freedom as the supreme ideal, had no taste for an author who preached obedience to collective rules and influence.

In 1963, an eminent historian and redoubtable liberal pronounced his verdict against *The Return to Religion* as "possibly the most consummate manual of philistinism and conformity every written in America."[22] Link had violated a fundamental taboo. He had exposed the necessary secret. And he was punished, first with obloquy, then with oblivion. Today, his name is forgotten, and his books are out of print.

It must be admitted that, however striking Link may have been as the prominent exponent of an unusual point of view, his perception of social realities was in many respects crude and shallow. He did not realize how much the American formula depends on motivation inspired by its first half, and accordingly, he did not understand that its efficient functioning would be hindered rather than improved by discouraging the illusory but idealistic belief in individual freedom. Although Americans are actually as conformist as Link said they should be, it is crucially important that they do not realize this fact. They must continue to think of themselves as hardy if not rugged individualists. The necessary secret must remain a secret.

The workings of the second half of the formula are far more subtle, sturdy, and supple than Link imagined. Like other persons of conservative temperament, he was disturbed by change and desired fixed and definite standards. Liberalism, he complained, had released people "from the traditions and restraints of the past without substituting an adequate set of restraints or ideals for the future."[23] He need not have worried. One of the essential qualities of America's strength in the second half of its formula is the ability to cope with change. Americans are instinctive conformists to change, chameleons to every emerging collective consensus. They readily adapt to shifts in public opinion or in a private clique, to the new rules of a new group or to an alteration in the existing rules of an old group.

This flexible conformity, which was analyzed at length in the previous chapter, is a necessary prerequisite for living and flourishing in the modern world. Neither in the public sphere of productive work nor in the private sphere of personal relations and material consumption have things stayed the same. Both these realms have posed challenges that the American formula has had to confront. Its responses have often been difficult, creative, paradoxical, and new—so much so that their true nature is not always immediately apparent. Something that may seem to be a symptom of failure (such as the rising divorce rate, which bothered Link so much) may actually be a sign of success. Such matters will be discussed in the subsequent third part of this book. The concluding fourth part will consider the larger subject of how the forces of modernity have evolved to the present day and how the American formula has struggled to cope with them.

KEEPING THE FORMULA IN BALANCE:
IDEALISM IN CONFLICT WITH REALITY

CHAPTER SEVEN

The Changing World of Work

—1—

A s the previous chapter explained, the two halves of the American
formula continue to operate in efficient tandem because Americans
are able to believe in the illusory predominance of the first half (specifically individual freedom) and to ignore the actual existence of the second
half (specifically group control). Maintaining this self-deception has never
been an easy task. In my previous analysis of economic individualism
and its foundation, the panglossian ideology of the free market, I noted
how, in holding to these articles of faith, Americans have had to disregard
unpalatable realities, such as the inequality of individual opportunities
and the fortuity of markets. Emphatically and persistently, they have
refused to accept the fact that external circumstances (specifically the
circumstances of social class) exert a decisive influence on a person's life.
It's all up to the individual, they insist; in a free and open economy, he
can rise as high as his personal effort and ability will carry him.

The task of keeping this dogma convincing and credible has not
grown easier with time. The development of the American nation has
created certain conditions that have posed a new threat to the doctrine of economic individualism. As the country advanced from the

Age of Jackson into the industrial age, its economy grew and became increasingly complex. To cope with the change, a new form of business organization emerged. It was the corporation, which rose from small beginnings until, by the end of the Nineteenth Century, it dominated the entire economy.

Utilizing, as it does, the national genius for collective, cooperative action, the corporation is one of the most prominent and important instruments of the second half of the American formula. It has played a crucial and indispensable role in the creation of goods and services and consequently in the growth of national wealth and power. Anyone who takes the trouble to search out the origins of the necessary, useful, and pleasurable items in everyday life will find that an overwhelming number of them were produced by corporations. They form an "envelope of existence," which has been called the "corporate surround."[1] It first began to be obvious around the beginning of the Twentieth Century, and it has increased in the subsequent hundred years.

Yet, despite all the benefits the corporation has bestowed, it has not been duly appreciated. It has received reluctant respect and grudging acceptance at best; at worst, it has provoked resentment and even hatred. According to one scholar, journalist, and commentator, "No other institution in American history—not even slavery—has ever been so consistently unpopular...with the American public. It was controversial from the outset, and it has remained controversial to this day."[2]

Such an assertion may sound startlingly extreme, especially to Europeans, given their predilection for substantial, established institutions. But it is quite true. Americans are disposed to think badly of corporations. Whenever the flagrantly illicit behavior of a few executives becomes national news, pundits seize the occasion to condemn the entire corporate world, as happened with the accounting and bankruptcy scandals of 2002. So strong is the prejudice that it erupted even in the midst of a book entitled *The Progress Paradox*, which was written to demonstrate the soothing and levelheaded proposition that life is getting better. The author made an exception for the misdeeds of corporate leaders and lashed out at them with indiscriminate and extravagant condemnation. A popular documentary movie entitled *The Corporation* (2004), and the book on which it was based, maintained in all seriousness that, since the law views corporations as persons, their personality should be diagnosed as psychopathic, because they are habitually predatory and ruthless.[3]

The following pages are an account of how this bizarre and problematical view of a vital, preeminent institution has come about, as Americans have struggled to preserve the ideal of economic individualism under threat, as they have tried to reverse the widening gap between conditions that they would like to exist and those that they perceive as existing. It has been, to employ a figure of speech that was used earlier, an attempt to correct an increasingly unbalanced equation between desire and reality.

During the early years of the Nineteenth Century, working life took the form of what contemporaries called "free labor" and scholars later called "small producers." Most men were neither employers nor employees. They owned their own farms or shops, where they worked for themselves, often with the assistance of their families. Each shoemaker, for example, bought raw materials, fashioned them into shoes, and sold them directly to customers. When a person hired himself out for wages, he usually intended to remain in that situation only a limited time—long enough to complete an apprenticeship or accumulate a nest egg—and then strike out on his own.

This state of affairs began to change with the rise of large manufacturing organizations. By organizing teams of workers, with each man performing a specialized task, they were able to produce more goods at lower prices than independent artisans could produce by their separate efforts. Innovations in the means of transportation and communication (railroads, steamships, and telegraph lines) opened up wider markets, which could absorb the increase of goods. Factories appeared and grew in size, and the larger ones naturally opted for the legal advantages of incorporation.

Before the Civil War, factories tended to be small and corporations few, but from the very beginning the public in general and workingmen in particular perceived them as a threat and a serious danger. They reduced the value of the individual worker. Instead of having a highly trained and experienced man construct an entire product for sale, they hired less skilled laborers at lower wages and assigned each one a specific and simplified part of the process. A former craftsman complained that, by working in a shoe factory as one of sixty-four people on the production line, he was functioning as "one 64th of a shoemaker."[4]

The new arrangements also reduced the independence of the individual worker. As an employee, he had to adjust his behavior to that of other employees and, far worse, to the dictates of superiors. His relationship to those outside the business also changed. A man who owned his own shop could stand up to an obnoxious customer, and he would lose no more than the trade of a single person. An employee who dared to maintain his dignity in this way risked losing his job.

In addition, the employee who remained an employee could scarcely hope that the future held something better in store for him. When a man had his own business, no matter how humble, he could always imagine that by the exercise of his own effort and ingenuity he might succeed in improving his lot, perhaps striking it rich. But as long as a man remained in a factory or other corporate organization, he would remain a subordinate, with all the disadvantages of subordination, and little or no prospect of improvement. Only a limited number of higher positions fell vacant, and these were handed out at the wish and whim of corporate management.

Whenever defenders of the South argued that the lives of their slaves were, as a rule, better than those of Northern workers, opponents had one formidable and cogent reply: the condition of a free laborer, no matter how low and unappealing, was not permanent; he could improve it by his own exertions. But that was not the case if he were to remain an employee. Workers and middle-class observers alike perceived this fact, and they looked with disapprobation and fear upon these new corporate organizations, which were growing in size and number, for they appeared to be contrary to everything that the ideal of freedom in general and economic individualism in particular had promised.

In the 1830s, the phrase "wage slavery" (along with "factory slavery") became popular. Comparisons were frequently made between this form of bondage and the bondage of Negroes, with the former being viewed as equally vile or at times worse than the latter. One operative in a New England mill complained that the factory bell was like "a slave driver's whip." A famous essay, "The Laboring Classes" (1840), condemned the entire system of working for wages as a means by which capital cheated labor: "A cunning device of the devil for the benefit of tender consciences, who would retain all the advantages of the slave system without the expense, trouble, and odium of being slave holders."[5]

Charges leveled against the corporation went far beyond anything it might do to its own employees. Since the hated banks were also corporations, Jacksonian and Anti-Masonic protest denounced all such organizations as dangerous tools of a wealthy minority, which was allegedly using them for the illicit advancement of its own interests and the subversion of democratic government by means of bribery and influence. The language and ideology of panglossianism stigmatized the corporation—with its limited liability protection and other features inexplicable to the layman—as a complex and unnatural contrivance that exploited hardworking people and corrupted public officials. It was charged with subverting the natural and simple relationships that ought to prevail among men, where each individual dealt with other individuals and not with faceless organizations and their subtle, sinister machinations.

So monstrous a thing did the corporation seem, that people believed it could be guilty of any social offense or transgression. An individual businessman, however debased his personal character, might shrink from wrongdoing because he feared public opprobrium and other penalties it would provoke. But sheltered behind the anonymity of a corporation, unscrupulous men would stop at nothing. "Corporations have neither bodies to be kicked, nor souls to be damned," declared a maxim often repeated. Such an organism was not so much immoral as amoral; it only wanted to increase its profits and power, and it would do anything to attain this end. A short story published in 1837 told of a corporation that persecuted a poor widow. In reply to the question of why it had done so, the author could only answer, "It was a corporation"—precisely the point made in a review of the film *The Corporation* over a century and a half later: "It's in their nature."[6]

Despite all the bad publicity and the calls for their reduction, corporations in antebellum American flourished and multiplied, because they were in fact an economically superior way of utilizing capital and labor. Some wealthy and sophisticated persons (like the Whigs) and their spokesmen (like Daniel Webster) deplored the loud and continual cry against "all banks and corporations," for these organizations were instrumental in promoting the prosperity of the country. Those who were closer to the popular mentality (like the Democrats) were often ambiguous, even hypocritical, in their treatment of the new institution. Many a politician denounced corporations on the stump and the hustings while supporting them in his backroom deals and with his legislative vote. One staunch and prominent Jacksonian argued, not that they should be abolished, but that they should be made available to all, including the poor, who would benefit from being able to form corporations to advance their own interests.[7]

In the years after the Civil War, corporations spread into all parts of the commercial world and all geographical regions of the country. They merged and grew ever larger, until by the end of the century they had become the dominant business institution of the nation. In some sectors of the economy, control was exercised by only a very few firms ("the big twos, threes, and fours").[8] Occasionally, it was only one, John D. Rockefeller's Standard Oil Company being the most notorious example.

This development was the result, not so much of personal ambition and opportunity, as of business necessity and demand. Chaos and misery, as well as growth, had characterized economic life during the later decades of the Nineteenth Century. Companies fought with each other in a frantic competitive effort of producing, buying, and selling, which created unpredictable waves of boom and bust. Prices would shoot up, driving consumers into panic, then plunge downward, bankrupting businesses and throwing people out of work. In an effort to protect themselves in the midst of this disorder, firms consolidated and merged. Each drop in the economy drove them to create larger organizations, until at last the great corporations emerged. Their dominance brought stability and an end to the wild, injurious, and extravagant warfare of competition.

Looking back over their success, the corporate leaders could be proud of what they had done. They had created tremendous material prosperity and power for the American nation, and they had established the conditions for its increase in the coming century. "Competition is no longer the life of trade...," declared one financier. "The spirit of cooperation is upon us...[which will] provide a more orderly conduct of business—freer from failure and abuse, guaranteeing better wages and more steady employment to labor, with a more favorable average price to the consumer...." John D. Rockefeller agreed: "The day of combination is here to stay. Individualism has gone, never to return."[9]

These captains of industry were not being prudent or discreet in praising the second half of the American formula and denigrating the first half. Later spokesmen of business would learn to speak more judiciously and less frankly, but at the moment they were carried away by the flush of triumph and the realities of the situation. That was especially true of Rockefeller, who had good reason to feel satisfaction. His Standard Oil Company was the largest corporation in the United States and the one others looked up to. It had brought stability and quality to an industry that used to be notorious for anarchic behavior and unreliable products. Individual entrepreneurs had formerly employed cutthroat tactics against one another, to the detriment of the consumer, who had paid for their wasteful rivalry with higher prices and worse.

At a time before electric lights appeared in ordinary households, kerosene lamps were the usual means of illumination. Each year, defective concoctions of inflammable liquids had caused thousands of explosions, which resulted in hideous injuries and deaths. Standard Oil, with its superior efficiency and size, bought up the small producers or drove them out of business. Almost all the kerosene the public now purchased came from Standard Oil. It was safe, its quality was high, and its price was low. For this achievement, Rockefeller might have expected to be applauded as a benefactor to humanity and the nation. Instead, to his evident surprise, he found that he had become "the most hated man in the world."[10]

—2—

Ordinary people, including ordinary businessmen, viewed the rise of the corporation much differently than did its proprietors and directors. The industrialization of the American economy in the second half of the Nineteenth Century had brought with it new demands. In factories, men were forced to be more punctual and to work faster, with machines regulating their movements. Assembly lines were introduced; time clocks appeared. Those who would not or could not adapt to these new demands for regularity and speed were expelled and replaced, often by immigrants, willing and ignorant, who were crossing the Atlantic in shoals.

In the white-collar world, the pace of business increased. Employees were expected to do more and to do it more quickly, at the slightest prompting from superiors—to "deliver a message to Garcia," as a contemporary phrase expressed it. A new disease reflected the new conditions and received a new name: "neurasthenia." Described as a breakdown of the "nerve force" resulting from mental exhaustion, it afflicted people involved in "brain work." The complaint was widely reported and discussed, and various cures or palliatives were devised, including "nerve tonics"—drinks like Coca-Cola (with its dose of cocaine)—which were supposed to restore one's depleted energies.[11]

Along with these new demands came something that provoked far more consternation—the loss of freedom itself. At the beginning of the Nineteenth Century, most people who were engaged in remunerative labor worked for themselves, in farms and shops that they owned. By the end of the century, most of them were working for someone else, on land or in a business that they did not own. Workers who would have been self-employed craftsmen or tradesmen a generation or two earlier were now employees in factories and other industrial organizations. Independent entrepreneurs found that it was increasingly difficult to survive in a world dominated by large businesses. Local merchants who had once been the self-sufficient pillars and patrons of their communities now had to endure the humiliation of taking orders from the bureaucratic officers of remote corporations.[12]

To many it seemed as if the most fundamental components and the most precious qualities of American life were in danger. All the accusations that had been directed at the corporation when it was in its infancy during the antebellum era were repeated with new urgency and intensity now that it had become a ruling power. If most Americans were to spend their lives working for such organizations, the results would be pernicious for both the men and the country. Individuals would have to renounce the hope of bettering their economic position and thereby realizing their full personal potential. Instead of being rewarded for ingenuity, initiative, and independence, as they presumably had been in the free market, the corporation would teach them the habits of obedience and docility, thereby transforming a free and active citizenry into a servile and passive one.

Such a degradation was profoundly unnatural, the popular panglossian logic insisted, and thus it could only be accomplished by means that were no doubt immoral and probably illegal. Corporations must, therefore, have risen to their present dominance by underhanded business practices, if not by outright fraud and crime. The public easily believed and eagerly repeated stories of their robbing widows and orphans, blowing up the plants of smaller rivals, and bribing politicians with their ill-gotten wealth. One muckraking tract entitled "The Treason of the Senate" (1906) asserted that a majority of the United States Senate was in the pay of the corporations. That same year, Ambrose Bierce defined "corporation" in his *Devil's Dictionary* as "an ingenious device for obtaining individual profit without individual responsibility."

As the richest man in the country and head of its largest business organization, John D. Rockefeller became the personal symbol of putative corporate wrong and the convenient target for the hatred it aroused. Henry Lloyd's *Wealth Against Commonwealth* (1894) declared that Rockefeller and his associates belonged in the penitentiary. The book achieved such popularity that contemporaries compared it to *Uncle Tom's Cabin* in importance and influence. But it was surpassed by Ida Tarbell's *History of the Standard Oil Company* (1904), a two-volume opus presenting a simple morality story, in which Rockefeller's greedy corporation, using unfair tactics, drove out of business honest, smaller competitors, of whom Tarbell's father had been one. The impact of her indictment was so enormous that a later historian pronounced it to be one of only three books that could be said to have exerted an actual influence on American history. Lloyd and Tarbell were only the most memorable accusers; there were innumerable others. As Tarbell herself said, "The public...has always been willing to believe the worst of the Standard Oil Company."[13]

Rockefeller was surprised and perplexed by the opprobrium. His company had not robbed widows and orphans or blown up rivals' plants. Its tactics were in fact no worse than those employed by other businessmen of the time, large and small, including the inefficient independent oil producers, whom Tarbell had idealized to a ridiculous degree and the Standard Oil Company had put out of operation to the public benefit. Supported by these facts, Rockefeller was sure that people would eventually come round to his way of thinking and recognize the good things his company and other corporations had bestowed upon the nation. It did not happen. When, in later life, he turned to philanthropy, his money was stigmatized as "tainted," and he was jeered at for attempting to relieve a guilty conscience and buy his way out of hell, to which his sins would justly assign him. Even today his reputation, like that of the other captains of industry (a.k.a. robber barons), is mixed at best.[14]

Faced with what they experienced or perceived as the threat of corporate power and abuse, people took action. Blue-collar workers joined unions. At an earlier time, when employers were small, an aggrieved individual could confront a boss on terms of man-to-man and, if he proved unreasonable, simply leave and hire out to another. This tactic had become increasingly difficult, since the firms doing the hiring had declined in number and grown to enormous size, and were now able to wield intimidating weapons like the blacklist against unsubmissive individuals. Under these new conditions, only by organizing and forming their own organizations could workers hope to acquire anything approaching the strength of their employers, as even the notorious spokesman of management Mark Hanna admitted.[15]

The unions that arose after the Civil War (most prominent among them, the National Labor Union, 1866–1872, and the Knights of Labor, 1869–1902) aimed at more than merely raising pay and improving conditions of work. They wanted to abolish the entire system of wage labor. This intention reflected the desires of their membership, who looked back to earlier days when a worker could set himself up as an independent businessman. They did not want to remain lifelong employees in a factory or other corporation. Their leaders agreed and declared that things such as low wages and long hours were superficial complaints. Their real goal was a change in the fundamental arrangements of work.[16]

Denunciations of "wage slavery," which had first been heard in the antebellum era, became louder and more widespread. They were shared and echoed by many sympathetic, concerned, and respectable people outside the ranks of labor. There was a general feeling that working for wages, in contrast to being in charge of one's own business, was injurious, both to the worker and to the country, limiting as it did a person's opportunities in life and turning him into a servile dependent instead of an independent citizen. One respected and influential journalist, the founder of the *Nation* magazine, urged workers to continue their union organizing and agitating, until "the regime of wages…has passed away as completely as slavery or serfdom, and until in no free country shall any men be found in the condition of mere hirelings…."[17]

Members of the middle class had a similar grievance against the corporations. They saw their own independent businesses falling under the domination of these expanding organizations and found themselves being transformed from entrepreneurs to employees. Their resulting anger and fear created what became known as the antitrust movement ("trusts" being the common name for large corporations in that era). In the 1880s, trusts were an obsession, and the "trust question" was a national issue. Both political parties denounced them, as did the major newspapers. State laws were passed to limit their power and growth. When these proved ineffective, the struggle was taken to the federal level. The entire effort culminated in the Sherman Antitrust Act of 1890, passed by Congress with only a single dissenting vote, to the general acclaim and relief of the public.

During the subsequent years, various antitrust prosecutions were launched, but corporations did not decline or diminish; if anything, they became larger and stronger. In the meantime, a new attitude began to develop, especially among knowledgeable and sophisticated persons. Corporations, they said, were a logical and inevitable result of economic evolution. Any attempt to abolish them was not only futile but in fact detrimental to society, for they were an essential part of modern civilized life and a basic source of national power. They did much tangible good in eliminating the inefficiency of small-scale operations and the waste of petty, vicious competition. They provided lower prices and better goods for consumers, as well as higher wages and steady employment for workers. If it was true that they sometimes abused their power and acted contrary to the public interest, the best remedy was for the government, not to abolish, but to regulate them.

At the same time as these ideas were beginning to be heard, the corporation was discovering a new ally in a very unexpected quarter—organized labor. The unions, as indicated above, had wanted to abolish the system of wages, but the alternatives they tried (including the Knights of Labor's extensive and prolonged efforts to set up its own "cooperative" enterprises in competition with those of capitalism) had come to nothing. Now a growing segment of the labor movement (in particular Samuel Gompers' American Federation of Labor) was advancing a different strategy. They accepted the inevitability of wage labor for their members and asked only for higher pay, steady employment, and better working conditions; in return they would provide an orderly, reliable workforce.

This approach was known as "business unionism" or "unionism pure and simple," and its proponents found that the large corporations were far more willing to agree to the proposed bargain than were smaller employers. With its established success and prosperity, a corporation could afford to take larger and more enlightened views and realize that well-paid workers would behave as motivated employees as well as ready consumers of its products. Businessmen conducting smaller operations tended to have narrower and less generous minds, as Gompers himself discovered. After all, an individual entrepreneur, obsessed with clawing his way to wealth, is naturally the meanest and most exploitative of employers. An employee might want to be such a person, but he certainly would not want to work for him.[18]

In time, more and more labor leaders stopped denouncing wage slavery and applauding small producers and instead began speaking of the need for workers to maintain "a living wage" and to enjoy "the American standard of living." But the change, however welcome to the corporation, did not please the general public, including many and perhaps most of the rank-and-file workers, who still dreamed of setting up their own independent businesses. When John Mitchell, president of the United Mine Workers, bluntly declared in his book *Organized Labor* (1903) that the average wage earner had come to the realization that he would remain a wage earner for his entire working life, it provoked an uproar. Editors and reviewers all over the country pounced on Mitchell's couple of sentences. No one needed to read a word farther, fumed one outraged critic: this "un-American" doctrine deprived the worker of hope and condemned him to permanent subservience, which would stifle productivity and lead to class warfare.[19]

There were similar outbursts of anger whenever anyone attempted publicly to defend the corporation and point out its advantages. One speaker did so at the Chicago Conference on Trusts, convened in 1899, and he had the temerity to say that those who wanted to abolish the corporations were like Luddites, the English laborers who in the early years of the century had tried to destroy the newly invented industrial machinery. The audience's furious reaction was so loud and disruptive that the chairman conducting the meeting threatened to have the galleries cleared to restore order.[20]

Opponents of the corporation did not want to hear that it had a good side. They brushed aside the claim that it produced lower prices. Such a benefit was only temporary, they insisted, and even if true, it was a minor consideration. As a justice of the Supreme Court declared in his opinion on one of the antitrust cases, lower costs for the consumer and the manufacturer were no compensation for "driving out of business the small dealers and worthy men whose lives have been spent therein" and thus bringing about "the ruin of such a class."[21]

The president of the United States agreed. In his 1896 annual address to Congress, Grover Cleveland referred curtly to the alleged and "incidental economic advantages" of the trusts, but spoke at ponderous length of the manifold social evils they inflicted, as they "crush out individual independence...hinder or prevent the free use of human faculties and the full development of human character...[and injure the] personal character, prospects, and usefulness" of citizens.[22]

Cleveland was expressing himself rather moderately, given the mood of the times. Possessed by the feeling that their country was facing a fundamental and immediate threat, fanatics blamed corporations for nearly every bad thing that had happened in the past or might happen in the future and called for their extirpation. A puzzled journalist from England reported that the governor of Michigan for one viewed "the trust as a kind of Antichrist," about to bring a reign of havoc and ruin upon the land.[23]

The case in favor of the corporation was logical and realistic, but it lacked wide support and emotional intensity. The idea of accepting corporations and having the government police them might seem attractive to a few people—often influential and discerning people (like Herbert Croly, founder of the *New Republic*)—but not to the general public.

Thomas Riley Marshall, vice president of the United States under Woodrow Wilson, probably spoke for most ordinary citizens. If some politicians could be said to understand "the psychology of the mutt,"

Marshall was politically gifted with the mind and mouth of the mutt, and being American it was an idealistic mutt. One of his pronouncements has persisted in the nation's memory to the present day: "What this country needs is a good five-cent cigar." On the subject of trusts, he scoffed at the notion that they "were a natural evolution, and that the only way to deal with them was to regulate them. The people are tired of being told such things," he declared. "What they want is the kind of opportunity that formerly existed in this country."[24]

It might have seemed that a disastrous, unavoidable collision was approaching. If the idealism of the American formula's first half prevailed and brought about the dismantling or even just the diminishing of the corporation, it would have ruined or at least seriously damaged the nation's economy. If a realistic recognition of the formula's second half had prevailed, and people gave up their dreams of economic individualism, it would have injured and perhaps destroyed productive motivation and morale. On the horns of this dilemma was many a politician, who realized the crucial and ineluctable importance of the corporation yet somehow had to appease the public cry against it.

As had happened before and would happen again, the national talent for beneficial self-deception emerged and found a way out of the predicament. The fundamental complaint against the corporation was its size. If it had remained small, independent small producers could have coexisted alongside it. Instead, as it grew larger and stronger, it swallowed up the independents. But even though size was the basic issue, the ground on which the antitrust advocates based their attack was that of moral behavior. People assumed that the corporation could have attained its present power and proportions only by means that were vicious and underhanded, and these formed the substance of the most persistent and angry charges. In the public mind, the two aspects of their enemy were intimately connected. Stop the corporation from employing unfair tactics and enjoying fraudulent advantages, and it would automatically and inevitably lose strength and contract to a diminished size or—most likely and hopefully—to nonentity.

This putative equation of large size and bad behavior gave the politicians who conducted antitrust campaigns the necessary space in which to maneuver. As they loudly proclaimed that they were going after the misbehaving corporations, they prudently added, or tacitly assumed, that they would leave in peace those which were not misbehaving. Thus there were two kinds of corporations: the bad and the good, although the public assumed that the ones in the latter category must be few or nonexistent.

Woodrow Wilson employed this distinction with remarkable explicitness and great audacity. On the one hand, he declared, there were the trusts; on the other, there was big business. A trust was an "artificial" contrivance, which had expanded to great size and power by illicit means, such as shutting potential rivals out of the market and bribing public officials. If the trusts were forced to play fair, new competitors, though initially much smaller, would be able to rival and surpass them.

"Every society is renewed from the bottom," Wilson told his audiences during his successful campaign for the presidency. "Limit opportunity…and you have cut out the heart and root of all prosperity…. Are you not eager for the time…when your sons shall be able to look forward to becoming, not employees, but heads of some small, it may be, but hopeful business, where their best energies shall be inspired by the knowledge that they are their own masters…."[25]

Having reassured the voters by invoking the ideals of the American formula's first half (economic individualism, including egalitarian opportunity and the free market ideology, as well as the panglossian contrast between the artificial and the natural), Wilson could then expend a few words on the realities of the second half. "Big business is no doubt to a large extent necessary and natural," he admitted. "The development of business upon a great scale, upon a great scale of cooperation, is inevitable, and, let me add, desirable." But these, as distinguished from the trusts, were "natural" organizations, which had become large and had surpassed their competitors by fair means, such as operating with greater efficiency and producing better products. "I am not afraid of" this kind of corporation, "no matter how big it grows," Wilson reassured his audience.

On the basis of this distinction between corporations that played by the rules and those that broke the rules, Wilson was able to proclaim, "I am for big business, and I am against the trusts." And he no doubt believed it, given his sincere idealism, which in the coming years he would turn from making America safe for "small...but hopeful" businesses to making the world "safe for democracy," with about an equal lack of actual success in both ventures.

Numerous other politicians were clever enough or naive enough to take a position similar to Wilson's. Theodore Roosevelt was one of them. He too drew a distinction between good and bad corporations, and he found a sufficient number of the latter to win himself a reputation as a "trust-buster." At times, though, he was more insightful or at least more forthright than Wilson in recognizing the permanent predominance of corporations and the utter futility and fatuity of any attempt to return to an economy of small producers.[26]

One natural and perhaps unavoidable consequence of self-deception is a gap between verbal declaration and real behavior. Historians have commented on the huge contrast between antitrust language and antitrust prosecution: the extravagant proclamations and pronouncements on the one hand, the paltry measures actually legislated and the negligible results actually achieved, on the other. This had been true from the very beginning. When the Sherman Act was passed in 1890, it contained little in the way of practical implementation or effective enforcement. The more astute politicians perceived the charade. One of them admitted that they just wanted "to get some bill headed 'A Bill to Punish Trusts'" which they could take "to the country."[27]

This set the pattern for future antitrust campaigns. They began with dire warnings about the peril facing the nation, and they ended, amid equal publicity and fanfare, with the indictment of a corporation or two that had been greedy and clumsy enough to commit an actual violation of the law. Theodore Roosevelt, with his talent for catching the public eye, was especially skilled in this kind of posturing. He once compared himself to an actor in a minstrel show who had to put on blackface and do a routine on stage.[28]

Antitrust performances were more or less tolerable, if not agreeable, to the parties concerned. They made ordinary people feel confident that the government was doing something to combat the malignant trusts, while the corporations themselves simply went on growing and consolidating. With its maximum publicity and minimal effect, the trust-busting of Roosevelt and others was reminiscent of Jackson's war on the BUS. Both the antitrust effort and the Jacksonian movement were, at a basic level, reflecting a persistent condition of American life—the unbalanced equation between reality and desire, specifically the fundamental conflicting dichotomy of the American formula.

———

During the national prosperity of the 1920s, fear of the trusts abated, but the feeling that replaced it was only one of tolerance. People did not have any affection for or confidence in the corporation; they did not even understand it. Magazine articles lamenting the decline of the self-made man and the family business continued to appear, and concerned citizens continued to worry about the pernicious effects of an economy where most workers were employees instead of independent entrepreneurs. One of the most prominent of the worriers was the Supreme Court Justice Louis Brandeis, a tireless advocate of the small businessman. When he published his miscellaneous papers in 1936, they appeared under a collective title, *The Curse of Bigness*.

An anti-chain store movement arose in the late Twenties and grew during the Depression years of the Thirties, as more and more independent merchants were driven out of business. The merits and demerits of the chains became a national issue, which saw the publication of actual handbooks and manuals to assist public debate on the subject. In 1936, the Robinson-Patman Act was passed—a piece of antitrust legislation that a historian later described as intended to "punish" the

A & P Company for inventing the supermarket.[29] But the cause was doomed to failure. However much people expressed their sympathy and concern for the small shopkeeper, they usually spent their money at the chains, which offered better products, a wider selection of goods, and lower prices. By the end of the Depression, the anti-chain store movement had vanished.

During the early years of the New Deal, the Roosevelt administration's approach to corporations was to advocate their regulation, not their abolition or reduction. But as the Depression persisted and for a time (during the recession winter of 1937–38) grew worse, the old prejudices and hopes, which had lain smoldering, burst into flame. The villain was identified, not as the occasional corporate miscreant, but as the entire tribe of corporate monsters. Perennial rabble-rousers of antitrust (like William Edgar Borah, senator from Idaho since 1907) acquired new popularity and trumpeted the old cause with a new energy.

In response to the growing discontent, President Roosevelt proposed and Congress approved a Temporary National Economic Committee (TNEC), which opened hearings in late 1938 amid great publicity and expectation. Many people genuinely believed that at last the corporations would be broken up, and the economy would return to a natural and healthy state of individualism, with each man able to run his own business and compete with others in a fair and free market.[30]

It all came to nothing. No sweeping antitrust legislation was passed. In 1941, the TNEC issued its final report, which failed to recommend any substantial, practical measures, much to the public's disappointment and exasperation. But they soon had other things to occupy their attention. Near the end of the year, the Japanese bombed Pearl Harbor, and the ensuing war effort not only ended the Depression but vindicated the strength and effectiveness of the nation's corporate economy.

—4—

The Great Depression of the 1930s was arguably the most influential event in twentieth-century American history. It had been more severe, and it had gone on longer (an entire decade) than any previous business downturn—so long, in fact, that it had seemed like a tremendous reversal of nature, contradicting Americans' panglossian optimism and their confidence in continual progress. The experience traumatized an entire generation. As a novelist born in 1932 later declared, "If there was one lesson my upbringing had instilled, it was our earthly insecurity."[31]

A pervasive fear colored the mood and mentality of the nation to the end of the 1940s, through the entire 1950s, and into the early 1960s. The soldiers of World War II grimly expected to return to a country that had relapsed into a new depression. Although this proved not to be the case, people thought that it might happen at any moment, just as the Great Crash of 1929 had unexpectedly followed the boom years of the 1920s.[32]

What gave the postwar era its unique character and made the Fifties (the convenient if somewhat inaccurate label for this stretch of years) so unusual, even incongruous and perverse, was the combination of internal fear with external prosperity. Previously, material abundance had gone hand in hand with social restlessness and experimentation, as it had in the Gilded Age and the Roaring Twenties. But the memory of the Great Depression, assisted by the present threat of the Cold War, cast a shadow over the new and unprecedented affluence. The Fifties were a time when the American economy experienced enormous and sustained growth, showering the public with abundant and proliferating consumer goods and providing them with steady employment and high wages. The Fifties were also a time when, as one contemporary put it, "You stuck with your job, you stuck with your wife, you stuck with everything."[33] People were too nervous and afraid to risk making changes.

Security was what everyone wanted, and many of them hoped to find it in the corporation. Working for an enormous company like AT&T might not be very exciting, young men graduating from college told each other, but there would always be an AT&T. The last thing they considered doing was to go into business for themselves.[34]

In addition to its promise of security, the corporation also gained prestige as the source of postwar prosperity. In 1946, an authority on management observed that only a few years earlier (while the TNEC hearings were in session) there had been a serious debate over whether large companies should exist or not; now the very question seemed "meaningless if not frivolous."[35]

Just as big business and its executives were increasingly viewed as essential pillars of the modern economy, small business seemed increasingly marginal and its entrepreneurs increasingly anachronistic. They lacked the means to compete against firms with such resources as scientific laboratories and marketing research. Those that survived did so by accepting the role of inferiors, following the lead of the corporations and providing services to them.

While sophisticated and realistic people accepted the dominance of the corporation and the eclipse of small business, there remained among the populace a feeling that tended in the opposite direction. Individuals might resign themselves to jobs as employees and enjoy the new affluence, but they continued to be discontent. They persisted in imagining that, if it were not for the interfering presence of big business (not to mention big government and big labor unions), they would be able to venture forth as successful, independent entrepreneurs.

These attitudes were strong and widespread enough to be echoed in the oratory of politicians. "Do we want an America where the economic marketplace is filled with a few Frankensteins and giants?" one senator in 1952 asked rhetorically. "Or do we want an America where there are thousands upon thousands of small entrepreneurs, independent businessmen, and landholders who can stand on their own feet and talk back to their government or to anyone else."[36]

Such opinions managed to proceed beyond mere verbiage and prompted a certain number of legislative acts and regulatory measures. From time to time, Congress would pass a bill aimed at helping to prop up small businesses by tax advantages or some other charitable assistance. And from time to time the federal judiciary would find a prominent corporation to harass. It seemed as if there was a cynical consensus among the government prosecutors. Since the general public was incapable of genuinely understanding or fully appreciating big business, one might appease their prejudices by throwing them an occasional victim.[37]

The gap between antitrust action and economic actuality yawned embarrassingly wide. As the economist John Kenneth Galbraith noted with characteristic irony, the corporations that foreign visitors came to see as "showpiece[s] of American industrial achievement" were the very same ones that federal attorneys scrutinized in their search for monopolistic wrongdoing. An antitrust case against IBM dragged on for thirteen years, cost the government hundreds of millions of dollars, and was at last mercifully dismissed. The ordeal prompted a Japanese graduate student to ask his American professor, why was the United States "government...pretending to want to break up IBM, the one American company" that Japan had been unable to rival? The professor had great difficulty answering the question, and the student found his explanation so inadequate as to seem duplicitous.[38]

The powerful and tenacious allure of economic individualism was reflected in the behavior, not just of politicians and antitrust prosecutors, but of corporate leaders themselves. In their effort to win over the popular mind, they did not attempt to refute individualistic values and attitudes; instead, they embraced them. During the late 1940s, they spent millions on an advertising campaign that defended gigantic, corporate business in terms of small, entrepreneurial business. It celebrated the free market as an arena where thousands of separate enterprises competed on a supposedly equal footing, winning or losing according to their merits and producing in the process the best products for society. Although the lavishness of the funding has probably never been equaled since—it gave rise to a "lesser literary flowering," in Galbraith's sarcastic phrase—the themes evoked and the ideals sounded have echoed down the decades in the free-enterprise inspirational literature that corporations feel a perennial need to produce, especially when they are trying to resist some government regulation or other.[39]

The masquerade went deeper than the paid propaganda of public relations. Then and in subsequent years, corporate executives have often struck the pose of entrepreneurs. "They pictured themselves as self-reliant men, individualistic, with a trace of justifiable arrogance, fiercely competitive and with a desire to live dangerously," in the words of Galbraith. These characteristics were notable for being the very opposite of those that were needed and in fact were present in the everyday conduct of corporate business. Its "group action" required, as Galbraith went on to observe, "not indifference but sensitivity to others, not individualism but accommodation to organization, not competition but intimate and continuing cooperation." Especially preposterous was the repeated cry raised by corporate spokesmen for more strenuous individualistic competition. If modern executives had been foolish enough truly and sincerely to heed this call, the consequence would have been destructive disorder of the kind which businesses had suffered from in the second half of the Nineteenth Century and which they had escaped by creating the corporation.[40]

The contradiction between occasional posturing by politicians, antitrust prosecutors, and business executives on the one hand and economic realities and practices on the other had a twofold source. First, and more fundamental, was the underlying contradiction between the realities of the second half of the American formula and the ideals of the first half. This disjuncture had always existed and, with the development of the modern corporate economy, had grown more pronounced. The intricate complexity and coordination of big business demanded that those who conducted its operations behave less individualistically and more collectively than they had when businesses were smaller and less organized.

If this had been the only element in play, the public's perplexity and distress during the postwar era would have been much less than it actually was. The second half of the American formula would probably have remained below the level of general conscious perception, as it had done during earlier times and as it would do after the Fifties. But there was another factor involved. The fear created by the Great Depression resulted in people demanding conformity and imposing social controls to such an exaggerated degree that neither the presence of the second half nor its divergence from the ideals of the first half could continue unnoticed.

The corporation of the Fifties required, not merely that its employees work together harmoniously and efficiently, but that they meet an additional range of social requirements which were petty, annoying, and arbitrary. This was the era of "the organization man" with his slavish obedience to the whims of superiors, to the punctilios of office etiquette, and, above all, to the norms of bland uniformity that society of the time pronounced and enforced. The corporate executive was supposed to be, not merely a dedicated worker and an effective leader, but also a normal, "well-rounded" person.

The balance between the first half and the second half of the American formula had been tilted so far in the direction of the latter that people could perceive it, and they began to call for more of the former. During the later years of the 1950s and into the 1960s, the complaints grew more widespread and more earnest. Appearing with increasing frequency and stridency were books and movies that criticized America in general and the corporation in particular for stifling personal freedom and limiting human potential (for example, *The Organization Man*, *Growing up Absurd*, and *The Man in the Grey Flannel Suit*). The prevalence of "conformity," the dominance of "mass culture," and the uniformity of "suburbia" became topics of public concern and the subject of incessant discussion and worry.

———————

At last the discontent moved from words to action. It could have been predicted. The contradictory combination of fear and affluence during the postwar years could not have persisted. But when the change finally came, it came as a loud, rude, and unexpected shock, beginning with the Free Speech Movement on the Berkeley campus in 1964. Although the subsequent youth protests and disorders received a fortuitous boost from opposition to the Vietnam War, they were fundamentally directed at the restrictions of the Fifties. One of their principal targets was the corporation—the rat race arena with its workaholics and uptight squares. The last thing rebellious young people wanted to become was an organization man. Instead, they demanded more of the freedom promised by the first half of the American formula.

The rambunctious Sixties initiated a readjustment of the balance between the formula's two halves. By the 1970s, the previous decade's effects had spread from college youth to the rest of the population. Since its main influence occurred outside the world of work, in the manners and morals of private life, it will be discussed more fully in the following chapter. What pertains to the present subject was the last phase of the process, the so-called entrepreneurial revolution of the 1980s.

This decade had an ambiguous character. In some aspects, it was a reaction against the Sixties. Loud and numerous voices denounced the excesses of personal liberation and called for a return to more traditional norms and standards, specifically those of the Fifties. But in other aspects, the 1980s were a continuation of the 1960s, a final reaction against the fears created by the Great Depression. It was during the 1980s that a cry arose for the restoration of individual freedom, not in the sphere of personal conduct, but in that of economic relations.

It was as if the most repressed and conventional people of the Fifties at last rose up and demanded that their dreams of economic individualism come true: that the corporations shrink and wither away, that small businesses flourish, that everyone have the opportunity to be an entrepreneur and get rich. In the 1980s, people thought these fantasies were about to become reality. They spoke of corporations as doomed dinosaurs, too big and sluggish to survive in the emerging business world, where quickness and maneuverability would carry the day. Small businesses, in contrast, were touted as the source of the economy's new jobs and new ideas. Faceless CEO's and bureaucratic executives were ridiculed and deplored, while spectacularly successful entrepreneurs were hailed as heroes. A number of the latter became national celebrities and reveled in the pose of straight-talking, risk-taking mavericks. The Eighties, under the banner of Reaganomics, appeared to be the very reverse of the Fifties: the death of the organization man and the revival of the self-made tycoon.

College students talked of founding their own businesses in tones of personal excitement and even idealism. Some of them—along with a number of nominal adults—believed they were part of a new movement that would change the world, just as in the 1960s the New Leftists had imagined they could do so with their radical politics and the hippies with their rural communes. "The years ahead should be a good time for dreamers and visionaries of the business world," stated a prominent management guru.[41] "Ordinary people" would be "doing extraordinary things," declared a cliche of the time. Such effusions sprang from the economic individualism of the American formula's first half, whose panglossian notions now assumed a wildly expansive and extravagant form. One could be an independent individualist, lead an adventurous life, earn millions, become a better person, and make the world a better place—all simply by going into business for oneself in the free market of the new economy.

Needless to say, it turned out to be an illusion. After the crash of 1987 and the depression of the early 1990s had popped the bubble, the world appeared much as it had been before. The financial frenzy of the 1980s, with its junk bonds and leveraged buyouts, had left some persons worse off, others far better off, and a few in jail. But corporations still dominated the economy, and the overwhelming majority of people remained employees. There were fierce accusations and recriminations among the ideologically devout: Reaganomics had never been adequately tried, it had been betrayed by cowardly politicians, it had been sabotaged by the villainous big three (big business, big government, and big labor), who had seen it as a threat to their domination.

But, as usual, the salutary optimism of most Americans kept them from looking back in anger or despair. They soon found a new source of hope in the booming high-tech companies, which were supposed to transform the entire economy. The downside of the business cycle would disappear, some claimed, and the stock market would never fall.

Throughout the rest of the 1990s, new versions of old promises were heard. Computers and the internet would free and empower the common man. Instead of being a cowboy capitalist in the Wild West economy of Reaganomics, he could become a console cowboy or internet entrepreneur—that is, a fierce independent, working on his own for himself in the free market of cyberspace.

The whole thing ended in another, even worse depression (2000–2003), leaving more people badly off, some others very rich, and a few more in jail. Once again, predictions of a new heaven and a new earth for the working stiff had come to nothing. That was not a novelty. Ever since Andrew Jackson slew the BUS monster, the populace of the United States has beheld a succession of optimistic economic mirages, each one appearing, then vanishing, only to be followed by another. This might seem like an endlessly agonizing punishment of Sisyphus, but one would be wrong to deplore it. As I have explained earlier, it is vitally important for their productive morale that Americans continue to believe in the idealistic first half of their formula, specifically in economic individualism and panglossian principles, no matter how far these may diverge from reality. In fact, it is precisely during those times when reality is most inimical and repugnant that Americans benefit most from their ability to cling to their illusions.

—5—

The need for beneficial self-deception has become especially urgent in recent years. Beginning in the 1980s, appearing in full and obvious form in the 1990s, then proceeding triumphantly into the new century, significant changes have been taking place in the world of work. The pace, scope, and complexity of business have increased. New communications technology has made possible greater speed and better coordination. That, along with improved means of transportation, has enabled markets to expand and include the entire world—a tendency that is frequently referred to as "globalization." An item sold in a local

store or used on a local construction site might come from another con-
tinent. Outsourced tasks and telecommunications-based services may be
performed by workers on the other side of the earth.

Sixty years ago, the United States was the only advanced industrial
nation to emerge intact from the Second World War, and as such it
dominated international trade and manufacturing. Today, it has rivals
all over the world, especially since economic superiority is now based
less on tangible assets than on knowledge. New ideas and new technolo-
gies can emerge from anywhere at any time and can become obsolete
just as rapidly.

The most obvious consequence of these developments is that people
now have to work harder and faster than they did in the past. Complaints
about exhaustion and burnout on the job became commonplace in the
1990s and the subject of numerous magazine articles, as well as a book
or two (e.g. Arlie Hochschild's *Time Bind*). A few authors pointed out
the similarity to the 1890s. Both decades experienced an increase in the
pace of doing business, as well as the resulting worries about mental
overload and breakdown. Both even saw the appearance of beverages
(called "nerve tonics" back then and "energy drinks" now) that promised
to pep up tired minds and raise sagging spirits.

One semi-facetious notion, which was current in the 1990s, suggested
that companies hire only young executives who were unmarried, since
the demands of work had become so great as to leave insufficient time
for normal family life. This stood in diametric contrast to earlier business practice, when being married was often a precondition, if not for
hiring, then for promotion. The latter had been a common policy in the
corporations of the 1950s—it even provided the basis for a TV sitcom,
NBC's "Occasional Wife"—since in those days marriage was considered
a reliable sign of personal normality, stability, and well-roundedness.

Not only has there been an increase in the speed and quantity of work,
there has also been a change in its quality. The assembly line, where
men imitated machines, is no longer a model for the organization and
coordination of labor. Mechanical robots are now able to perform routine
tasks, leaving the more difficult work for people. A similar development

has been taking place in the white-collar world. Computers can do things that offices full of clerks and accountants used to do. They and their managers now find that they need to function on a higher level.

The word that keeps reoccurring is "entrepreneurial." Employees are supposed to exhibit the attitudes and motivation of someone who owns his own business. Limiting one's attention to a narrowly defined job and merely performing its assigned tasks is no longer enough. An entrepreneurial employee is supposed to be constantly on the lookout for opportunities to improve operations and to take the initiative when he discovers them. Instead of referring problems to higher authorities, he should confront them himself and come up with creative solutions. This is no place for the bureaucratic functionary who is putting in his time. "You don't 'just work here' anymore," a slogan warned the easy-going and lackadaisical. Entrepreneurial employees should "be taking the business 'home in their stomach.'"[42]

Management has justified these demands by invoking the first half of the American formula. Yes, the work is exhausting, so the argument runs, but it is fulfilling and empowering. An individual is exercising his latent talents and realizing his inner potential. Work should be "a source of self-realization…continued growth and challenge…more individualized options and personal autonomy." At their more heady moments, the advocates of the "reenchanted workplace," as it has been called, sound like Ralph Waldo Emerson reincarnated as a CEO: "Creativity [in business] is about connecting to your inner self…we are talking about divinity…we're turning business into a spiritual discipline…the emerging paradigm is inner wisdom, inner authority, wholeness."[43]

On a somewhat less exalted level, one of management's arch-gurus and enthusiasts declared, "I want my company to be so attractive…it makes your head swim. I want to give you an exciting work environment…. In turn, I demand that you give your all…. You must perform and grow as you've never performed and grown before." A more skeptical and detached observer recently noticed that the word "passion" has been appearing with increasing frequency: people are being told they should feel passionate about their work. Genuine personal enthusiasm is supposed to ignite "the fire in your belly," which American business occasionally used to expect from its new recruits and which it is now coming to expect from everyone.[44]

The champions of this brave new workplace cannot announce their program often enough or loud enough: they are dismantling the old bureaucratic corporation, decentralizing its hierarchical structure, abolishing its rigid rules. From the ranks of authoritarian superiors and cowering inferiors, a multitude of liberated, creative people is emerging. Gone are the stodgy, buttoned-down bosses of the past, whose watchwords were loyalty, responsibility, and maturity. In their places are executives who talk like bold innovators, even radicals. The more unrestrained of their public statements and the splashier of their media advertisements explicitly proclaim their resemblance to revolutionary movements. Revitalized business organizations are the new Vietcong and Khmer Rouge; their leaders are latter-day Che Guevaras.[45]

Management has been making a deliberate effort to conjure up the old hopes and promises of the Sixties, which were based on individualistic ideals and panglossian assumptions. When a hip new CEO declares, as many of them do, that the purpose of his company is not to make money but to enable people to be free and creative, he is not being consciously hypocritical. He is relying on the following implicit chain of panglossian logic: if one is free, then one will be creative; if one is creative, then one will be productive; and if one is productive, then one will make money. Like every generation of Americans before him, he wants and expects to realize higher purposes in life at the same time as he gets the cash. The doctrines of the new workplace are a turbocharged and technologically updated version of the old ideology of the free market, gilded with a patina of the daring and the cool.[46]

As always, when the first half of the American formula stokes up the motivation, the second half steps in to keep things from getting out of control. The informality of personal interaction, the increased scope for individual initiative, the extension of greater responsibilities down the chain of command—all these are necessary practices for a company seeking to flourish in the new economy. But they also have their dangers. A workstation in one ultramodern office displayed a sign proclaiming that the word "madman," which had been used to "gag all innovation," should instead be regarded as "a title of honor."[47] Such an attitude may encourage creative thinkers, but it may also unleash those who mistake the voice of their restless ego for the promptings of actual talent.

The latter possibility seldom becomes reality—or at least seldom reaches the danger point of causing serious disruption—thanks to the persisting and subtle power of the formula's second half. Despite the absence of explicit rules and overt commands in the new workplace, an employee quickly perceives signs of approval or disapproval from those with whom he interacts, and, being a properly conditioned American, he adjusts his behavior accordingly. This is especially the case in the dealings of superiors and inferiors. The hip CEO and his managers may dress like aging hippies and go on occasional retreats where they play like children, but when it comes time for a serious decision to be made, the CEO's word is decisive. Of course he listens to what his subordinates have to say, but the final verdict is his. In spite of all the free-for-all frankness with which they voice their opinions, they never forget this reality, and—you may be sure—neither does he.[48]

Underneath the incessant talk about liberation, empowerment, creativity, and self-fulfillment on the job, the employee still remains an employee. When a man owns his own business, he understandably works hard in the knowledge that any profit he makes will be his own. That is not the situation of the employee. He receives a salary or commission; the profits go to the employer. This kind of arrangement lends itself to exploitation: the harder an employee can be induced to work, the more profit the employer receives.

In the new, reenchanted workplace, the employee is required to work harder than before in exchange for the promise, not of an additional material reward, but of an additional emotional one. Such compensation can easily lose its allure. The work that at first seemed exciting and fun can become dreary and burdensome—no longer worth the sacrifice of long hours and extra energy.

The ugly and brutal fact is that today's employee, subject to the new demands of work, is supposed to behave like an entrepreneur without the prospect of an entrepreneur's reward (that is, the profits that go to the owner of a successful business). He may get a bonus or some other limited award, but only at the boss's whim and discretion. Often, all he receives is his continuing employment at salary or commission—and sometimes not even that.

—•—

During the 1980s the corporation initiated a strikingly new practice, which became widespread in the 1990s and has continued to the present day. It has been laying people off—not just blue-collar employees, who had always been liable to this treatment, but white-collar employees, and not just lower-level white-collar employees, but managers. This was not a temporary measure, instituted to meet some urgent and dire emergency. It has proceeded apace even during good times, when business is booming and productivity is soaring.

Corporations acted much differently in the past. It used to be that after a person was hired at the managerial level, as long as he did not commit some enormously egregious blunder, he would always have a job. If the task that he was performing was no longer needed or if the unit in which he worked was phased out, he would be reassigned to somewhere else in the company. For the generation that came of age during the Great Depression and accordingly sought security above all else, this policy and practice was profoundly reassuring, and it persisted through the 1970s.

Then things began to change. With the development of computer technology, corporations found that machines and software could perform the functions, not just of many lower-level employees, but of many middle-level ones. With rapid transformation becoming the norm in the economic world, corporations wanted to be able to discontinue, relocate, or merge various lines and functions of business as quickly as possible. Instead of trying to reassign all the people that these changes had displaced, they simply began getting rid of them.

The way in which the corporation views and handles an employee has altered drastically. Formerly, its own internal rules and procedures had determined his worth and compensation in relation to other employees: what level does he occupy on the organization chart, how long has he been with us, how old is he? Now, it is the external market that increasingly decides the evaluation and the compensation: how do his skills and salary compare with what we can hire off the street, how important is it to retain someone with his experience and abilities? Everywhere the old promotional ladders with their precise gradations of power, pay, and privilege have been disappearing, and along with them the ceremonial awards for long years of service to the company.

These new arrangements have obvious advantages for the corporation. Its ability to shed employees the moment it no longer needs them enables it to operate with greater speed and flexibility. The new arrangements also have a certain attractiveness to the employees themselves. Conditions created and requirements set by the outside market are more real, that is, closer to actual business needs, than those which corporations used to devise for themselves or allow to develop. No one can regret the present declining importance of office politics, with its Machiavellian intrigue among coworkers and subtle sycophancy to superiors, which were highly developed and incessantly practiced arts among the old organization men.[49]

It is also true, however, that working for a corporation driven by market forces is far more dangerous and unpredictable than working in one filled with backstabbing peers and tyrannous, arbitrary bosses. In the old days, the worst a manager had to fear was being stopped in his upward rise through the corporate hierarchy and being frozen permanently at his current level. Avoiding any action that might turn out to be a "career killer" used to be a persistent preoccupation of executives. Today the penalty for miscalculation is much harsher. You have devoted months or years to some particular project; tomorrow, management decides that it is not sufficiently profitable or is otherwise no longer desirable, and you are on the street. After years with a company, you have worked your way to a position with a large salary; tomorrow, management discovers it can hire younger people who will do jobs like yours for significantly lower pay, or it learns of another firm to which it can outsource these jobs for less, and you are on the street. Your technical training and experience have put you in some high-flying sector of the company; tomorrow, a new technology is discovered, making your skills suddenly out of date, and you are on the street. Not only is today's employee supposed to act like an entrepreneur without the possibility of an entrepreneur's rewards, he is also supposed to do so while running an entrepreneur's risks.

As it has happened many times in the past when discouragement and disillusion threatened, the illusions of the first half of the American formula (the promises of individualism and the assumptions of panglossianism) have stepped in and proceeded to conceal the grim reality of the situation. Far from facing disaster or even disadvantage, they now declare, someone who loses a corporate position has before him a splendid personal opportunity. He needs to give up his cowardly and futile desire for security and stability. The market contains abundant rewards for those who anticipate and embrace change. A former manager should become a "free agent," welcoming new experiences, discovering his real talents, growing as a person, and expressing his inner-self. Brazen cant of this sort has often been heard from business motivational speakers and at counseling sessions for the laid-off. It attained its most pithy and pungent expression in the form of a little story or parable entitled *Who Moved My Cheese?* which became a best-seller in 1998.

The actual experience of middle-aged managers who lose their jobs has proved to be somewhat different. They do not emerge as bold, energetic entrepreneurs; the very idea is ludicrous and pathetic. Most of them end up in inferior companies at inferior salaries. Some sink from the upper-middle to the lower-middle class, with woeful consequences for their family relationships and their own self-esteem. Of course, free-market enthusiasts and advocates of corporate downsizing—as the layoffs were euphemistically called when they first came into fashion—blame the misfortune on the victims' own failure to heed and genuinely take to heart the lessons of *Who Moved My Cheese?* and similar words of pan-glossian counsel.

Those corporate employees who happen to escape the ax have indeed learned a lesson, but it is not the one being openly preached. They live in fear for their jobs. Rather than share the fate of their unfortunate colleagues and be thrust into what has been touted as the free market of splendid opportunities, they are willing to submit to whatever demands the market-driven corporation makes of them. This is the enchanted workplace's stick of coercion behind its carrot of enthusiasm. If the latter fails to provide sufficient motivation, the former will. Some companies, most notoriously General Electric under Jack Welch, have adopted it as a formal technique of managerial practice. Every year superiors rate the performance of their subordinates. Those who reach a certain score at the top of the scale are promoted. Those who fall below a certain score at the bottom are discharged. If you don't have a fire in your belly, somebody will light one under your rear.[50]

—6—

In view of these new circumstances, one might worry that efforts to disguise the unattractive realities both inside and outside the corporation are putting a strain on America's talent for self-deception. The illusions of individualism and panglossianism could possibly be wearing thin. How are Americans actually bearing up under the new demands of work? one might ask. The answer is, surprisingly well.

The managers who were laid off have not organized themselves into a lobby with grievances. They have not denounced the corporations as exploiters who have used and then discarded them. Instead, they have behaved as Americans usually behave when they fall victim to economic misfortune. They became confused and bewildered. ("Why aren't things working the way they used to?") They blamed themselves. ("I should have made different moves. I should have taken more risks.") These reproaches are a testimony to their persisting faith in economic individualism and its panglossian view of the world. They see themselves as having failed to live up to their system of values, rather than their system of values as having failed to deliver on its promises.

Chronic layoffs are not the corporation's only problem that has proved easier to handle than might have been feared. Since the 1970s, the salaries and other compensation for top management and especially for CEO's have been steadily increasing at such a rate as to provoke embarrassing publicity and critical comment. At the lower levels of the organization, superiors determine the pay of inferiors; at the highest level, in the absence of superiors, peers determine each other's pay, and in doing so they prudently if not piously follow the golden rule. As a result, CEO's receive astronomically more than people in the lower ranks, they continue to accumulate their princely remuneration even when the companies they direct are losing money, and if they are finally discharged, they leave with the ransom of a king rather than the penalty of a failure.

So flagrant and scandalous are these practices that they have drawn complaints even from commentators on the political right, like Irving Kristol, who read "with a kind of despair those recurring accounts of corporate executives who, having brought their corporations to the brink of ruin, and their stockholders to the brink of desolation, 'resign' with huge cash benefit." Since "they do not take the risks of entrepreneurs," Kristol was at a loss to understand why they should receive an entrepreneur's rewards—a situation precisely the opposite to that of most corporate employees. In 2003, *Fortune* magazine, a cheerleader of business and regular reading for executives, put a pig in a business suit on one of its covers, as an illustration for that issue's leading article, "Oink! CEO Pay Is Still Out of Control." "Their performance stank last year," it stated, "yet most CEO's got paid more than ever."[51]

The political left has seized upon evidence of this kind to bring charges of a more general nature against the present economic system and against corporations in particular. Social inequalities are enormous, according to this indictment, and they are growing worse. People at the top are living like the robber barons of the Gilded Age, while people in the middle and at the bottom are struggling just to get by. These victims should recognize their common plight and organize politically to rectify it. Corporations should be prevented from buying influence and advantage from the government. Occasionally, there is even a rumble or two of the old thunder: use the antitrust laws to break up these concentrations of economic power.

Much to the exasperation of the left, the public persistently refuses to respond to its calls for action. It is undeniably true that people at the top have made out far better in the last two or three decades than everyone else, but this has often happened in the past. As has been explained in chapter two, Americans, unlike Europeans and most other people, lack the perceptions and animosities of social class and accordingly refuse to view the mere fact of inequality as automatic evidence of injustice and privilege. So long as his own situation is not getting obviously worse, the ordinary citizen does not care if some people far from his own immediate experience have had the luck to become filthy rich. If anything, he finds their example encouraging.

It is true that the new demands of work have fallen more heavily on some than on others, but the mentality described above as being produced by the American formula's first half has prevented this disagreeable fact from becoming a serious and disruptive issue. During the Fifties, a single paycheck was sufficient for most families to maintain an acceptable standard of living. To do so now, many couples find that both husband and wife need to take remunerative jobs. And they have done so, without complaining or even noticing that people at more privileged levels of society do the same from choice rather than from necessity. Even the glaring inequity of CEO pay probably arouses real bitterness only within that limited stratum of tantalized executives who find themselves just below the level at which the largess is flowing. For others, it provokes envy rather than hatred, cynical shrugs rather than rage.

The general response has been to shoulder the new burdens of work and get on with one's life, rather than to become discouraged and angry. This has been typical of Americans' behavior in the past, and it is now especially remarkable at the lower levels of society, which are having the most difficulty coping with the changes imposed by the new economy.

As countless pundits and surveys have been proclaiming for years, education is becoming increasingly important as a means, not merely to attain higher social status and larger personal income, but simply to maintain a decent standard of living. More and more entry-level positions require, not just a high school, but a college degree. The old basic skills of reading, writing, and arithmetic—accompanied by the old basic attitudes of reliability, obedience, and a willingness to work—are no longer enough. Today's jobs now expect the employee to be able to do such things as use computers, solve problems by devising and testing solutions, and function efficiently in teams composed of persons from diverse backgrounds.[52]

This puts a new and significant liability on lower-class people. Not only are they less likely to have the money to fund the necessary years at school, but equally telling and more insidious is the fact that the decision to seek higher education has to be made at a young age, when an individual is strongly under the influence of his parents and peers and largely ignorant of the long-term consequences of his choice. The pull of lower-class culture, with its social pleasures and claims of allegiance, its impatience at deferred gratification and prejudice against book learning, can easily lead a youngster of high potential into a life of low-wage labor and family ties, from which he will have tremendous difficulty escaping, even supposing that he might want to.

A number of studies have claimed that the rate of upward social mobility in the United States has been declining in recent years. Their warnings have been repeated frequently and seriously enough to have found their way—on one occasion at least—into the pages of a conservative business journal, much to the entertainment and indignation of a left-wing journal that had been saying such things for decades.[53] The charge may well be true, and, in view of the increasing tendency of education to be the chief path to upward mobility, it should continue being true and may even increase in validity.

But it hardly matters. As chapter two explained at some length, even though the people at the lower levels of society have always suffered under greater disadvantages than those at the higher levels, the workings of the first half of the American formula have kept the former from realizing the significance and extent of their disadvantages. That the first half is still performing this venerable and vital function can be seen in the recent behavior of people on welfare.

Reacting to the new demands and liabilities of work in the late Twentieth Century, the middle class did not form an allegiance with other elements under threat lower down the social ladder, as the left hoped and expected they might. Instead, they did the very opposite and demolished what remained of the old welfare system. They were saying, in effect, if we are to be put at risk and forced to work harder, those below us will share the burden. The welfare reform act of 1996 imposed time limits on benefits and obliged able-bodied individuals to work. The left predicted that widespread misery would result from these changes and looked forward to an explosion of political protest. Neither occurred. Instead, the chief outcome of welfare reform has been nothing more or less than a significant reduction in the number of people on the welfare rolls.

———

So far, the examples I have given of Americans coping with the new economic situation may seem rather grim. But there is one element of society that has responded, not merely with gritty determination, but with energetic initiative and a genuinely positive spirit. I refer to the youth of the upper-middle class. For their distinctive behavior, one can thank the parents, who have realized that the new technological and globalized economy was creating a more difficult and competitive world, in which their children would have to struggle harder than they themselves had done to secure and maintain a high position in life.

The efforts of such parents may begin well before birth, as they play classical music to stimulate the fetus in the womb and enrich its environment. Once they have the actual infant in their possession, they ply him with toys and other devices that promise to help "build baby's brain" or otherwise give him an edge in the coming marathon. They monitor his progress constantly, and any failure to exhibit some form of developmental behavior by the expected age fills them with acute anxiety, triggering nervous consultations with other parents and, if the deficiency persists, with medical experts.

As the time for formal schooling approaches, the worry increases. Parents want to get their offspring into the right preschool program as the first step on the top educational track. Some highly prestigious preschools require an IQ test for entrance, and although preparatory coaches can be hired to help boost the child's score, it may nevertheless fall short, to the agony and anguish of the parents. Failing at the age of four is thus a real possibility.[54]

Once in school, the pressure continues and grows. There is a galaxy of professional support available to address the needs of the child: homework helpers, special subject tutors, testing trainers, career counselors, psychological therapists. In total, they, along with the core component of parents and teachers, constitute what has been dubbed an "achievatron," a congeries of adults all working for the same purpose: to mold and shape a youngster so that he possesses the optimal equipment—intellectual, emotional, and social—for success in the world.[55] At times, under the duress of circumstances, the means employed can descend to the low and raw: manipulating the kid emotionally (your mother won't love you unless you achieve), offering him cash or other bribes for better grades, putting him on medication to calm him down or pep him up.

As education proceeds, the final goal of the parents looms into view: getting their teenager into one of the nation's top colleges. This has become increasingly difficult since these institutions have raised the standard for entrance. It used to be that their notion of the ideal freshman was someone with a high school record of top grades and ample social activities—in short, a "bright, well-rounded kid." Today,

BWRKs, as admissions officers derisively call them, are the norm among applicants, thanks to the efficient functioning of the achievatron.[56] The elite colleges are looking for something more, something impressively outstanding; exactly what, they are not all that sure—which adds an element of frustrating unpredictability to the whole process.

I hardly need to discuss further the prolonged and torturous experience of the children who, with the active urging and assistance of their parents, take up the college quest. This has been the subject of numerous books and articles (e.g. "Give Me Harvard or Give Me Death"). What is important for the purposes of the present discussion is the end result—the students who finally do succeed in arriving on the campuses of the most prestigious institutions. The journalist David Brooks took a look at them and reported his findings in a piece he called "The Organization Kid." The title was deliberately and carefully chosen. In 1956, William H. Whyte's *Organization Man* depicted people who willingly adapted to the demands of the working world in that era; in 2001, "The Organization Kid" found a generation ready to meet the demands of today's workplace.[57]

These youngsters have accepted and internalized the values of their parents. They want to reach the top (society's most lucrative, prestigious, powerful, and interesting positions, which will be theirs someday if they continue to perform at a sufficiently high level). They have also heeded the warnings (relaxing or taking a wrong step may cause them to lose their advanced position in the race, which they may be unable to recover). They do not complain about the pressures they impose upon themselves or the efforts they feel compelled to make, any more than a potentially champion athlete complains about the rigors of his training and the difficulty of the contest. They are simply doing what they feel they need to do, and they want to do it.

Their unrelenting industriousness and efficiency are truly remarkable. Each day, they prepare their schedules in advance, allotting the necessary time to various tasks. Then they proceed through the agenda in swift and steady progression, finishing each and moving on to the next without hesitation, diversion, or delay. Brooks characterizes them as "workaholics." Not having enough time is a common and persistent problem. Some of them find that they have to schedule appointments for informal activities, like talking with friends; otherwise such things would be swept aside by the press of more urgent and important business.

Equally remarkable is the detached, instrumental way in which they approach their labors. "Sometimes we feel like we're just tools for processing information," declared a student. One might characterize their behavior as selfless self-seeking. They do a thing, not because they find it personally appealing or because they consider it intrinsically admirable, but because it is another step in the direction of their self-conditioning and self-advancement. When they embark on a new task, they first determine what ground rules are in operation, that is, the established and often unstated premises and assumptions. Once these are understood, they proceed to adapt themselves and to function according to them. They are highly respectful and attentive to any person in authority, since he acts as an arbiter of the rules and a judge of their performance.

Organization kids have learned to behave in this way, whether they are undertaking a course of study or a remunerative job. They accept the premises and discharge the tasks of the situation at hand, under the assumption that their successful performance will enable them to advance to further and superior situations, where there will most likely be different premises and tasks. The undergraduate who masters the radical and subversive theoretics of postmodernist literature, for example, may with smooth nonchalance proceed to a postgraduate career of capitalistic moneymaking on Wall Street. A professor interviewed by Brooks observed that his students "work for Save the Children and Merrill Lynch and they don't see a contradiction." Of course they don't. In either case, they are simply engaging in an activity that society considers laudable and useful. Wherever the organization kid happens to find himself, he adjusts to the circumstances—quickly and willingly.

This is American flexible conformity pushed to a high degree of development, and it is just what is needed in today's workplaces, with their varied and changing norms. Although organization kids are only a minority of college students, they have a significance greater than their numbers. They represent the most advanced edge of a general tendency, which extends its influence far and wide.

———

As the demands of productivity extend into an ever larger part of personal life and into ever more remote sectors of the population, the American formula has continued to function with remarkable effectiveness, proclaiming the promises of its first half while concealing the realities of its second. Now, as in the past, Americans continue to lay their human sacrifice on the altars of economic efficiency, not in a spirit of resigned submission to bitter necessity, but willingly, even happily, in the conviction that they are engaging in an exciting enterprise that will realize their personal dreams and bring out the best in themselves.

American men have always prided themselves on how much and how hard they work, turning the originally pejorative word "workaholic" into a boast.[58] And they have done so while believing that they were acting freely—the freest people on earth—choosing to devote themselves to tasks that promoted their own best interests as well as those of society as a whole and the world at large.

American women displayed a similar attitude when the economy of the 1970s obliged them to leave their homes and provide "an available, cheaper, and typically more acquiescent labor pool." They had to do so because a double income was now necessary for a married couple with children to maintain an acceptably middle-class standard of living. The bosses, coworkers, and customers that they had to deal with might be far more demanding and far less affectionate than the husbands and children of traditional homemakers. Even at the higher end of the market, female employees are often no more than "the gilt-edged peons of the corporation." But like the men, the women too believed that they were acting freely and willingly. Taking a job was an act of liberation and fulfillment, they claimed.[59]

At last, when America called for the children to be handed over to a discipline that would produce the latest and most advanced generation of the myrmidons of modernity, their parents agreed gladly, and the children themselves have responded enthusiastically. "'I want to be this busy,'" declared one of Brooks' organization kids in all sincerity, after describing a daily schedule that would be condemned "as slave-driving if it were imposed on anyone."[60]

CHAPTER EIGHT

The Changing World
Outside Work

—1—

O ne of the most important activities outside work is the acquisition of goods produced by work. These range from necessities,
through conveniences and ordinary pleasures, to luxuries. During its
entire history, the American economy has been manufacturing consumer
goods in an increasing quantity and variety and has been distributing
them throughout the population to remote regions and down the social
ladder. The mechanical complexity of life and the standard of living
have risen steadily, as yesterday's luxuries become today's conveniences
and tomorrow's necessities.[1]

Americans are notoriously ardent in the pursuit of these goods because
they are motivated, not just by the universal human desire to better one's
material condition, but also by three attitudes which are prominent in
their culture. First, as was mentioned in chapter three, they have a bias in
favor of the new, which they assume will be superior to the old. Ready to
buy whatever novelty the market offers, they are, according to one international comparison, "the most receptive consumers on earth."[2] Second,
as was discussed in chapter five, the possession of more expensive goods
is a mark of higher social status. Pleasure in the actual enjoyment of a

luxury is often secondary to its owner's proud conviction that it confirms his personal superiority, both in his own estimation and in the opinions of others. Third, by making choices as consumers, they feel that they are expressing their freedom as individuals. The more goods they buy, therefore, the more freedom they are exercising. President Franklin D. Roosevelt once declared that if he wanted to convince the Russians that the American way of life was unquestionably better than theirs, he would send them, not documents expounding elevated and abstract liberties (like the Declaration of Independence, the Constitution, or the Gettysburg Address), but copies of the Sears, Roebuck catalog.[3]

Advertising plays upon these three attitudes, and upon others that are more universally human and less distinctively American, as it seeks to attract potential customers. Its basic strategy is to invest a specific, tangible product with alluring, intangible qualities, and it often does so with much artfully insinuating subtlety and persuasive success. For this, it has been criticized and even excoriated as a mercenary deceiver of the public, inducing them to buy things they do not need and cannot afford.

The charge is superficial and misguided. Advertising does indeed "commodify desires" (as the practice has been called), but attributing intangible merits and virtues to tangible phenomena is something that Americans have always done, as may be seen, for example, in their views on the moral and psychological benefits of prosaic and routine religious practice or on the ability to make money as a reflection of personal excellence (discussed in chapters three and two respectively). It may be reassuring for anyone who is disgusted by the vulgar excesses of commercialism in the United States to blame, not the low taste and materialistic desires of the people, but the manipulation of advertising. Actually the latter does no more than encourage or, if you will, exploit the former, which were present and thriving in national life long before the latter made its appearance.

Like advertising, consumer goods have themselves been the target of superficial complaints. For centuries, old-fashioned moralizing has stigmatized "luxuries" and blamed them for exerting a baneful influence on personal conduct. During the Twentieth Century, the indictment was updated in terminology, and since the prosperity of the 1950s, pundits have, from time to time, lamented the decline or loss of what they call "the Protestant ethic" or "the Puritan ethic" or simply "the work ethic." This is their way of referring to a putative decrease in self-denial and a corresponding increase in self-indulgence, as the public crowds the shopping malls and accumulates ever larger amounts of credit card debt.

Contrary to these shallow and automatic grumbles, the more knowledgeable social historians recognize that Americans have always scrambled after material possessions, the only difference being that there are many more goods available today than there were in the past, and many more people with money to spend on them. In addition, the more discerning among the social commentators admit, with varying degrees of approbation, resignation, or aversion, that such behavior is an essential ingredient of national productivity.

Even in the early days, there were occasional observers of the social scene who refused to join in the automatic and indiscriminate "cry against the evil of luxury" and who pointed out that the longing to acquire more expensive possessions led men to engage in useful labor and enterprising businesses.[4] Less noticed but equally important is the other side of the productive cycle: once goods are produced, it is necessary that people should want to buy them. Fortunately, the insatiable appetite for a higher standard of living drives both sides of the economic wheel, with Americans functioning as both eager producers and enthusiastic consumers.

The danger for the individual is that the intensity of his desire to acquire luxuries may cause him to forget the necessary priority of production over consumption and tempt him to buy things before he has accumulated sufficient funds to pay for them. Self-help books and their earlier equivalents (from Benjamin Franklin's "Way to Wealth" in 1758 to Robert T. Kiyosaki's *Rich Dad, Poor Dad* in 1998) have warned against this tendency. The indefatigable optimism of Americans, driven as it is by powerful cultural currents of panglossian self-deception, has beguiled many a hapless spender into assuming that new gains in the future would compensate for new expenses in the present. Rates of savings in the United States are notoriously low compared to those of other countries. In the words of one buoyant entrepreneur, "Saving too much is practically un-American."[5]

However deluded and self-damaging many consumers may be in the conduct of their personal finances, their behavior has a larger, positive dimension to it. They are like those eager producers described at the end of chapter two—the farmers, workers, and businessmen who went forth, and whose descendants continue to go forth, confident that they can attain their dreams of wealth. Most of them met with disappointment, as do their descendants, but their efforts have contributed to the prosperity of the nation as a whole. In a similar way, whatever frustrations profligate consumers may experience in their personal lives, their spending contributes to the demand for more goods and for more employees to produce them, thus helping to promote society's collective well-being.

A second important focus of activity outside work is sex. Unlike traditional societies, where parents and relatives have played an important and even decisive part in determining the marriage partners of young people, American society has from the very beginning endorsed the principle of free choice by the individuals most directly and intimately involved. In 1787, a character in an American play proclaimed, "In our country, the affections are not sacrificed to riches or family aggrandizement"—an opinion that Thomas Jefferson himself echoed when he stated, in reference to his own daughter's selection of a husband, "According to the usage of my country, I scrupulously suppressed my wishes, that...[she] might indulge her own sentiments freely."[6]

The intense mutual affection that was supposed to form the basis of marriage has remained "as much a part of the American dream as every boy's chance to become rich...." During the 1930s, a visiting Frenchman remarked on the endless stream of love songs that he heard gushing from radios. In contrast, he estimated that three out of every four songs in his own country were about politics. France has changed since then, I understand, but not America. The tendency has persisted and is shared by Americans in all walks of life. In 1982, the author of a book called *The Redneck Way of Knowledge* observed, "The chief theme of popular music is love.... I think falling in love is the only religious experience my generation legitimizes.... Romantic love is the only mumbo-jumbo we all agree upon."[7]

In this land of free marriage, there was a problem, and it has been present from the very beginning. After one chose a partner, one was supposed to remain bound to that decision for life. But, as innumerable couples have discovered, a relationship which began well might turn out badly, and the marriage could become distasteful and even intolerable. The obvious solution was divorce. One of its early and vocal advocates was Thomas Paine, the idealistic revolutionary. Just as he believed society need not endure the legacy of the past with its accumulation of miseries and mistakes but could "begin the world over again," so he believed couples ought not continue in loveless unions but should separate and begin marriage over again with new partners: "Each has his mate somewhere or other; and 'tis our duty to find each other out, since no creature was ever intended to be miserable."[8]

Many Americans agreed, including Emerson, who referred to the discarding of unsatisfactory sexual soul mates and the search for better ones in his customarily exalted diction and metaphor: "When half-gods go, the gods arrive." So began the familiar practice of having more than one spouse, but only one at a time—"serial monogamy," as it has been facetiously called, or "rotating polygamy."[9] The raw and youthful society of the West, which offered a new start for those who had failed economically, did the same for those who had failed maritally. As the frontier advanced, a succession of boomtowns (from Indianapolis, Indiana, to Reno, Nevada) provided relatively quick and easy divorces to newcomers arriving from out of state.

Some wanted to go further. During the Nineteenth Century, a few bold individuals advocated in printed literature and at times from speakers' podiums a doctrine that became known as "free love." It maintained that law and public opinion should no more attempt to regulate the sexual activities between men and women than they did the business transactions between merchants and customers. Its goal was the creation of a free market in sexual relations similar to the free market in economic relations.

Although the arguments of individual liberty and the presumptions of panglossian social benefits could logically support and were actually employed to defend this doctrine, it proved to be far in advance of its time. The overwhelming majority of Americans rejected "free love" as an abomination. Throughout the Nineteenth Century, divorce in the United States was highly disapproved of, rarely resorted to, and, in most localities, difficult to obtain.

But sexual restrictions were slowly weakening, and they were doing so as economic conditions improved. Through the decades and up to the present day, there has been a connection between the two phenomena. By 1900, industrial productivity was bringing an array of new consumer goods to the public, advertising was learning to broadcast emotional enticements as well as factual information, and venturesome people were declaring that individual self-expression and personal growth were more important than the dictates of duty, respectability, and social restraint. This last development was reflected in a popular slogan of the time—"the rights of the heart"—which enjoyed advocacy and support from various progressive and reform-minded individuals. The desire for more freedom in private life demanded a "freer granting of divorce," and divorce itself was becoming more frequent.[10]

These tendencies in both consumerism and sex increased during the prosperous years of the 1920s. There were more goods, and more people had money to spend on them. Buying on credit became widespread. Advertising increasingly ignored the tangible aspects of the products it was selling and instead appealed to the hopes or fears of consumers, including their libidinous ones. Trendy books and magazines denounced repression and puritanism and claimed that their abolition would improve society in general as well as the lives of individuals. Movies purveyed fantasies of erotic adventure. Automobiles became available as a means of escaping the scrutiny of parents and neighbors. One worried contemporary (the brother of a former president) remarked that ordinary young people were now being lured by "distractions and temptations" that used to be available only to "the small circle of the very rich."[11]

The advancing tide of new opinions and new behavior provoked much opposition and controversy. Public moralists urged men and women to "subdue the beast that is in us" and blamed selfish individuals for putting the gratification of their base appetites above the higher good of the community. The warnings and worries intensified during the 1920s, as information about birth control began to be made available to the public, and divorces began to be granted for nothing more than personal incompatibility and the mutual loss of affection. When Judge Ben B. Lindsey, who was nationally famous as an advocate of permissive attitudes, published a book entitled *Companionate Marriage*, it was vehemently attacked as "nothing but free love" and "barnyard marriage." One young woman in Georgia exclaimed that if society went the way the judge was recommending, people would soon be exchanging sexual partners with the same nonchalance as they exchanged partners at a dance.[12]

—2—

With the arrival of the Great Depression, the country's slow and acrimonious drift toward a free market in sexual relations came to a halt. The change starkly demonstrated how much material prosperity is a necessary precondition for erotic license. With one of every four workers unemployed, people lost their inclination or tolerance for personal indulgence. In the previous decade, sexual experimentation and unconventionality had been a daring and controversial option; now they were universally condemned as frivolous and irresponsible. Even liberals and radicals began to talk about the requirements of social life and the need for people to curb their individual desires and to function as part of a larger social collectivity.[13]

All this was more than a momentary, passing phase. The economic catastrophe of the 1930s produced long-term effects and counter-effects that extended through every decade during the rest of the century. Its most immediate and obvious influence was on the postwar years, from the 1940s to the early 1960s. As indicated in the previous chapter, the Fifties (the abbreviated name for that era) were a time of pervasive and persisting insecurity. People believed that a new depression might happen at any time. In their desire for "security" (a contemporary buzzword), they avoided innovation and risk and accepted existing rules and conventions. "Adjustment" was the word that came into vogue. One was supposed to adjust oneself to social conditions as one found them. In the language of the times, an individual demonstrated "maturity" by behaving as a "well-adjusted" person.

Given these prevailing attitudes, the Fifties became an era of conspicuous, even sanctimonious domesticity. Rates of marriage and childbirth went up; rates of divorce came down. "Family-" became an all-purpose, positive prefix in advertising copy. "Togetherness" emerged as a popular new concept. Religion, as was usual in the United States, extended powerful sanction and assistance to the dominant social agenda. Church attendance rose, "under God" was added to the Pledge of Allegiance, and highway billboards proclaimed, "The family that prays together, stays together."

America, in obedience to the second half of its national formula, is a society that enforces and obeys social norms with extraordinary strength and thoroughness, and its pursuit of normality naturally engenders the persecution of abnormality. During the Fifties (as was mentioned in the previous chapter), this tendency reached extremes far beyond the customary and necessary practice. Companies routinely administered psychological tests to applicants for jobs, to make sure that they were sufficiently mature and well-adjusted. An influential book of the time recommended that all men who remained unmarried over the age of thirty should be subjected to punitive tax rates and "encouraged to undergo psychotherapy." It also recommended that elderly unmarried women be prohibited by law from teaching school, so as to prevent their "emotional incompetence" from harming young children.[14]

One article in a popular magazine went as far as to declare in its very title that it was "smart to be stupid," and it proceeded to explain that too much intelligence resulted in various forms of self- and socially destructive behavior, including "marital infidelities, excessive drinking, mental depression, major and minor crimes, and assorted delinquencies." The principal of one junior high school evidently agreed, for he declared that he felt sorry for "parents of bright children" and referred to a little girl with an IQ of 162 as "poor thing," because she was "cut off from the rest of us."[15]

The preceding examples may have been somewhat extreme, even for the times, but they were only exaggerated reflections of a mentality that dominated the country. Anything that appeared deviant, strange, or unusual provoked strong and automatic disapproval. People who lacked the actual qualities of prescribed conventionality, who were not happily married family men or devoted mothers and housewives, quickly learned to act as if they were or suffer the consequences of hostility and ostracism. "There was a lot of camouflage in the Fifties," observed Ted Morgan, a sophisticated French immigrant who had changed his name from Sanche de Gramont. "It was hard to tell who was who or what was what."[16]

The climate of contemporary political opinion reinforced the mood of caution and conformity. It was the depth of the Cold War and the height of McCarthyism, and the public was ready to apply the epithet "Communist" to anything that annoyed or disconcerted them. During his travels around the country, a novelist found that people avoided talking about politics: "Strong opinions were just not stated." In the words of a contemporary historian, it was a case of "the bland leading the bland." A visiting British cartoonist noticed a change from earlier years. The old stereotype of the loud, vulgar American was out of date: "Voices are quieter, manners less rugged."[17]

So deep were the prevailing fears of the Fifties that they did not stop at disparaging and discouraging individualism as an actual practice and—in the writings of Henry C. Link, for example—as a theoretical ideal, they even went so far as to cast doubt on the validity of panglossian principles. An outlook on reality that came to be called "the tragic view of life" gained popularity among reflective minds during those years. It maintained that human nature was fundamentally flawed and limited, that a certain amount of evil and misery in the world was consequently inevitable and ineradicable, and that one should therefore accept the situation and not hope for perpetual progress or ultimate perfection. Some thinkers with a religious bent expressed similar ideas under the rubric of "original sin." Though utterly at odds with traditional American attitudes of optimism, these pessimistic convictions had sufficient currency and cogency to influence the popular mind. Many people expressed doubts about the ability of scientific knowledge to solve social problems and declared that "the real problem is in the hearts of men."[18]

The Fifties contained a fundamental contradiction. It was a time of fear, which was the legacy of the Great Depression. It was also a time of prosperity, as the postwar economy initiated and sustained an unprecedented boom of consumer affluence. With the passage of the years, the fear subsided as memories faded; at the same time, confidence grew, as prosperity persisted. People became increasingly restive under the existing social restrictions.

The national faith in the ideal of individualism and the principles of panglossianism, which had been languishing since the Depression, began to revive. A few psychologists and sociologists began to attack the concepts of adjustment and maturity; to defend the personal quest for autonomy, growth, and self-expression; and to assert that spontaneous impulses were intrinsically good. Some novelists depicted the conventional lives of middle-class people as circumscribed, warped, and miserable, and the unconventional lives of socially marginal people as adventurous and exciting. Norman Mailer, one of the more prominent of the intellectual insurgents, carried the new tendency to extremes in his notorious essay "The White Negro" (1957), which applauded violence and the destruction of "social restraints," yet asserted the utterly panglossian conviction that freedom, creativity, and goodness could be the ultimate outcome, since underneath violence "is finally love and the nuances of justice," and "the real desire to make a better world exists at the heart of our instinct...."

Opinions of this kind were confined to small, avant-garde circles, where "alienation" had become as much a buzzword as had "adjustment" in the larger society. At the same time, less extreme postures of discontent were being more widely expressed. Among the popular purveyors of high-minded opinion, an outcry arose against "mass culture." This became a fashionable topic for the sophisticated and the articulate, and it was later joined by a clamor against suburbia.

But the incessant, fretful chatter over these two hobgoblins paled in comparison with the stir created by the appearance of a third—"conformity." By the late 1950s, people were talking about conformity as if it were a major national problem. Everyone—left, right, and center—deplored it. Classes of graduating seniors had to listen to interminable speakers expatiating on the inevitable topic. They all seemed to be taking their text from Emerson: "Whoso would be a man, must be a nonconformist." A characteristic example of their preaching was the following fervent appeal by the theologian Paul Tillich: "We hope for nonconformists among you, for your sake, for the sake of the nation, and for the sake of humanity."[19]

There was an air of unreality in all this talk. It provoked no significant, immediate change in actual behavior. Mass culture remained as popular and as banal as ever. Suburbia continued to be the choice of families who could afford to buy a house there. And the efforts against conformity, as was mentioned in chapter five, prompted Americans verbally to condemn conformity with uniform expressions and in uniform tones, while privately they worried about how they might find some socially accepted standard of nonconformity to which they could conform.

But all the verbiage from Tillich and countless others directed at members of the younger generation was not entirely in vain. Their discontent was growing. They were the segment of the population that was the least influenced by the old fears and the most coddled by the new affluence. The word "teenager" had appeared in common usage during the 1940s to signify an always precarious and now increasingly significant stage in life, between the controls of childhood and the responsibilities of adulthood. "Juvenile delinquency" was a perennial topic of discussion among nervous parents and an uneasy public throughout the Fifties. Possessing a certain amount of spending money, teenagers became a new class of consumers, who created a market for new kinds of products, including those that reflected their dissatisfaction with adult norms of caution and respectability. Prominent among their enthusiasms that irritated and disturbed the grown-ups were rock and roll music (especially as performed by the downmarket sex idol Elvis Presley) and movies featuring a "crazy mixed-up kid" as hero (epitomized by James Dean in *Rebel Without a Cause*).

With the advent of the Sixties and the election of the young and glamorous John F. Kennedy as president, the restless energy of juveniles—at least a certain number of them—took an idealistic and political turn. Some college students traveled to the South and joined the struggle of black people for civil rights. When a number of them returned to the University of California at Berkeley for the fall semester of 1964, they indignantly realized that the college administration was restricting their own rights of free speech. Like most every other institution of higher education at the time, Berkeley prohibited political advocacy on the campus. The student activists decided to do something about it. They formed the Free Speech Movement (FSM), which organized demonstrations, culminating in the famous sit-in at Sproul Hall and ultimately forcing the administration to concede.

A long, slow fuse had burned its way to a keg of powder, and the ensuing explosion shook the nation. The example of FSM was imitated in subsequent semesters at other institutions. Throughout the rest of the Sixties, various forms of conspicuous protest—rude and noisy, and at times disorderly and destructive—became a familiar feature of higher education. Adults everywhere reacted with fascination, incredulity, astonishment, and horror. Their compulsive Fifties' propriety and respectability were being outraged. In particular, their notion of college life as a placid and amiable world of fond memories or fantasies was being ferociously execrated and ruthlessly desecrated.

Even those who had urged young people to be bold and daring, not to play it safe but to follow their dreams and desires, were often appalled and dismayed at the results. This was not what they had intended. They were rather like Emerson, the philosophical theorist of a sublime democracy, confronting the unsavory vulgarities of real Jacksonian democracy. I recall one middle-aged man remarking that he had hoped the younger generation, in contrast to himself and his contemporaries, would display a more sophisticated attitude toward sex; instead, the kids were shouting four-letter words in public.

—◦—

In retrospect, the disruption and disorder of the Sixties can now be perceived and understood as obviously inevitable. The Great Depression of the Thirties had disturbed the harmony between the two halves of the American formula by moving the balance far in the direction of the second half (social controls). This new arrangement made sense in circumstances of material privation, but it could not persist into the future, as economic conditions improved, thereby stimulating desires for the promises of the first half (the ideal of freedom and panglossian optimism). When the young radicals challenged the caution and pessimism of their elders and demanded more freedom, more openness, and more trust in human nature, they were attempting to throw the balance of the American formula in the opposite direction, far toward the first half.

Extremism in reaction to the Fifties was a dominant characteristic of the New Left (the collective name for the politically oriented protest movements of the Sixties), and it often assumed a puerile and destructive form. Its anger was fueled, not by the resentment of the deprived and the subjugated, but by the impatience of the comfortable and the privileged who had been kept too long under unnecessary control and irksome supervision. "You are the spoiled brats of the bourgeoisie!" one eminent European professor at the University of California is said to have exclaimed. (I think it was the poet Czeslaw Milosz, who had known real oppression in Communist Poland.)

During my years at Berkeley during the Sixties, I recall noticing how readily the activists inflated trivial grievances into major issues, how easily they moved from complaints about specific conditions on campus to general indictments of American society, and how quickly an initial cause of contention was forgotten, once the surge of anger and action had exhausted itself. A spirit of festering hostility prevailed among the leaders, who were always on the lookout for some new grievance to serve as justification for a new wave of demonstrations.

I remember one well-intentioned liberal professor asking some of the student radicals what they would do if the university administration offered to fund whatever innovations they proposed. The possibility took them aback. They had given no thought to positive goals. They had no idea of any new institutions that they might want to build. They simply wanted to overturn the old ones, to launch a program of "creative destruction," as they called it, deliberately creating disorder in the hope and expectation that something good would arise from the chaos. This was panglossianism gone wild. So was their incessant advocacy and quest for indiscriminate experience—for any and all experience beyond that of middle-class respectability—especially for extreme forms of experience involving drugs and political violence.

It was a bizarre posture that the radical youth of the Sixties displayed—vague, naive, idealistic words often combined with specific, nasty, malicious behavior—neatly and accurately skewered in a cartoon by Jules Feiffer, which displayed six pictures of the same bearded face, uttering the following sequence of statements: "I occupy buildings, raid files, scream obscenities, throw rocks, and call cops pigs, in an attempt to humanize this brutalized society." Lurching and stumbling, the whole sorry cavalcade—an "age of rubbish" one historian called it—would have come to an end much sooner than it finally did, but the national agony over Vietnam gave it a new cause that kept it going through the second half of the Sixties.[20] When the war ended, the New Left vanished, as suddenly and as unexpectedly as it had appeared.

During the later years of the 1960s, youthful discontent developed a cultural agenda, and the political radicals had to share the stage of public attention with lifestyle rebels called hippies. These successors to the previous decade's beatniks intended to counteract the Fifties world of organization men, uptight squares, and role-playing conformists by seceding from it and forming their own society. The resulting communes (as their inhabitants called them) exhibited a maximum amount of personal freedom, which was based on drastically panglossian assumptions about goodness, harmony, and simplicity—assisted by the ingestion of contraband substances. Although the hippies lasted a little longer than the New Leftists, the would-be utopias they founded inevitably fell into decline and vanished during the 1970s.

––––

Despite all their frustrations and failures, the Sixties were unquestionably successful in shifting the balance of the American formula. By the Seventies, ordinary adults were seeking new liberties in their personal lives. During the Fifties, people had been preoccupied with obeying the established rules and dominant practices of society; now their attention turned to the individual self. In 1976, a journalist dubbed it "the Me decade," and the cliches and buzzwords of the time reflected this orientation. You were supposed to have "the freedom to be yourself." Your first obligation was "to yourself." Everyone was, or should be, engaged in a quest to find one's "authentic self," with "self-fulfillment" and "self-actualization" as the goal.[21]

The first and foremost item on the agenda was sexual liberation. Its advancement, which had halted with the Great Depression, restarted among small groups of youths in the 1960s, then began spreading through the rest of the population. Its underlying foundation was material prosperity, as it had been in the 1920s and during previous times.

The link between affluence and sexual freedom had a conspicuous precursor in the Fifties. *Playboy* magazine, the object of avid teenage interest during those repressive years, was more than a purveyor of erotic titillation and an advocate of sex outside marriage; it also provided advice to young people on how to behave as informed and somewhat sophisticated consumers in the newly prosperous postwar society ("how to buy a sports car, what kind of hi-fi set to buy, how to order in a restaurant, what kind of wine to drink with what kind of meal").[22]

In *Playboy*, freedom was intimately connected with affluence. The same was true of the Sixties. Despite all their talk of simplicity and denunciation of materialism, New Leftists took for granted a high level of prosperity, both in their personal lives and in the life of the nation. For them the chief problem was the equitable distribution of all these goods and services. Charles Reich, one of the most prominent theorists among the young radicals, applauded the advance of technology and the invention of laborsaving machines, because these gave every person "a new freedom to choose how he would live."[23] It hardly needed to be said that a prominent feature of their new lives was to be sexual liberation.

The Seventies realized this specific promise, and it did so mainly by a change in the attitudes and behavior of women, a change that was itself based on material conditions. Not only had women gained ready access to birth control, they were also taking jobs outside the home and in the process accumulating money of their own. The resulting financial independence made possible the transition from the subordinate and confined "angel of the house" to "the independently passionate woman," who selected and discarded sexual partners in sole obedience to her carnal appetite and changing desires.[24] Men, needless to say, were not slow in becoming active participants in the new liberation. At last, at long last, the free market in sexual relations had arrived.

Some pundits had foreseen this development and had predicted that when neither public opinion nor economic necessity kept married couples together, marriages would become better and more secure— bound, as they would be, solely by the ties of mutual affection. The imaginative optimism created by the Sixties took strong hold of some authors and social commentators as they attempted to describe the nature of the new marital relationship, for example, "the equality of two self-actualizing spiritual beings who connect at the level of their beingness," or couples who "individuate [sic] together and explore their wholeness with each other."[25]

Reality quickly contradicted the utterly panglossian presupposition of natural harmony between the sexes. Animated by an ethos of self-realization rather than self-denial or self-restraint, people in the Seventies entered marriage with high expectations. Spouses, according to one assessment, were supposed to be passionate lovers, sympathetic friends, and skilled mutual therapists.[26] If the requirements of either party were not met, he or she felt justified in ending the marriage and going off to look for a more suitable partner. Divorce rates, which had remained stable through the 1950s and most of the 1960s, began to soar.

—3—

From the outset, the new sexual freedom aroused much controversy. Conservatives charged that it weakened the fundamental bonds of society by undermining the family and that it was especially harmful to children, who were damaged emotionally by mothers leaving the home to work and by parents getting divorced. Down the social ladder, the effects were reported as being even worse, as ever larger numbers of unmarried, impoverished mothers and their unruly offspring produced a growing culture of dissipation, destitution, dysfunction, and disorder.

People of a more liberal inclination were quick and vociferous in expressing contrary opinions. They asserted that by perpetuating bad marriages, dominating children, and restricting women, traditional family life was responsible for curbing human freedom and limiting human potential. Anything that weakened or destroyed such tyranny benefited all involved, including the children, who—far from being emotionally injured by working or divorced parents—would now grow up in a better and more liberating environment. This applied as well to single mothers and their children at the lower levels of society, though class snobbery and authoritarian rigidity might fail to perceive it.

The clash between these two points of view went on for years. It was a part, and probably the most acrimonious part, of a larger dispute over the salutary or baneful influence of the Sixties, which came to be known as "the culture war" (or "wars"). Voices on the right, in various tones of admonition and desperation, declared that American society was on the road to ruin: People were questioning any and all established rules, merely because they thought it was liberating to do so, and some were actually breaking rules, for selfish advantage or from personal whim. Everything seemed up for grabs and subject to the approval or rejection of each individual. The consequence was increasingly repulsive and pernicious behavior, reflected and promoted by an increasingly vile and degenerate popular culture.

Voices on the left claimed the very opposite: All Americans, low as well as high, were at last beginning to exercise the full freedom promised to them by the ideals of their culture. Nervous conservatives naturally found the effects of this development disconcerting, and at times there might actually be a few instances of unfortunate excess, but the overall trend was positive, and it deserved to be welcomed and encouraged. Actions that appeared at first to be offensive and unconscionable transgressions might actually turn out to be valuable and empowering innovations. And even if they did not, they were at least the result of individuals' healthy urge to express themselves and try out new options. Lifestyle individualism was as legitimate, as logical, and as natural a practice as economic individualism, even if historically the latter had enjoyed far more public approval than the former.

Such were the opinions of the two opposing sides. Having started up in the 1970s, the culture war proceeded to rage on through the 1980s. The effect of the conflict in the latter decade was to move the balance between the two halves of the American formula away from the first half, toward which the Sixties had pushed it, and back toward the second half. People became more and more dubious about the benefits of unrestrained individual freedom and extreme panglossian assumptions. The rates of murder and other violent crimes had been rising precipitously since the 1960s, accompanied by an increase in various disturbing phenomena, including drug abuse, teenage pregnancy, welfare dependency, and single motherhood, all of which were widely assumed to have been caused by a decline of the family, specifically by broken or nonexistent marriages. The liberals' assertion that such things were no more than an expression of alternate lifestyles and liberated mores sounded ever more unconvincing to a public that was becoming ever more worried about growing social degeneration and disintegration.

Even people on the left started having second thoughts. The excesses of the Sixties and their persisting influence had already scared a number of them into the ranks of what later became known as neoconservatism. And the trend to the right continued. Celebrations of freedom and innovation diminished, as social critics began deploring antisocial behavior, talking less about individuals' rights and more about individuals' responsibilities, and calling for "more community, more civil society, more moral cohesion."[27] It had been one of radicalism's old platitudes, repeated endlessly, that the family was an instrument of conformity and control which capitalism utilized to suppress human freedom and frustrate social justice. Now a new platitude replaced the old one: the family is a source of social bonds and personal affection, and it is under threat from the forces of ruthless commercialism and relentless change unleashed by capitalism. The new version has likewise been repeated endlessly.

This is not to suggest that, since the Eighties, the nation has been on its way back to the norms of the Fifties. People reject the extreme expressions of the new freedom introduced by the Sixties, but they do not reject the new freedom itself. They may favor the traditional practices of family life in the abstract—the babble about "family values" goes on incessantly—but when it comes down to actual behavior, they want to retain for their own personal lives the options of divorce, unmarried cohabitation, and (if necessary) abortion. Even the old conviction that an unhappily married couple should stay together for the sake of the children receives only a small percentage of assent in the opinion polls. The frequency of divorce is as high among "born-again" Christians as it is for all Americans, and the liability of marriages to fail is now accepted everywhere as a simple if unfortunate fact of life, with some realistic brides and bridegrooms changing their vows at the altar from "until death do us part" to "until our love dies."[28]

A certain element of the political right would like nothing better than to lead the country back to an age of prudish controls and priggish manners, but it has been continually frustrated in its attempts. Politicians have found that advocating a stricter standard of sexual morality loses them votes, especially among the young or affluent. It may be all right for a virtuous constabulary to harass a welfare mother, who can be viewed as having forfeited her genital freedom by her irresponsible economic conduct (living on the public dole). But no one wants the sex police in one's own bedroom or in the bedrooms of one's peers and pals.[29]

The great opportunity and great disappointment of the Comstockian conservatives was the impeachment of President Clinton in 1999. By exposing and arraigning his carnal misdeeds, they hoped to achieve a symbolic condemnation of the Sixties and their lubricious liberties, of which Clinton was product and exemplar. But the wave of public outrage and indignation that should have swept him from office failed to arise, and he was acquitted. A few partisans of the right retired in bitterness and disgust, muttering that it was too late, the virus of a foul decade had already infected a majority of the American population.[30]

Conservatives themselves concede that they are losing or indeed have lost the culture war. Not only have they failed to inspire a return to the behavior of the Fifties, they have also failed to curb even the public representation of objectionable behavior. Popular culture has continued to become more coarse, violent, and obscene, and for all the complaints one hears, people—at least a significantly large number of them—like it. If that were not the case, it would not attract paying audiences of a sufficient size to keep itself in business. Pornography has gone from backstreet, under-the-counter operations to open, mainstream enterprises, and its customers are no longer furtive, skulking deviants but ordinary citizens, including perhaps many of those who, on other occasions, praise family values and deplore their decline.[31]

In view of this reality, it is not surprising that the right wing's attempts to crack down on offending media usually come to nothing, for example, the Southern Baptist Convention's call to boycott Disney in 1996–97. Conservatives have been further weakened by a crucial division in their own ranks. As chapter four explained, Americans who declare themselves to be on the right politically are not traditionalists of the European kind. They are champions of free enterprise, and many of them frankly, even proudly, declare that the market gives the public whatever it wants—everything (as a prominent libertarian boasted in *Reason* magazine) from the staid moralities of William Bennett's *Book of Virtues* (1993) to the raw degradation of a rock group called Nine Inch Nails.[32]

Such a stance is generally popular, as one right-winger in the traditionalist mode discovered to his frustration and chagrin. Whenever he spoke in favor of the government censoring the violent and obscene products of popular culture, he encountered opposition even from the respectable and the sedate, who agreed with the liberal principle that "people ought to be allowed to see whatever they wanted to see."[33] It was the ideal of freedom trumping the idea of control, which is what normally happens on the level of theoretical discourse, unless specific considerations prompt an opposite verdict.

Whether they are listening to someone on the right, on the left, or in the center, Americans want to hear about unlimited opportunities and expanding choices, about bright futures and cheerful prospects, where they can realize their personal ambitions and indulge their personal fantasies. They do not want to be told that they need to cultivate more self-control and exercise more self-denial. If that is suitable advice for anyone, it is only for a small minority of criminals and dysfunctionals who abuse freedom and misuse liberty. For everyone else (the vast majority), the individual self is sacred—something, not to be restrained and confined, but to be nurtured, strengthened, and expanded—as the first half of the American formula proclaims. In the face of so powerful a collective conviction, the realities of the second half must remain hidden.

For decades, the national psyche suffered from the effects and counter-effects of the Great Depression. It began by shifting the balance between the two halves of the American formula so far toward the second half that by the 1950s the machinery of social regulation had become excessive and obnoxiously obvious. The 1960s erupted in reaction and moved the balance so far toward the first half that by the 1970s the disorderly behavior of liberated individuals had become excessive and obviously disruptive. This provoked a reaction in the opposite direction during the 1980s (the era of the so-called Reagan revolution), which was followed by a counterreaction in the 1990s (the era of multiculturalism and political correctness), until, by the arrival of the new century, the balance came to rest in the middle. At last, the ideological dingdong of the decades had exhausted itself: the traditional equilibrium between the two halves of the American formula had been restored, and after seventy years of discomfort and disorientation, the country could be said to have escaped from the noneconomic effects of its worst economic disaster.

The new balance appeared first and most unmistakably at the top of society. From the margins of the Democratic Party, one can still hear denunciations of corporate greed and exploitation. From the margins of the Republican Party, one can still hear calls for a return to old-fashioned sexual morality. But among affluent people in the higher ranks of both parties, a consensus has emerged. In the sphere of economics, they favor a maximum of free enterprise and a minimum of government regula-tion. They have no desire for a revival of the tax-and-spend programs of Sixties' liberalism. Democrats in particular are careful to distance themselves from their traditional opposition to the powers of finance capital. In the aftermath of a national outbreak of corporate scandal at the beginning of the Twenty-first Century, the Democratic Leadership Council (DLC) was emphatic in warning its party faithful to avoid sounding "anti-business and class warfare themes."[34]

In the sphere of personal life, sophisticated and well-to-do people, whether Republican or Democrat, are intent on retaining the freedoms won by the Sixties, though without their destructive excesses. Even abortion, as an examination of the statistics reveals, "turns out to be an indispensable part of the normal middle-American toolkit." When the other choices available are your daughter marrying some nutcase or becoming a single mother instead of going to college, no one with any sense hesitates.[35]

"Today, the culture war is over," declared David Brooks, "at least in the realm of the affluent." His book *Bobos in Paradise* (2000) presents a semi-humorous portrait of the new, upper-middle-class phenom-enon—a hybrid springing from the personal liberation of the Sixties and the economic conservatism of the Eighties—the Bobo, short for bourgeois bohemian. Such a person cannot understand why liberals and conservatives continue to argue. He has transcended their conflict. He is (it has often been remarked) on the right economically and on the left socially.[36]

He wants "low taxes," complained one right-wing journal, but also "low morals"—that is to say, low sexual morals by the standard of the Fifties. While he welcomes the new liberties, he rejects their extremes. He does not accept the naive panglossian notion of the Sixties "that maximum personal freedom will automatically produce a dynamic but basically wholesome order." He believes that social bonds and institutions are highly important and that they must be deliberately fostered and assiduously maintained.[37]

The social maladies created by the Sixties have been diminishing. Crime rates and the other indicators of national distemper have been going down. But they have not vanished or even subsided back to the levels they were at in the Fifties. This is a matter of special concern in regard to those below the age of adulthood. As one teacher of long experience observed, although schools are "about as bad" as they always have been, "the world beyond the school is [now] much harsher toward children."[38] The possibility that one's kids might "get in with the wrong crowd" has always been a parental fear. Today, with the proliferation of drugs and gangs since the Sixties and the lax discipline in schools resulting from the rights revolution begun in the Sixties, wrong crowds are far more conspicuous and behaving far worse than they used to.

Middle-class parents, especially upper-middle-class ones, have perceived this reality and have taken action accordingly. They plan and supervise what their youngsters are doing and with whom they are doing it, to such an extent that David Brooks pronounced them "probably the most supervised generation in human history."[39] Free, unstructured time has diminished perceptibly; children are no longer told simply to "go out and play." Instead, moms and dads set up elaborate schedules of activities and take care to see that their sons and daughters proceed from each one to the next on time.

All this monitoring serves the negative purpose of keeping children out of trouble. It also has the positive effect of preparing them for conditions of work in the adult world. The "color-coded charts on the refrigerator indicating where each kid has to be at each moment of the week" are the junior version of an executive's day planner, and some adolescents have actual day planners of their own.[40] The optimal product of the process, the organization kid, has already been described in the previous chapter.

—4—

During the last decades of the Twentieth Century, the demands of work have increased significantly, as was detailed in the previous chapter. They have also, as a consequence, impinged significantly on life outside work. Social activities unrelated to a person's job have been in noticeable decline; people no longer have the time to participate in them. This was the source of the widely deplored and equally widely misunderstood phenomena of "bowling alone" (as was mentioned in chapter five). Domestic chores that one used to do for one's self are being purchased from commercial firms. The "home-meal replacement market," for example, is a booming business. Some large companies provide services like auto repair and dry cleaning, so that employees can concentrate more of their energy and attention on their work. Dating agencies are available for those who are too busy to engage in the slow and laborious procedure of unassisted courtship.[41]

In such an environment, the leisure time that remains has acquired a distinct character. For the ambitious and energetic, it tends to resemble work, with all its competition and stress, as the participants in a particular sport or hobby scrutinize, evaluate, and criticize each other's performance according to its seriousness and success. But more generally and more commonly, life outside work serves as a source of relaxation, recuperation, and reward.

A comparison with certain traditional, hierarchical societies is instructive. Cultures that assign a fixed, obvious, and rigid position to each of their members often take care to provide specific occasions when these constraints can be ignored and flouted. Days of carnival and other such wild but limited festivities function as a safety valve, periodically releasing tensions and frustrations that would otherwise build up until they exploded at unpredictable moments and with damaging effect.

A somewhat similar arrangement has developed between requirements on the job and liberties outside the job. During the second half of the Twentieth Century, the world of work has been imposing more demands (more time, effort, attention, commitment, cooperation, risk). During the same period, by way of compensation, the world outside work has been bestowing more rewards (more consumer goods, more sexual liberties).

Imperceptive and moralistic critics, especially those on the right, have viewed the resulting changes in private life with alarm, as if they were evidence of social degeneration and moral corruption. It is nothing of the sort. It is only hard-working people letting off steam after hours. One criticism of contemporary society points to the "contradiction" between the disciplined norms of work and the hedonistic norms of private life.[42] The relationship would be better described, not as a contradiction, but as a complement, in which two different elements assist and reinforce each other, while at the same time functioning as a check on each other's possible excess. The more one works and earns, the more one needs to indulge oneself outside work and the more one can afford to do so. The more one indulges oneself outside work, the more one needs to work and earn, in order to pay for the expense of one's indulgence.

I leave it to some subtle philosopher who, with recondite and recherché calculations, might total up the gains and losses in the various compartments of human existence and pronounce a verdict as to whether Americans today actually possess a sum total of more, less, or the same freedom, compared with what they had in the past. The precise reality is not important; the crude perception is. Whatever changes there have been in life at work or outside work, Americans continue to believe they are a free people, the freest in the world. Once again, as ever in the past, the ideals of the first half of the formula overshadow and disguise the realities of the second half. The necessary secret remains a secret, with its beneficial self-deception continuing to go about its vital and quiet business.

In exercising their carnival options, some people at the higher levels of society superficially imitate the behavior of those at the lower levels. The man who dons a leather jacket and rides a motorcycle on weekends is a respectable banker during the rest of the week. The woman who flaunts a tattoo and dresses like a hooker off-hours is an efficient businesswoman on-hours. The adolescent who listens to music that celebrates the most depraved emotions and the vilest behavior is heading for an Ivy League education. The college student who has sex with no intention of marriage is deliberately postponing the responsibilities and distractions of a family until his or her career is safely under way.[43]

Once again, there are impulsive moralists who observe the superficial conduct and jump to the wrong conclusion—that there is rot at the top, that the vices of the underclass are infecting the rest of society. Closer attention and better understanding would calm their worries. This applies as well to the fear that the fashionable gutter modes of the affluent are sending the wrong message and providing the wrong example to the nonaffluent. It might seem likely that the unfortunate and underprivileged view the displays of apparent wildness at higher social levels, as reflected in various media of news and entertainment, and imagine that these are acceptable social norms, rather than what they actually are—a temporary release from the restraint and discipline of social norms. But most Americans, low as well as high, have never been totally deluded and led astray by the freedoms that the first half of the formula exhibits and proclaims. Although, in accord with the necessary secret, they refuse to recognize it consciously, they nevertheless perceive and obey the realities of regulatory control that the second half demands and imposes.

There is another reassuring aspect to the new arrangements. The lower-class postures of affluent people help to reinforce America's egalitarianism ethos. When the impecunious youth glimpses those above him, flaunting their wealth and indulging themselves in the context of a vulgar popular culture, he is not discouraged by unattainable elegance or repelled by incomprehensible refinements. Instead, he sees conduct that appears immediately understandable and obviously desirable, and it sends him a message of motivation and encouragement: climb up to that level and you will be able to pig out and gross out all you want.

He is deceiving himself, of course. His prospects for spectacular economic advancement and social mobility are unlikely, for reasons explained in chapter two. And even if he does succeed, the process of his ascent will have inculcated traits of moderation, prudence, and restraint that will prevent him from making the wild splurge that he dreamed of. But his personal disappointments or perplexities are of little importance; what is important is the productive effort that he has been induced to make.

Statistics suggest that this is in fact the way in which the lower classes have been responding. Rates of violent crime have been going down, and so have other indicators of social dysfunction (such as illegitimate births, welfare dependency, and drug abuse), whose rise in previous decades had been the source of so much anxiety and lamentation. It would appear that most Americans of whatever background understand that if they wish to enjoy the pleasures of a materially abundant and sexually indulgent culture, they first need to possess sufficient self-control to hold a job and earn an adequate income. The lesson of Benjamin Franklin's "Way to Wealth" is as valid today as it always was: the requirements of work are primary and must be satisfied first; only then is it safe to gratify one's appetites outside work.

Of course, there are always those, especially at the lower levels of society, who try to make a quick grab at the carrot, and for them there is the stick. America has always condemned and, whenever possible, punished those who try to cheat the system by taking the fruits of productivity without being productive themselves. Over the past decades, the penalties have become harsher. For many years, public-spirited and high-minded people were in the habit of telling each other that crime could only be prevented by first curing its "root causes"—that is, by eliminating general social ills like poverty and unemployment. During the Nineties, this notion lost currency, and it was replaced by the conviction that the best way to prevent crime is to punish it, especially in its initially minor manifestations, as the new "broken windows" theory of criminal motivation and appropriate countermeasures has stipulated.

And it worked. At least the general public has concluded that it worked, since rates of crime have been going down as rates of incarceration have been going up. Putting an ever larger number of criminals away for ever longer periods of time—accompanied by an execution every now and then—sends in louder and harsher language the same message as did the expulsion of the able-bodied from the welfare rolls: get ahold of yourselves and become responsible, productive citizens—or else.

KEEPING THE FORMULA IN BALANCE: MODERNITY'S CHALLENGE FROM THE LEFT

CHAPTER NINE

The Growth of Higher Ideals (Remedial and Transcendent)

—1—

I n analyzing the conflict between the ideals and the realities associated with the American formula, the previous two chapters have
emphasized realities—how they have changed and how they have consequently affected ideals and the behavior of those who believe in them.
The present chapter and the following one will focus on ideals—the
ways in which they too have changed and the social transformations
that have occurred as a result. At the outset, in this first section of the
chapter, the perspective of the discussion will expand, as it proceeds to
explain the development of idealism and its encounter with reality in
the larger context of modernization in the Western world. Once this
has been accomplished, the investigation will return to the realm of
specifically American phenomena.

In 1675, Madame de Sévigné, aristocrat and lady of fashion, whose
letters would become a classic of French literature, expressed her amused
contempt at the miseries of some lower-class people who were being
driven from their homes, tortured, and executed. When Alexis de
Tocqueville, also an aristocrat, quoted her remarks in the second volume
of his *Democracy in America* (1840), he hastened to assure his readers

that Madame de Sévigné was actually a woman of tender sentiments and sympathetic feelings and that she "treated her own vassals and servants with kindness and indulgence." But, like her contemporaries in general, she could not help viewing those who occupied an inferior level of society as an inferior form of the human species. Tocqueville further asserted that no one in the present age would dare to speak of the common people as she had done. Even if an individual's callousness and brutality prompted him to do so, the prevailing attitudes of the time would forbid it.[1]

Between Sévigné and Tocqueville, the Eighteenth Century had intervened. During its years a profound change occurred in the sensibilities of the Western world. At the outset, elites viewed the masses with traditional and customary indifference and disdain. But gradually a new conviction took hold and began to spread. It became the fashion for persons of idealistic temperament and liberal views to assert that ordinary people possessed admirable qualities and large potential, which only the unfortunate circumstances of birth prevented from achieving full and remarkable expression. Many a "mute inglorious Milton" or a Cromwell unknown to fame must lie in the humble cemeteries throughout the land, John Gray mused in his highly popular "Elegy Written in a Country Churchyard" (1751).

Along with these new panglossian ideas about the universality and excellence of human nature came related ideas about society and government. During the Eighteenth Century, an increasing number of articulate and influential voices called with increasing urgency for new institutions that would promote the abilities of individuals at the same time as they advanced the common good of the entire body of citizens. In place of a society where the high positions and honors of life were the prerogative of the hereditary few, there should be a society that employed talent of all origins and encouraged participation from all quarters. Instead of a government whose legitimacy rested on genealogical succession, there should be a government whose right to rule derived from the consent of the entire population and whose tenure in office depended on its promotion of their general welfare.

Such was the tenor of idealism and imagination during that age. At the same time, in the world of mundane economics and politics, developments were taking place that tended in a similar direction. By the end of the Eighteenth Century, they began to reveal themselves in tangible facts and obvious conditions that would translate the higher valuation of ordinary people from a philosopher's dream into a practical demand. In the coming century, every successful actor in public life, including self-seeking politicians and cynically calculating heads of state, would have to recognize the importance of the formerly despised and neglected masses.

This adamantine feature of the emerging modern age appeared in spectacular form during the French Revolution. In the midst of all the fustian, cant, and gas about the realization of "the fairest aspirations of the human mind" and the "very heaven" of being young at that hour, a new hard reality was making itself known.[2] When revolutionary France launched its armies into the field, they presented striking and undeniable evidence of the power and dynamism of a nation animated by the egalitarian spirit. In the past, war had involved only limited numbers of the population, with mercenaries and vassals filling the ranks. Now, in a France where "liberty, equality, and fraternity" were proclaimed, war called forth the full effort of an entire people. The *levée en masse* of 1793 designated all able-bodied men as liable for service, and everyone not actually enlisted was expected to support the troops both morally and materially. Even the most hidebound and unsympathetic conservatives of Europe could not help perceiving the superiority of this new military machine. Other countries realized they would have to contrive something similar or be at a lethal disadvantage.[3]

Warfare was not the only task in which a nation entering modernity induced its people to take a larger and more energetic part. By the early Nineteenth Century, they had become similarly engaged in a range of useful and practical activities. This was not an option but a necessity. The new and growing industrialized economy demanded ever larger amounts of collective participation, social cooperation, and personal attention. Managing a railroad, for example, was far more arduous and exacting a task than managing a farm, and the penalties for apathy and error were far more grievous.

Reform movements of the Nineteenth Century reflected the new demands. They proclaimed the dual objective of bettering the lives of the low and unfortunate and at the same time improving the moral health and material strength of the nation. Temperance was one of the most prominent and popular of the reformist causes. In earlier times, respectable and responsible persons could view the intoxicated behavior of the lower classes with indulgence and indifference. This was no longer possible. "A drunken field hand was one thing, a drunken railroad brakeman quite another."[4]

The result of these developments was a tremendous and triumphant advance in material progress, which has often been described and applauded, not least by Marx and Engels in their *Communist Manifesto* of 1848: the middle class with its science, its industries, and its finance capital was destroying the stagnant traditions of aristocrats and peasants; shrinking the distances of the globe, abolishing provincialism, and imposing its ways upon the peoples of the world; clearing entire continents for cultivation and conjuring whole populations out of the ground; bending nature to its will and raising monuments greater than those of any previous civilization.

The superiority of modern societies is apparent even in their worst behavior. The body count accumulated by wars and mass executions during the first half of the Twentieth Century no doubt dwarfs any atrocities committed during previous ages. This is evidence, not of greater viciousness, but of greater thoroughness and efficiency. Nazis and Communists could not have hated their victims more than did the religious fanatics of earlier times. The latter perpetrated less slaughter only because they were less organized and disciplined. Their actions were like those of a mob, with its spontaneous, haphazard behavior. In contrast, whenever a modern regime undertakes something, whether for good or for evil, it carries out its work with the unflagging pace, undeviating attention, and unvarying consistency of a machine.

The accomplishments of the Western world in the Nineteenth and Twentieth Centuries have been the result of continually increasing efforts by ever larger numbers of people. To inspire and sustain this rising level of participation has been one of the chief tasks, if not the chief task, of modern society. It was assisted by—and it may have even prompted—the rise of nationalisms and their creation of traditions, symbols, and fetishes. It was a major and incessant preoccupation of the three new forms of government (democracy, socialism, and fascism) that have emerged during the past two centuries, as it had never been for older forms of government, like monarchy and aristocracy.

The tremendous collective exertions of modern national economies did not occur without great conflict and controversy. In return for their new and increasing contributions of disciplined labor, the masses demanded new and additional compensation, which social elites did not willingly grant. During the early years of industrialization, the question of what constituted fair and appropriate remuneration for its workers was already a matter of dispute. As industrial economies grew, this issue grew with them. People on the lower levels of society laid claim to a larger share of social advantages, political power, and economic prosperity; those on the upper levels resisted their claims.

The cause of the masses attracted sympathy and support from outside their own numbers. Sensitive and high-minded individuals were appalled at the living conditions of the poor and blamed them on the indifference, arrogance, and greed of the rich and powerful. The tone of their complaints was no longer the subdued sadness of Gray's elegy but the ferocious indignation of Edwin Markham's "Man with the Hoe" (1899). In the reform movements and radical politics that began in the Nineteenth Century and have continued, with fluctuating size and strength, up to the present day, inarticulate and unsophisticated workers have seldom lacked eloquent allies and cultured advocates from more privileged backgrounds.

"Remedial idealism" is the term that may be used to designate the entire cause carried on in behalf of the underprivileged and disadvantaged, in all its various forms and directions. Its common theme is the plight of those who have not received a sufficient and just portion of the benefits that they have helped to create by participating in the modern economy. It argues that these unfortunate and exploited people should receive more—better wages, better working conditions, better housing, better health care, better education, et cetera.

The thrust of remedial idealism is very familiar. It is reflected in the opinion pieces of today's more high-toned magazines and newspapers. And it has been repeated for over two hundred years. But it has never been enough, for the same reason that the very world it seeks to reform has itself never been able to find adequate justification for the productive tasks it imposes. Near the end of chapter two, I mentioned the actual benefits of American life and noted that they do not, by themselves alone, provide motivation sufficiently strong enough to inspire the effort that is necessary to produce them. This unbalanced equation between social reality and human desire, as I have called it, is a fundamental condition, not just of one country, but of modern existence in general.

Despite all the obvious advantages that industrial society and its successor technological society have created, and all the benefits they have bestowed, they always lacked a certain degree of fundamental legitimacy and basic attractiveness. Even after the middle class had managed to oust the aristocracy from its position of social leadership, they and their occupations continued to arouse contempt from both left and right for their ignobility and vulgarity.[5] However useful and important their work has been, they have never escaped the taint of the dreary, the mundane, and the low.

From the beginning, the very word bourgeois received a pejorative coloring that it still retains. Commerce, declared a character in one Victorian novel, "is very necessary, and may, possibly, be very good; but it cannot be the noblest work of man...."[6] In earlier times, works of art immortalized the ideals of aristocratic and religious cultures. In modern times, high art has held itself aloof from the norms of society or made outright attacks against them. No masterpiece ever celebrated the businessman, the industrialist, or the technician.

This profound deficiency of modern life would remain, no matter how fairly its rewards were distributed among all its various groups and classes, no matter how much opportunity for personal advancement were extended to people of low origin. Attaining only the goals of remedial idealism would result in just more of the same—more middle-class people and middle-class occupations. "The entire dream of democracy is to lift the proletariat up to the bourgeoisie's level of stupidity," growled Gustave Flaubert, the supreme master of realism in French literature.[7]

Even as early as the Eighteenth Century, idealists realized that something more was needed. They were not satisfied with the idea of lowborn people having a better life and being able to develop their personal talents. That was supposed to be only one part of a much larger agenda. Again and again, in moments of enthusiasm, writers and orators called for a general transformation and elevation of the entire society, which would take place as everyone, of every station in life, threw off the crippling restraints imposed by the past—traditional customs and inveterate superstitions, artificial structures and hereditary authorities—and realized their full and natural potential.

This hope for a marvelous flowering of human achievement and virtue may be called "transcendent idealism," since it accepts but goes beyond remedial idealism. Like other high-minded notions of the Eighteenth Century, it became part of the ideological bedrock of the new American nation, where it acquired an especially bold and radical form—the idea, not merely of a natural aristocracy for the talented few, but of a mass elite that would include everyone. It was the vision of a world filled, not merely with useful citizens, obeying the demands of a materially productive society, but with people realizing their most fanciful personal dreams and, at the same time, attaining the highest capacity of human beings. This was what Thomas Jefferson had in mind when he imagined a direction of progress, induced by "our democratic stimulants," that would result in "every man" becoming "potentially an athlete in body and an Aristotle in mind."[8] Ralph Waldo Emerson assumed the role of philosophical champion for this visionary future, and Walt Whitman emerged as its poet laureate.

On the European side of the Atlantic, where traditional hierarchies and oligarchies were stronger and more numerous, remedial idealism faced greater opposition and accordingly required more attention and effort. As a consequence, transcendent idealism was less emphatically and confidently proclaimed. But it has always been present, even in the most discouraging moments and circumstances. *The Communist Manifesto* urged the "workers of the world" to throw off their chains, but it also called for a society in which "the free development of each is the condition for the free development of all"—a sentiment that could just as well have been uttered by Marx's contemporary, Emerson.

Whenever the battalions of the left have unfurled their banners and sounded their trumpets, the themes of both remedial and transcendent idealism have been heard. After the workers of the world had risen up and seized the power and wealth that were legitimately theirs, they were not supposed to stop at this point but to proceed forward and lead the entire population on to the creation of utopia and the development of "the new man." The achievement of the latter, in the opinion of that prominent if unfortunate Communist revolutionary Leon Trotsky, would result in "the average human" becoming "immeasurably stronger" and rising to "the heights of an Aristotle."[9]

There is an intimate and naturally symbiotic relationship between the remedial and the transcendent aspects of modern idealism. Remedial idealism is the more tangible and immediately powerful of the two. It provides most of the specific complaints and objectives of practical programs. Its battle cries resonate with the urgency and force of the actual, rallying supporters and intimidating opponents. Without remedial idealism, transcendent idealism would seem vague and dubious, containing little more than unconvincing arguments and unreal dreams.

Transcendent idealism, on the other hand, gives larger meaning to the issues raised by remedial idealism. It imbues them with glamour and loftiness. It supercharges the energy and conviction of their advocates, who believe they are fighting, not merely for the relief or rights of some limited group, but for the advancement and elevation of all humanity, themselves included. Without transcendent idealism, remedial idealism would seem low, petty, and mundane. Since by itself remedial idealism promises nothing more than better remuneration for the exploited and better opportunities for the disadvantaged, its ultimate result would simply be a larger supply of willing and able workers for the modern economy. The task of turning demoralized drudges and marginalized indigents into motivated employees and professionalized technicians is unquestionably a necessary one in a society with an ever-increasing demand for efficient productivity. But who can get excited about it, any more than Flaubert could become enthusiastic about the prospect of proletarians becoming bourgeois?

In practical operations, the remedial and the transcendent usually reinforce each other, often blend with one another, and are inevitably found together. But however strong their mutual need may be, their association is by no means simple and harmonious, for in certain crucial ways they are not genuinely compatible and congruous. By itself, remedial idealism would be able to reach an accommodation with the realities of the modern world. Remedial idealism's ultimate goal of the disadvantaged becoming fully participating members of society, of their contributing to productivity as well as sharing in the rewards, is something even opponents are able to accept, at least as an abstract principle. Disagreement arises over the specifics: what are the appropriate and practical means for achieving a suitable remedy, what precisely is either side supposed to give and receive? But in such controversies, negotiation and compromise are possible.

That is not the case with transcendent idealism. It does not want to strike a better deal with present realities but to transform them. It does not want simply to gain something more for disadvantaged people but to create something entirely different and better for everyone. It would not be satisfied to see the poor become busy, prosperous employees in the workplaces of the modern economy; it wants them and everyone else to become a mass elite of independent men and women, all of them realizing their splendid inner potential, as Emerson preached and Whitman sang.

Those who do not share this vision find it chimerical. But transcendent idealism is seldom so foolish as to arouse vehement criticism from the unsympathetic by appearing alone and making an open proclamation of its visionary hopes. Instead, it seeks the company of its more prosaic and acceptable ally, remedial idealism, and prudently keeps in the background when the two present themselves in public. The advertised priorities of an idealistic agenda are inevitably its immediate and specific remedial measures. The vaguer and larger transcendent developments are something that will come later. First, the workers need to escape poverty, or racial discrimination must cease. A utopian dictatorship of the proletariat or a harmonious integrated society will follow afterwards, sometime in the unspecified future.

The presence of these two elements, remedial and transcendent, in a single party, movement, or person, can result in behavior that appears confusing and contradictory. But this is a basic characteristic of modern idealism, and its often puzzling manifestations can only be understood by perceiving its dual nature, which the present and the following chapter will attempt to demonstrate and analyze.

As an initial example of the phenomenon, one may consider the striking dichotomy in leftist attitudes toward the people at the bottom of society on the one hand and toward those at the level above the bottom but below the middle class on the other. The former receive nothing but praise and sympathy; their faults are disregarded or excused. They are seen as innocent victims who are heroically struggling against deprivations and prejudices that the rest of society has heaped upon them. As such, they are assumed to deserve the humane attention and assistance of every decent person.

Those just above the bottom but below the middle class receive a diametrically opposite evaluation. They are dismissed as ignorant and vulgar, animated by blind fears and vile intolerance—people who rigidly adhere to a code of petty proprieties, who reject higher principles and think of nothing but guarding what little they have from the supposed threat of the ones beneath them, who have even less.[10]

Considered from the perspective of remedial idealism alone, the left's judgment of the people at the bottom is too favorable and its judgment of the people on the next level up is too negative. Bad qualities and unattractive behavior are hardly more abundant among the latter group than they are among the former. If anything, the reverse is true. As for misfortune and exploitation, a good amount of that exists at both these levels, yet the champions of humanity recognize and respond to it only at the lower one.

The explanation for this apparent inconsistency of mind and definite contradiction in fact is transcendent idealism. Although remedial idealism could find victims worthy of its attention and assistance in every stratum beneath the middle class, it is overruled by transcendent idealism, which realizes that only at the lowest depths are people alienated and destitute enough possibly to favor the idea of fundamental change. Only here are the promises and norms of middle-class life sufficiently weak and remote that the inhabitants, with proper instruction and leadership, might be capable of supporting a radical movement that would bring about a transformation of society.

This hope vanishes the moment one passes from the bottom to the next level up. Here people cling to their limited possessions and narrow respectability with fearful tenacity, condemning and shunning those underneath them in an effort to assert a fragile superiority. They would never make common cause with their proletarian inferiors to oppose the bourgeoisie or work to found a classless society, but they might join a fascist organization if they felt sufficiently threatened and insecure. The idealistic left turns away from such persons with automatic and utter revulsion, with a loathing so profound, consistent, and intense that (in the words of one journalist with international experience), "It sometimes seems" to be "the only thing which unites Marxists the world over...."[11]

—2—

In America, the two aspects of modern idealism have developed in a distinctively indigenous way. Remedial idealism evolved from the ideology of individualism. Like all other Americans, reformers on the left begin by declaring that every person should have the opportunity to rise to a level worthy of his talent and effort. They then proceed to point out that some people have had much less than their fair share of opportunity—specifically the members of certain groups whom society has discriminated against, exploited, or otherwise placed in a disadvantageous position. Clear evidence of their victimization is the fact that they have attained less of the world's goods than would be their proportional lot according to their numbers. Society, the remedial idealists conclude, should end its unfair treatment of such people and should give them special assistance, so that their acquisition of wealth, power, and prestige will correspond to their percentage of the population.

The American version of transcendent idealism has likewise risen from native foundations. It is based on panglossian principles and proclaims an Emersonian mass elite. It goes beyond the remedial ideal of genuine equal opportunity and its putative natural outcome, a fair distribution of the goods of the world. Instead, it calls for absolute equality. In its view, all inequalities, whether proportional to the size of participating groups or not, are artificial, unjust, and deleterious. Every person contains within himself splendid talents and potential. If the structures of society could be altered to allow these to develop fully and freely, there would be no failure or inferiority, no one would be destitute or despised, all would be prosperous and respected. Instead of individualistic rivalry and suspicion, mutual trust and a harmonious community of equals would prevail. Instead of a shabby commercial culture of exploiters and scam artists, there would be a magnificent growth of human achievement and a stupendous elevation of the human spirit.

Together these two, remedial and transcendent, may be designated under a collective name: America's higher idealism. As a program for practical life and politics, it has not had an easy time. From the very beginning, its remedial notions ran into opposition from the self-deceptions of the American formula. As was explained in chapter two, programs for redistributing wealth, like socialism, have made little headway against the adamant popular belief in economic individualism. Ordinary Americans, including those of humble origins, have persisted in rejecting, rather than taking up as their own, the grievances of leftist preaching. Its condemnation of social inequalities leaves them unmoved. Since they are convinced that every person can improve his material condition by his own efforts, they conclude that anyone who remains in a low and unsatisfactory situation has no one to blame but himself.

Transcendent ideas have enjoyed even less popular appeal than remedial ones. While Americans accept the concept of an equality of opportunities as a desirable goal, the notion of an equality of results (all winners, no losers) arouses their utter skepticism. They think competition is a natural, practical, and admirable activity. They see it as separating out the good from the bad, the ambitious from the lazy, the efficient from the inefficient—and they have little sympathy for anyone who falls into the latter categories of these pairs. The idea of a society of economic equals strikes them as absurdly unreal. So does the rest of the agenda of transcendent idealism. They want a house in an attractive suburb, not some vaporous fantasies of a harmonious community. They want more consumer goods, not an elevation of the human spirit.

As a consequence of the peculiarly American configurations of social class and personal conviction, it has taken higher idealism, in both its remedial and its transcendent forms, a long time to gather strength and become a significant force and factor in national life. During the early years of the republic, a small number of individuals worried about the condition of certain unfortunate groups (such as Indians and Negroes) and deplored the narrow, materialistic attitudes of their fellow countrymen. Such scruples were overwhelmed by the demands and preoccupations of the majority, who wanted nothing more than to seize the opportunities present in a new and thriving land and to increase both its prosperity and their own. But gradually, as the level of national affluence continued to rise, and more and more people came to enjoy security and comfort, an increasing number of them became dissatisfied with merely accumulating more money and more luxuries. They began to adopt wider perspectives, to cultivate loftier tastes, and to pursue more high-minded interests.

This tendency first became noticeable as a collective phenomenon in the late Nineteenth Century. Some young people from privileged backgrounds, like Jane Addams, discovered in remedial idealism an inspiring cause, and they dedicated themselves to improving the condition of the poor and disadvantaged. But their motivation consisted of something more than altruism; it included a distinct and unmistakable ingredient of transcendent desire. They saw the objects of their charity as possessing a special attractiveness, as having qualities that made them more admirable even than those who stood above them and patronized or despised them. In the words of one social worker, writing in 1902, "More and more I feel how much we have to learn from these people whom too often we are expected to teach. They are braver, simpler, better than we are; more generous, more helpful...."[12]

After experiencing a spurt of growth during the Progressive Era, the impulses of higher idealism were curbed by a contrary national mood in the years of World War I and the subsequent prosperity of the 1920s. During that decade, the public was obsessed with making money and spending it. Then came the Great Depression of the 1930s, and for idealists a glorious opportunity seemed to have suddenly and unexpectedly arrived. Economic distress created a mass of angry unemployed workers, who appeared ready to form a genuinely radical movement. The nation itself acted as if it were ripe for fundamental change, with pundits and leaders calling for bold new social experiments. These were the circumstances behind a contemporary's observation that the "fundamentally benevolent and humane" intellectuals of America "loved their fellow countrymen in distress far more than they could ever love them in prosperity."[13]

Encouragement for higher idealism arrived from abroad as well, specifically from the new revolutionary regime of the Soviet Union. In future years, the question would often be asked how otherwise intelligent and sophisticated people in the Western world could have been attracted to this brutal regime, how they could have accepted its flimsy lies and ignored the blatant oppression that it was inflicting on its own people. This remains a puzzle as long as one considers the subject only from a perspective of remedial idealism. If Western observers had viewed Russian Communism as nothing more than the attempt of a remote and downtrodden country to put an end to deprivation and tyranny and to establish fairer economic and social arrangements, they would have had no difficulty recognizing that it was a laudable effort that had gone unfortunately astray.

But Communism represented something much more. To the idealists of the West it promised the fulfillment of their transcendent desires—a society that appeared to be heading toward the realization of "the highest possibilities of human life," in the words of one literary witness and participant. Confronted with such a prospect, many ordinarily skeptical people surrendered their critical faculties, even as far as to compromise on their standards of remedial idealism—or at least on its immediate application. They dismissed out of hand the reported violations of human rights and human dignity as fabrications or exaggerations or, at the very worst, temporary measures required by exigencies of the times and circumstances. It would all come right in the end, they reassured themselves. Meanwhile, anyone who condemned this utopia in progress was scorned as being "deficient in goodwill"—that is, callously indifferent to the aspirations of mankind. In the words of two slogans that were frequently repeated during the 1930s, a Communist was nothing more than a democrat (or a liberal) in a hurry, and Communism itself was simply twentieth-century Americanism.[14]

———

All these expectations turned out to be illusions. After the end of the Second World War and with the onset of the Cold War, they collapsed. The New Deal had instituted some measures of reform, but American society had not altered fundamentally. The Soviet Union had ceased to be the greatest hope of the future and had become instead the greatest threat of the present, the archenemy of human freedom rather than the realization of human dreams. Its social achievements were exposed as hallucinations and fabrications, whereas its atrocities—which apologists had denied with brazen falsehoods or palliated with inexhaustibly ingenious sophistries—turned out to be all too real.

Most distressing of all was the behavior of America's putatively revolutionary proletariat. During the Great Depression, liberals and radicals had celebrated the "moral superiority" of "the masses" and had proclaimed them to be the source of national salvation. But "the workers" had not risen to the occasion, and now, in the midst of the Cold War, they actually applauded as their former adulators were called dupes and traitors by zealots and demagogues of the right, like Joe McCarthy. Lower-class Catholics and lower-class Protestants, once the bitterest of enemies, joined together in a common effort to revile the exponents of 1930s idealism—the radicals and their liberal sympathizers—who, by the 1950s, had become "a generation on trial." "There is one thing that the American people know about Senator McCarthy," declared a commentator in a notorious summary of the new political climate: "He, like them, is unequivocally anti-Communist. About the spokesmen for American liberalism, they feel they know no such thing. And with some justification."[15]

If the working class failed to respond to the preaching and proselytizing of leftist spokesmen and ideologues during the miseries of the Depression, it was all the less inclined to do so during the rise of prosperity after World War II. This continued to be the case even when the political mood changed in the 1960s, and young people from the New Left went into the factories with the intention of "raising the consciousness" of the workers. Their efforts were pathetic—a parody of 1930s intellectuals trying to radicalize and lead the masses—and the results were nil or negative. Blue-collar employees wanted nothing to do with these middle-class college kids who were pretending to be proletarians and playing a game they called revolution.

Outside the United States, left-wing causes have enjoyed more popularity. Large numbers of lower-class people accepted transcendent ideals because they responded to the preaching of remedial grievances. They agreed when they were told that they were exploited and oppressed, and in the course of joining a struggle to improve their material and political situation, they naturally adopted the movement's utopian pronouncements, no matter how remote and incomprehensible such language and ideas may have seemed to their unsophisticated imaginations. After all, the fantastical promises of religion have a similar appeal for such people.

The situation has been different in America. Here the dominance of the ideal of individualism, specifically economic individualism, assisted by an ethos of egalitarianism, has inoculated the lower classes against the doctrines of the left. In addition, material progress has played an unkind trick on the development of higher idealism by simultaneously affecting the opposite ends of the social scale in different ways. Through the course of the Twentieth Century, at the more affluent levels, an increasing number of people have felt secure and free enough to be sympathetic to the remedial needs of the less fortunate as well as to indulge their own restless longings for some transcendent purpose. But during the same time, at the less affluent levels, a decreasing number of people have felt deprived and disaffected enough to follow the leadership of their idealistically discontented superiors—or even to give the appearance of being ready to do so.

As a result of these contradictory tendencies, there has been an increasing scarcity of individuals with genuine lower-class credentials in the ranks of American left-wing organizations and among their supporters. During the search for Communists in the 1950s, the suspects and their defenders turned out to be of noticeably higher social standing than those who pursued them or applauded the hunt, much to the puzzlement and indignation of the anti-Communists. In the 1960s, it was students from affluent families who joined the New Left, and the more prestigious campuses that were disrupted. This tendency has continued to the present day. Recent studies have found that whereas Europeans in general are worried and unhappy about social inequality, in the United States the only people that it bothers are "a sub-group of rich leftists."[16]

Ever since the Sixties, liberals and radicals have occasionally put forward the idea of creating an alliance and joining forces with the entire sector of the population located below the middle class. After all, its members can still be said to stand in need of a certain amount of remedial justice. Their wages have often not kept pace with the growing economy. Their trades are threatened with obsolescence, and their jobs are threatened with outsourcing to cheaper labor abroad.

But this strategy never comes to anything. Most workers—specifically, white lower-class people—are simply not destitute and alienated enough to inspire the compassion of remedial idealism or the dreams of transcendent idealism. They have become too much a part of the system of national productivity. They have attained too much prosperity and have acquired, along with it, too many middle-class attitudes. They do not want to go beyond the norms of respectability and the products of a low materialistic culture. The former seem unquestionably right and salutary to them, and they only want more of the latter. Leftists who condemn both arouse their incomprehension and hostility.

It is not just that the workers have rejected the left; the left itself has given up on the workers. The image of the heroic and noble proletarian in the 1930s seems as remote from present-day reality as an ice-age hunter of woolly mammoths. By the second half of the Twentieth Century, only the most besotted ideologue or dreamy idealist could think of blue-collar employees as potential revolutionaries at the bottom of society, since most of them were ensconced at that repugnant level well above the bottom if still below the middle class.

During the 1950s, study after study, sponsored by prestigious institutions and conducted by respected social scientists, proclaimed that inhabitants of this odious social stratum were averse to the higher ideals of American egalitarianism, that they harbored paranoid fantasies and exhibited authoritarian behavior. Since the 1960s, cartoonists in the more upscale and trendy publications have exhibited these same people in vilifying caricature. They appear as fat, ugly, badly dressed slobs and brutes, carrying misspelled signs and exhibiting the trashy emblems of debased popular culture. These images reflect an accepted stereotype.

Among high-minded members of the middle class—especially those tending toward upper-middle-class status—lower-class white people have come to be viewed as little more than a psychological junkyard for obsolete ideas, pernicious prejudices, and repulsive attitudes.[17]

—3—

Having lost the masses, the devotees of higher idealism needed to find other recipients for their remedial compassion and other allies in their transcendent quest. And they found them, by elevating a formerly secondary category of concern (persecuted or otherwise disadvantaged minorities) to the rank of principal importance. The criteria for inclusion were rough and loose: any victims of discrimination based on a hereditary or at least an involuntary condition. The result was a wide and disparate variety of groups, ranging from blacks and Hispanics to homosexuals and the handicapped, and including what is in fact a majority—women (hence the often parodied left-wing tag line in news stories: "women and minorities hardest hit"). Since the amount of each group's past suffering and present disadvantage determined its position in the hierarchy of grievance and attention, black people held the pride of place.

Around this new orientation, a number of convictions formed and soon achieved the status of an accepted orthodoxy. First, minorities were assumed to be free from any responsibility for their own unfortunate situation. To claim that they acted in ways that were antisocial and self-defeating was to "blame the victim." On the contrary, blacks in particular were said to display admirable qualities, specifically "resourcefulness" and "resilience," in coping with hostile treatment from the rest of society.

Second, whatever bad behavior minorities did exhibit was viewed as a rational and understandable response to the conditions that had been imposed upon them. The bigoted majority had gotten things precisely wrong and upside down. Minority crime, violence, drug addiction, or any other nasty conduct one might name did not cause poverty and justify prejudice; on the contrary, poverty and prejudice had themselves produced the nasty conduct.

From these premises arose certain conclusions. To persist in the old strategy of telling the poor that they should acquire better habits of living was not merely outrageously unfair, it was ineffective and futile. Society, not its minorities, needed to change. It needed to end discrimination against them, and it needed to improve their material situation. This would eliminate the "root causes" of poverty and its attendant maladies.

Idealistic activists translated these conclusions into practical measures. Public welfare programs changed in character from a reluctant charity to a means for distributing extra income to the poor, with case workers now endeavoring to hand out as much as they could to as many as possible. Formerly, for the able-bodied, welfare had been a shame, a mark of irresponsibility and incompetence. Now, it was proclaimed a right, a just if inadequate compensation to minorities for society's mistreatment of them.

An iron logic and a rigid procedure developed for identifying discrimination and imposing rectification. One first determined the percentage of a particular minority in a certain school, neighborhood, or business. Next, one compared the figure to the percentage of that minority in the population at large. If the former was smaller than the latter, then bias and intolerance by the majority were automatically assumed to be the cause of the discrepancy, and action needed to be taken to increase the numbers of the minority. The specific means for doing so ranged from the compulsory busing of schoolchildren to the imposition of hiring and promotion preferences (called euphemistically and inaccurately "affirmative action").

From the very beginning, this way of thinking and its practical agenda aroused much opposition. But the activists working in behalf of minorities had the advantage of idealistically higher ground. They held the Emersonian and panglossian premise that members of minority groups, like all human beings, started life with innate virtues and potential equal to that of the rest of mankind. Consequently, they should have achieved their statistical share of the good things in life. Since they had not, the fault must lie with external forces, that is, with conditions created by the majority. Society had thus done the damage; it was therefore society's responsibility to repair it, even if this meant, not only stopping discrimination and guaranteeing civil rights, but also giving preferential treatment to groups that it had neglected and abused.

To counter this position, opponents resorted to the principles of economic individualism: the right means for improving the situation of any group had been and should be the industrious efforts of its individual members, not the favors they might receive collectively from the rest of society. This was the way in which initially disadvantaged and despised immigrants (such as those from Ireland, Italy, and Eastern Europe) had improved their lot. Even when they benefited from collective and mutual action, it was a result of their own initiative and organization. The Tammany Irish, for example, did not receive their government jobs as a result of the sympathy and guilt of a white Anglo-Saxon Protestant elite.

These arguments were logical and accurate, but they had the disadvantage of appealing to a lower ideal, specifically that of self-help and self-interest, even if it was enlightened self-interest. Aside from inspiring a small if vocal group of ideological libertarians, economic individualism (like the concept of the free market, which it underlies) tends to receive its support and defense from those who have benefited materially from it or hope to do so. This is, in fact, its most potent ingredient, and it has always been so, ever since immigrants began arriving in the New World with the intention of bettering their condition. In the past, economic individualism was the undisputed, ruling ideology of the American people. But, as explained above, the steady rise in the level of national affluence gradually undermined its dominance. As people satisfied their immediate and primary needs for material security and comfort, their allegiance to a doctrine of self-interest relaxed, and they became susceptible to the call of higher ideals.

The eventual result was an alteration in the country's moral sensibility, which can be seen in a comparison between two American presidents. Both Abraham Lincoln (b. 1809) and Bill Clinton (b. 1946) often spoke to audiences about the disadvantages they personally had encountered early in life, but each interpreted his experiences in a different way, and the contrast illustrates the distance between what was once the popularly accepted stance and what it is now. Lincoln declared that his success in overcoming difficulties was proof other persons of low origin could do likewise and encouragement for them to make the effort. Clinton declared that his own misfortunes enabled him to understand the misfortunes of others, that he could "feel your pain," and that this sympathy would prompt him to promote governmental policies for the relief of pain and suffering and for assistance to the disadvantaged, so that they could enjoy a better life.

Personal exhibitions of misfortune in the manner of Bill Clinton have become a standard performance and a customary posture in the political arena. At electoral conventions, particularly Democratic ones, the candidates' recollection of past personal agonies are now a familiar and expected ritual. If a politician cannot claim fellow feeling as the result of his own agony, he can compensate by making especially emphatic protestations of allegiance to the disinterested altruism and noble magnanimity of higher idealism in its remedial form.

Faced with such confident self-righteousness, even the most stalwart advocates of self-reliant economic individualism feel intimidated and on the defensive. Whenever politicians on the left have stigmatized their opponents as being selfish and callous, as not caring about unfortunate and mistreated minorities, as lacking "compassion" (a popular buzzword in political rhetoric since the 1970s at least), politicians on the right have scurried about, at times clumsily and unconvincingly, to escape or refute the accusation. It continues to spook them, as was seen, for example, in President Bush, Jr.'s prominent and persistent efforts to advertise himself as a "compassionate conservative."

So incessant was the parade of victims and grievances and so continuous were the demands to show sympathy and profess responsibility that eventually a complaint of "compassion fatigue" was heard. As one listened to public radio or network news, it almost seemed as if the prediction made over two centuries ago was in the process of coming true: the cause of humanity would triumph and the entire world would become one enormous hospital in which everyone would act as each other's compassionate nurse.[18]

In addition to their moral edge, the advocates of higher idealism enjoyed an advantage as a result of their superior social position. They had the time, the money, the confidence, and the knowledge, not merely to utilize the obvious tools of political action, but, far more important, to influence powerful agencies and personnel that lay behind the scenes and beyond reach of the ordinary democratic process. Since they realized that it would be very difficult to induce the majority to accept their agenda in behalf of minorities, they abated their efforts in the laborious and often frustrating tasks of popular politics (proposing initiatives and referenda, passing legislation, putting forward candidates for election). Instead, they bypassed adverse public opinion and secured the institution and enforcement of their programs by the decisions of unelected judges in the law courts, of remote bureaucrats in government regulatory agencies, and of high executives in foundations and corporations. These were "deceptively easy victories," one activist later admitted. There was "remarkably little public discussion"; policies in favor of minorities were simply imposed from above. But the success came at the price of widespread and "enduring resentment" among the majority, whose interests had been ignored and whose feelings had been scorned.[19]

The resentment was all the more intense thanks to the personal behavior of the idealists, who were themselves usually able to avoid the unpleasant consequences of the measures they had devised, championed, and implemented. When members of minorities were hired or promoted instead of more qualified nonminority candidates, the jobs tended to be in nonprofessional occupations or at levels safely below their own. When prestigious colleges and universities accepted the children of minorities instead of the more qualified children of nonminorities, their own children were often protected by alumni preferences. When city schools and neighborhoods were integrated by means of busing and low-income housing, they remained safe in their suburban homes and communities. On those rare occasions when the changes threatened to touch their own schools and neighborhoods, they either redeployed their lobbying skills and repelled the menace, or relocated to more secure localities. Occasionally, they justified their actions with some frankness, for example, "I don't want to sacrifice my children to the experiment of public education."[20]

People without these social and economic advantages lacked the means to resist effectively or to flee, and it was they on whom the burden of the idealistic programs fell. "We have watched like frightened sheep," declared one pastor in his angrily demotic idiom, "as do-gooders sniveling about the underprivileged gleefully grabbed our children by the nape of the neck and rubbed their faces in filth to create equality."[21] Such complaints were dismissed as the ignorant and vicious yelping of bigots. Confident in their moral superiority and prudently distant from the realities of the situations they had created, middle-class idealists were pleased to think that lower-class whites should learn to live with lower-class blacks and like it, for the good of both parties and of society in general.

Affirmative action—the most pervasive program of the minority agenda and, after welfare, the most unpopular—had originally been intended only as a temporary measure, which would give the former victims of discrimination and the inheritors of their disadvantages a compensatory boost upward. After an initial period of assistance, they were supposed to be able to proceed on their own, working and competing as equals with people of other backgrounds.

That had been the hope, but by the 1980s, after two decades of affirmative-action preferences, blacks had not achieved anything approaching educational or economic parity with whites, nor, to judge from their slow progress, did they seem likely to do so any time in the near future. Their rates of crime, drug abuse, and other socially destructive behavior were far higher than those of the rest of the population.

If remedial idealism alone had been involved, it would probably have been able to cope with the obvious though distressing reality. It could have taken the position that society's prolonged mistreatment of blacks in the past was responsible for their present internal as well as external deficiencies, and that society therefore had a duty to assist them in bettering themselves. But implicit in such a stance is the assumption that blacks, on their part, needed to recognize their personal misconduct and make an effort to improve it. That would have been anathema to transcendent idealism. To accept the idea that a minority has to adapt itself to the standards of the majority would be to give up any hope of a mass elite, of a future where individuals would all develop their splendid unique potential. It would be to resign oneself to nothing but more of the grim and hectic present: a rising generation of select black organization kids taking their place alongside select white ones. Only the skin coloring would be different.

Faced with such an unappealing prospect, higher idealism acted as it had done in the past and set itself against reality. Activists who had been supporting the minority agenda clung tenaciously to their original convictions. Launching a barrage of excuses, obfuscations, and at times simple denial, they rejected the evidence of black dysfunction and disorder. The persistence of white racism was to blame, they angrily and loudly insisted, and they called for more of the old remedies: more measures to give blacks preferences and to punish whites, who were assumed to be discriminating against them.

But the tide of public opinion was moving in an opposite direction. Its tendency first became apparent among lower-class whites, who had suffered the most from the programs of integration and affirmative action. When they complained about black criminals infesting their communities or unqualified blacks being hired and promoted, middle-class liberals condemned them as racists. When they defended themselves or struck back, mainstream news media depicted them as behaving like the Ku Klux Klan.[22]

In response to this treatment, they changed parties. Their traditional allegiance had been with the Democrats, who had supported New Deal reforms and labor unions. But since the 1960s, Democrats had become active and vocal supporters of the minority agenda. Their advocacy of racial preferences, their favors to welfare recipients, their leniency toward criminals, and their indulgence of misbehavior of all sorts dismayed and repelled the blue-collar workers, who began to desert in ever larger numbers to the Republicans. Although this was the party of their traditional antagonists (management and big business), at least it spoke the language of law and order, of personal self-discipline and responsibility—economic individualism, in short. The Democrats, in contrast, employed the language of remedial and transcendent idealism—specifically, expressions of collective guilt, tolerance for any personal lifestyle, individual rights for social deviants, and compensatory benefits for minorities.

At the same time, a change in the larger climate of opinion was taking place. Slowly but inevitably, as higher idealism persisted in its perverse opposition to reality, a contrary trend emerged and began to grow. The advocates of the minority agenda had generally been referred to as "liberals" and their ideology as "liberalism." As they persisted in pushing their programs and repeating their orthodoxies no matter what the results, the very word "liberal" acquired a negative connotation, implying "sanctimonious stupidity," which it has retained to the present day.[23] In public discourse, it became an epithet to be hurled at opponents, and people on the left learned to avoid applying it to themselves or their policies. ("Progressive" has served as a more appealing substitute.)

Open and outright objections began to be heard, challenging one of the basic assumptions of higher idealism. Doubts were expressed as to whether white racism still actually posed the principal or even a significant obstacle to the advancement of minorities, including black people. It had certainly not stopped the Asians, who had suffered more discrimination in the past than Hispanics yet had achieved more success. The Hispanics themselves were looking like traditional immigrants, with a steady rise in economic and occupational status.

Increasingly, the finger of blame was being pointed at the attitudes and actions of blacks. Magazine articles and television documentaries examined the dysfunctional behavior and emotional pathology of "the underclass," that is, the residents of "ghettos" (as black slums had come to be called since the 1960s). Senator Daniel Patrick Moynihan's report on the fragilities and deficiencies of the black family, which had been widely condemned for "blaming the victim" when it first appeared in 1965, was revived in the 1980s and applauded as a work of candor and discernment.

These opinions were all the more telling for being expressed, not just by people on the right, but also by a certain number of those on the left. Jim Sleeper and Christopher Lasch, for example, authors with solid liberal credentials and sentiments, admitted that the lower-class whites who resisted the programs of indiscriminate school and neighborhood integration had been justified in doing so. However extreme and misguided they might have been at times, they were not as much in the wrong as the blacks who brought crime and disorder to their schools and neighborhoods, or the liberals who refused to admit the realities of the situation. There were even some black authors (such as Shelby Steele, Thomas Sowell, and John McWhorter) who agreed. With outspoken frankness, they criticized blacks for using white racism as an excuse for their own misbehavior, and they condemned white liberals for encouraging the practice.

By the end of the Eighties, efforts to integrate schools and neighborhoods had stalled. Opposition to welfare for the able-bodied was growing and would eventually lead to its abolition by the welfare reform legislation of 1996. Opposition to affirmative action was also growing, and it would result in statewide initiatives and referenda against the policies of racial preference. In the world of judicial opinion and decision, 1989 was "a year of second thoughts."[24] The Supreme Court undercut the iron logic of minority percentages by ruling that the mere fact of statistical underrepresentation was not sufficient in itself to prove a case of discrimination; actual intent had to be demonstrated as well.

In addition to these setbacks for higher idealism inside the United States, there had been reverses abroad as well. Since the very beginning of the nation, Americans have occasionally looked to foreign countries for inspiration and alliance in what they assumed was the common cause of human progress. Their ignorance and imperception, assisted by the barriers of geographical distance and cultural difference, helped both to create the mirage of transcendent idealism emerging into life and to screen the reality of remedial idealism being betrayed.

The cycle of soaring hope, adamant denial, and eventual disappointment made its first appearance with Thomas Jefferson and other radical republicans, who applauded the French Revolution as a great victory for the freedom and progress of mankind, while they dismissed reports of the bloody excesses of the Terror as untrue or excused them as unfortunate necessities.[25] This syndrome of foreign illusions, as it might be called, reached a high point in the 1930s, when, as described above, the Soviet Union seemed to be in the process of building a socialist utopia.

Once Russian Communism had been discredited during the years following World War II, the left turned its hopes to a succession of other countries (China, Cuba, North Vietnam, Nicaragua) and to a succession of revolutionary leaders (Mao Tse-tung, Fidel Castro, Che Guevara, Ho Chi Minh, and Rigoberta Menchu). As one observer on the left complained, numerous political pilgrims trekked to Nicaragua to express their sympathy and admiration for a new and exciting regime, but not a single person traveled to Flint, Michigan, to express solidarity with the unemployed factory workers, who had long ago lost their attractiveness in the hearts and minds of idealists.[26]

Each of these foreign illusions faded in turn, to be replaced by another, until at last the final disillusion came in 1989. The Berlin Wall fell, the Cold War ended, and the Soviet Union broke up. "A dream long corrupted has now been shattered," admitted one prominent cultural critic and lifelong socialist.[27] Those few countries, like Cuba and North Vietnam, that remained committed to some form of anticapitalist ideology now appeared, not as heralds of a promising future, but as moribund dinosaurs of the past.

Over half a century earlier, President Franklin D. Roosevelt had claimed that copies of the Sears, Roebuck catalog would convince the Russians that the American way of life was superior to theirs. Now, in 1989, Soviet President Boris Yeltsin, on returning from a trip to the

United States, declared that his citizens needed to view the abundance of food in American supermarkets and so learn what their rival had to offer.[28] The rest of the world understood and agreed without having to make an actual visit. They wanted to make money and enjoy consumer goods—that is to say, they wanted their own version of American economic and lifestyle individualism.

The people of Western Europe in particular shared this desire. While their elites might grumble about the vulgarity of American culture and American business, the masses wanted nothing more than to enjoy the affluence and entertainment of their transatlantic neighbor. The actual trend of events was in that direction. Throughout the 1980s, as European populations were acquiring American products and imitating American norms of behavior, their governments and political parties were dismantling the socialistic elements of their programs and policies and turning instead to private enterprise.

Prominent in the transition was Britain under Margaret Thatcher, an energetic opponent of both right-wing traditionalism and left-wing collectivism. Not only did she break the power of the labor unions, she opened up her own political organization to the ambitions of the despised lower-middle class, her own people. Among the English, it was said that she had taken the Conservative Party away from the estate holders (landed proprietors) and had given it to the estate agents (real estate dealers). In essence Thatcherism was classical American economic individualism.

—4—

By 1989, higher idealism was obviously and seriously under threat both at home and abroad. Whenever something similar has happened in the past, that is, whenever reality has contradicted what idealistic Americans have desired, their facility for self-deception has emerged and brought them relief. In this instance, it took the form of something called "multiculturalism." A sociologist who later searched for the word in a database of major newspapers found no mention of it in 1988. Then it appeared 33 times in 1989, more than 100 times in 1990, over 600 times in 1991, and so on, increasing by about 300 each subsequent year.[29]

With the invention of multiculturalism, higher idealism attempted to steady and strengthen its faltering cause. Up to this point, minority groups had carried a taint of the negative. Even if their misfortunes were not considered to be their own fault, many people nevertheless viewed them as substandard and therefore as needing to change and improve. Multiculturalism sought to abolish all presumption of inferiority. It proclaimed minority groups as totally positive, as the possessors of rare and precious qualities, which could benefit the rest of society. In what seemed an instant, the character of higher idealism's minority agenda changed, and it began to demand, not just compensation for past injuries, but reward for unique contributions.

According to this new perspective, the members of a minority group brought with them the special gifts and talents of their tradition. Formerly, it had been widely assumed that they would prosper by giving these up and adopting the ways of the majority. Now, multiculturalism proclaimed the very opposite: they should retain and cultivate their heritage. By doing so, they would become more valuable participants in the life and work of the larger society, and they would accordingly gain occupational advancement and win general appreciation.

Once minorities had learned to esteem themselves sufficiently and the majority had learned to value them correctly, their multifarious activities would produce an amazing burst of human accomplishment and achieve a marvelous fulfillment of human potential. It would be something like the realization of Emerson's mass elite, or at least an enormous step in that direction. And it would all come about simply by adding to the remedial negative ("end prejudice and discrimination") a transcendent positive ("celebrate diversity"). The latter slogan became the watchword of the multicultural movement, and it was repeated incessantly.

Advocates of affirmative action quickly adopted the new, inspiring rhetoric. They asserted that having more minorities on campus would benefit not merely the minorities themselves but the rest of the student body, who would profit from association with fellow students who had different experiences and ideas. Similar notions were repeated in the business world: because minorities were different, hiring more of them would bring new perspectives and more innovative solutions to the problems of work.

Far from supplanting remedial idealism's complaints of grievance and postures of compassion, transcendent multiculturalism reinforced and supercharged them. Society now stood accused, not only of mistreating the weak, but also of discarding the valuable. Members of a minority group could continue to advance their cause as innocent victims, and in addition they could do so as the proudly indignant inheritors of unfairly disregarded strengths and virtues. The criteria for guilt expanded accordingly. The dominant majority could now be blamed, not just for exploiting or oppressing minorities, but merely for ignoring or (in multiculturalism's terminology) "marginalizing" them.

As a result of all this encouragement, the multiplicity as well as the virulence of the aggrieved parties increased. National Public Radio became the unofficial "Voice of Multiculturalism," broadcasting an almost daily report "on the victimization of this or that minority group by the dominant straight white male European culture, or on the brave struggle of this or that ethnic sliver to maintain its identity in the face of Anglo supremacism."[30]

The expanding effort and agenda did not stop with the human species. An apparent increase in shark attacks on swimmers prompted an editorial in the *New York Times*, which may stand as a paradigm for multicultural advocacy. One need change only the details, which appear below in parentheses, and the general substance could be applied to any abused or neglected group:

1. Society is unjustifiably prejudiced against this minority. ("Cultural hysteria about sharks...induced by the movie *Jaws*.")
2. The minority is not to blame for its apparent misbehavior. (The attacks are "not the result of malevolence or a taste for human blood on the shark's part but instinctive feeding behavior and a case of mistaken prey...every shark attack is unusual.")

3. Society has in fact mistreated the minority. ("50 million" sharks are "killed annually by fishermen.")

4. The minority deserves assistance. (Shark "populations have plummeted globally…they desperately need protection.")

5. Society has committed misdeeds of arrogance. (Humans are "routinely polluting and overfishing…the earth's oceans.")

6. In a more suitably humble state of mind, society could actually benefit from the minority. ("How much we have to learn about them [sharks] and their waters.")[31]

The partisans of higher idealism had reason to be well pleased with these new developments, which ushered in the 1990s and persisted through the decade. Not only had multiculturalism rejuvenated their cause in general, it also promised to solve two specific, persistent problems. Under its dispensation, there was no longer a danger that people on the bottom, in their rise up the social ladder, would come to resemble the loathsome creatures on the level above the bottom but below the middle class. On the contrary, a principal tenet of multiculturalism was for members of minority groups, not to imitate the ways of those in higher social positions, but to retain their own characteristic behavior. This was part of their unique heritage, which would assist and accompany them in their upward mobility and which the rest of society would learn to understand and appreciate as a contribution to diversity and difference.

In addition, they would not fall prey to the temptations of individualistic ambition and abandon group ties and allegiances to join the competitive pursuits of American life. On the contrary, the essence of multiculturalism was for members of minorities to remain members of minorities, to retain their traditional feelings of solidarity, even as they rose in the world. This was, in fact, the old dream of transcendent idealism—individual self-development in a collective context ("an association in which the free development of each is the condition for the free development of all")—suddenly appearing in a new and unexpected setting and configuration.

While the 1930s promised an egalitarian mass movement building a socialist society, the 1990s promised an egalitarian movement of minority groups building a multicultural society. Although enthusiasts failed to predict and proclaim a "new man" of multiculturalism (on the lines of "the new man" of socialism), it was only because such a term would have been unacceptably restrictive, implying the exclusion of women and limiting their paragon to a single form—a poor and inadequate representation of the future growth of multiculturalism in all its splendid variety.

—•—

It seemed too good to be true. And that was just the problem. Multiculturalism has even less connection with reality than Marxist socialism had. To begin at the most basic level, in human as well as animal societies the individual who is different has always posed a difficulty and a threat. The outsider arouses instinctive suspicion and automatic hostility. He must first prove himself suitable and compatible before a group will accept him. From the new kid on the block to the new hire in the office, the onus of adaptation is on the newcomer. This is especially the case if he represents, not just an isolated oddity, but a group of similar deviants.[32]

Multiculturalism has attempted to abolish this intrinsic and instinctive fear simply by asserting that the stranger, the alien, or "the other" (as it called him) poses no real threat of danger or disruption. On the contrary, when properly appreciated, he is capable of making positive contributions and bestowing real benefits. What about all the bitter and bloody strife that has gone on among clashing ethnicities and cultures for millennia? They were just wrong to reject "the other"; they should have welcomed him. Now America could set an example to the world by becoming a new model society in which different peoples retain their hereditary group identities, yet at the same time interact peacefully with each other for the enrichment of all.

Such a fanciful vision of utopia sprang from native roots and appealed to native illusions. It was concocted from panglossian presumptions of abundant goodness and natural harmony. It won the support of higher idealism's desperate believers, who enthusiastically embraced and automatically broadcast the tenets of their new faith. America was not, or at least should not be, a single culture with a unified set of values, they declared. To the extent that such a thing did exist, it was a pernicious and illegitimate creation, imposed by a dominant white Anglo-Saxon Protestant male elite, and it should be rejected and dismantled as quickly as possible. A generation or so earlier, professors of American studies had been arguing over what made America great; now they were arguing over whether there was such a thing as an American identity or an American mainstream, or whether America should even be regarded as a single nation. Did something as accepted and commonplace as a national biographical dictionary make sense any longer, one historian asked.[33]

To the proponents of multiculturalism, the idea of assimilation was anathema. They asserted that America had never been, and should never have tried to be, a melting pot. In its place, they substituted new metaphors, such as a mosaic, a salad, or a kaleidoscope, in which the separate components retained their distinct natures. They faulted the immigrants of the past for giving up their native cultures and condemned the public schools and other institutions of majority domination for pressuring them to do so. The future would be different, they proclaimed. From now on, immigrants would retain their native cultures, and new multicultural curricula in the public schools would assist them in doing so.

The fantasies just described are entirely divorced from any reality past or present. Throughout its history, America has indeed managed to cope with a great diversity of peoples, and it has done so, not by preserving their uniqueness, but by turning them into Americans. The process and means by which it accomplished this were described in chapter four. They are, as was explained, a major component of the second half of the American formula, and they have continued to operate, contrary to the delusions of multiculturalism.

Through the 1990s and up to the present day, cultural diversity in America has been decreasing rather than increasing. Judging by any of the obvious and significant measurements of assimilation (such as intermarriage, acquisition of English, geographical diffusion, educational attainment, or occupational level), at the turn of the Twentieth Century the immigrants from Asia and Latin America have been and are being absorbed into the mainstream as rapidly, and probably more rapidly, than their predecessors from Ireland, Italy, and Eastern Europe had been at the turn of the Nineteenth Century.

Especially among the young, the powerful solvent of American life still does its work with undeviating and unremitting thoroughness. "We're not even Indians anymore," remarked a girl at a school attended by Native Americans and dedicated to the promotion of their culture. An exasperated partisan of the left agreed, "She and her classmates dress and talk in the same pseudo-urban way that characterizes students of all races, from downtown Portland to suburban Baltimore." A commentator on the opposite side of the political spectrum came to the same conclusion about the country's various races and mixed races, immigrant and native: "What all these people have in common is that their dress, patois, and tastes are becoming homogeneous."[34]

The advocates of multiculturalism made a similar error in perceiving a trend toward greater diversity, not just in the United States, but over the entire globe. During the 1990s, it was almost a platitude to assert that, contrary to previous expectations, the world was becoming more complex and varied rather than more uniform, and to cite as proof the numerous conflicts that were breaking out everywhere.[35] The conflicts were real enough, but their cause was the contraction of space rather than the growth of differences. In earlier ages, peoples with contrary ideas or customs could live at a distance and in ignorance of each other; today, new means of communication and the growing rate of commercial interaction have been forcing them to confront one another, often with disagreeable and at times explosive results.

The steamroller of modernity, which was described so vividly and dramatically in *The Communist Manifesto* of 1848, has been proceeding on its way at accelerating speed, assisted by continual boosts from scientific innovation. The elite executives and technical experts of the various nations who conduct today's globalized business tend to act and think in a similar manner, and the rank and file—at least certain elements of them—are not far behind. "The world is flat," declared the title of a best-seller in 2005. It warned that the younger generation in places like India and China has been acquiring the standard knowledge skills and personality traits needed to function efficiently in the modern economy and now looks ready to rival the Americans at their own game.

Those unfortunate people who, for whatever reason, cannot or will not accept the changes and rise to the challenges of modernity no longer have a place to hide. The new technology, with its ever more numerous and intrusive devices, has been carrying the lure and the threat of America to the most remote corners of the planet. Some persons and groups, especially religious fundamentalists both inside and outside the United States, have reacted by turning to political action and even to terrorism. They do not represent a growth of diversity; they are the opponents of modernity with their backs to the wall.

So remote from reality are the notions of multiculturalism that it may seem a wonder they became so widely popular. "We are all multicultur-alists now," admitted the title of a book by one of its former opponents. And indeed, during the 1990s, the celebration of ethnicity became auto-matic, almost mandatory. Cliches sprang up and were repeated every-where with nonchalant certainty: the only thing we have in common is our diversity; we are all different; diversity is our strength.

When one prominent pundit on the right asserted that "subcultures have replaced a national culture," an old iconoclast of liberal orthodoxies had to step up and correct him by pointing out, "Those subcultures do not exist." It was all a myth, he complained, foisted on the public by opinion-makers of the left.[36] That was true, but the general acceptance and persistence of the myth had deeper cultural and psychological roots than he and other unsympathetic observers may have realized.

Multiculturalism sprang from the native soil of panglossianism. The optimistic assumption that bringing together different cultures and ethnicities will result in concord and synergy rather than conflict and disorder is based on a panglossian faith in the latent goodness and innate harmony of mankind. The newly fashionable conviction that a person can participate and flourish in the larger society while at the same time preserving the habits and attitudes of his inherited ethnic tradition is a version of the old idea (analyzed in chapter three) that one can gain the collective benefits of social life without having to modify one's personal inclinations or sacrifice one's individual freedom.

Prompted by multiculturalism, Americans have been going about declaring that society at large has no right to impose its culture upon the cultures of minority groups (just as they have always asserted that society has no right to direct the behavior of individuals, and have assumed that in fact it does not do so).[37] The new slogans ("we are all different" and "diversity is our strength") are rather like the old ones ("we are all individuals" and "individual freedom makes this country special"), even if the former contain a coloring of the collective and the vicarious that is lacking in the latter.

Just as the ideals of the first half of the American formula stand in utter contradiction to the realities of the second half, so do the ideals of multiculturalism to the realities of national life. In both cases, people escape the dilemma in the same way: by self-deception, specifically by consciously believing and professing the ideals while at the same time subconsciously perceiving and obeying the social realities.

This has resulted in multiculturalism being both highly popular and extremely superficial. In middle-class social settings, a person of obvious ethnic derivation often finds that he attracts favorable attention, even enthusiasm, but he quickly discovers that his interlocutors have no genuine affinity for his culture and very little knowledge of it; they are simply demonstrating that they "value diversity." A well-meaning American might sample a foreign cuisine and learn a phrase or two in a foreign language, but he is not going to do much more than that.[38]

The ethnics themselves have been behaving in a similar manner. In America, children of immigrants seldom accept their heritage as an unmodified totality. Instead, they select which of its elements they will keep and maintain. By the third generation, their heritage becomes tenuous indeed, especially if they have attained middle-class status. The fashion for multiculturalism has prompted them to nurture some vestiges of their fading traditions—a "symbolic ethnicity" cultivated for the sake of personal distinction and vanity, or a "narcissism of minor differences," as it has been called.[39]

Even in the schools, which since the 1990s have viewed themselves as the proselytizing champions of multiculturalism, superficial treatment has become the practical rule. In addition to the initial difficulty of finding time for a new subject in the midst of the standard academic curriculum, there has been the persistent problem of deciding which minority cultures should be taught and how much of each. Shallow, innocuous instruction has been the natural consequence, featuring things such as food, costumes, and holidays from various countries. At the same time, the serious, difficult, and lengthy task of learning foreign languages has in fact declined.[40]

One exception to this tendency toward the superficial was bilingualism, which represented a real attempt to promote genuine multiculturalism. The program obliged children from non-English-speaking homes to receive all instruction in their native language and learn to read and write in it before making the transition to English. The rationale was that, having first gained confidence and pride in their own languages and cultures, students would then perform all the better in mastering English and other subjects presented in English.

The actual result was a failure to learn English, and after much acrimonious dispute, bilingualism was demoted from mandatory to optional in most schools. It only went on for as long as it did because its victims had been the children of poor, uneducated immigrants. Although many of the parents sensed the danger of this counterproductive curriculum and avoided it, large numbers were trapped and intimidated into accepting it, thanks to the efforts of middle-class multiculturalists and their middle-class ethnic allies, whose own children were never subjected to the ordeal.[41]

Similar things were going on in the corporate world. As in academia, there was an initial rush to embrace multiculturalism. Throughout the

1990s, CEO's and their top executives asserted again and again that a diverse workforce was a business necessity, that teams and departments containing only people of one background (specifically white middle-class men) could not adequately cope with the variety of global markets, and that employees from minority groups would bring special insight and creativity to their jobs. "Managing diversity" was the term used to designate this new priority, and it was accompanied by recruitment programs to hire more minorities, as well as by "diversity training" programs to increase the receptiveness of nonminority employees to the new developments.

As has been the case with many a fad in management technique and business organization, the reality on the ground was rather different from the cloud of rhetoric descending from above. Aside from specific and limited circumstances, such as a black salesman dealing with products for black consumers, an employee's minority background does not give him an edge over other employees in coping with difference and diversity. There is no evidence that a businessman of Puerto Rican origins, for example, would be better able to deal with Sri Lankans than would a businessman of Anglo-Saxon origins. On the contrary, the success of the Japanese in the global marketplace is testimony in favor of cultural uniformity—that is, the uniformity of the right culture.[42]

Far from contributing assets, minority recruits often bring with them liabilities. Chapter two discussed the deficiencies in the social capital of the lower class in comparison with the middle class. Members of disadvantaged minorities are prone to suffer from a similar lack of subtle but crucial emotional attitudes and patterns of behavior, which can vitiate whatever natural talents they may possess or technical qualifications they may have acquired. That, incidentally, is the reason why white women have benefited far more than any other group from affirmative action. As the daughters, sisters, and wives of those with social capital, they have naturally received a good amount of it themselves, so that once preferences came their way, all they needed to advance in the world of work was personal ambition and practical training.

NATIONAL LIES: THE TRUTH ABOUT AMERICAN VALUES

Corporations have continued their efforts to hire and retain minority employees, but once on the job they are supposed to act like everyone else and demonstrate that combination of initiative, cooperation, and quick flexibility which is characteristic of the American worker at all levels. Although a manager might show a good deal of patience and even indulgence toward his minority recruits, his hope and expectation is that eventually they will adapt to the norms of the business organization. This would be assimilation, and while it may have been proceeding apace in real life, it is a far cry from the multicultural promise of tapping into the supposedly splendid qualities of cultural diversity.

That should not be surprising. In the practical world, affirmative action itself is a matter of superficial differences. The organizations that employ it want to create staffs that are diverse only in external appearance, that contain an acceptable number of obvious minorities who are otherwise very much like their colleagues. After President Clinton, an incessant mouthpiece of multiculturalism, chose a cabinet which he said would reflect the nation's variety ("look like America," in his words), it was pointed out that, whatever their differences in gender or ethnicity, its members were people with conventional establishment careers, mostly lawyers.[43]

Given their vulnerability to accusations of indifference, if not of outright prejudice, politicians on the right were quick to see the need for superficial diversity. President Bush, Jr., has been especially active in finding women and persons of color who support his policies and placing them in highly visible positions. Opponents on the left are bitterly sarcastic about this "tokenism" and "hypocrisy," but their grousing has failed to arouse any serious protest or objection. Hypocrisy in this instance is the tribute that realism pays to idealism, precisely to higher idealism.

—5—

Multiculturalism was not the only prominent phenomenon of the 1990s; there was also something called "political correctness" ("PC" for short). The two were closely connected, with multiculturalism functioning as the elevated and positive partner, and political correctness as its low and negative associate. As was explained above, multiculturalism did reinforce and promote remedial idealism's complaints about the denigration and marginalization of minorities, but its distinctive and characteristic stance was one of transcendent idealism, stressing the contributions that minorities could make to the rest of society and the attractive future that would result if diversity were able to flourish. Political correctness, in contrast, was predominantly an expression of remedial idealism, with only an occasional note of the transcendent. In contrast to the vague notions and cloudy rhetoric of multiculturalism, PC activities had a very specific and practical goal: to rectify and punish offenses committed against minorities.

Ever since higher idealism adopted minorities as its chief object of protection and concern, it has been on the lookout to discover and denounce the wrongs they have suffered at the hands of the majority. But with the passage of civil rights and civil liberties legislation and the public's growing aversion to acts of overt bigotry and discrimination, the task of finding occasions for serious grievance and complaint had become increasingly difficult in the years leading up to the 1990s. Political correctness solved this problem by expanding the criteria for what it considered to be a culpable offense. Since cases of tangible injury were disappointingly few, it turned its attention to incidents of mere insult and embarrassment.

PC zealotry first appeared on college campuses, with the imposition of both informal censorship and explicit speech codes aimed at derogatory language. Among the groups declared to be under protection were blacks, Hispanics, and other ethnics, but also women, homosexuals, the handicapped, and other miscellaneous classifications of disadvantage. In some places, such as Smith College with its female sensitivities, coverage extended further to include the fat and the ugly.[44]

Like the rules themselves, their violations were defined with wide and generous latitude. A blameworthy act might include anything from a deliberate personal slur to an ethnic joke, a stereotyping generalization, or a word like "niggardly" (strictly innocent but with unfortunate associations). Formerly inoffensive expressions were singled out and condemned for literally if not intentionally objectionable content ("a nip in the air" or "calling a spade a spade," for example, might be considered demeaning to Asians and blacks respectively).[45]

The inherently sexual, or sexist, dimension of the English language was the source of much vexation and trouble. Conscientious or fearful people struggled to devise new expressions that they could substitute for words denoting gender. Changing "chairman" to "chairperson" was easy enough, as was referring to a seagoing vessel or a nation of the world as "it" rather than "she." But when the pronouns "he" and "his" were deemed to be no longer suitable for application to both sexes, it set off a search for acceptable alternatives that still goes on. In the avant-garde and outré purlieus of academe, "women" began to be spelled "womyn," and "ovular" was suggested as an alternative to "seminar."[46]

From the moment it appeared in public, political correctness aroused much ridicule. But that did not keep it from spreading beyond the campus. Television announcers and talk show hosts were soon making a conscious effort to avoid sexist language. One of them, interviewing an actor, carelessly stated, "You play a Frenchman," then instantly corrected himself, "French *person*." "Men at work" signs disappeared from the roadways. Sports teams were encouraged to discard their Indian names and regalia. Corporations announced to their employees that they were not to make remarks or tell stories that might offend any "protected class." The highest court in the state of New York came one vote short of banning ethnic jokes.[47]

Although the ridicule continued, PC sensibility has persisted to the present day (over a decade and a half after its emergence), and its activities still appear in the news, with the more outlandish of them compiled into regular reports, like the one that used to be published in John Leo's column. Activists have kept protesting against sports teams with Indian names (to the annoyance of the Indians themselves, who generally like the practice). Zealots have tried to eliminate offensive words from official scrabble contests. And "niggardly" continues to get people into trouble no matter where it appears. Journalists still struggle manfully—sorry, I should have said, mightily—against the inherent sexism of the language. They recently began referring to athletes' "sportslike" conduct, instead of "sportsmanlike" conduct. And Smith College, having long ago banished male pronouns, has now excluded "she" and "her" from its student constitution, because, in the words of its Director of Institutional Diversity, "a growing number of students identify themselves as transgender and say they feel uncomfortable with female pronouns."[48]

During its heyday in the 1990s, political correctness was remarkable, not just for the busy ingeniousness with which it identified new offenses, but for the high-handed and ferocious methods with which it dealt with the old ones. A student or professor who made a casual remark that could be considered derogatory to any of the standard protected groups might find himself—or herself—accused and reviled, as if he—or she—were a flagrant sinner surrounded by puritans who had assumed the role of agents for the wrath of God. One novelist described how a charge of racism could ignite a campus community: "Simply to make the accusation is to prove it. To hear the allegation is to believe it. No motive for the perpetrator is necessary, no logic or rationale is required. Only a label is required. The label is the motive. The label is the evidence."[49]

The campus administrations' disciplinary bodies that handled such cases tended to act like star-chamber inquisitions. When there were no corroborative witnesses, the word of the accuser was usually accepted over that of the defendant, because, as one university's statement of policy declared, "People almost never make false complaints about discrimination." The truth of the objectionable words was no defense. To declare, for example, that "black athletes are failing their academic courses" or that "women don't do well in this field" was considered culpably offensive to blacks and women, whether or not the statement was factually accurate.[50]

The typical victim of a PC tribunal was the naive undergraduate who, in a paper for one of his classes, had expressed a negative opinion about the social behavior of some minority. His punishment customarily took the form of submitting to a program of politically correct indoctrination or psychological counseling and making a public statement of apology and recantation. Professors received similar sentences for imprudent comments from the lectern. In the more egregious cases or at the hands of the more ardent prosecutors, reeducation and humiliation were not considered a sufficient penalty, and the malefactors were expelled or fired. The law school faculty of the New York State University at Buffalo announced that, not only would it punish such miscreants while they were students, it would also pursue them into their professional lives and attempt to ruin their careers, by writing to any bar at which they applied for license to practice and informing it of their sins.[51]

Draconian punishment was not confined to the campus. An off-handed disparaging quip by a businessman at the lowest or the highest organizational level could result in his summary discharge. Corporations instituted programs for all employees, so that they would understand the subtleties of behavior now expected of them and realize the dire consequences of seemingly casual infractions. Recruits from foreign countries found the indoctrination especially bewildering, and when reports of the new American obsession over minority sensitivities crossed the Atlantic, they provoked comments about the United States being "the world's greatest madhouse."[52]

Gaffes continued to be made, and most of them no doubt remained private matters that were dealt with privately. But when one happened to find its way into the news, the consequences could extend far beyond the punishment of the individual responsible. A customary ritual developed, in which the head of the company would go on television, would admit that the sin of prejudice (usually labeled as "racism") existed in his organization, would declare that it was to be extirpated by an extensive program of discipline and reeducation, and would promise that the members of the offended minority group would be compensated with raises and promotions. An incident in 1996 at the oil company Texaco was especially noteworthy. Not only were the acts of contrition and retribution duly performed, they continued to remain in force even after it was discovered that those accused were in fact innocent and that the offensive remarks had never been made.[53]

Elated by a feeling of moral superiority combined with a certain amount of success, the proponents of political correctness were eager to extend their influence into every corner and over every sector of American life. The First Amendment of the Constitution prevented them from simply outlawing objectionable speech, but they got around this obstacle to some extent by passing laws against what they called "hate crimes" or "bias crimes." Such legislation, which was frequent during the 1990s, stipulated that when a person was convicted of a criminal act against another, his punishment would be increased if he had expressed animosity toward the minority affiliation of his victim. The precise groups named in the statutes varied from state to state. There were the old standbys (race, religion, ethnicity, sexual preferences, and disability, though never gender—evidently the men who wrote the laws were not going to give venomous ex-wives even more legal advantage than they already had), as well as some new categories, contrived by fertile imaginations ("personal appearance, family responsibility, matriculation…political affiliation…[military] service," even "position in a labor dispute"). Had the word "scab" become legally recognized hate speech?[54]

PC zealots had less trouble overcoming obstacles on campus. It has long been a platitude in the academic world, repeated endlessly in commencement speeches and in the prefaces of college catalogs, that higher education is a place where all ideas, however controversial, should be freely expressed and openly discussed. A few rash and stubborn individuals maintained that this included opinions which might offend minorities. But others, who were usually more numerous or at least more impassioned, insisted that such opinions inflicted psychological damage which was so grievous as to outweigh the right of free expression. According to this point of view, calling a black man a nigger was almost like stringing him up. "Racial epithets are not speech," declared one law professor. "They are bullets." In their righteous ardor, the defenders of minorities seldom distinguished between vulgar slurs and right-wing opinions. To them, the former were merely a logical extension and forthright expression of the latter. Derogatory remarks about feminism they declared to be a form of rape; opposition to affirmative action, a kind of lynching.[55]

College administrators either shared the inflamed mentality or were sufficiently intimidated as to go along with it. Whatever an institution's theoretical pronouncements about free speech and open inquiry happened to be, a student quickly discovered that if he voiced a critical opinion about feminists, black welfare recipients, or homosexual lifestyles, he could be in for real trouble. His punishment, however, might be considered a salutary experience, reinforcing as it did a lesson about submitting to the dictates of the immediate and dominant social ambience that he, like every American, should have already learned. As this book has taken some trouble to explain, believing in the liberties expounded by the first half of the national formula is not enough; a well-functioning citizen also needs to recognize and obey the controls and restrictions—whatever they may be in specific cases and contexts—imposed by the second half.

The student's professors had already learned the lesson. Although many of them detested political correctness, they did not dare to criticize it openly, despite their tenure and academic freedom, which had been deliberately intended to protect controversial ideas. Even when they thought multiculturalism was nonsense, they voted to support it rather than face the disapproval of their colleagues. In those rare instances when their very academic specialties were touched, they remained prudently silent, as did the Egyptologists when Afrocentrist cranks declared that the ancient Egyptians were a black race. A journalist telephoned seven professors in the subject. All of them rejected the idea as "completely untrue," but not one was willing to be quoted by name. I do not think that Egyptologists are more timorous than other academics, or that academics are more cowardly than other people. They are all just Americans, properly conditioned and socialized by the national culture.[56]

The politically correct fanaticism of the 1990s has puzzled many observers. Actual conditions in the United States were not such as to justify so extreme a response. College campuses were not places where minorities were being assailed with derogatory speech. It was not a problem until the PC activists turned it into one, by seizing on trivial or imaginary incidents and inflating them into the dimensions of a bugaboo. When a freshman orientation program at the University of Pennsylvania sought to warn its new students about the danger of verbal assault against minorities, it had to invent instances of harassment, which it presented as real examples.[57]

The same was true of American life in general. Tensions between majority and minority groups were not high. Nor were acts of intolerance numerous. This is apparent from the statistics collected on hate crimes. In 1997, for example, there were 1,022,492 aggravated assaults in the entire country; of these, 1,237 had been hate crimes (less than 1 percent: 0.12 percent precisely). In 1999, there were 12,658 murders, of which 17 had been hate crimes (0.13 percent).[58]

Misguided activists were attacking the wrong targets—this was a charge that was heard during the 1990s with increasing frequency and exasperation, not just from people on the right, but from some on the left. The latter's complaints had a particular edge and trenchancy, criticizing, as they did, the entire practical effort of higher idealism for ignoring matters of substance and wasting its time on superficial and trivial issues. Instead of building a mass movement, it had become bogged down in multicultural identity politics, which divided the aggrieved against one another. Instead of confronting real economic inequalities and social injustices, it was expending its energies on tracking down insulting behavior and punishing disrespectful language.

The complaint was accurate, but changing their practical strategy or actual behavior was not a realistic option for the activists. As was explained above, the cause of higher idealism had lost the possibility of appealing to a majority and had been obliged to turn to minorities. Instead of a mass movement, there was now a spoils system, handing out benefits to disparate categories of disadvantaged persons. Rivalry and bickering among the various victim groups naturally and inevitably ensued. From the beginning, little affection or fellow feeling had existed between members of different ethnicities. One survey revealed that they viewed negative stereotypes of minorities—other than themselves, of course—as valid and accurate, to a far greater extent than did the white majority.[59] Having to compete in an affirmative-action contest over who had endured the most suffering or was laboring under the greatest distress only increased their mutual animosities.

A more basic difficulty was the lack of obvious, demonstrable, and significant grievances. As mentioned above, higher idealism after the 1960s had been having an increasingly hard time coming up with convincing complaints to present to the public. Since it could no longer point to overt acts of discrimination and injury, it had to claim that more subtle forms of prejudice persisted and, as evidence of these, PC activists cited the derogatory remarks that people continued to make.

This concern aroused a certain degree of sympathy and compliance from the public at large. It was not asking them to redistribute more money to the poor (that had been off the political agenda since the failure of President Johnson's Great Society program). It was not asking them to receive dangerous and obnoxious elements into their schools and neighborhoods (the flood of integration had by now slowed to a trickle). It was only asking that they stop using offensive language in reference to minorities.

Petty, moralistic reform of this kind has traditionally appealed to the panglossian simplicity of Americans, promising, as it does, great benefits in return for a small inconvenience or a minor expense (as was explained in chapter three). Improving language would supposedly improve perception, which in turn would perhaps improve behavior. As one carefully subtle advocate of politically correct speech claimed, "Surely we give up little and perhaps gain much in substituting 'average workers' for 'the average workingman.' And to substitute 'people who are blind' for 'the blind' is to encourage perception of the person as a human being who happens to lack the ability to see rather than as someone defined by that disability."[60]

At a less imaginatively hopeful and more mundane level, the idea of avoiding insults to minorities agreed with the general social tendency among Americans to avoid upsetting people, in a word, to be "nice." No one could object to that, just as no one could object to the apparently innocuous avowals of multiculturalism that it only wanted people from different backgrounds to "live together in harmony and respect each other's cultural heritage."[61] The possible benefits were unexceptionable—more social grease to keep the interactions of personal life as well as the wheels of productivity moving along smoothly.

The partisans of political correctness took this mild permission that the public gave them and pushed it to the limit. Since they could not lead a workers' uprising against oppression or even a sit-in to protest the abridgment of some minority's civil rights, they poured all the wrath of their frustrated idealism into the trivial issues of offensive speech. After perpetrating a misguided media feeding frenzy like that at Texaco or some other crazy excess, they would, by way of excuse, profess their pure and lofty intentions. They had only been trying to stop the verbal viciousness that some people inflict on others. In the words of one grand old liberal, the PC zealots of the campus were prompted by "the same outrage against cruelty which moved the students and faculty of Charles University in Prague to resist the Communists in 1948, and the students and faculty at South African universities to resist apartheid laws."[62] Attempting to excuse low behavior by citing high motives is an old and practiced tactic of fanatics and their apologists. I recall hearing it during the Sixties, when kids threw bricks through bank windows and set government cars on fire. (Remember the Feiffer cartoon cited in the previous chapter.)

—6—

Despite all the promises multiculturalism made and all the controversies political correctness stirred up, by the first years of the new century it is difficult to believe that higher idealism has gained significant ground. If anything, it is in a worse situation now than before the exhausting and confusing struggle of the 1990s began.

In the world of practical affairs, adverse forces are as strong as ever. Contemporary capitalism, with its proliferating technology and its expanding markets, continues to press its demands upon the peoples of the world with unrelenting insistence and power. In the United States at least, the response has been positive, even enthusiastic, as organization kids hurry from the campus into the workplace, and the public makes best-sellers of books that warn them to prepare for a life of competition in the global economy.

It seems as though the only ideals left in the world—at least the only ones with real cogency and practicability—are the low promises of economic individualism. If a person wants to accomplish something important and to serve humanity, the best he can do is to start a business and grow it successfully. The panglossian workings of the free market ("The Market as God") will supposedly translate all the separate efforts of energetic entrepreneurs into collectively beneficial results for all mankind. According to the enthusiast George Gilder, the upshot will be a kind of utopia, sarcastically described by one left-wing journalist as a "reverse-communism in the sky, where the state really does wither away, and the dreams of all the heroic soda pop bottlers and real estate operators that inhabited Gilder's earlier books would come true at last."[63]

However distasteful this vision of the future might be, higher idealism no longer has anything that it can propose as a convincing or even a plausible alternative. By 1989, at the latest, whatever remained of any serious plans for a socialist economy or a workers' state had been dumped into the Marxists' "garbage can of history." Multiculturalism was in actuality a declaration of bankruptcy. Its panting eagerness to welcome and celebrate "the other" was a desperate cry for any other, for something else—anything else—other than what reality was forcing down its throat. Political correctness was a frantic attempt to discover any issue, however trivial, to justify controversy and resistance, rather than submit to the agenda of an increasingly dominant technological world and global economy.

Higher idealism now finds itself in a situation like that of an ideological guerrilla army—battered and wretched. It is too weak to engage in open combat and frontal attacks, so it slinks and scuttles around the peripheries of the hostile zone, greedily looking for the occasional oversight or mistake committed by their enemies. Its misery is exacerbated by the frustrating contradiction between an awareness of practical inferiority and a conviction of moral superiority. Despite the disadvantages under which they labor, its partisans believe that their motives are incomparably more noble than those of their opponents. This combination of impotence and self-righteousness has produced an angry hunger and along with it a reckless opportunism, resulting in a readiness to grasp any chance and exploit it without scruple or restraint.

Moderate liberals have occasionally been taken aback at the hysteria and fanaticism with which their more zealous allies on the left attempt to advance their cause, seizing upon minor complaints and superficial grievances and inflating them to the dimensions of vile crimes and heinous offenses. There should be no cause for surprise. They are moralistic desperados who are ready to seize any opportunity, however small and unpromising, that happens to come their way.

Since the 1990s, anyone who makes a derogatory comment about what is perceived to be a disadvantaged minority runs the risk of becoming the instant prey of famished idealists. They howl in rage, demanding his public humiliation and the ruin of his career, and at times they succeed in getting what they want. Although the incidents they provoke no longer reach the dimensions or the intensity of those they instigated a decade ago during the heyday of political correctness, they are still capable of exacting the occasional sacrifice to the chronic neurosis of their frustrated idealism.

While this is the condition of the zealots of higher idealism, that of their putative beneficiaries, the minority groups—more accurately, the activist elements and self-proclaimed leadership of these groups—is hardly much better. The rich and powerful have learned to say nice things about them and to toss them an affirmative-action bone or two, which they fight over.

CHAPTER TEN

The Chronic Neurosis of
Frustrated Idealism

—1—

D uring the last decades of the Twentieth Century, a new intellectual
tendency rose to prominence. It appeared under various names,
such as "poststructuralism" or "deconstructionism," but it became generally known as "postmodernism." The doctrine it advanced was radical
and disconcerting. Instead of proposing a better and more accurate
version of the truth, as countless new ideologies had done in the past,
it questioned the very idea of truth, which, it maintained, changed
according to social context and served the interests of those in power.
Thinkers and savants who had claimed to seek or to have attained a
detached and objective view of reality had been doing no such thing;
they had actually been propounding ideas that benefited established
authority and reinforced accepted prejudice.

"All thought is ideological...all knowledge is political."[1] This applied
to science as well as to other departments of human knowledge. If anything, science was more culpable, because its influence and prestige were
greater. Gleefully and incessantly, its postmodern detractors cited the
racist, misogynistic, and homophobic theories that it had endorsed in the
past and now recalled with acute embarrassment. They blamed it, not for

a failure to employ scientific methodology with proper rigor, but for the methodology itself, for the very attempt to ascertain truth and understand reality with a dispassionate mind employing impartial means.

Postmodernism derided logic as no more preferable or more accurate than intuition or emotional conviction. It viewed reason as nothing but a "form of domination masquerading as rational," and in some circles, the very word "rational" became as pejorative as the word "elitist." Occasionally one even heard denunciations of clear writing as being contrary to "complex and critical thinking."[2]

By the arrival of the Twenty-first Century, the postmodern stance had achieved the status of orthodoxy in many parts of the academic world, where it had come to be considered a mark "of intellectual sophistication and moral rectitude." As the dean of a school of psychology declared, "Twenty-five years ago, we were convinced that science could allow us to know everything. Now…we think we cannot know anything." Papers in the scholarly journals of the humanities and social sciences regularly appear with the words "truth" and "objectivity" set off by ironic quotation marks. The same is often true for "fact," "knowledge," and "evidence." In some classes, students' papers are graded down if they fail to put quotes around the word "reality."[3]

While postmodernism has naturally aroused much opposition from spokesmen on the right, it has also stirred up protests from people on the other side of the political spectrum. With much earnest distress, they insist that they themselves are by no means conservatives or reactionaries, and that they believe in the same progressive social goals and programs as the postmodernists. They concede that postmodernism has done useful and valuable work in excoriating the vile purposes that science has at times served and in exposing the pernicious motives that have often hidden beneath the professed search for truth. But the effort has gone too far, they complain. Instead of doubting truth, scorning science, disparaging logic, and avoiding clear, forceful prose, their postmodern comrades should accept all these things with enthusiasm and use them against the lies, prejudices, irrationality, and obscurantism of their enemies on the right.

Such is the criticism that ordinary, well-meaning liberals have directed at postmodernism. Their naive faith is touching, but one may wonder where they have been for the last few decades. They assume that reality (and thus truth, along with the means for attaining it, like logic, reason, etc.) is fundamentally and inevitably on their side, the side that both they and the postmodernists share, specifically the side of higher idealism; whereas in fact, as the preceding chapter has explained at some length, the very opposite is the case. Reality has been giving higher idealism a continual battering ever since the enthusiasms of the 1960s cooled down.

Many of those actively engaged in the struggle have sensed that something basic was going wrong. When they attempted to advance their cause by utilizing scientific proof, rational argument, logical analysis, and clear evidence, they have more often than not seen their political opponents take up these very implements and employ them with greater effect. In the agony of discomfiture, some of the combatants on the left have been driven to realize and even to exclaim in dismay that truth can be "a weapon of the right" and a "source of oppression."[4]

In the midst of so desperate a situation, a desperate strategy was needed, and postmodernism has provided one: demote the truth. It does not seek to abolish truth entirely, although postmodernists may sometimes sound as if that were their goal. After all, one wants to be able to resort to the truth when it happens to be on one's side, so postmodernism provides for truth to be used selectively, at one's discretion and choosing. It does this by weakening the authority of the truth. Formerly, truth trumped all other values; now, according to postmodernism, it is only one of a number of values, others of which may on occasion outweigh it. The possession of high idealistic motives is thereby able to trump a claim to the truth. From this perspective, the foremost consideration in discourse and debate becomes, not whether something can be presented as accurate or logical, but whether it can be viewed as promoting progressive rather than reactionary or conservative social values, in a word, whether or not it advances the cause of higher idealism.

A striking example of this metaphysical gerrymandering, as it may be called, occurred during a panel discussion held at New York University in

1996. The question arose as to the distinction between Native American creationism and Christian fundamentalist creationism. A number of people on the left had rejected the scientific theory that the ancestors of Indians migrated across the Bering Strait to America and had accepted instead the Indian myth that their ancestors had always been present in the Western Hemisphere, having "sprung from the earth." If leftists were willing to believe that, asked a member of the audience, why shouldn't they also accept the Christian fundamentalists' assertion that God had created the earth and all its inhabitants during a single week around ten thousand years ago? Andrew Ross, a prominent postmodernist, was not at a loss for an answer. He explained that the difference lay in "the inequality of power relations" between Native Americans and white Christians, the former being the most "screwed over" and "marginalized" minority in the history of the United States. Thus victim status trumps truth.[5]

This kind of thinking and arguing is more a spontaneous tendency than a conscious and deliberate application of philosophical doctrine. It is a way that a growing number of idealistic people have found for coping with an increasingly uncongenial reality. Although this strategy may be conveniently referred to as postmodern, most of those who employ it do not necessarily think of themselves as postmodernists and may have little or no knowledge of the formal theories of the postmodern school. But even if the phenomenon is not explicitly identified or labeled, it is widespread in many academic institutions as an actual mode of argumentation.[6]

To support a doctrine by citing facts and evidence can often be a difficult and disappointing task. Evidence may prove inadequate, and facts may turn out to be adverse. How much easier it is simply to assert that one is on the side of the angels. When criticism is rampant and the strength of one's position is dubious, how reassuring it is to be able to declare, as did Martin Bernal, the author of *Black Athena*, that, even if his theories could not be proved right or wrong, they were superior to those of others "on ethical grounds," because his, unlike theirs, agreed with "the general liberal preferences of academia."[7] This is a commonplace stance among scholars these days: proclaiming an idea to be superior or inferior according to whether it is on the right or the wrong side politically, socially, and morally.

Equipped with so convenient a club of authority, some professors have not been delicate in using it on mere students. Questioning left-wing views that proceed from the lectern is likely to provoke, not a "dispassionate examination of the issues at hand," but an outright assault on the rash questioner's "moral character and integrity."[8] This, of course, is in accord with the postmodern tendency: the important thing is what's in your heart, not what's in your head, if anything.

A few decades ago, it was an orthodox belief among academics that their disinterested pursuit of the truth would result in an accumulation of verified knowledge, which would in turn assist the effort to improve the human condition.[9] Although the ensuing years have seen many advancements in the material circumstances of life, the goals of higher idealism, such as economic equality and a mass elite, seem as distant as ever. Animated by an awareness of this failure, a growing number of professors have given up on the attempt to determine objective reality and have instead become more deliberately and directly engaged in what they regard as the promotion of a better society.

When their research turns up something that will advance a politically progressive agenda, they are eager to study it and quick to broadcast their discoveries. When, however, they find something that threatens to do the opposite, they are just as quick, if not quicker, to ignore and conceal it. Some of them have publicly, emphatically, and righteously declared that if they ever encounter anything that they might regard as possibly having a socially damaging influence—such as evidence of the unattractive characteristics of a minority group—they would, as a matter of moral principle, refuse to publish it.[10] So much for academia's old vow and vaunt: to advance the discovery of the truth no matter where it leads. Truth is not so good or so important as to deserve such blind devotion, as postmodernism now admonishes.

Those who fail to obey this new ethical agenda receive sharp disapproval and actual coercion from its zealous adherents. One professor

of psychology warned his colleagues that if they venture into controversial areas like "daycare, sexual behavior, childhood memories, [or]
the treatment of substance abuse," they may find themselves subjected
to "vilification, harassment, intervention by politicians, and physical
assault." Even a subject as seemingly innocuous as left-handedness can
prove dangerous. When two psychologists "published statistics in a
medical journal, showing that lefties on average had more prenatal and
perinatal complications, are victims of more accidents, and die younger
than righties," they were attacked with "the threat of a lawsuit, numerous
death threats, and a ban on the topic in a scholarly journal—from
enraged left-handers and their advocates."[11]

If this is the reaction to politically incorrect discoveries on such a
marginal subject, it is no wonder that scholars become acutely nervous
handling more sensitive and inflammatory matters. When one sociologist was doing a study on children's attitudes toward work and found
that those of blacks were much different than those of whites, he simply
discarded the racial data he had collected. Such an action has not been
at all unusual, prompted as it is by a persuasive combination of two
cogent motives, low prudence and high-minded idealism.[12]

Suppressing unfavorable evidence is not a new practice, even—or,
one might say, especially—in issues involving elevated moral purpose.
Neither is shifting one's ground when one is getting the worst of an
argument, nor is applying double standards to avoid being caught in an
unfavorable situation. Only now, postmodernism allows its followers and
their allies to employ these underhanded tactics with a clear conscience.
Reassured by the postmodernist conviction that truth is uncertain
and changeable—being relative, contextual, and contingent in its very
nature—double-dealing idealists can play fast and loose with the truth
whenever they find it convenient to do so, in the confidence that such a
minor and fluctuating obstacle should not hinder them in the advancement of their noble goals and lofty aspirations.

During the course of their checkered and often adverse fortunes, they
have had much need for this assistance. The issue of free speech is a
case in point. Years ago, when the United States was still in the grip of

the fears and repressions of the Cold War, idealistic leftists strove long and passionately to defend the right of free speech. They often repeated the classic argument that by allowing the expression of all ideas—even those which many people considered deleterious and reprehensible, such as Communism—the best ideas would emerge obvious and victorious. Then, with the arrival of the 1990s, the sudden popularity of multiculturalism and political correctness lifted these previously defensive combatants to an unexpected position of power, where they immediately began proclaiming that there were certain ideas—specifically those critical of minorities—which were so deleterious and reprehensible as to deserve, require, and demand suppression and punishment. The former champions of free speech became the energetic inquisitors and eager prosecutors of bad speech. And so they no doubt would have remained to the present day, but in 2001 the terrorist attacks of September 11 occurred. When a number of pundits and professors on the left responded in a way that a large number of Americans viewed as insufficiently patriotic, degenerately perverse, or even outrightly treasonous, and politicians began to threaten them with censorship and dismissal, radical activists and their liberal allies at once reverted to the old position. Loudly and righteously they revived the cry for freedom of speech and insisted that it should include even speech which some members of the public might regard as deleterious and reprehensible.

However successful such maneuvering has proved in the short run, it has created lasting odium and mistrust. The tergiversations over free speech may seem entirely justifiable to a staunch idealist of the left, since with each shift of position he remains an advocate of what he regards as the highest cause in play at the moment, and that, from a postmodern perspective, is more important than ideological consistency. But to those who do not share his assumptions, his behavior seems like nothing but low opportunism. His paramount concern is obviously for one kind of speech only—his own. When he is in a position of weakness, as a tactical move, he will advocate free speech as a general principle. When he is in a position of power, he will discard the rhetoric of free speech and become as ferocious a suppressor of enemy ideas as the anti-Communist right-wingers were when they were in power, although he may accompany his repressive actions with much more denial, hypocrisy, and idealistic rationalization.

The entire enterprise of postmodernism is permeated with the odor of dishonesty and deception, including self-deception, an obvious symptom of which can be found in the style of the prose it produces. One of the main causes of bad writing, perhaps even its chief cause, is a disjunction between perception and desire: what the writer wants to believe contradicts what his actual experience tells him, and in his effort to bridge the gap between the two, his writing suffers, since it must now perform the function of deception rather than elucidation. This is especially the case in higher education today, being the bastion of postmodernism and its project of demoting truth and disparaging reality.

Academic prose has always tended toward the ponderous and pretentious, but in the past two or three decades, as many have noticed, it has taken a turn for the worse, with a proliferation of sesquipedalian jargon, excruciating circumlocutions, vague abstractions, clotted syntax, and long, tortuous sentences. Since the mid-1990s, there has been an annual Bad Writing Contest, in which university publications inevitably emerge with top honors. The winners and the runners-up are often postmodernists outright or at least authors who have been influenced by postmodern ways of thought and explication.

Impenetrable prose functions as a form of defense, like a squid's ink, concealing those who produce it from their enemies. To step forward with a clearly stated position into the open arena of intellectual combat is to risk being crushed and humiliated. The guerrilla fighters of the left have learned from bitter experience to avoid that situation. Throughout the 1990s (as one of their allies has noted), with each attack from their right-wing opponents, their own writing became more egregiously convoluted and evasive.[13]

From time to time, despite all their obscurantism and obfuscation, the postmodernists have been caught out. Probably the most embarrassing incident of exposure was the Sokal Hoax. In 1994, the physicist Alan Sokal, a liberal in the traditional mode, wrote a paper stuffed full of postmodern cant and posturing, but also deliberately larded with scientific gibberish and errors of the most elementary kind. *Social Text*, the foremost journal of postmodern opinion, was no doubt elated to have an actual scientist appear on its side and published the paper with much seriousness and fanfare. When the hoax was revealed, it created a storm of ridicule and criticism. Some of the postmodernists retreated in confusion and embarrassment. Others proved more staunch and brazen. Acting in accord with their doctrines, they attacked the motives of their opponents.[14]

—2—

It might be tempting to dismiss the postmodernists as contemptible and insignificant—a few sour academics, inhabiting the "most neglected" sectors of higher education (in particular, the English and history departments), exuding the bile of their discontent.[15] But, however noxiously repulsive and wildly wrongheaded postmodern tendencies may be, they are important as the most advanced symptom of a profound social and psychological conflict.

To understand this large significance, it may be useful first to summarize (in this and the following three paragraphs) the main arguments of my book up to the present chapter. Since the Eighteenth Century, modern life, in the process of promoting the modern economy, has imposed demands without granting adequate rewards. People have been obliged to supply the engines of productivity with enormous amounts of personal energy, attention, cooperation, and self-discipline. At the same time, the benefits they have received in the form of consumer goods and services, though conspicuous and highly valued, have not been sufficient to inspire the required efforts of the producers.

In coping with this unbalanced equation between the realities of the world and the desires of human nature, America has been remarkably successful. Its dual formula of arousing enthusiastic participation by proclaiming an ideal of freedom (specifically in the form of economic individualism), while at the same time surreptitiously exercising regulation and control, has enabled it to disguise the demands of modernity while exaggerating the rewards. From the very beginning, America has practiced this beneficial self-deception, which continues to motivate its citizens and make them highly productive.

But the demands of the modern world have not remained stationary; they have increased. Today's technological economy requires wider participation, more profound compliance, and quicker adaptation than did yesterday's industrial economy. It is a far more difficult task—involving far more subtle, elaborate, and prolonged operations—to educate an organization kid in 2000 than it was to train a factory manager in 1900.

At the same time, the rewards expected from modernity have also increased. Economic individualism no longer exerts the universal allure or commands the overwhelming allegiance that it did in the past. An increasing number of people want something more, which has taken a form that the present and previous chapters have analyzed under the name of higher idealism. This is not an entirely novel contrivance; it is in fact derived from the more elevated aspects of individual freedom, which Emerson expounded long ago.

The conflict between these two forces, the reality of economic production versus the aspirations of higher idealism, permeates modern society. It is conspicuous in the world of higher education, especially among the more prominent institutions. On the one hand, prestigious universities are the source of experts and expertise that the nation needs to keep functioning. They are the places where the children of the middle class seek entrance, to advance their lives and careers. On the other hand, these same universities are also the source of idealistic criticism and discontent. At one moment (of faculty self-congratulation), you can hear professors extolling the achievements won by the rigor of scientific logic, the impersonal standards of merit, and the disinterested quest for knowledge. At another moment (of postmodern prompting), you can hear professors condemning logic, merit, and disinterestedness as pretexts for majority dominance and disguises for elitist arrogance. Sometimes a single person is capable of expressing both points of view.

This conflicting dichotomy is not confined to the campus. It exists among the members of the American middle class, especially at its upper levels. The productive side of their lives does not need to be stressed. They are the ones who occupy the highest positions in the modern economy. Their energetic commitment to the enterprises of the working world was detailed in chapters seven and eight, specifically in David Brooks' depiction of what he termed the "bourgeois bohemians" (Bobos) and their offspring, the "organization kid."

But the upper-middle class has another side to it, which Brooks also perceived: "This has got to be one of the most anxious social elites ever."[16] They fear that in a constantly changing world their success may be transitory and the prospects of their children may be dubious. Their nervousness and uncertainty have a more profound cause as well. They sense that, in the process of achieving material productivity and occupational success, the values they have maintained and the traits they have cultivated are humanly inadequate and leave them emotionally unsatisfied.

They display their wealth and status, but with subtlety and careful restraint, while at the same time regarding them with attitudes of ironic detachment and even disparagement. They are continually talking about such things as roots, traditions, community, and religion, although these play a tenuous and subordinate part in their lives, if at all. Most of them have left far behind whatever roots and traditions they had, and they are ready to abandon community and religious ties if these come into conflict with their careers or thwart their personal desires, as statistics of geographical movement, marital divorce, and changes in religion demonstrate.

Feelings of inadequacy and incompleteness lead naturally to a romanticizing of people who are different. During the 1950s, the upper-middle class was already experiencing a tendency in this direction, as a study of their favorite periodical reading in those years has demonstrated. They were multiculturalists long before the word itself came into popular use. When an actual multicultural movement arrived in the 1990s and became a national fad, they led the way. Students on Ivy League campuses packed the classrooms where things such as American Indian religion were being taught. Movies like *The Horse Whisperer* achieved the status of cautionary fables. Its story, in David Brooks' one-sentence summary, was the following: "Oversophisticated New York magazine editor comes to Montana, finds simple honest man who communes with horses and helps her rediscover the important things in life."[17]

Going hand in hand with an attraction for "the other" is a sympathy for radical or at least liberal politics. As the previous chapter explained, well-to-do people in America have gravitated in increasing numbers to the programs and promises of higher idealism. They feel the need to prove to themselves, their peers, and the world at large that they are not grubby low philistines, obsessed with making money and maintaining the petty decorum of bourgeois society. As transcendent idealists, they can pose as bold, free spirits, ready to adopt liberated mores and to appreciate cultural innovations from which their immediate social and economic inferiors, the lower-middle class, would shrink in fear and distaste.

At the same time, they want to show that they are not selfish and greedy, preoccupied with their own personal interest and advancement. They want to see themselves as high-minded and altruistic, as taking an interest in the welfare of others and of society in general. Remedial idealism enables them to do this and to confirm their superior status as well. By championing the cause of the disadvantaged and expressing their solicitous concern over the rights and conditions of minorities, they display the bounty and strength of a rich patron and demonstrate to everyone that they are wealthy and confident enough to rise above their own self-interest and the prejudices of others, in contrast to the blinkered and small-minded inhabitants of the social level just below their own.

The exodus of large numbers of lower-class people (specifically the white working class) from their traditional home in the Democratic Party to the Republicans is a phenomenon of the last three decades that has often been observed and commented upon. Less noticed but equally significant has been a shift in the opposite direction. At the same time as blue-collar employees were moving to the right, high-level white-collar people were moving to the left. It used to be that corporate executives and members of the professions inevitably voted Republican; now they are more likely to vote Democratic.

The Democrats have gone from being the party of the unprivileged and ordinary majority to the party of an enlightened upper-middle-class elite. This transformation was not accomplished without certain adjustments. The Democrats' old strategy of tax-and-tax/spend-and-spend had to be abandoned. Their old rhetoric denouncing exploitative bosses and greedy businessmen had to be silenced. Corporate managers and technicians needed to be able to support the programs and repeat the rhetoric of their new party without the fear that they were undermining their own occupational productivity or acting against their own economic interests.[18]

The prevalence of the minority agenda and the rise of multiculturalism greatly facilitated this accommodation. Upper-middle-class members of the Democratic Party would have balked at the old labor union and collective bargaining platform; now, in contrast, they can celebrate diversity with easy acceptance and even warm approval. They can favor modest and minor measures protecting the rights or promoting the identity of this or that specific group, instead of having to stomach legislation (such as the institution of universal health insurance) that would benefit workers in general and impose significant costs or restraints on business and industry.[19]

In making the transition from conservatives in the Republican Party to liberals in the Democratic Party, the upper-middle class has done its best to straddle the divide between economic realism and higher idealism. On the one hand, they can now view themselves as noble remedial idealists, altruistically concerned with the plight of disadvantaged minorities, as well as glamorous transcendent idealists, boldly welcoming liberated forms of personal behavior from the margins of society. On the other hand, they continue to retain their positions at the top of the economic pyramid, where they exercise the power and enjoy the privileges that have always been the prerogatives of persons in that station.

The affluent advocate of left-wing politics who intends and expects to retain the personal advantages of his high status is a figure that appeared early in American life, and he immediately provoked the charge of hypocrisy. In the 1830s, voices from the incipient labor movement sneered at factory owners in the northern states who condemned black slavery in the South while ignoring the existence of their own exploited wage slaves. During the early Twentieth Century, middle-class Marxists were derided as "parlour pinks." In the second half of the century, their successors, supporters of the minority agenda, received the epithet "limousine liberals."[20]

The basic type continues to flourish, having grown in number along with the growing popularity of higher idealism. After the attacks of September 11, audiences were perhaps amused or scandalized by the public postures of the media mogul Ted Turner, at one moment sympathizing with the terrorists as avengers of "abject poverty" in the world, at the next indignantly rejecting the suggestion that he should grant the public access to his vast private land holdings in the state of Montana.[21]

Accusations of hypocrisy are heard, not merely from the right, but especially from the left—specifically from frustrated and resentful zealots, middle-class individuals with much education and intellectual sophistication but not all that much money and even less power. They function as the bad conscience of higher idealism, always on the lookout for persons on their own side whose actions fail to match their words. They have plenty of opportunities to exercise their self-righteous disapproval. As well-meaning and well-to-do people continually vacillate between idealistic urges and realistic perceptions, their indecisive and inconsistent behavior presents a large and inviting target. During the Sixties, the true believers of the New Left directed a steady stream of opprobrium and ridicule at "wishy-washy liberals"—"ten degrees to the left of center in good times, ten degrees to the right of center if it affects them personally," in the words of the folksinging radical Phil Ochs.

The game has continued through the decades. At present, whenever there is a community meeting in one of the more upscale neighborhoods, some suburban Savonarola is likely to stand up and berate his fellow residents for not being "diverse" (that is, for not having enough people of color as neighbors). In a less affluent milieu, the audience would most likely jeer at him and shout him down. But here, his reproaches are received with intimidated silence and embarrassed discomfort—perhaps punctuated by a clumsy evasive excuse or at worst a grumble or two—for his is the voice of higher idealism, which upper-middle-class people respect to a remarkable degree, even while they perceive its absurd fanaticism and bridle at its sniveling, hectoring tone. Their ambivalence is an expression of their divided soul and an instance of their consequent hypocrisy—the tribute that their realism pays to their idealism.

—3—

With reality standing in opposition, the zealots of higher idealism have not been able to accomplish all that much in the way of tangible measures and practical programs. But one thing they have achieved. They have managed to make people feel guilty—so much so that the phrase "liberal guilt" has long been a cliche, referring to an amorphous and pervasive feeling that characterizes much of the middle class.

Guilt itself is the necessary first step on the road to moral advancement. One must first recognize one's shortcomings before one can desire to improve and then act to achieve improvement. This applies to collective consciences as well as to those of individuals, and for centuries, preachers have harangued audiences on their sins in an effort to make them feel guilty.

In the modern age, a new kind of admonitor appeared. Adam Smith discerned his presence as early as 1759, when he spoke of "those whining and melancholy moralists who are perpetually reproaching us with our happiness while so many of our brethren are in misery" and urging our "commiseration for those miseries which we never saw, which we never heard of, but which we may be assured are at all times infesting such numbers of our fellow-creatures...."[22]

This type of guilt has two prominent characteristics. First, it is experienced by people who are not themselves responsible for creating the evil complained of but who nevertheless feel guilty simply because the evil exists. Human beings caused it, and since they too are human beings, they consider themselves implicated in the misdeed. Second, they feel this way even when the evil is remote from their actual experience and perception.

The United States, with its panglossian aspirations and their persistent frustration, provided a fertile soil for Adam Smith's kind of moralist to take root and multiply. As was mentioned in chapter three, the American Jeremiah has long been a familiar figure. Emerson himself spoke of encountering angry abolitionists who expressed an "incredible tenderness for black folk a thousand miles off" and whose "love afar is spite at home."[23]

The feeling of guilt has always accompanied America's higher idealism, and as the latter increased and extended its influence, so did the former. By the 1920s at the latest, guilt had become associated with left-wing politics, even if the exact phrase "liberal guilt" may not yet have appeared. Though widely recognized, the actual phenomenon was still quite limited in social extent. On college campuses in the 1950s, it became a dominant ethos only at certain private, highly exclusive institutions, such as the one satirized in a contemporary novel, which suggested that the following motto should have been inscribed over its entrance: "Ye shall know the truth, and the truth shall make you feel guilty." (On the postmodern campus, that might be updated to read: "You will be unsure of the truth, and it will make you feel even more guilty.")[24]

During the 1960s, guilt acquired a louder and more extended voice. The Vietnam War provoked denunciations, not merely of a misguided or even an immoral foreign policy, but of America in general. Opponents of the war often asserted that it was a manifestation of fundamental faults and failings in the nation as a whole. One example of this attitude appeared as a paid advertisement in the *New York Times* under the headline, "War Crimes—Genocide." It proceeded with a statement of collective culpability: "We, the American people. We: affluent, corrupt, dehumanized, brutalized, chauvinistic, racist white America—who share the guilt for U.S. policy and for the atrocities."[25]

Such language reflected something more than the transient extravagance of a heated political moment and a hotheaded faction. Many articulate, affluent, and otherwise stable people were ready, even eager, to recite a litany of putative national sins, and some did so with positive glee. A larger tendency was at work, and it became all the more obvious when the war ended, but the guilt did not stop. Instead, it turned to other complaints.

This was not the first or the only instance of emotional transference from one cause to another. As the previous chapter explained, underneath the specific grievances of remedial idealism, transcendent idealism is at work, exaggerating the seriousness of the injuries suffered and inflaming the anger of the victims and their advocates. When the burning outrage of the moment starts to lose its appeal—public attention having wandered and public sympathy having flagged—another cause is discovered and pumped up to take its place.

Since the beginning of the Cold War, it had been a commonplace in speech and writing to make sorrowful or indignant reference to the likelihood of humanity destroying itself with nuclear weapons. But when relations between the United States and the Soviet Union improved, and the possibility of World War III faded, a new threat appeared. Ecology, pollution, the environment—subjects that had formerly been associated in the public mind with little more than Boy Scout conservation projects—were suddenly elevated to the status of an urgent national priority and an international problem. Soon it became a commonplace in speech and writing to make sorrowful or indignant reference to the likelihood of humanity destroying itself by mistreating the earth.

During the 1970s, 1980s, and 1990s—when higher idealism turned of necessity to a minority agenda, then saw it falter and stall, and finally resorted in desperation to multiculturalism and political correctness—guilt grew and spread. In some sectors of society, such as the more prestigious universities and churches, it has become a prevailing climate of opinion. This development was only natural. Since idealists have been frustrated in the realization of their actual goals, they have made all the more effort to create an emotional atmosphere which they hope will eventually turn an insufficiently responsive populace to their way of thinking. The more a people persists in waywardness and indifference, the louder its preachers denounce sin.

The chief difficulty with the ongoing moral crusade to make Americans feel guilty is the lack of obvious, immediate wrongs in a sufficient quantity and of a sufficient magnitude. Most people's lives at home, at work, and in the community are not so bad as to excite shame and repentance or to make witnesses and participants want to join a movement of reform. Faced with this inhospitable reality, the preachers of guilt have resorted to things remote from common perception, to localities and events that ordinary citizens have never visited or viewed. There are advantages to dealing with distant arenas of action. When an audience cannot use their own experience to verify or negate what they are told, an exhorter finds it easy to make his case by a judicious selection of facts, by loud assertion and little evidence, or by any of the tricks and dodges, described above, that the example and influence of postmodernism encourage.

The condition of the environment is a convenient and popular subject for inducing guilt. Secular preachers go on at length as to how the human race (especially the greedy, extravagant United States) is using up the natural resources of the earth and poisoning the planet with its waste. They may be right, for all the ordinary listener or reader knows. Resource depletion and environmental pollution are highly technical subjects, of which the speaker or writer who moralizes about them may himself be ignorant. But the emotional heat of his declaration carries the day and drowns out the less strident voices of skepticism and moderation. When the dire prophecies of these ecological Jeremiahs do not come to pass, they simply make new ones and assert them with the same vigor and conviction that they employed in making the earlier ones.

Time furnishes an argumentative advantage and a polemical convenience similar to that of physical distance. Unlike the present, which contains witnesses who may be hostile and spectators who may be unsympathetic, the past offers an easier ground on which the indignant idealist can operate. Liberal and left-wing academics dominate the knowledge and study of history, and many of them have willingly, even enthusiastically, accepted and promoted the agenda of guilt. In the more extreme of their writings, the story of America is mainly a tale of genocide, slavery, and other mistreatments of various victim groups, beginning with Columbus and continuing to the present day. When an eminent scholar published a massive account of the new market economy in the Age of Jackson, a reviewer remarked that it painted such a negative picture of the "undemocratic and inhumane" practices of capitalism, the reader must wonder how the entire enterprise ever managed to succeed. Historian after historian has put the Founding Fathers—or any subsequent generation of American leaders—in the docket, tried them according to the politically correct standards of the late Twentieth Century, and found them guilty. As unsympathetic observers have remarked, the field of American studies would be more accurately called "un-American" or "anti-American" studies.[26]

The tribunal did not stop at the nation's borders but extended its scrutiny and judgment to the entire Western world. Any country that had ever abused a minority or carried on an aggressive war might find itself condemned as an enemy of mankind. The Victorians in particular were exhumed, desecrated, and exhibited on gibbets of scholarly construction. Their chief sin was to have established an international empire of colonies, thus oppressing the peoples of the non-West. Whenever the non-Western natives had themselves acted badly, the academic inquisitors either ignored their misbehavior or attributed it to the malign influence of their colonizers.[27]

This was more than a random and casual trawl through the misdeeds from the past; it was a fundamental attack on the pride and self-proclaimed superiority of Western civilization. The West was accused, not merely of occasional lapses, but of an inherent and irrepressible viciousness. What had formerly been considered its highest achievements and most noble moments were tainted and suspect, as persistent criticism of the eighteenth-century Enlightenment sought to demonstrate. Once, scholars had regarded this period as having initiated the best things in modern life, such as science, material progress, rationality, humanitarianism, and democracy. Now, they were blaming it for all the evils that have plagued the modern world, "from inhuman city planning to deification of technology, super-rationalism, pollution, totalitarianism, and racism," not to mention nationalism, colonialism, slavery, genocide, and fascism. One book appeared with the title *Hitler as Philosophe: Remnants of the Enlightenment in National Socialism.*[28]

As the cavalcade of guilt proceeded ever further into more distant regions and earlier times, its connection with reality became, if possible, more tenuous and its proclamations more fantastical. Having declared that the West was wrong in claiming superiority over the non-West, it went on to assert that civilization itself should not be regarded as superior to so-called uncivilized cultures. The busy and inventive minds of many naively idealistic authors performed remarkable work in palliating and disguising or in rationalizing and defending the nasty, benighted, and self-defeating practices of primitive peoples, while enhancing and celebrating any of their qualities that might seem attractive. A few scholars have challenged this favorable picture of tribal life in prehistoric ages or at remote locations, especially the assumption that the natives were peaceful and protective of the environment. But such notions have remained popular, satisfying as they do the need for an ennobled savage to stand in contrast to vilified modern man.[29]

Even the most remote corners of history and anthropology did not satisfy the restless urgings of guilt. It penetrated into the realm of the imagination and found literature, specifically classical Western literature, to be blameworthy. Some observers of the contemporary scene have been surprised to find the last dying remnants of Marxism, as well as the most radical voices of emerging postmodernism, among the faculty of English departments. Students too have perhaps been disconcerted to hear professors whose official duties were to teach drama and poetry repeating stale and dubious complaints about capitalism, derived second- or thirdhand from a socialism that had long ago lost its credibility among economists and other social scientists.[30]

In a realm where the functioning of the imagination enjoys its widest liberty and where obstinate and contrary facts obtrude the least, the purveyors of guilt have enjoyed a free and open range for their enterprise. They began by denouncing the literary achievements of Western civilization as the product and expression of its worst sins. Acting as Torquemadas of a new cultural orthodoxy, they subjected to contemporary moral scrutiny the lives of the authors, their written works, and the characters they had created. These may have appeared a hundred or several hundred years ago, but they were now rudely shaken from their repose, hauled into the forum of political correctness, and condemned for having failed to promote such things as "gay rights or equal opportunities or multiculturalism or anti-imperialism." Of course, they were all guilty. What else could they be, since they were nothing but "dead, white males."[31]

Along with the dismissal and degradation of the old miscreants of literature, the judges of the new dispensation proclaimed that books written by women, primitives, non-westerners, revolutionaries, the downtrodden, and various ethnic minorities were to be elevated in status and taught as classics in their own right. Did these works lack intellectual sophistication and aesthetic accomplishment? No matter. The right social origin and the correct political stance trump artistic merit, as postmodernism allows. When the Nobel laureate Saul Bellow had the temerity to ask who was the Tolstoy of the Zulus, he was denounced as "ignorant," "parochial," "arrogant," "arguably racist," "insensitive to the value of Zulu culture," and "reflect[ing] a denial in principle of human equality."[32]

———————

In their efforts to promote feelings of guilt, the partisans of higher idealism have found reality to be a persistent opponent. Usually they manage to circumvent it, but occasionally their desire for success induces them to underestimate the dangers involved. American foreign policy provides an easy target and temptation. Most people know little about it, especially its history. In addition, it is a prerogative of the federal government, which they are inclined to mistrust and dislike. Taking advantage of public ignorance and prejudice, leftists discovered long ago that they could denounce government misconduct abroad without having to provide much in the way of evidence to support their indignation. When the United States intervenes in some disaster in another country, they accuse the government of overweening arrogance; when it fails to intervene, they accuse it of callous and inhumane indifference. There is a well-known slogan that refers to the practice of automatically finding cause for national shame in foreign affairs: "Blame America first."

Every so often, however, the enterprise gets out of hand and brings glaring discredit on its perpetrators. That happened in 1995, when the Smithsonian Institution was constructing an exhibition to commemorate the fiftieth anniversary of dropping an atomic weapon on Hiroshima. It was named for the airplane that had carried the bomb, the *Enola Gay,* and it included statements such as the following: "For most Americans, this war was fundamentally different than the one waged against Germany and Italy—it was a war of vengeance. For the Japanese, it was a war to defend their unique culture against Western imperialism."[33] When organizations that represented the American veterans of World War II learned about the text of the exhibition and its photographs of Japanese suffering, they were outraged, and they took their complaints to Congress.

As a result of mounting popular protest and political pressure, the exhibition was cancelled, but its creators were unrepentant in the conviction that their high moral purpose of making Americans feel guilty outweighed any other consideration. "Do you want to do an exhibition intended to make veterans feel good," asked one museum official, "or do you want an exhibition that will lead our visitors to think about the consequences of the atomic bombing of Japan?" That is, an exhibition to make the veterans and the rest of the public feel bad.[34] In recalling their defeat, some of the Smithsonian's participants and sympathizers looked forward in hopeful anticipation to a time when the veterans would all be dead, and future purveyors of guilt could present this historical incident to the public without arousing the misguided interference and low-minded contradiction of contemporary witnesses.

The *Enola Gay* exhibition was a rather small misstep. A very large one occurred in 2001 after the terrorist attacks of September 11. On the very day that the World Trade Towers collapsed in a fiery ruin, causing over 3,000 deaths, one schoolteacher explained to her pupils that people hate America "because we're bossy." Another informed her class that the United States and its allies had killed even more civilians in the bombing of Dresden during World War II. These two minor but typical responses characterized in a mundane and low-key mode the reaction of the liberal left, in those social spheres where it held sway.[35]

In a variety of tones, from regretful to exultant, the proponents of higher idealism and promoters of collective guilt declared that the attacks had been a reaction to American greed and arrogance abroad, that the terrorists represented people living in utter and hopeless poverty, and that the United States must change its behavior and address itself to this "root cause" or else terrorism would persist. (Such a belief, by the way, closely resembled another article of leftist faith, that efforts against crime must eliminate its root cause, also assumed to be poverty.) The people who said such things ignored all contrary facts, including the middle-class and even upper-middle-class origins of the terrorists. They did not bother to argue their case or present evidence; they simply stated it as self-evident.

Some extremists proclaimed that America itself was the world's greatest exporter of terrorism and that it had inflicted more human misery than any conspiracy of religious fanatics ever had or ever could. They compared the guilt of the United States to that of Germany. Just as the latter had confronted and attempted to atone for its Nazi past, the former needed to recognize the evil it had caused, to change its ways, to perform significant penance, and to make sufficient compensation.

Following this train of logic, Ward Churchill, a professor of ethnic studies at the University of Colorado, referred to the technicians and other professionals who had been killed in the World Trade Towers as "little Eichmanns," since their work had contributed to America's oppressive power, just as the work of Hitler's minions had promoted the tyranny of the Third Reich. Alexander Cockburn, a columnist in the prominent—perhaps the premier—left-wing magazine the *Nation*, applauded Churchill's statement as a "voice of sanity."[36]

The rest of the country was puzzled and angered at these sentiments from the intellectual elite, at least as much as they were able to hear of them. For the moment, mere prudence, perceiving the feelings of the majority, restrained the expressions of guilt from being too loud or inflammatory or from getting too much publicity.[37] Churchill's remarks, for example, only became widely known and provoked national indignation three years after they first appeared in an obscure radical publication.

But enough reached the public forum to cause controversy among the pundits and opinion-makers. Spokesmen of the right denounced it as treasonable decadence and self-hating degeneracy. Even on the other side of the political spectrum, many were disgusted and dismayed. Michael Walzer, editor of the journal *Dissent*, declared that "the leftist critique [of the United States]...from the Vietnam years forward...has been stupid, overwrought, grossly inaccurate...." And he asked in the title of an article, "Can there be a decent left?"[38]

One might be tempted to dismiss these obsessions of guilt as the practice of a small if conspicuous number of people. It is true that the tendency is most prevalent among the intellectual few, but they represent the advanced sector of a general trend. During the last decades of the Twentieth Century, guilt had been growing in both intensity and extent. By the arrival of the new century, it had become a prominent national ethos or miasma.

It has become especially strong in the world of education. In the last generation or so, there has been a noticeable change in the curriculum of the primary and secondary schools. Children used to be taught that America was the greatest country in the world, that other nations were right in imitating it, and that the world was getting continually better. Now, they are receiving lessons of a much different kind: that America is guilty of great faults, that other nations should pursue their own traditions, and that the world faces serious and lethal dangers.

Many parents are not happy with the change. To their anger and dismay, their sons and daughters come home repeating such things as they have learned in school: that America was a better place before the Pilgrims arrived or that everyone may die as a result of mistreating the environment.[39] It is a symptom of both the strength of this new climate of opinion and the weakness of the old that most of the upset parents see no hope of changing the situation and limit their discontent to private verbal complaints.

Meanwhile, the pedagogical inculcators of guilt continue with their work, intent and confident that they are improving the moral conscience of the new generation. Their theme of white majority culpability proceeds relentlessly through the grades, from primary to secondary and on to higher education. It provides, in fact, the one unifying element in a miscellaneous multicultural curriculum. No matter what the subject, from the history of China to the ethnography of Peru, the story is always the same: a "passion play of victims and oppressors, colonizers and colonized...."[40]

At the college level, where the modern proliferation and diffusion of knowledge has long ago demolished any common program of studies for undergraduates, guilt is the one thing that is on offer everywhere and that administrators have determined the impressionable young minds shall not escape. In many institutions of higher learning, there is only a single course that all students are required to take. It goes by a variety of titles and descriptions (such as non-Western study, American ethnicities and multiculturalism, pluralism in the United States, diversity seminar, respecting difference), but it contains the same predictable moralizing content. At my own alma mater (I should say my *amara mater*), UC Berkeley, the recipients of this force-feeding snidely branded it with the name of a college institution from the distant past: "compulsory chapel."[41]

If idealistic adults have been eager to inflict an ethos of guilt upon the young, they have been just as ready to impose it upon themselves. During the 1990s especially, it was fashionable for middle-aged, middle-class white men to make offhand, derogatory comments about the behavior of their own kind in both the past and the present. Some of their remarks were clumsily contrived and bizarre, such as a sociologist referring to Max Weber and Emile Durkheim, the illustrious pioneers in his field, as "comfortable white boys."[42]

While this posture of self-derogation has naturally been most emphatic and prevalent in the academic world, it also appeared, to some extent, in the general culture. The movie *Dances with Wolves*, which depicted settlers and soldiers in the American West as vile and vicious and Native Americans as noble and humane, enjoyed great popularity. "It makes you ashamed to be white," remarked a spectator leaving the theater. There have been many other films with similar themes and moral lessons. One cartoonist summed up the mood of the times with a figure repeating to himself again and again, "I am not just a fifty year old white guy."[43]

I recall an encounter that must have been repeated numerous times. A self-righteous, moralistic self-flagellant would speak in deploring tones about an alleged incident of turpitude perpetrated by privileged and arrogant white people in the past (anything from upper-class passengers on the Titanic to Arctic explorers dealing with Eskimos). Another person would challenge him and present evidence that his view of the matter was inaccurate, that the people involved had not behaved all that badly or badly at all. Eventually, the person who had brought up the subject would yield to his opponent's superior knowledge and arguments with the grudging admission, "Well, you may be right." He was not relieved, but disappointed. He wanted to feel guilty.

People could be quite adamant in maintaining their culpability, and not always at a safely vicarious distance. One of the nasty, personal applications of guilt proceeded from the recently expanded and popularized definition of "child abuse," which could mean anything from emotional unresponsiveness at one end of the scale to forcible incest at the other end. Soon, respectable, middle-aged men began admitting that they themselves might have abused their children.[44] Although the deed was obviously shameful, they regarded their declaration of its possibility almost with pride, as an act of honesty, responsibility, and high moral consciousness. To have rejected it outright and out of hand would have been a benighted act of denial, something that one might expect from those lower down the social ladder.

The prevailing practice of guilt operates that way. One is supposed to admit to the charges or at least to their possibility. Not to do so is a moral dereliction. This is even more the case in matters of collective blame, as may be seen in the popular act of public apology. Whenever something bad happens in the political arena or whenever something nasty is dug up from the past (usually something that was done to a minority group), the zealots of higher idealism immediately begin calling for an apology. They may not be able to inflict punishment on the offenders or obtain compensation for the offended, but at least they can get someone to apologize.

Like professions of suffering and compassion, statements of apology have become a standard ritual or gesture to be performed by politicians. President Clinton's administration was notorious for apologizing on almost any occasion and for almost any transgression, no matter how distant (the deposition of Hawaii's monarch in 1893, for example, or the massacres that followed the Crusaders' capture of Jerusalem in 1099). The practice became so frequent that it provoked a complaint of "apology inflation": their excessive use was diminishing their worth, assuming they had any to begin with.[45]

—4—

Among all the things that Americans are able to feel guilty about, race holds pride of place. The idealistic purveyors of guilt have identified white racism as the nation's first, worst, and most enduring sin, and they are obsessed with it. On no other issue have they been so determined to make their fellow countrymen repent and reform, and on no other issue have they ignored and transgressed reality so extravagantly, ingeniously, and persistently.

During the last decades of the Twentieth Century, racist groups like the Ku Klux Klan were in decline, and polls indicated that whites' attitudes toward blacks were improving. Far from welcoming this news, the partisans of higher idealism were upset and incredulous. They were losing the greatest justification for guilt that they could possibly wave in the faces of their fellow countrymen. They were not about to allow this to happen, so they swung into action with objections and arguments to the contrary. Racism was still present, they insisted; social disapproval and punishment had merely forced it underground. People had learned not to express it openly, especially to pollsters. Scratch the surface, and one would find the same old intolerance and hostility.

Such an explanation might apply to naturally bigoted lower-class whites, but what about all the decent and respectable members of the middle class, who genuinely believed they had shed any former prejudices and who repeated liberal pieties in private as well as in public? Here the inquisitors of higher idealism were able to discover a more subtle and insidious form of racism. According to the prevailing definition, proclaimed and enforced by the full force of political correctness, any negative generalization about black people was racist. But, as the most cursory observation or casual experience revealed—supported by an overwhelming body of clinical and sociological evidence—the actual behavior of black people was conspicuously inferior to that of other Americans.[46]

When confronted with the black susceptibility to, if not predilection for, things like crime, violence, drugs, marital abuse, educational failure, and welfare dependency, even the most pious and gullible liberal could not help lapsing into occasional, involuntary negative generalization. At that moment, the Torquemadas of racial guilt had their evidence and pronounced their verdict. It was a case of "racism among the well-intentioned," as one speaker declared. "Even the most compassionate among us harbor racist attitudes." As a result of their inadvertent "discrimination and stereotyping," asserted a columnist, "it is mostly nice, nonhating people who perpetuate racial inequality."[47]

The good liberals were bitterly chagrined, but they accepted their chastisement as just. So they have continued to lurch and quiver back and forth between the contrary and irreconcilable poles of actual reality and desired belief: perceiving black misbehavior one moment, then reproaching themselves the next for succumbing to the negative generalization of a stereotype, however accurate it might be. As one woman admitted while she struggled with these contradictions, "The best I'll ever be is a recovering racist."[48]

But guilt did not stop here. Even if individual whites were able to expel from their consciousness and subconsciousness every last bad opinion about blacks, there would still be racism. The name for it is "institutional racism." The invention of this term (like the substitution of "ghetto" for "slum") shifted the onus of blame from blacks to whites. Whenever an institution imposes any criteria of judgment (such as an examination of academic competence or an assessment of professional qualifications) that results in blacks receiving lower scores or experiencing a higher rate of failure than whites, the institution is guilty of institutional racism.

Even though the test itself was administered fairly and impartially, it was nevertheless racist because, as its very outcome demonstrated, it favored the cultural characteristics of whites over blacks; that is, it measured things which whites had more of an opportunity to acquire and more of a likelihood of possessing than blacks had. The Supreme Court may have disallowed the iron logic of minority percentages in formal litigation, but the concept of institutional racism restored its legitimacy as a practical argument and rationalization.

The implications of institutional racism agreed nicely with the postmodern agenda of denigrating unacceptable reality. During the 1990s, the more ideologically nimble and fashionable spokesmen of the left began repeating statements like the following: Standards reflect "what white men value about themselves." Merit is "white people's affirmative action." "There is no such thing as intrinsic merit...the tendencies, skills, or attributes of white America" set the "standards for performance." Even "the finest and proudest of American values" (such as "self-reliance, individual initiative, the desire to achieve and to excel—above all, the master idea of individualism") are guilty of producing racially discriminatory results. In brief, institutional racism decreed that any qualification or standard which blacks had more difficulty meeting than whites was ipso facto racist.[49]

This pronouncement threw an additional burden upon the already beleaguered liberals. Even if they could somehow manage to purge themselves of the last traces of racial stereotypes and negative thoughts, nevertheless they still found themselves charged with involuntarily and automatically receiving the favors of an unfairly advantageous social and cultural heritage. As the "unwitting beneficiaries of white skin privilege," claimed one typical remark of the times (and typically appearing in the

New York Times), "millions of 'good white people'" were "more responsible for preserving and entrenching the racial pecking order" than the few remaining conscious racists.[50]

Once again, the liberals did not shrink from the accusation of guilt. Like genuinely repentant sinners, they accepted it with determination and even eagerness. One woman, to remind herself of her culpable advantages, compiled a list of forty-six instances of "white privilege" that she personally enjoyed in ordinary daily life and black people did not.[51]

Convincing whites that they were guilty of racism was only half of the work at hand, however. It was also necessary to persuade them that blacks were innocent of any bad behavior, which might possibly justify or at least excuse racism. This was no easy task. Evidence of black misconduct and dysfunction are overwhelming. Especially obvious and seemingly undeniable are the statistics showing high rates of black violence and criminality.

Faced with such a challenge, the idealistic ideologues of guilt did not cower and withdraw. Instead, they boldly stood up and declared that the high crime statistics were proof, not of black misbehavior, but of white racism, specifically of the biased attitudes and discriminatory actions of law enforcement personnel and authorities, who focused their efforts against the kinds of criminal activity that blacks but not whites preferred. This was said to be apparent in the law's harsh punishment of street crime, in which blacks predominate, as compared to its more lenient treatment of white-collar crime, in which whites predominate.

"You can't stop crime in the streets until you stop crime in the suites." To that popular adage, imaginative leftists added their assertion that white-collar crime actually causes more social damage than street crime. Of course, the very reverse is true. Violence, which is the essence of street crime, involves a fundamental attack on social order and safety, and as such it has always been the first thing that the government of every civilized culture worthy of the name seeks to put under control and regulation. To treat it as if it were on a par with white-collar crime is patently ludicrous. Would anyone, black or white, want to live in a neighborhood with street criminals rather than in one with white-collar criminals?

Blacks, as a matter of fact, commit more than their share of white-collar crimes as well as street crimes. If the amounts of money they steal are smaller than those stolen by whites, this discrepancy is a result of blacks occupying lower positions in the corporate and occupational hierarchy, where they have less access to the big sums. The gap will no doubt close if affirmative action ever achieves its objectives.

Explaining, excusing, or arguing away high rates of black crime proved less effective than simply making the mention of them taboo. Journalists have performed notable service in furthering this agenda. Whenever a white person (especially a police officer) kills a black, they give the story maximum coverage and impute motives of racism to the perpetrator. Whenever a black person kills a white (including a police officer), they play down the story and attribute the act to motives of personal grievance, economic need, mental derangement—anything but racial hatred. It hardly needs to be said that they never cite the statistical fact that blacks commit hate crimes at a rate three times higher than that of whites.[52]

One must understand that the people in the reporting and entertainment media are prompted by what they would regard as the highest of motives. On the one hand, they want to make white people feel guilty for the sin of racism. On the other, they want to suppress or at least limit bad publicity about blacks, so that it will not reinforce the prejudices of whites. This agenda has affected news coverage from the days of forced busing to the present. Watching television and reading newspapers, the public learned all about the white resistance to integration, but absolutely nothing about the similarly ferocious opposition of the black middle-class to integration with the black poor.[53] When the media celebrity Bill Cosby recently denounced the misbehavior of black youth, the foremost concern of the earnest and distressed white reporters from National Public Radio was that his remarks might confirm and encourage white prejudice, not whether they were accurate.

Vigilant racial sensitivities in the media have prompted a variety of actions, ranging from the historical past to current events. One television company rejected a series dealing with the slave trade because it was historically accurate in depicting African natives taking part in the procurement and sale of other blacks. When film footage from the aftermath of a hurricane in Jamaica showed only black people looting the wreckage, the "sensitivity patrol" at the CBS network became acutely distressed. Ninety-five percent of Jamaica's population is black, and the cameramen had not been able to find even a single person who could serve as a token white looter.[54]

One may perceive the misbehavior of black people, but one cannot talk about it, and above all one may not draw any negative generalizations from it. That has become a rule of conduct, not just for the media, but for the more affluent sectors of the middle class and for those who aspire to membership therein. One upwardly mobile young man of humble origins embraced the required doctrine with all the eagerness of a parvenu. In recounting an incident from his childhood when some blacks had beaten him up, he declared, "I had no business being there in that neighborhood."[55] If the situation had been reversed, and a gang of whites had beaten up a black kid for being in their neighborhood, this newly minted liberal would no doubt have expressed the customary and expected horror and outrage.

Not everyone is able to master racial double standards with such conviction. It is especially difficult for those who have had actual experience in dealing with the minority group in question. But the idealists soldier on, despite their twitching discomfort when confronted with contradictory facts. One example of their fortitude was the academic father and mother who earnestly lectured their son that "most black boys are not thieves," after his black playmates but not his white ones had victimized him, and he had drawn the logical conclusions. "Contact does generate prejudice," admitted a psychologist, "even among professionals who ought to know better." Yes, reality can have that effect, even among those who have been conditioned to deny it by years of indoctrination, including the excuses of their parents, the preaching of their teachers, and the consensus of their fellow professionals.[56]

In the midst of such adverse and uncomfortable circumstances, draconian penalties are necessary to enforce the taboo of silence. When the head of the New Jersey State Police stated in a newspaper interview that certain minority groups had a tendency to be involved in drug trafficking, the governor of the state (Christie Todd Whitman) fired him immediately. When a New York journalist published an article describing the fear that white commuters felt for black assailants, a group of her colleagues at once began to shun her and to petition the management that she be fired.[57] That happened at the conservative *Wall Street Journal*; one can imagine what the consequences would have been at a more liberal publication. There have been a number of similarly notorious incidents, as well as many others too minor to make the news but sending a message nonetheless.

Carefully avoiding the subject of black misbehavior in general and black crime in particular may be the most prudent and the most popular strategy for most middle-class people, but there are a few who have engaged the offensive phenomena with a bolder and more active stance. They frankly recognize and openly accept black crime against whites as understandable, justifiable retribution for all that black people have received from whites. This position is rather like the one that some people on the left adopted in response to the terrorist attacks of September 11: America is itself chiefly to blame for the evil it has suffered. In both cases, there was a wide range of emotional tones in the admission of guilt. Some spoke with regret, some with satisfaction, and a few (like Ward Churchill) with positive exultation.

Churchill's equivalent on the topic of black crimes against whites is Frank Lentricchia, professor of English at Duke University. When a predominately black jury acquitted O. J. Simpson in 1995, black people all over the country spontaneously burst into gleeful and public celebration at the fact that he had murdered two white people and gotten away with it. In 1997, after presumably sufficient time for considered reflection, Lentricchia declared his enthusiastic sympathy and solidarity with the black reaction: "It's about time that payback was delivered…no more whining and moaning…white America needs the experience, now and then, of having 'injustice' shoved down its throat, by blacks…."

Lentricchia's statement was not simply a spew of hateful rancor, however. His apparently vicious vindictiveness had an ultimately positive and idealistic purpose. Sounding notes of hope and reconciliation, he announced: "I don't know what it would take for a white person truly to bond with the humanity of a black person, but I suspect that a common experience of searing injustice might help…a rageful response to racism, in the Simpson criminal trial, may have been a step in the right direction. Let us pray."[58]

Thus a howl of vileness and degeneracy presents itself as the voice of high-minded idealism and moral righteousness.

———————

Racial guilt, in all its perversity, irrationality, and downright craziness, has had significant, practical effects. It has been sufficiently widespread, pervasive, and powerful to influence significant individuals, sway actual groups, and thus create real damage and disorder in social life, most of whose victims turn out to belong to the very minority that the promotion of racial guilt was supposed to help.

New York City provides a paradigmatic case in point. In the 1990s, Mayor Rudolph Giuliani launched an attack on street crime. This involved large numbers of police stopping and searching potential suspects, in accord with the new "broken windows" tactics of prevention. The crime rates dropped, and city residents, including those in the black districts, where crime was most prevalent, were generally pleased.

But many white, middle-class idealists, who lived elsewhere than in the affected areas, were not. As the police effort proceeded, their complaints became increasingly frequent and loud. They charged that authoritarian and racist white officers were punishing trivial infractions and singling out minorities for mistreatment. At last, when some nervous cops shot a black suspect who turned out to be unarmed, a storm of righteous fury burst forth from pundits and the media. In response, the police curtailed their efforts, and crime rates started back up again, especially in the black districts.

A similar sequence of events occurred in other cities (Cincinnati in particular). Here as elsewhere the real victims were the same—ordinary, law-abiding black people who simply wanted the police to clear the crime out of their neighborhoods. The police were in the process of doing just that, but it did not fit the white liberals' obsession with racial guilt. The latter were looking for another scenario, that of bigoted and ignorant cops entering black urban communities, treating minor incidents of informal behavior as menacing acts of disorder, and imagining crime and vice where there was actually nothing but neighborly association and sociability. "Over the past few years, police brutality has become America's preoccupying race trauma," gasped a prominent liberal journal in 2001.[59]

The black residents could have told a different story, one of drug dealing, violent assault, robbery, rape, and murder perpetrated by other blacks. But the idealistic liberals did not want to hear it. Instead, reporters from the *New York Times* and representatives of the American Civil Liberties Union (ACLU) found other black witnesses who confirmed their social and racial fantasies. Articulate and inventive local criminals posed as the unoffending victims of white policemen. Black political demagogues and professional militants—some homegrown, others trained in the best Ivy League universities—emerged from below and arrived from afar to denounce white racism and police brutality.[60]

Since the 1960s, when the celebrated black author James Baldwin discovered a profitable and perhaps enjoyable line of work by threatening white audiences with forecasts of a bloody tide of racial revenge, observers of the American scene have occasionally wondered at the readiness of white leaders and opinion-makers to accept and even to applaud and support the most violent—that is, the most verbally violent—extremists as appropriate and genuine spokesmen of their race. In the words of a black trade union official, "Financing the man who says, 'Burn whitey,' isn't common sense." But racial guilt has its own overriding imperatives, and a certain number of enterprising black people have long ago learned to play to them.[61]

There are two influences fueling the motivation of affluent whites that induce them to ignore black moderates and to indulge black extremists. The first is a combination of vicarious excitement and social vanity. As chapter eight explained, those who submit to the discipline and control of society's productive agenda need to indulge in a simulacrum of liberty during their off-work hours. One of their ways of doing this is to experience vicariously the wild behavior of black people. Rap music, for example, with its celebration of unrestrained sex and violence, probably makes most of its sales to privileged white teenagers. The posturing of black militants serves a similar purpose. By countenancing their vengeful rants, a member of the upper-middle class shows that he is sophisticated and avant-garde, attuned to and appreciative of the exciting aspects of political radicalism and social innovation.[62] At the same time, he also achieves another purpose, mentioned in chapter one, that of differentiating himself from his nearest social inferiors. He demonstrates that he has the generosity of spirit and elevation of conscience to respond positively to the enraged cries of the oppressed, which only repel and terrify members of the lower-middle class, with its small minds and hardscrabble self-interests.

The second influence was analyzed at length in chapter nine: transcendent idealism prompts prosperous people to esteem those on the very bottom of society while scorning those at the level just above the bottom. This tendency is evident in the attitudes of affluent white idealists. The last thing they want is for blacks to adopt the norms of nervous white respectability. The Emersonian dream of everyone realizing their inner potential and forming a mass elite is certainly not going to emerge into reality from that source. The behavior of lower-class blacks may not be genuine freedom, or freedom in its highest and best form, but in the imagination of higher idealism it is closer to freedom than the repressed and narrow behavior of lower-class or lower-middle-class whites. Who would feel a thrill of accomplishment and uplift if the effort for racial liberation ultimately produced nothing more than black corporate employees who dress, act, and think like white corporate employees?

This potent combination of motives has warped and clouded the minds of white people in their attempt to promote what they believe is racial equality and justice. When, a few years ago, they discovered that police officers stop, search, and arrest black motorists at a higher rate than white motorists, they created a national uproar over "racial profiling," which they called "the civil rights movement of this generation." They did not bother to notice that blacks were guilty of a higher rate of traffic violations than whites, or that the searches turned up illegal weapons and narcotics at a higher rate for blacks than for whites. Instead, they imposed new and intrusive official scrutiny on the actions of police officers, who accordingly developed their own system of racial quotas. Once they reached a certain number of stops, searches, or arrests of black motorists during a given period of time, if they noticed any more suspicious drivers of that race, they simply let them go on their way unhindered. The result has been more guns and drugs ending up in black neighborhoods.[63]

A similar sequence of events has occurred in the management of school discipline. When administrators imposed strong new codes of conduct to curb the increasing incidents of violence and disruption both inside and outside the classroom, it resulted in black students receiving far more than their numerical share of the punishments. That was only logical, since they committed far more than their numerical share of the infractions. But the obvious connection between these two phenomena did not halt the resulting wave of racial indignation, which included the familiar ingredients of self-righteously vicarious guilt from remote and influential whites, combined with automatic anger from professional black demagogues and militants, some of whom denounced "disciplinary profiling." The upshot of it all was that school disorder continued, which has harmed the education of black children far more than it has that of white children, whose parents are more likely to have the financial means to transfer them to better regulated private institutions or to move their homes to safer localities with safer schools.

The basic problem is that black people and their self-appointed white defenders are motivated by fundamentally different needs and preoccupations. Whereas the blacks have yet to acquire the basic ingredients of ambition and self-discipline that constitute the American formula, the whites in question have already done so automatically and unconsciously and have subsequently proceeded upward into a stratosphere of higher idealism, from which they are incapable of understanding the realities below. In the midst of this morass of contradiction and incomprehension, a clever and unscrupulous black minority panders to white guilt with postures of militancy and accusation for the enhancement of their own profit and power. The unthinking black majority enjoys the immediately pleasurable sensation of hearing whites being excoriated and browbeaten. And the few blacks who perceive the damage done to their community remain silent in public, so as not to be branded as traitors, though privately they excoriate the race hustlers and opportunists.[64]

An example of the resulting imbroglio and the harm it has inflicted on those least able to protect themselves can be seen in the regulation of public housing, where minorities predominate. In recent years, residents have agitated for stricter measures to keep out the hooligans, thugs, and criminals. They want the screening of new applicants for arrest records and drug usage, the installation of metal detectors to discover guns, and the issuing of identification badges to separate occupants from intruders. At times, the residents have succeeded in obtaining some of these things, but it has only been in the teeth of opposition from liberal advocacy groups, like the ACLU. Representatives from these organizations have argued earnestly and persistently that the proposed policies and devices will discriminate against members of minorities, especially against blacks, and in general against individuals who fail to conform to hidebound and blinkered standards of social propriety. The white judges and administrators who decide public housing controversies have often accepted such arguments, based as they are upon the rationalizations of remedial idealism and the prompting of transcendent idealism. The resulting decisions only serve to assist the actions of destructive deviants and violent assailants.[65]

—5—

If race is the most acute and perplexing source of guilt, its one aspect that has provoked the most prolonged controversy and produced the most agonizing muddleheadedness is the strategy of racial preferences known as affirmative action. As chapter seven explained, the later decades of the Twentieth Century have brought with them an increasing demand for productivity and efficiency, beginning with the education of the young and leading directly to their occupational employment as adults. A college degree has become a basic prerequisite for the better jobs, and institutions of higher learning have themselves been raising their requirements for entrance and graduation. The technological and globalized workplace keeps calling for more and better qualifications from its entry-level candidates and insisting on greater amounts of initiative and effort from its employees at all levels.

This trend has had one highly distressing consequence. If the rising standards—or even the current standards—of ability and performance were imposed uniformly and impartially, the result would be that the numbers of black students in the better schools and black executives in the more important organizations would shrink to minute size. That would be intolerable to the high-minded and guilt-ridden white people in positions of power, to the corporate as well as to the college presidents, with their allegiance to the principles of remedial idealism in general and specifically to the belief that minority groups should receive a proportional share of the good things that society has on offer.

The problem was recognized as early as the 1960s, and a remedy was quickly devised. Under the name of affirmative action, black applicants for education and employment were given preference over white applicants with higher qualifications. The practice, though widespread, was generally surreptitious, and it was intended as a temporary measure. Once black people overcame their initial disadvantages—in a generation, at the very most—they were supposed to function and compete as the genuine equals of everyone else, without the benefit of special assistance.

It did not turn out that way. Instead, affirmative action led to the creation of an enduring and inferior black track that extends through the world of education into the world of employment. Having entered college with lower levels of preparation and achievement, black students earn lower grades and are more likely to drop out. After graduating from law or medical school, they have difficulty passing the bar examination or achieving board certification. When they take positions in organizations, they tend to end up in the less important and less demanding areas, such as personnel rather than production.[66]

In the world of work, with its multifarious variety of jobs and occupations, a curtain of privacy, maintained by the competitive rivalry of business enterprise, has enabled the black track to persist and grow, largely unnoticed by outsiders. But in the world of education, with its smaller number of institutions, which are vulnerable to the interest and scrutiny of the public, the existence of the black track became increasingly difficult to conceal, though campus administrators did their frantic best to do so.

The result has been an endemic swamp of contradiction and obfuscation. One page of a college entrance application will declare that it judges and selects candidates "without regard to race, gender, religion, ethnicity, or national origin"; the next page presents a list of victim groups and encourages the applicant to declare if he belonged to any of them. When someone complains about the preferences granted to minorities, a college spokesman explains reassuringly that these give the beneficiaries only a slight advantage; if anyone has the temerity to suggest that, since the preferences are so negligible they might be abolished, the spokesman reacts with horror at the momentous consequences—the prospect of minorities all but disappearing from the campus. One moment a university president may be bragging about the high test-score requirements for students at his institution; the next moment, in reference to the low scores of blacks, he is denouncing the same tests as racist and asserting that it is "simple-minded" and "incorrect" to regard them as a standard of "qualifications."[67]

The parade of confusion and deception, especially self-deception, has proceeded onward into the graduate division. In one illustrative incident, an examination was held to determine membership on the Yale law review, and the authorship of all the test papers was carefully kept secret from those who evaluated them. Only two black candidates emerged successful. This plunged the entire school into a long, loud, and angry altercation, during which various charges of recondite racial bias were voiced and repeated. No one dared to mention the obvious explanation. The school's affirmative action admissions policy had accepted blacks with inferior qualifications, which produced inferior results.[68]

The same obstinate denial of reality occurs in the world of work. An organization is accused of not having enough blacks or of not promoting them. The organization typically admits its shortcomings, even confesses to harboring some recalcitrant form of racism, and promises to institute new programs or hire special diversity consultants, so as to remedy the defect. The real problem of black underperformance is not raised or discussed. In demanding, high-level occupations, there are few blacks with even the basic qualifications, and they tend to be a mediocre lot at best. "Many black associates struggle mightily with legal writing," an honest partner at a top law firm admitted to a persistent reporter, but only under the promise of ironclad anonymity.[69]

Controversy over the existence of racial preferences and the resulting black track is something that people in positions of power strenuously try to avoid. Their preferred tactics are simple: conceal the reality, lie about it when necessary, and denounce—as well as injure, if possible—anyone who tells the truth. During the Nineties, there were a number of nationally prominent uproars over such disclosures, for example, in 1990, the federal government's practice of "race norming" (fiddling the results of its employment examinations so that the scores for blacks reflected only their competition with other blacks); in 1991, the gap between black and white students' LSAT scores at Georgetown University Law School; in 1995, the *Washington Post*'s hiring of substandard black reporters and writers. In all these cases and in others like them, the individuals who revealed the unpalatable facts were vilified and slandered by an awesome array of outraged persons and organizations, ranging from bosses and colleagues at their own workplace to the public news media.[70]

Such formidable hostility and the punishment it can inflict have managed to impose silence on many who might have spoken out. But anger at the blatant unfairness of affirmative action and revulsion at the obnoxious presence of the black track may, from time to time, overcome prudence. Young people, who have had to struggle to make it into the better colleges and universities and who are struggling to enter the better occupations and attain the better jobs, do not look kindly on some of their contemporaries being given an easy ride and a soft birth on the basis of their skin color. In the past year or so, their resentment found cute and clever expression in the staging of what they called "affirmative action bake sales," in which they sold cookies and cakes at higher prices to whites and at lower prices to women and minorities. Campus administrators were not amused and forced the perpetrators to desist, under the threat of receiving a permanent black mark on their academic record.[71]

The adverse consequences of affirmative action and its black track have fallen with notable effect on two social groups in particular. The first and most obvious is the white lower class. Since their social position stands just above that of the disadvantaged minorities, it is they who tend to lose jobs and promotions to minority preferences. Exacerbating their resentment is the knowledge that the middle-class whites who champion affirmative action have largely escaped such personal costs, as was noted in the previous chapter.

An additional source of complaint is the fact that affirmative action chiefly benefits, not the deprived and destitute black lower class, but the comfortable black middle class. The former usually lack the minimal social and intellectual skills to satisfy even the low standards of the black track, which has ended up being filled by persons from the latter. And, if that were not enough, children of the black bourgeoisie tend to have lower test scores than children of lower-class whites. Consequently, the better colleges and universities accept the sons and daughters of black businessmen and bureaucrats, while excluding the academically superior sons and daughters of white mechanics and laborers.[72]

In their relations with the high-minded idealists of the middle class, lower-class whites have long been subjected to a double standard. Liberal opinion blames them for the same behavior that it ignores or excuses when exhibited by blacks. The caricature of the faggot-bashing, minority-hating, sexist hard hat has been around since the Sixties and is still going strong. The same people who continue to repeat that stereotype are deliberately blind to the existence of black homophobia, misogyny, and ethnic prejudice (especially against Hispanics and Asians). Whenever a black (most notoriously Tawana Brawley in 1987) is caught contriving a racial incident, pundits on the left solemnly declare that, however bogus the specific case may be, it points to a larger incontrovertible truth, the persistence of racism in America. Whenever the opposite occurs (whites contriving a racial incident), one never hears the opposite excuse (that it points to the general truth of black crime and misbehavior). Raging winds of liberal opinion would howl that down in an instant.

When lower-class whites have complained about the unfairness of affirmative action and the damage it has done to them, they receive no redress and fail to elicit the slightest expression of sympathy. Instead, they are subjected to nothing but condemnation, some of it outrageously preposterous in its calumny, accusing them of being unused to competition from minorities and thus feeling a threat to their sense of entitlement as white men. A few piously vindictive idealists—along the lines of Professor Lentricchia—growl that the injured whites are getting what they deserve, as retribution for their racist conduct in the past and their racist sentiments in the present.

Behavior of this kind on the part of self-righteous moralists does not contribute to the general trend in the direction of racial reconciliation and harmony. During the 1960s, lower-class whites were coming to the slow and grudging realization that blacks had been unfairly treated, that they deserved to be given an even break and an opportunity to show what they were worth. This was the bargain that has been offered to other minority groups past and present. They took it (and continue to take it), and they succeeded (and continue to succeed), though often with much effort over many years.

Affirmative action has had a contrary effect. It demanded immediate equality of results along with immediate equality of opportunity, and when the former failed, it created an inferior black track, accompanied by a flood of obfuscation, rationalization, prevarication, subtle mendacity, and brazen lies. Lower-class whites have been intimidated and confused but not fundamentally and successfully deceived. They had always regarded blacks as underperformers. Now, they see them as coddled underperformers.

———

The other social group to suffer from the bad effects of affirmative action has been the blacks themselves. The experience created by affirmative action is one of sink-or-swim. It does not attempt to instruct its beneficiaries in the ways of the white majority; it simply throws them into the mainstream and assumes they will adapt. Many do not, as the high rates of failure and dropping-out indicate.

Those who survive—the ones who can swim sufficiently to make their way along the black track—usually succumb to a more subtle debility. They refuse to do anything more than meet the minimal requirements. Why should they expend any further effort? After all, as the advocates of the minority agenda in general and of affirmative action in particular have stated repeatedly, the inferior situation of blacks is the fault of the white man, so it is his responsibility to improve it. Accepting this comfortable presupposition, they proceed to slide through school and into the labor market. Their natural and consequent attitude is one of "you owe me."

The ethos of multiculturalism and its celebration of diversity, assisted by the spirit of postmodernism, have encouraged the easy riders on the black track in their sloth and resentment. If black culture is as good as white culture, then blacks employed in the professions are justified in complaining, as they often do, that they have to learn and understand the ways of whites, but whites do not have to learn and understand theirs.[73] Furthermore, whites have no right to apply such things as standards, merit, or qualifications to blacks. These are the judgments of a single culture, and it is arbitrary and arrogant to impose them on the members of another culture. Their chief function is, after all, to maintain the odious domination and artificial superiority of the white race.

Both blacks and their white supporters have applauded and repeated these ideas, as they have applauded and imitated a rather less sophisticated position that certain black spokesmen have taken up. In defense of their mediocre performance in the world of work, they point with sarcastic indignation to the poor and shoddy work that whites have supposedly gotten away with in past and that some allegedly still get away with. Now it's our turn, they say. This is quite a different stance than the one that other outsiders, specifically immigrants, have traditionally adopted when seeking a place in the American economy. They asserted and still assert, "I am as good as you are" and "I am equal to your best." The blacks, in contrast, have been proclaiming, "I am no worse than some of you were in the past" and "I am no worse than your worst."[74]

At the same time as they receive its assistance, the beneficiaries of affirmative action's racial preferences persist in complaining that they still suffer from racial discrimination. They repeat the belief, as if it were an obvious and unimpeachable truth, that a black has to be twice as good as a white to receive the same reward in the white world. And their malaise continues even after they have attained occupational positions in the middle class. During the 1990s, it was widely reported that the more successful blacks became economically, the worse they felt. Far more than the impoverished members of their race, they were unhappy with their lot, feared the future, mistrusted whites, and believed in paranoid conspiracy theories.[75]

Affirmative action is itself chiefly responsible for this paradoxical phenomenon. By creating an inferior black track, it has allowed people to enter middle-class occupations and receive middle-class incomes without genuinely earning them and, in the process, without having to acquire intimately and fully the values and attitudes which are their necessary prerequisites. Those who find themselves in such a situation cannot help sensing its precariousness and insubstantiality, and their reaction is understandably one of nervous discontent. Whites also perceive the reality, and it naturally creates doubts in their minds as to the competence and genuineness of the entire black middle class. Blacks in turn, including those who happen to be both competent and productive, react to the blanket of suspicion with discomfort and distrust.

Contributing to this poisoned atmosphere is the climate of politically correct opinion that dominated the 1990s and still lingers in the air. As soon as the white zealots of higher idealism became ferociously intent on elevating trivial insults to the status of major grievances, discontented middle-class blacks were ready and willing to assist them. Books like Ellis Cose's *Rage of a Privileged Class* accused whites of incessant verbal offenses, both deliberate and unintentional, that struck "repeated blows to the soul" of black people. Black celebrities declared that, despite all their wealth and prominence, they still felt oppressed and always would, since racism would always remain in the hearts of white people.[76]

In view of all the bad things that affirmative action has produced, one might think that there must be a better way of dealing with racial problems in the United States. In fact, a number of reform-minded individuals have pursued what would seem to be an obviously sound and practical strategy. They began by recognizing that black people lack certain crucially important skills and attitudes which are necessary to lead a productive and adequately remunerative life in American society. They then proceeded to identify the deficiencies, and finally they devised an educational curriculum aimed at remedying them.

But they have found, to their puzzlement, that their efforts failed to arouse the interest and encouragement that they might have expected. As one sociologist observed, there are a number of schools where blacks and other minorities have learned to do well academically, yet these successes have been ignored or disparaged. "Failure attracts more money than success," he concluded in bewildered frustration.[77]

These reformers have also discovered, to their further consternation, that their most impassioned and vociferous opponents are not on the right but on the left—their very own side. Idealists possessed of a more radical temperament than theirs and stoked with a higher ardor of moral indignation have condemned the strategy of improving the personal behavior of the disadvantaged rather than their external situation. Society is responsible for the deplorable condition of black people, they insist. It is the recalcitrant indifference, selfishness, and bigotry of the intransigent majority that need to change, not the conduct of their victims, the members of the minority.

This is a position that many prominent and influential people, including pundits and policymakers, maintain with adamant and undeviating conviction. The very suggestion that the cultural norms of blacks—or of any minority, for that matter—might produce undesirable behavior seems to them nearly as abhorrent as the belief that inherited genetics might do so. "The sky will fall" before they admit the simple and obvious truth, exclaimed one journalist in exasperated disgust. Instead, with weary and automatic predictability, they continue to denounce white racism as the villain.[78]

What is the reason for this stubborn denial of reality among otherwise intelligent and informed people? Why do they persist in rejecting what is the clear and sensible explanation for persistent underperformance by blacks and what would be its logical and practical solution? The answer is twofold. First, accepting such an explanation and solution would satisfy the goals of the remedial half of their higher idealism (including the iron logic of minority percentages), but at the same time it would negate those of the transcendent half. Blacks would achieve genuine academic and occupational success in percentages equal to those of the white majority, but they would do so by reproducing the objectionable characteristics of the white majority, including its inequalities.

Blacks would begin by submitting to the basic and elementary restraints on behavior which are characteristic of the higher levels of the lower class (including that detested group of people just above the bottom of society). Some blacks would succeed in going further and acquiring the tastes and interests of the lower levels of the middle class. And a few would manage to master the subtle manners and elevated outlook of the upper-middle class. The result would be a black replication of white America's social hierarchy, with the percentage of the total of both races at each level diminishing equally as one proceeded upward.

The idea of such a future is contrary to transcendent idealism's dream of equality with its vision of an inspiring, exciting life for everyone, as all human beings realize their highest potential and an Emersonian mass elite comes into being. The previous chapter explained how the hope of attaining this goal has fueled the passion of people who have been applauding and advancing the cause of disadvantaged minorities since the Sixties. Because a realistic assessment of black failure and its realistic remedy would lead obviously and naturally to a future devoid of transcendent idealism, the response among the social activists and their allies is one of anger, dismay, and disbelief. This cannot be the end which they have been working to achieve, with all their prolonged and selfless effort.

The prospect of higher idealism being diminished and degraded by the loss of its transcendent half is a powerful incentive to aversion and denial, but there is a second and more profound motive involved—the imperative of preserving America's necessary secret. Black people have been notably unsuccessful in business enterprise, whether as corporate employees or as independent entrepreneurs or even as members of criminal organizations.[79] The explanation is not white racism, as the left claims, nor is it simply a lack of individual initiative and effort, as the right believes. It is, in fact, almost the opposite of the latter notion.

As the basic thesis of this book has argued, American achievement rests on a delicate and dynamic balance which it has managed to maintain between the two halves of a formula consisting of individualism and conformity. Black society lacks this balance; it is overabundant in the first half and deficient in the second. As sociologists have observed—back when they could speak more frankly on racial matters than they can today—black men in their natural environment behave as rampant individualists, each one out for himself, ready to use savage force or cunning fraud to achieve his own dominance and advantage.[80]

Excessive individualism upsets the efficient functioning of collective enterprise, whether in business or elsewhere, which requires the harmonious interaction of individual participants and the smooth coordination of their respective efforts. The American workplace accordingly imposes what I have called flexible conformity, which allows for individual initiative within limits set by peer groups. Black culture lacks this supple regulation of the self by the collectivity. The black employee is not a team player; his ego is always engaged and easily aroused. He resents orders or criticism from superiors, black or white, as a personal affront. When disagreements arise, he exacerbates them with a loud, angry, and automatic defense of his position, whatever it may be, right or wrong. Blacks actually enjoy office meetings that accomplish nothing more than a venting of emotions, as each individual allows his ego to roar with complete spontaneity and no restraint.[81]

"The expressive lifestyle," as it has been called, functions contrary to the thick layers of social grease that facilitate personal relationships in American organizations. Blacks complain about the dishonesty and inauthenticity of corporate life, which obliges them to suppress their real emotions and pretend that they like people whom they actually dislike. They are not comfortable with the degree to which a person is expected to subordinate his individuality to the demands of the job and, at the more professional levels, to merge his individual identity with that of his occupation. White people "even look like what they do," remarked a black manager. "A white accountant looks like an accountant, a white lawyer looks like a corporate lawyer." Welcome to the world of American productivity, blackie. You have just met the myrmidons of modernity.[82]

Incompatibility between behavior acquired from their culture and behavior expected on the job is the fundamental source of black frustration and failure. As numerous employers have observed, the difficulties of black employees arise less from their lack of specific skills or technical knowledge than from their general attitudes. That, incidentally, is the source of a nugget of truth behind the popular black complaint that one has to be twice as good as a white employee to achieve the same reward. Being conspicuously superior in the external qualifications of formal knowledge and know-how is one way of compensating for a deficiency in the internal qualities of emotional self-control and social rapport.

Some black people try to adapt to the world of work by totally repressing their natural reactions and becoming lackeys and yes-men. Black women are more likely to employ this strategy than black men. Like women in general, they are more willing than men to endure supervisors, colleagues, rules, and tasks that they dislike and even detest, just so that they can provide for their families. But submissiveness alone will carry one only so far. Black women have surpassed black men in percentage and levels of employment, but they still remain in the lower positions of the workforce, and rightly so.

The American labor market is a shrewd and discerning judge of its workers. In allowing access to its higher places, it requires more than passive obedience and a willingness to perform drudgery. It demands that candidates for advancement have a keen and active commitment to their work, that they possess the emotional as well as the technical skills necessary to interact efficiently with others. External compliance and automatic imitation are not enough. One must have absorbed into one's mind and spirit the fundamental presumptions and subtle qualities of the American formula.

How black people can do this—how any minority group can do this after its culture has taught them different and contrary lessons—is the question. In addressing it, one would need to investigate the situation at a thorough and fundamental level. That will not and must not happen. Anyone who seeks to determine what are the crucial characteristics that most Americans have and that most black Americans lack will come face-to-face with the collective controls of the second half of the national formula and their dominance over the ideals of the first half. At this moment, he must draw back and retreat.

To proceed further would result in the violation of a necessary secret and its dire consequences, which were explained in chapter six. As a result, public discussion of race in America has remained and necessarily must remain at an ignorant and superficial level. People on the left continue to blame white bigotry and call for more racial preferences under the name of affirmative action. People on the right keep preaching the traditional line of economic individualism and its beneficial self-deception: blacks should just work harder and everything will be all right—as if this were a panglossian world, in which effort alone will achieve success. Neither side could do otherwise, however. White people cannot possibly be honest with black people because they cannot be honest with themselves. The necessary secret must be preserved at all cost.

—6—

Since the last years of the 1990s and during the first years of the new century, a change has been taking place in the tenor of American life. It has been especially noticeable in race relations: the tensions and hostility between blacks and whites have been decreasing. Electoral contests and results reflect the tendency. Race is no longer an important issue on the candidates' agenda. Districts with white majorities as well as those with black majorities have been electing and reelecting black politicians with moderate views. Militants, both black and white, continue to trumpet the old rhetoric of outrage, but the public has become increasingly indifferent. When, for example, they proclaimed the plight of black hurricane victims in New Orleans as if it were flagrant evidence of injustice and discrimination, the charge received a cursory nod of attention from the rest of the country and then was quickly forgotten.

The rhetoric of racial oppression has become less popular even among blacks. In 2005, Bill Cosby decried the ugly, irresponsible, and self-destructive behavior of young black men, to the indignation of veteran black activists but also to the applause of ordinary black people. Of course, racist attitudes continue to exist among whites, and they result in random minor insults. But they are just that, as John McWhorter has insisted—random minor insults. They are not the life-blighting and soul-crushing acts that Ellis Cose and other racial obsessives made them out to be a decade earlier.[83]

This tendency toward moderation has not been confined to the subject of race. The burning issues of the 1990s in general have simmered down. One can still hear the occasional complaints: a vapid appeal for diversity here, a prissy complaint about politically incorrect speech there. But the old war cries have become less frequent and less strident. On campus, the culture war between left and right is "not exactly over," according to one witness. "The situation is more like a Korean armistice—with periodic saber-rattling on both sides" but "most of all, a feeling of exhausted confusion about what all the fuss had originally been about."[84]

The left has come up with some new versions of its old causes, such as the "racial profiling" of Arab terrorist suspects and "gay marriage" as a civil right for homosexuals, but these have failed to arouse anything like the old passion in behalf of civil rights for black citizens or even the outcry in the 1990s against the racial profiling of black motorists. Activists grumble that left-wing politics have become nothing but a superficial stance and an empty gesture for most people, who repeat idealistic pieties and give cursory attention to the issues of the day, while they invest their significant time and real effort in personal careers and private life. The complaints extend to prominent spokesmen and ideologues, who are criticized for trying to act like stars of popular culture rather than genuine revolutionary leaders.

It is all part of a general trend that chapter eight explained. By the year 2000, the prevailing figure at the higher levels of American life had become David Brooks' Bobo, the bourgeois bohemian, an upper-middle-class person who had absorbed and reconciled the personal liberation of the 1960s with the economic conservatism of the 1980s, and who therefore saw no reason for serious conflict or controversy. Underlying the new moderation, the prolonged and disruptive influence of the Great Depression was at last coming to an end, with the two halves of the American formula finally regaining their original state of balance and equilibrium.

The emerging mood of this historical moment found early expression in the popularity of the phrase "the end of history," derived from the title of an essay and later a book by Francis Fukuyama, who had been inspired by the end of the Cold War. The situation in the world at large was similar to that which prevailed within the United States. Abroad as at home, "all of the really big questions had been settled."[85] The clash of international ideologies was over; capitalism and democracy had won. America was the only remaining superpower, and it provided the social model for other nations.

The dramatic emergence of Islamic radicalism onto the world stage, signaled by the terrorist attacks in 2001, has not completely invalidated this view of reality, as some are inclined to think. Islam does not pose a fundamental challenge in the way Communism and fascism did during the early years of the Twentieth Century. Both members of that pernicious pair seriously disputed the future of modernity with capitalistic democracy. Both aspired to be the social and political system that was best able to manage the changes created by the rise of industrialism and specifically to win the allegiance and participation of the masses. Islamic radicalism, in contrast, does not seek to lead modernity but to destroy it and return to a religious past. Its ideas, consequently, have no attraction or appeal for the modern inhabitants of the West. It has not won any significant number of converts and fellow travelers, as Soviet socialism did in the 1930s. It can cause damage and create disorder, but little more than that.

Does this mean America is now approaching a permanent state of perpetual domestic tranquility, where the populace will go about busily producing and happily consuming, and the complaints of dissatisfaction on both the left and the right will subside to a low if not inaudible murmur? Alas, it cannot be so. The fundamental dilemma of modernity, an unbalanced equation between human desires and the realities of the world, remains unsolved.

It was already present by the turn of the Eighteenth Century, as the beginning of chapter nine explained. Philosophers and other men of letters chattered on about the marvelous natural harmonies of human society and the wonderful future prospects of mankind, when people everywhere would realize their limitless innate potential. At the same time, the world was getting to work, herding vast and motley populations into barracks to form peoples' armies in behalf of peoples' states, then driving them into factories to produce the material abundance and strength characteristic of industrial economies in the Nineteenth Century.

The contrast continues today. Earnest and idealistic citizens worry about the rights and opportunities of women and minorities, while educational and occupational realities proceed with the grinding, mundane business of converting this previously underutilized human raw material into the reliable and replaceable parts of a technological economy. As academics proclaim that their obscure writings are "unmasking patriarchy" or "discrediting hierarchy" or in some other way promoting what they believe is the cause of human freedom, the practical world pushes relentlessly onward, molding the uniformity and imposing the discipline that it needs to achieve its productive agenda.

Assisted by their national formula, Americans have coped with the unbalanced equation of modernity more successfully than other peoples, but they have done so by telling themselves lies—and lies, even beneficial ones, have consequences. Among these is a neurosis of frustrated idealism, some of whose festering manifestations I have analyzed in the preceding pages of this book. At the present moment, it is in a state of comparative quiescence, but one can predict that eventually it will revive and grow, until it produces some new variety of moralistic miasma to distract and dominate the national consciousness. This would not be a new development, only the recrudescence of a chronic condition—one of the persistent liabilities of life in the modern world.

The distemper was diagnosed long ago. In the late Nineteenth Century, a philosopher appeared who deserves to be called the Copernicus of sublunary reality or the Magellan of the human spirit. He viewed the great corporate organizations of modernity and perceived their inherent ethical weakness: everything about them was false. He even identified a precise symptom of their inadequacy: confusion in the language of good and evil. Then he turned to what society has regarded as its highest ideals and dared anyone who was curious and reckless enough to look into the dark factory where they were manufactured and see that they were counterfeit, that wretchedness and impotence had been transformed into virtues.[86]

The ardently self-righteous and assiduously fraudulent moralists that he exposed spoke the language and repeated the dogma of religion. Today, their lineal descendants are secular in word and mind—even ferociously so, with an abiding aversion to traditional faiths. But as they proclaim their compassion for the miserable and oppressed of all humanity, as they vaunt their own selfless altruism and moral sensitivity while excoriating the prejudices, the egotism, and the apathy of others, they are carrying on the work of their pious progenitors. They will, no doubt, have similar progeny of their own.

An Afterword with Sonny

The work of the vivisector is finished. The internal organs of the body politic (the cleft heart, the clouded brain) lie exposed—bloody and twitching—to the sight of my audience. At this moment, I can imagine a somewhat familiar figure stepping forward to express his displeasure—perhaps not Sonny himself but someone like Sonny.

"Surely you don't mean to end here."

Well, yes. The exposition of my ideas is complete. I have done my best to extend my theory to its largest dimensions, to pursue its furthest implications, and to draw out its ultimate conclusions.

"But you have ended on a negative note. That is not suitable for an American book. The public wants something positive, something that will make it feel good."

Consider the entire work. It does not necessarily oblige a reader to feel downcast and pessimistic. It does not preach decline and ruin. One might peruse it and logically conclude that over the long run things will proceed much as they always have—continuing material progress accompanied by a certain amount of inevitable discontent. The American formula with its beneficial self-deception has overcome difficulties in the past. It would seem reasonable to expect that it will continue doing so in the future, that Americans will go on "puzzled and prospering" (as Jefferson predicted)—though, in the case of my readers, I hope somewhat less puzzled.

"I was puzzled myself that you should describe as beneficial something which most people would view as detrimental. The idea that we are better off because we have deceived ourselves—what a paradoxical thesis for a book!"

You might regard it as a *Praise of Folly* for the Land of the Free.[1] Perhaps there is a glimmer of wisdom in the popular saying, "God looks after fools, drunkards, and the United States of America." Of course, one needs to be a particular kind of fool. Not all foolish people or peoples prosper.

"That last statement at least is certainly true. But aside from the overall import of your work, you cannot deny that you are often critical and occasionally derogatory of the various social conditions and behavioral practices that you take up and discuss. Now when someone identifies anything as less than optimal, he has an obligation to suggest how it can be made better. That is a rule of American practical thinking, as you surely must admit, in view of what you have identified as panglossianism."

You are correct in your general observation but wrong in applying it to me. Considerations of length alone would have limited the present work to description without prescription. Since I had to introduce and explain ideas that I knew readers would find unfamiliar, novel, and at times dubious, it was clear that abbreviated and abstract statements alone would not suffice to convey understanding and win conviction. I needed to add arguments and illustrations, and these increased the expenditure of words and space. So did the very nature of the subject. A theory that seeks to explain a significant part of social reality necessarily entails the presentation of a large number of phenomena both past and present, including the treatment of subordinate points that support larger ones and of minor causes that combine to produce major effects.

In view of all this prolonged exposition and complex analysis, the suggestion that I should also offer remedies and improvements is not a request that I would have been able to grant. Even if I were rash and presumptuous enough to proceed from the role of vivisector to that of redesigner, to become a kind of sociological Dr. Frankenstein who would attempt to discover, not just how the body politic functions, but also how it could be refashioned to function better—even if I were foolhardy enough to undertake such a task, the length of the present work would forbid it. It would need to be the subject matter of another book.

As for the present one, if it has any claim to merit, that must rest on the accuracy, depth, and originality of its insights, and those are the criteria on which I hope readers will judge it, not on its failure to present plans for practical betterment. I have constructed a theory that addresses two fundamental questions: Why has the United States become the most powerful and prosperous nation in the world? and Why, despite this achievement, are so many of its citizens so discontent? I should think that such an undertaking would satisfy anyone with a normal intellectual appetite.

"Very well, but I come back to my original objection as to your ending. One may frankly and openly confront an audience with negative things—in fact, one can arouse their serious attention by doing so—but one must conclude on a note of uplift. It is not enough to say that the country and the world will stumble along as they always have. People want to be told that they can, may, or will get better—internally as well as externally, emotionally and morally as well as materially. That is true for all public discourses, high and low alike. A hellfire sermon spends most of its time threatening its listeners with the inferno, but at last it extends to them the possibility of heaven. An expostulation on the current state of humanity or the nation may be filled with portentous (that is, pretentiously portentous) warnings, but it needs to assume a stance of dogged, gritty persistence: yes, we have problems, but we are able to confront and master them; yes, at times we slide backwards, but eventually we regain the ground we have lost; and slowly, painfully, overall we are making progress forward. That is the kind of conclusion which I and—I venture to say—most other readers want to hear."

Your argument, I admit, is cogent and convincing. And I believe that, in this matter at least, I may be able to "comply with the taste of the town" (or rather, with the American temperament).[2] Even at this late hour, I suppose I could wrap things up with a look at the positive side rather than the negative or the neutral. So let me see what I can do.

An Optimistic Conclusion

I n the process of coping with new and difficult conditions that have
arisen during the course of its social and economic development,
America has devised many new and surprising measures that have
misled observers and critics. What initially appeared as unsound and
repugnant (such as the conditions detailed at the beginning of chapter
one) has at times, with further development and deeper examination,
turned out to be sensible and positive. Among contemporary candidates
for inclusion in this general category are three phenomena. Although at
present they are too amorphous and inchoate to be understood fully or
evaluated with final certainty, they are indicative of the bold innovation
with which America continues to engage and shape its future, and as
such they may form a fitting conclusion to this book.

(1.) "Relativism" is a subject that arouses much controversy. Professors
have found that one of the few things their students have in common
is the disbelief in a universal standard of morality. These young people
are adamant in maintaining that ideas of right and wrong vary from
group to group and from culture to culture, and who is to say that one
culture or subculture's values are superior to another's? They have difficulty condemning even practices that are blatantly vicious or stupidly
self-destructive, when these are presented as what some tribe or other
distinct group of people freely accepts and willingly promotes.[1]

As is usually the case, the young are only reflecting in exaggerated
form an attitude that prevails among their elders. Contemporary higher

education itself teaches instrumental competence not ultimate values. Long ago, it stopped talking about "character" and "virtues" and gave up worrying about what qualities constitute an "educated person."[2] From the professors themselves, one can hear any number of arguments in favor of relativism: It reflects tolerance, democracy, and freedom, in contrast to moral absolutes, which impose judgment upon others, thereby promoting authoritarianism and control. Besides, the United States, not to mention the world, is far too diverse to have a single code of conduct.

Similar if less explicitly rationalized attitudes are popular among the general public. Each individual asserts the fully equal worth of his own outlook compared with that of anyone else on earth, as he declares in response to some sentiment with which he disagrees, "I have my own opinion, and you (or he) have yours (or his)"—end of discussion. An English visitor was struck by the nonchalance with which talk show guests who expressed the most debased and perverse attitudes were received, as if "everyone has a point of view worth hearing." The Eleventh Commandment of contemporary America seems to be "Thou Shalt Not Judge," and in fact "judgmental" has become a highly pejorative word.[3]

Some pundits, especially on the right, are greatly distressed by this climate of relativism. They think it is leading to moral anarchy and a society where anything goes and everything is up for grabs. Their fears are unfounded. Today's relativism is only an advanced form of flexible conformity, a trait which, as chapter five explained, has always characterized Americans. An individual who believes that values vary with times and circumstances will be susceptible to the values of whatever group he happens to be a member of, and he will thus function as its cooperative and obedient participant. This, of course, is precisely what the engine of American productivity has needed in the past and continues to need all the more now, when speed and change are increasing in the world of work, and employees are called upon to be "focused, fast, friendly, and flexible"—especially the last.[4] The youth whose only firm conviction is that standards of conduct are relative should become the adaptable worker of the future.

(2.) Another development that has given rise to conventional misgivings is the devaluation of private domestic life. As a number of social commentators have complained, the home is becoming less and less a warm and secure place where one can find refuge from the indifference and adversity of the outside world. One social critic compared the new character and emerging functionality of the home to that of a "railway station," where individual family members stop for fuel and rest as they go about their busy and separate lives.[5]

Not only has the bond between husband and wife become fragile and problematical—liable, as it is, to be broken at the wish of either party—even when it persists, its benefits and attractions are now appraised at far less than they used to be. A reviewer of two "perfectly good books," one about divorced people and the other about lasting marriages, found it difficult to say which was the more depressing. A survey of parental happiness was surprised to find that "the highest level of satisfaction is reported not within intact marriages but by divorced dads! Evidently, the less time one spends with one's children, the more positive is one's parenting experience. The more active and engaged are the parents, the more they report feelings of inadequacy, negativity, and ambivalence."[6]

While this anti-domestic tendency has been widely noticed and deplored, some observers have perceived a related trend: as the home has been declining in value, work has been rising. It is not just the fact that work is absorbing more time and attention at the expense of private life; work is increasingly viewed as the more desirable of the two. People admit that they feel more competent and more appreciated on the job than with their family, that the former provides a more varied and interesting environment than the latter. With the attenuation of other forms of social life, such as neighborhoods and kinship groups, work is now the chief place where one can find friends and a sense of community. For women especially, it has become a source of, not just financial, but also emotional security in an age of troubled and precarious marriages. One journalist specializing in the domestic life of women has even predicted that the day is approaching when mothers will voluntarily choose to spend more time on the job rather than with their children.[7]

There are, admittedly, certain contradictions and shortcomings involved in the substitution of work for home. Emotional relationships are not necessarily efficient productive relationships. One's personal feelings and needs often have nothing to do with, and at times run counter to, the requirements of one's role as an effective worker. The overriding purpose of work is getting a job done with maximum speed and optimal results, not satisfying people's desire for friendship and community, and it is only a panglossian delusion to think that the two naturally coincide.

This becomes all the more obvious the higher one goes in the world of work. The situation where a number of people have been doing the same job together over a long period of time and have built up personal bonds in the process is increasingly a phenomenon of the past. Today it persists, if at all, at the lower levels of employment. Among better paid and more professional employees, change prevents and transience dissolves strong emotional ties. It is normal procedure for a team of specialists to be brought together to accomplish a particular assignment and, once that is done, for the individual members to go their separate ways.

However unsatisfactory this may be in human terms, it is what the modern economy needs, and the human aspects of the process have to be kept subordinate to the process itself. Lasting and significant personal relationships may actually interfere with productivity rather than assist it, for example, "I want to work with Jack, not with that jerk Bill, even if he is the better technician" or "Jim is my friend, how can I fail to promote him, even in view of his inferior performance?" Superficial amiability—the social grease mentioned in chapter five—is the functional desideratum, not deep friendship or enduring community.

(3.) The decline of domesticity creates further issues. There has been much worrying during the past decade or two over the effects of the new conditions on children. One has often heard the fear expressed that broken marriages and mothers at work will result in offspring who are emotionally needy, who are shallow, vulnerable, and insecure because they lack a firm grounding of certainty and a solid sense of self. This may be true, but it may also be the source of socially desirable rather than undesirable traits.

Chapter five mentioned the ungrounded quality of American life and the rootlessness of Americans, and it explained that these were the obverse and negative side of the positive and necessary qualities of cooperation and flexible conformity. The latter are what the second half of the American formula needs and promotes—people who obey the will of their productive peers and function as cooperative working parts—not independent, egotistical individuals, each insisting on his own agenda, as the ideals of the first half of the formula might suggest.

Judging from the results, one should feel reassured that certain conditions of contemporary childhood—absent parents, unconfident adults, a climate of relativism—favor the second half. Instead of the fractious and headstrong youth of the Sixties, we have the organization kids, who accept the conditions laid down by society and do their best to adapt to them. In time, they should develop into full-scale adult form as protean men, ready to adapt to any circumstance and to comply with anything that is expected of them.

The emotional lives of such persons may not be particularly attractive. Protean man is not the man of nobility or the man who has realized his highest potential. He is the hollow man, uncertain and restless.[8] But this is precisely the motivation that may result in highly productive functionality. After he attains a new level or accomplishes a new task, he still feels unsatisfied and proceeds on to the next in an endless and futile quest. The same thing is true of a person who seeks friendship and community on the job. The results are never all that he hoped for, but he goes on, spreading the grease of friendliness and thereby greasing the wheels of business operations. The insatiable consumer acts in a similar way as he joins the numberless throng of shoppers in the mall. "I buy things I don't need, with money I don't have, to impress people I don't like," declares a cynical commonplace. However unsatisfactory such behavior may be to its practitioners, it unquestionably helps to stoke the engines of manufacturing and to drive the endless cycle of acquiring and creating commercial products.

If protean man served only the requirements of the second half of the American formula, that would be enough, but he does more. He reinforces belief in the ideals of the first half by presenting the appearance of freedom—protean man as free man. This can be seen in the changing themes of self-help books. During the 1970s, and long thereafter, popular literature spoke incessantly of the need for every individual to rediscover his unique self. In recent years, this has changed, and books are now talking, not about a person having a single self or core identity, but multiple selves and identities: "We all put on masks and discard them as we wish." This is not a pretense because "once donned, mask becomes reality...we are, in effect, what we pretend to be.... The healthy, happy human being wears many masks."[9]

As I indicated at the outset, the foregoing speculations are tentative, and they may seem excessively optimistic, even panglossian. Admittedly, it is difficult to view apparently unattractive things as the source of good. But one should consider the conditions that existed in the early United States. The beginning of chapter one described the low business practices, vile politics, wild religion, debased culture, and ugly manners which characterized that time and which some contemporaries, including Thomas Jefferson, found highly distressing. Yet those very features were symptoms and elements of an egalitarian ethos, which has played a fundamental role as part of the American formula in building the country's prosperity and strength. Should it come as a surprise, if in the challenging times of the present, the nation manages once again to achieve an outcome of utility and profit with ingredients that seem worthless and harmful?

Let us have faith in Americans' ability to deceive themselves. It has worked to good effect in the past. We should wish that it may endure into the future. The naked ugliness of reality discourages hopes and efforts. Generations of Americans have turned their eyes away from it and persisted in their dreams and their striving. For this they—as a nation, if not individually—have been rewarded with power and riches unprecedented in the history of the world. If those who now possess such bounty wish to retain it, they need to preserve the illusions and persevere in the conduct that brought it into being. Long may they continue to do so.

NOTES

Introduction

1 For Sonny Then, see: Neil Chesanow. *The World-Class Executive*. NY, 1985. p. 11, 20, 55, 75, 85; for Sonny Now, see: *Spectator* (London). Oct. 30, 1993. p. 7.

The bibliographical references in this book serve two purposes: (1) to give the source of actual quotations and specific facts; (2) to cite documents that will amplify points made and illustrate subjects presented. References of the second kind are necessarily a selection, drawn from literally thousands of notes accumulated during years of research. They appear less frequently in the later chapters because the topics discussed there are less historical and more contemporary, for which the reader's own memory can furnish illustration and amplification.

Chapter 1

1 Thomas Jefferson. Letter to John Page. May 25, 1766; Thomas Jefferson. Letter to Giovanni Fabbroni. June 8, 1778; Thomas Jefferson (1800) quoted in: Henry Adams. *History of the United States of America During the Administrations of Thomas Jefferson*. v. 1, ch. 6.

2 Daniel Webster quoted in: Richard Hofstadter. *The American Political Tradition*. NY, 1954. p. 67; Daniel Webster. Letter to Abijah Fuller. Aug. 29, 1802; Alexis de Tocqueville. *Journey to America*. Westport, CT, 1981. p. 162, 287, 363–64.

3 Francis J. Grund. *The Americans in Their Moral, Social, and Political Relations*. Boston, 1837. p. 204.

4 John Fenimore Cooper. *Home as Found*. ch. 2: the character Aristabulus Bragg; Alexis de Tocqueville. *Journey to America*. Westport, CT, 1981. p. 113; Victor Jacquemont. *Correspondance Inédit, 1824–1832*. Paris, 1877. v. 1, p. 173; William Miller. *Men in Business*. Cambridge, MA, 1952. p. 17.

5 Frances Trollope. *Domestic Manners of the Americans*. NY, 1949. p. 301–302 (ch. 28), p. 359 (ch. 31); Edgar Allan Poe. "Diddling, Considered as One of the Exact Sciences"; George Combe. *Notes on the United States of North America*. Philadelphia, 1841. p. 268.

6 Frederick Marryat. *A Diary in America*. Edited by S. W. Jackman. NY, 1962. p. 458; Nancy Aycock Metz. *The Companion to Martin Chuzzlewit*. Westport, CT, 2001. p. 221; Neil Harris. *Humbug: The Art of P. T. Barnum*. Boston, 1973. p. 77.

7   Thomas Jefferson. Letter to Henry Middleton. Jan. 8, 1813; Thomas Jefferson. Letter to Nathaniel Macon. Jan. 12, 1819.

8   Gustave de Beaumont. *Marie (1835)*. Baltimore, MD, 1999. p. 224; Neil Chesanow. *The World-Class Executive*. NY, 1985. p. 75.

9   Durand Echeverria. *Mirage in the West*. Princeton, NJ, 1957. p. 195; Charles Dickens. *American Notes*. NY, 1985. p. 225 (ch. 18); John Kenneth Galbraith in: *Sydney Morning Herald*. May 22, 1982.

10 Michael Lewis in: *Spectator* (London). May 23, 1992. p. 16; Neil Chesanow. *The World-Class Executive*. NY, 1985. p. 20, 22, 27.

11 Thomas Jefferson. Letter to Edward Carrington. Jan. 16, 1787.

12 Frances Trollope. *Domestic Manners of the Americans*. NY, 1949. p. 124 (ch. 12); Richard Slotkin. *Regeneration Through Violence*. Middletown, CT, 1973. p. 308.

13 Frederick Marryat. *A Diary in America*. Edited by S. W. Jackman. NY, 1962. p. 438–39, 466; Richard L. Bushman. *The Refinement of America*. NY, 1992. p. 430.

14 Martha Bayles in: *Times Literary Supplement*. Feb. 14, 1997. p. 15.

15 Thomas Jefferson. Letter to Walter Jones. Jan. 2, 1814; Thomas Jefferson quoted in: Derek Bok. *The Trouble with Government*. Cambridge, MA, 2001. p. 71; Alexis de Tocqueville. *Journey to America*. Westport, CT, 1981. p. 251.

16 Mark Twain. *Following the Equator*. v. 1, ch. 8; Henry Adams. *The Education of Henry Adams*. NY, 1931. p. 261 (ch. 17).

17 Thomas Jefferson. Letter to Benjamin Waterhouse. June 26, 1822.

18 Merle Curti. *American Paradox*. New Brunswick, NJ, 1956. p. 42.

19 Harry S. Stout, D. G. Hart. *New Directions in American Religious History*. NY, 1997. p. 195.

20 Orville Dewey. *Letters of an English Traveller*. Boston, 1828. p. 73–74.

21 Thomas Jefferson. Letter to Thomas Cooper. Nov. 2, 1822.

22 Ralph Waldo Emerson. *The Journals and Miscellaneous Notebooks*. Cambridge, MA, 1971. v. 9, p. 381 (May 1, 1846): "corpse-cold Unitarianism."

23 Harold Bloom. *The American Religion*. NY, 1992. p. 257; John Graves quoted by Christopher Hitchens in: *Vanity Fair*. Sept. 2005. p. 238. Perhaps Graves is entitled to something like the ironic sympathy ("Alas, good man!") that the historian Edward Gibbon in his memoirs extended to the theologian Thomas Edwards, who found himself similarly disappointed by the behavior of his coreligionists.

24 Francis Wheen. *Idiot Proof*. NY, 2004. p. 100; Katha Pollitt in: *Nation*. Dec. 6, 2004. p. 12; Katha Pollitt in: *Nation*. Oct. 3, 2005. p. 10.

25 Thomas Jefferson. *Notes on the State of Virginia*. ch. 14.

26 Thomas Jefferson. Letter to Peter Carr. Aug. 10, 1787; Jacob Duché. *Observations on a Variety of Subjects*. Philadelphia, 1774. p. 29–30 (letter 2: July 10, 1771).

27 George Bancroft in: Joseph L. Blau. *American Philosophic Addresses, 1700–1900*. NY, 1946. p. 103; John Fenimore Cooper. *Home as Found*. ch. 14.

28 William C. Dowling in: *Society*. Mar.–Apr. 2000. p. 32; Frances Trollope. *Domestic Manners of the Americans*. NY, 1949. p. 328 (ch. 29); Nathan O. Hatch. *The Democratization of American Christianity*. New Haven, CT, 1989. p. 27–30.

29 Gordon S. Wood. *The Radicalism of the American Revolution*. NY, 1991. p. 361; Thomas Jefferson. Letter to John Adams. July 5, 1814.

30 Alf Mapp. *Thomas Jefferson, Passionate Pilgrim*. Lanham, MD, 1991. p. 340–41; George Tucker. *The Life of Thomas Jefferson*. Philadelphia, 1837. v. 2, p. 478–481.

31 Richard Hofstadter. *Anti-Intellectualism in American Life*. NY, 1963. p. 272–282.

32 Thomas Hamilton. *Men and Manners in America*. Edinburg, 1834. v. 1, p. 365; James Truslow Adams. *Our Business Civilization*. NY, 1929. p. 195, 215–16; Thomas Hughes in: *Time*. Aug. 7, 1995. p. 64; Thomas Hughes in: *New York Review of Books*. Apr. 23, 1992. p. 23.

33 Van Wyck Brooks. *The Confident Years, 1885–1915*. NY, 1952. p. 218–19: the "cave-man tendency" in modern American literature; Michael Foley on Raymond Carver in: *London Review of Books*. May 2, 1985. p. 12.

34 Dan Kurzman. *Fatal Voyage*. NY, 1990. p. 177.

35 James A. Michener. *Sports in America*. NY, 1976. p. 6; Katha Pollitt in: *Nation*. Sept. 17 & 24, 2001. p. 10.

36 Ambrose Bierce. *The Devil's Dictionary*; James A. Michener. *Sports in America*. NY, 1976. p. 188; Chester E. Finn in: *Commentary*. Oct. 2001. p. 55.

37 Adam Davidson in: *Harper's*. Aug. 2001. p. 48, 54.

38 William Hazlitt. *The Plain Speaker*. "On the Look of a Gentleman."

39 Thomas Hughes. *Tom Brown at Oxford*. London, 1864. p. 92 (ch. 10); Esther B. Aresty. *The Best Behavior*. NY, 1970. p. 191 (cf. the peasants' food orgy in Luis Buñuel's 1961 film *Viridiana*); W. J. Rorabaugh. *The Alcoholic Republic*. NY, 1979.

40 Catharine Sedgwick quoted in: Stow Persons. *The Decline of American Gentility*. NY, 1973. p. 50, 123.

41 Francis J. Grund. *Aristocracy in America*. NY, 1959. p. 10; John Steinbeck. *Travels with Charley*. NY, 1962. p. 211; James Muirhead. *The Land of Contrasts*. London, 1900. p. 96.

42 Esther B. Aresty. *The Best Behavior*. NY, 1970. p. 259, 280.

43 Roger Butterfield in: *Pennsylvania Magazine of History and Biography*. v. 74 (Apr. 1950). p. 165; John W. Gardner. *Excellence*. NY, 1984. p. 29.

44 Neil Chesanow. *The World-Class Executive*. NY, 1985. p. 274–75.

45 Nora Ephron in: *Esquire*. Sept. 1977. p. 140; Bruce Curtin in: *American Heritage*. Nov. 1989. p. 50.

46 Hal Draper. *Berkeley: The New Student Revolt*. NY, 1965. p. 141; Laura Miller in: *New York Times Book Review*. Sept. 1, 2002. p. 9.

47 David Brooks. "Manly Upscale Proles." *New York Times*. Oct. 4, 2003; Tom Wolfe. *Hooking Up*. NY, 2000. p. 10–12.

48 Alexander Eliot. *Three Hundred Years of American Painting*. NY, 1957. p. 36; Diana West in: *Public Interest*. Fall 1997. p. 129.

49 Alexis de Tocqueville. *Journey to America*. Westport, CT, 1981. p. 44; Robert W. Smuts. *European Impressions of the American Worker*. NY, 1953. p. 4–5; Henry Fairlie. *The Spoiled Child of the Western World*. NY, 1976. p. 228.

50 Werner Sombart. *Why Is There No Socialism in the United States?* White Plains, NY, 1976 (originally published in 1906). p. 110; George Orwell. *The Collected Essays, Journalism, and Letters*. v. 3 (1968). p. 21: "The English People"; James Bryce. *The American Commonwealth*. NY, 1893–94. v. 2, p. 752 (ch. 109); Harriet Martineau. *Society in America*. NY, 1837. v. 2, p. 163.

51 Joanne B. Ciulla. *The Working Life*. NY, 2000. p. 92; Werner Sombart. *Why Is There No Socialism in the United States?* White Plains, NY, 1976. p. 111; Jacques Barzun. *God's Country and Mine*. Boston, 1954. p. 44.

52 Todd Gitlin. *Twilight of Common Dreams*. NY, 1995. p. 43; James Fenimore Cooper. *Home as Found*. ch. 4; Judith Martin. *Common Courtesy*. NY, 1985. p. 54; Richard L. Rapson. *Britons View America*. Seattle, WA, 1971. p. 68: "I'm not your man."

53 Robert T. McKenzie, Allan Silver. "Conservatism, Industrialism, and the Working Class Tory in England." *Transactions of the Fifth World Congress of Sociology.* Washington, DC, 1962. v. 3, p. 199.
54 George Bailey. *Germans: The Biography of an Obsession.* NY, 1991. p. 380–81; Geoffrey Gorer. *The American People.* NY, 1964. p. 41: J. P. Morgan and the midget; Steven Nicastro in: *Hartford Courant.* Aug. 15, 1997. p. E3.
55 Johan Huizinga. *America.* NY, 1972. p. 120; Todd Gitlin. *Twilight of Common Dreams.* NY, 1995. p. 43: "egaliarian irreverence"; P. J. O'Rourke. *A Parliament of Whores.* NY, 1991. p. 233.
56 D. H. Lawrence. *The Rainbow.* ch. 1; Norman Mailer. *The Armies of the Night.* NY, 1968. p. 257–58; Ted Conover. *Newjack.* NY, 2000. p. 262–63; Alex Heard in: *New Republic.* Aug. 22 & 29, 1994. p. 11–12.
57 Nathaniel Hawthorne. *The House of the Seven Gables.* ch. 8.
58 Garry Wills. *Mr. Jefferson's University.* Washington, DC, 2002. p. 130.
59 Carl E. Prince. "The Great 'Riot Year.'" *Journal of the Early Republic.* v. 5, no. 1 (Spring 1985).
60 Frances Trollope. *Domestic Manners of the Americans.* NY, 1949. p. 348–49 (ch. 30).
61 William T. Stead. *The Americanization of the World.* NY, 1972. p. 132.
62 Lewis Lapham. *Money and Class in America.* NY, 1988. p. 86; *Fortune.* Feb. 27, 1989. p. 54.
63 Charles Loring Brace. *The Dangerous Classes of New York.* NY, 1880. p. 27; James Q. Wilson in: *New Republic.* Aug. 25, 1997. p. 38.
64 Alexis de Tocqueville. *Journey to America.* Westport, CT, 1981. p. 224; Frederick Marryat. *A Diary in America.* Edited by S. W. Jackman. NY, 1962. p. 161–62.
65 Jack Katz. *Seductions of Crime.* NY, 1988. p. 44; Elliott Leyton. *Men of Blood.* London, 1995. p. 235–39.
66 Frances Trollope. *Domestic Manners of the Americans.* NY, 1949. p. 163 (ch. 14); *Spectator* (London). May 23, 1992. p. 4; Robert D. Putnam. *Bowling Alone.* NY, 2000. p. 310.
67 J. A. (John Alfred) Spender. *Through English Eyes.* NY, 1928. p. 130; Charles Barkley quoted in: *Newsweek.* Aug. 17, 1992. p. 15.
68 Jeremy Rabkin in: *Public Interest.* Fall 2002. p. 100; James Q. Wilson in: *New Republic.* Aug. 25, 1997. p. 41; Gavin De Becker. *The Gift of Fear.* Boston, 1997. p. 309.
69 Sousa Jamba in: *Spectator* (London). Mar. 11, 1989. p. 42. In a savagely ironic twist of history, by the year 2000 England itself seems to have become what it had always suspected America of being. See: Charles Murray. "The British Underclass." *Public Interest.* Fall 2001. For more details, consult the writings of the doctor and social commentator Theodore Dalrymple.
70 Harriet Martineau. *Society in America.* Paris, 1837. v. 1, p. 83–90.
71 Alexis de Tocqueville. *Journey to America.* Westport, CT, 1981. p. 75; Nixon quoted in: Theodore H. White. *The Making of the President, 1968.* NY, 1969. p. 147.
72 Seymour Martin Lipset. *Continental Divide.* NY, 1990. p. 100.
73 Benjamin Soskis in: *New Republic.* Apr. 17 & 24, 2000. p. 26; Michael Massing in: *New York Times Book Review.* Apr. 22, 2001. p. 12; Henry P. Lundsgaarde. *Murder in Space City.* NY, 1997. p. 163–66.
74 Gunnar Myrdal. *An American Dilemma.* NY, 1944. p. 16–19 (ch. 1); Frances Trollope. *Domestic Manners of the Americans.* NY, 1949. p. 219 (ch. 20).

75 Dinesh D'Souza. *Letters to a Young Conservative*. NY, 2002. p. 198; Bharati Mukherjee in: Bill Moyers. *A World of Ideas, II*. NY, 1990. p. 8; Lewis H. Lapham in: *Harper's*. Jan. 1992. p. 46–48.

76 Bryan R. Wilson. *Religion in Secular Society*. London, 1966. p. 101; Bryan Wilson in: *Times Literary Supplement*. Aug. 3–9, 1990. p. 831.

77 Alexis de Tocqueville. *Democracy in America*. NY, 1945. v. 2, p. 121 (bk. 2, ch. 8). Translation slightly revised.

78 Koenraad W. Swart. "'Individualism' in the Mid-Nineteenth Century." *Journal of the History of Ideas*. v. 23 (Jan.–Mar. 1962); Yehoshua Arieli. *Individualism and Nationalism in American Ideology*. Cambridge, MA, 1964. p. 193; Tony Judt in: *New York Review of Books*. May 1, 2003. p. 27; William McLoughlin, Robert N. Bellah. *Religion in America*. Boston, 1968. p. 104.

79 Pierre Victor Malouet in: Durand Echeverria. *Mirage in the West*. Princeton, NJ, 1957. p. 213; Max Weber. *From Max Weber*. NY, 1958. p. 57, 310; Gregg Easterbrook in: *New Republic*. Jan. 4 & 11, 1999. p. 22.

80 Thomas Jefferson. Letter to John Adams. Jan. 21, 1812.

Chapter 2

1   Unless otherwise noted, the Emerson quotations in the following paragraphs are from these two essays.

2   Ralph Waldo Emerson. *Journals and Miscellaneous Notebooks*. Edited by A. R. Ferguson. v. 4 (1964). p. 342.

3   Peter L. Berger. *The Capitalist Revolution*. NY, 1986. p. 103.

4   Daniel Bell. *Communitarianism and Its Critics*. Oxford, 1993. p. 12.

5   Jonah Goldberg in: *National Review*. Oct. 23, 2000. p. 64.

6   Ralph Waldo Emerson. "Politics."

7   Robert N. Bellah et al. *Habits of the Heart*. Berkeley, CA, 1985. p. 143.

8   Ralph Waldo Emerson. "The New England Reformers."

9   Barbara Ehrenreich in: *New Republic*. Apr. 2, 1990. p. 31; John Taylor Gatto in: *Harper's*. Sept. 2001. p. 62; *Time*. May 10, 1963. p. 24; John William Ward in: Earl F. Cheit. *The Business Establishment*. NY, 1964. p. 76.

10 *North American Review*. v. 223 (Mar.–May 1926). p. 57.

11 Alexis de Tocqueville. *Democracy in America*. NY, 1945. v. 2, p. 99 (bk. 2, ch. 2); Rupert Wilkinson. *American Social Character*. NY, 1992. p. 293.

12 Anyone who doubts the truth of this statement may do himself the pleasure of perusing the fourth book of Schopenhauer's *World as Will and Idea*. A shorter alterative would be the maxims of La Rochefoucauld pertaining to *amour propre*. If both are too elevated for the reader's taste, the first couple of chapters of Dale Carnegie's *How to Win Friends and Influence People* should be sufficient.

13 Mary Ann Glendon. *Rights Talk*. NY, 1991. p. 8; Noel Ignatiev, John Garvey. *Race Traitor*. NY, 1996. p. 120.

14 Arthur Danto in: Suzi Gablik. *Conversations Before the End of Time*. NY, 1995. p. 286.

15 Arthur S. Link. *Wilson: The Road to the White House*. Princeton, NJ, 1947. p. 514.

16 Neil Chesanow. *The World-Class Executive*. NY, 1985. p. 89; Stuart Miller. *Painted in Blood*. NY, 1987. p. 61; Francis Fukuyama. *Trust*. NY, 1995. p. 114; Stanley Hoffmann et al. *In Search of France*. Cambridge, MA, 1963. p. 258.

17 Rush Welter. *The Mind of America, 1820–1860*. NY, 1975. p. 147: William A. Alcott in 1834.

18 Alexis de Tocqueville. *Journey to America*. Westport, CT, 1981. p. 185: "a gambler who risks only his winnings"; Hugo Münsterberg in: Henry Steele Commager. *America in Perspective*. NY, 1947. p. 266; Edmond About. *The King of the Mountains*. NY, 1924. p. 15: the character John Harris.

19 Alexis de Tocqueville. *Democracy in America*. NY, 1945. v. 2, p. 129 (bk. 2, ch. 10).

20 Henry Adams. *The Education of Henry Adams*. NY, 1931. p. 328 (ch. 21); Lewis Lapham. *Money and Class in America*. NY, 1988. p. 59: New York and Paris.

21 Stuart Miller. *Painted in Blood*. NY, 1987. p. 99–100.

22 Diana B. Henriques. "Personal Business." *New York Times*. Nov. 29, 1998.

23 Alexis de Tocqueville. *Democracy in America*. NY, 1945. v. 2, p. 152 (bk. 2, ch. 18) and p. 237 (bk. 3, ch. 18); Francis J. Grund. *The Americans in Their Moral, Social, and Political Relations*. Boston, 1837. p. 206; Antonio Gramsci. *Selections from the Prison Notebooks*. London, 1971. p. 305.

24 Albert Jay Nock. *Memoirs of a Superfluous Man*. NY, 1943. p. 111–12: "an army on the march," "go and get it"; Lewis Lapham. *Money and Class in America*. NY, 1988. p. 81–82: "nomad camps"; Jane Walmsley. *Brit-Think, Ameri-Think*. NY, 1987. p. 64: "go for it"; Stuart Miller. *Painted in Blood*. NY, 1987. p. 56: "sharks."

25 John Bristed. *The Resources of the United States of America*. NY, 1818. p. 427; Charles A. Murray. *Travels in North America during the Years 1834, 1835, 1836*. London, 1839. v. 1, p. 148; Alexis de Tocqueville. *Journey to America*. Westport, CT, 1981. p. 162; James M. Jasper reviewed by Andrew Stark in: *Times Literary Supplement*. May 25, 2001. p. 11.

26 Mary Beard in: *London Review of Books*. Apr. 4, 1996. p. 25.

27 The literature dealing with social mobility in the United States is notoriously vast and complex. I do not feel a need to provide any bibliographical citations because I believe the content of this paragraph is not controversial and would meet with general acceptance among specialists, however surprising and disconcerting it might be to ordinary Americans.

28 Christopher Jencks, David Riesman. *The Academic Revolution*. NY, 1968. p. 133, 146–47; Lena Williams. *It's the Little Things*. NY, 2000. p. 236–37.

29 Christopher Lasch. *The True and Only Heaven*. NY, 1991. p. 488–89.

30 Alfred Lubrano. *Limbo*. Hoboken, NJ, 2004. p. 131, 136, 138–39, 143–47, 156.

31 *Commonweal*. May 8, 1981. p. 271.

32 John P. Marquand. *Point of No Return*. Boston, 1949. p. 203–205: high school graduation address.

33 Jay MacLeod. *Ain't No Makin' It*. Boulder, CO, 1995. p. 266; Richard Rorty in: *Dissent*. Spring 1992. p. 267; Paul Fussell. *Class*. NY, 1983. p. 15; Diana Trilling in: *New York Times*. Feb. 19, 1989. p. A1: "if you so much as mention it."

34 Arthur Marwick. *Class*. NY, 1980. p. 311; Richard L. Zweigenhaft, G. William Domhoff. *Jews in the Protestant Establishment*. NY, 1982. p. 90–91.

35 Tom Wolfe. *Mauve Gloves and Madmen, Clutter and Vine*. NY, 1976. p. 219–220; Richard Kahlenberg in: *New Republic*. Apr. 3, 1995. p. 24.

36 Christopher Matthews. *Kennedy and Nixon*. NY, 1996. p. 75, 100, 120; on the other side of the political spectrum, William F. Buckley also arose from a parentage that was wealthy, though far from patrician. His striving for unmistakable gentility produced, not what he doubtless wanted, the accent of "a tenth-generation Old

Etonian" (James Fallows. *More Like Us.* Boston, 1989. p. 64), but an idiosyncrati-
cally artificial and outlandishly affected manner of speaking.

37 Andrew Sullivan in: *New York Times Magazine.* Nov. 15, 1998. p. 59; Toby Young
in: *Spectator* (London). Oct. 18, 1997. p. 15; Judith Martin. *Common Courtesy.* NY,
1985. p. 41.

38 Daniel J. Boorstin. *The Americans: The Democratic Experience.* NY, 1973. p. 91–92;
David Riesman. *The Lonely Crowd.* New Haven, CT, 1950. p. 74; Alan J. Stern,
Donald D. Searing in: *British Journal of Political Science.* v. 6, pt. 2 (Apr. 1976).
p. 191.

39 Robert Chesshyre. *The Return of a Native Reporter.* London, 1987. p. 10; James
Baldwin quoted in: Christopher Hitchens. *Unacknowledged Legislation.* London,
2000. p. 232.

40 Michael Lind in: *Harper's.* June 1995. p. 37; Theodore Dalrymple in: *Spectator*
(London). June 19, 2004.

41 Jacob Duché. *Observations on a Variety of Subjects.* Philadelphia, 1774. p. 29–30
(letter 2: July 10, 1771).

42 Hermann Keyserling. *America Set Free.* NY, 1929. p. 239–240; Alan Ryan in: *Dissent.*
Fall 1992. p. 471; Richard Hammer. *The Helmsleys.* NY, 1990. p. 270–71.

43 Tad Szulc. *Innocents at Home.* NY, 1974. p. 489; David Brooks in: *New York Times.*
Jan. 12, 2003. section 4, p. 15; George Santayana. *Character and Opinion in the
United States.* NY, 1921. p. 198 (ch. 7).

44 M. Harrington in: *Harper's.* Mar. 1984. p. 48; Tad Szulc. *Innocents at Home.* NY,
1974. p. 159–160; Michael Novak. "The Conservative Mood." *Society.* Jan-Feb.
1994. p. 14.

45 Haynes Johnson. *Sleepwalking Through History.* NY, 1991. p. 423: cancer clinic;
Everett Carl Ladd. *The American Ideology.* Storrs, CT, 1994. p. 79–80: international
poll.

46 W. H. Auden. *The Dyer's Hand.* NY, 1962. p. 335; Michèle Lamont. *Money, Morals,
and Manners.* Chicago, 1992. p. 68; Kin Hubbard. *Abe Martin: Hoss Sense and
Nonsense.* Indianapolis, IN, 1926. p. 29.

47 Bluford Adams. *E Pluribus Barnum.* Minneapolis, MN, 1997. p. 34–35; Margaret
Morganroth Gullette in: *American Scholar.* Spring 2000. p. 106.

48 Robert E. Lane. *Political Ideology.* NY, 1962. p. 61, 69, 79; Philippe Bourgois. *In
Search of Respect.* Cambridge, UK, 1995. p. 54.

49 Daniel Webster. "Lecture Before the Society for the Diffusion of Useful Knowledge."
Boston: Nov. 11, 1836.

50 Jean-Paul Sartre in: *Dissent.* Winter 2001. p. 36; Barbara Tucker. *Samuel Slater
and the Origins of the American Textile Industry.* Ithaca, NY, 1984. p. 254; Richard
Hofstadter, Seymour Martin Lipset. *Turner and the Sociology of the Frontier.* NY,
1968. p. 215.

51 Edwin L. Godkin in: *North American Review.* v. 105 (July 1867). p. 178; Seymour
Martin Lipset. *The First New Nation.* NY, 1967. p. 147.

52 Quoted in: Earl F. Cheit. *The Business Establishment.* NY, 1964. p. 52.

53 Michael Mann. *The Sources of Social Power.* Cambridge, UK, 1993. v. 2, p. 635.

54 Werner Sombart. *Why Is There No Socialism in the United States?* White Plains, NY,
1976. p. 9–10.

55 Leon Samson. *Toward a United Front.* NY, 1935. ch. 1 (quoted in: John H. M.
Laslett, Seymour Martin Lipset. *The Failure of a Dream?* NY, 1974. p. 439).

56 David Montgomery. *Beyond Equality*. Urbana, IL, 1981. p. 210–19; Werner Sombart. *Why Is There No Socialism in the United States?* White Plains, NY, 1976. p. 20, 22–23, 110.

57 Michael McGerr. *A Fierce Discontent*. NY, 2003. p. 66.

58 Ibid., p. 285.

59 Earl F. Cheit. *The Business Establishment*. NY, 1964. p. 201: small-town editors; Lawrence K. Frank. *Society as the Patient*. Port Washington, NY, 1969. p. 1: "sick society"; Irving Howe in: *New Republic*. Oct. 15, 1990. p. 45: "rotten structure"; Christopher Lasch in: *New Republic*. Aug. 10, 1992. p. 33; Charles A. Beard. "The Myth of Rugged American Individualism." *Harper's*. v. 164 (Dec. 1931). p. 22.

60 Robert and Helen Lynd in: Richard H. Pells. *Radical Visions and American Dreams*. Middletown, CT, 1984. p. 320; Michael J. Sandel in: *New Republic*. Feb. 3, 1997. p. 27.

61 Jean-Paul Sartre in: *Dissent*. Winter 2001. p. 33; Russell W. Davenport. *U.S.A.: The Permanent Revolution*. NY, 1951. p. 225.

62 Werner Sombart. *Why Is There No Socialism in the United States?* White Plains, NY, 1976. p. 112; Robert W. Smuts. *European Impressions of the American Worker*. NY, 1953. p. 21; Ronald Dore. *Taking Japan Seriously*. Stanford, 1987. p. 144.

63 Werner Sombart. *Why Is There No Socialism in the United States?* White Plains, NY, 1976. p. 20; Robert W. Smuts. *European Impressions of the American Worker*. NY, 1953. p. 23.

64 David Brooks in: *Atlantic*. Dec. 2001. p. 57–58.

65 Edward Everett. "Speech at the Mercantile Library Association." Boston: Sept. 13, 1838.

66 Thomas Frank in: *London Review of Books*. Mar. 21, 2002. p. 20; Thomas Frank. *What's the Matter with Kansas*. NY, 2004. p. 1, 248.

67 Dinesh D'Souza. *The Virtue of Prosperity*. NY, 2000. p. 75; Leon Trotsky. *My Life*. NY, 1930. p. 271; Tom Wolfe in: *Harper's*. June 2000. p. 77.

68 Michael Lynch, Katherine Post in: *Public Interest*. Summer 1996. p. 34–35; Peter Brown. *Minority Party*. Washington, DC, 1991. p. 38.

69 David Brooks in: *Atlantic*. Nov. 2002. p. 33.

70 James Fallows. *More Like Us*. Boston, 1989. p. 187.

71 David McClelland. *The Achieving Society*. Princeton, NJ, 1961. p. 222; Bray Hammond. *Banks and Politics in America*. Princeton, NJ, 1957. p. 281–82.

72 Joyce Appleby. *Inheriting the Revolution*. Cambridge, MA, 2000. p. 58; Richard Hofstadter. *The Age of Reform*. NY, 1955. p. 43, 46.

Chapter 3

1 Ralph Waldo Emerson. "Self-Reliance."

2 Richard Hofstadter. *Anti-Intellectualism in American Life*. NY, 1963. p. 338: democracy and science; George Bancroft in: Joseph L. Blau. *American Philosophic Addresses, 1700–1900*. NY, 1946. p. 102; Charles E. Wilson quoted in: Piers Brendon. *Ike: His Life and Times*. NY, 1986. p. 241.

3 Lawrence Frederick Kohl. *The Politics of Individualism*. NY, 1989. p. 162; Paul Leinberger, Bruce Tucker. *The New Individualists*. NY, 1991. p. 237–38.

4 David Boaz. *Libertarianism, A Primer*. NY, 1997. p. 16–18; William A. Donohue. *Twilight of Liberty*. New Brunswick, NJ, 1994. p. 320; Susan Sontag in: *Ramparts*. Apr. 1969. p. 10.

5   Jacob Burckhardt quoted in: Daniel Bell. *The End of Ideology*. NY, 1965. p. 13; Richard Hofstadter. *The American Political Tradition*. NY, 1954. p. 230 (ch. 9, pt. 3).

6   David Brooks. *On Paradise Drive*. NY, 2004. p. 229–230.

7   Thomas Paine. *Common Sense*. 1776.

8   Gordon S. Wood in: *New Republic*. Oct. 23, 1995. p. 40.

9   William M. Gouge. *A Short History of Paper Money and Banking in the United States*. Philadelphia, 1833. pt. 1, p. 91–96, 132–140; Andrew Jackson. Veto message to Congress. July 10, 1832: "…when the laws undertake to add to these natural and just advantages artificial distinctions…."

10 Arthur B. Shostak, William Gomberg. *Blue-Collar World*. Englewood Cliffs, NJ, 1964. p. 549.

11 Ralph Waldo Emerson. *Journals and Miscellaneous Notebooks*. Edited by A. R. Ferguson. v. 4 (1964). p. 297; Ralph Waldo Emerson. "The New England Reformers." and "Politics."

12 William Finnegan quoted by Joyce Carol Oates in: *New York Review of Books*. July 16, 1998. p. 14; the sculptor Richard Serra interviewed in: *New York Times Magazine*. Oct. 8, 1989. p. 41; Oliver Stone quoted in: Lynne V. Cheney. *Telling the Truth*. NY, 1995. p. 158.

13 Eva Hoffman. *Lost in Translation*. NY, 1989. p. 175.

14 George F. Will in: *Newsweek*. Nov. 11, 1996. p. 96.

15 Thomas Donohue quoted by Sam MacDonald in: *Reasononline* (www.reason.com). Jan. 21, 2002.

16 Alexis de Tocqueville. *Democracy in America*. NY, 1945. v. 1, p. 404 (ch. 18); Jacob Weisberg. *In Defense of Government*. NY, 1996. p. 32.

17 Irving Kristol in: *Times Literary Supplement*. May 26, 2000. p. 14; Alexis de Tocqueville. *Journey to America*. Westport, CT, 1981. p. 106; Joginder Singh Rekhi in: *National Geographic*. v. 126, no. 4 (Oct. 1964). p. 558.

18 H. G. Wells. *The Future in America*. NY, 1987. p. 15 (ch. 2): "optimistic fatalism"; James Fallows. *More Like Us*. Boston, 1989. p. 3.

19 John William Ward in: Earl F. Cheit. *The Business Establishment*. NY, 1964. p. 76.

20 Ralph Waldo Emerson. "The New England Reformers."

21 Dinesh D'Souza. *The End of Racism*. NY, 1995. p. 275; Andrew Sullivan in: *New York Times Magazine*. Sept. 26, 1999. p. 55; David Samuels in: *New Republic*. Sept. 18 & 25, 1995. p. 36.

22 Mickey Kaus. *The End of Equality*. NY, 1992. p. 160.

23 John Poppy. "New Era in Industry." *Look*. July 9, 1968. p. 64–76.

24 Walt Whitman. *Leaves of Grass*. "Over the Carnage."

25 Alexis de Tocqueville. *Journey to America*. Westport, CT, 1981. p. 219.

26 Raoul de Roussy de Sales. "Love in America." *Atlantic*. May 1938. p. 648.

27 Robert Moore, Douglas Gillette. *The King Within*. NY, 1992. p. 56.

28 H. L. Mencken. *Prejudices: Third Series*. NY, 1922. p. 16; Jonathan Rauch. "The British Disease." *Reason*. July 1996. p. 39.

29 Robert Stone in: *New York Review of Books*. Mar. 26, 1998. p. 25.

30 Dwight D. Eisenhower in: *New York Times*. Dec. 23, 1952. p. 16.

31 Will Herberg. *Protestant, Catholic, Jew*. NY, 1960. p. 2; George Gallup, Jim Castelli. *The People's Religion*. NY, 1989. p. 18, 60.

32 Giovanni Antonio Grassi in: Oscar Handlin. *This Was America*. Cambridge, MA, 1949. p. 148; Harriet Martineau. *Society in America*. NY, 1837. v. 2, p. 325–26.

33 George Gallup, Jim Castelli. *The People's Religion*. NY, 1989. p. 252; Anthony Trollope. *North America*. NY, 1951. p. 278, 281; David Brooks in: *New York Times*. Dec. 30, 2003. p. A21: "faith-hopping"; William McLoughlin, Robert N. Bellah. *Religion in America*. Boston, 1968. p. 95–96.

34 Bryan Wilson in: *Times Literary Supplement*. Aug. 3–9, 1990. p. 831; Robert N. Bellah et al. *Habits of the Heart*. Berkeley, CA, 1985. p. 221, 228.

35 Vice President Thomas R. Marshall quoted in: W. T. Colyer. *Americanism: A World Menace*. London, 1922. p. 44; vice-presidential candidate Joseph Lieberman quoted in: *Nation*. Sept. 18 & 25, 2000. p. 10.

36 Harriet Martineau. *Society in America*. NY, 1837. v. 2, p. 324–25; Alexis de Tocqueville. *Journey to America*. Westport, CT, 1981. p. 70–71; Wendy Kaminer in: *New Republic*. Oct. 14, 1996. p. 24; Ron Reagan on "The Larry King Show" (June 23, 2004); Martin E. Marty. *Modern American Religion*. v. 3 (Chicago, 1996). p. 300.

37 H. L. Mencken. *A Mencken Chrestomathy*. NY, 1949. p. 80–81; Diane Ravitch. *The Language Police*. NY, 2003. p. 145–46; Michael Barone. "Religion Shouldn't Be Ridiculed." *Philadelphia Inquirer*. Sept. 24, 1986.

38 Katha Pollitt. "God Changes Everything." *Nation*. Apr. 1, 2002. p. 10.

39 G. Lowes Dickinson in: *The English Review*. Jan. 1910. p. 199.

40 Robert N. Bellah. *The Good Society*. NY, 1991. p. 94; Norman Vincent Peale quoted in: Mark Pendergrast. *For God, Country, and Coca-Cola*. NY, 1993. p. 270.

41 Michelle Mary Lelwica. *Starving for Salvation*. NY, 1999. p. 77; Thomas P. Hunt quoted in: Michael S. Kimmel. *Manhood in America*. NY, 1996. p. 23; Earl F. Cheit. *The Business Establishment*. NY, 1964. p. 53 (1901); George Santayana. *Character and Opinion in the United States*. NY, 1921. p. 15; Alan Brinkley. *Liberalism and Its Discontents*. Cambridge, MA, 1998. p. 273, 351; Paul Heelas. *The New Age Movement*. Oxford, Eng., 1996. p. 95.

42 H. Richard Niebuhr. *The Kingdom of God in America*. Chicago, 1937. p. 193 (ch. 5): "A God without wrath brought men without sin into a kingdom without judgment through the ministrations of a Christ without a cross."

43 Russell E. Richey, Donald G. Jonels. *American Civil Religion*. NY, 1974. p. 79.

44 William Graham Sumner quoted in: Frederick Allen Lewis. *The Big Change*. NY, 1952. p. 68; Daniel J. Boorstin. *The Genius of American Politics*. Chicago, 1953. p. 179.

45 Harvey Cox. "The Market as God." *Atlantic*. Mar. 1999; Kenneth Lay quoted by Thomas Frank in: www.salon.com (Dec. 13, 2001); Philip J. Romero quoted in: *New York Times*. Feb. 4, 2001. section 4, p. 6.

46 David Brooks. *On Paradise Drive*. NY, 2004. p. 115.

47 O. A. Ohmann. "Skyhooks" (1955). *Harvard Business Review—On Human Relations*. NY, 1979. p. 448.

48 Henri Herz. *My Travels in America*. Madison, WI, 1963. p. 36; Frederick Marryat in: Allan Nevins. *America Through British Eyes*. NY, 1948. p. 187–88; Frances Trollope. *Domestic Manners of the Americans*. NY, 1949. p. 159 (ch. 14).

49 Harold E. Stearns. *Civilization in the United States*. NY, 1922. p. 440; Margot Asquith. *My Impressions in America*. NY, 1922. p. 201; H. L. Mencken. *Newspaper Days, 1899–1906*. NY, 1941. p. 38; *Economist*. June 10, 1995. p. 26.

50 John A. Hawgood. *The Tragedy of German-America*. NY, 1940. p. 296–97; Golo
    Mann. *Vom Geist Amerikas*. Stuttgart, 1954. p. 71: "Der arme Kaiser...war in
    Amerika ungleich mehr gehasst worden als Hitler."
51 James Carroll. "The End of the Dream." *New Republic*. June 24, 1991. p. 22–25;
    Lord Chesterfield. Letter to his son. May 8, 1750.
52 Lewis Lapham. *Money and Class in America*. NY, 1988. p. 137–38; Konstantinos
    Doxiadis quoted by C. Vann Woodward in: *American Scholar*. Summer 1997.
    p. 350.
53 Richard Hofstadter. *Anti-Intellectualism in American Life*. NY, 1963. p. vii.
54 G. K. Chesterton. *The Man Who Was Chesterton*. NY, 1946. p. 54.
55 Richard L. Rapson. "The American Child." *American Quarterly*. v. 17 (Fall 1965).
    p. 533; Norman Sherry. *The Life of Graham Greene*. NY, 1989. v. 1, p. 593; Tatyana
    Tolstaya in: *London Review of Books*. June 1, 1989. p. 23.
56 Richard Madsen in: Alan Wolfe. *America at Century's End*. Berkeley, CA, 1991.
    p. 441–42; Stanley Hoffman. *Gulliver's Troubles*. NY, 1968. p. 126–27.
57 Frederick Lewis Allen. *Only Yesterday*. NY, 1959. p. 182; Edward Behr. *Prohibition*.
    NY, 1966. p. 238.
58 Thomas Jefferson. Letter to William Short. Jan. 3, 1793; Dwight Macdonald.
    Discriminations. NY, 1974. p. 49.
59 Graham Greene. *The Quiet American*. 1955.
60 Ralph Barton Parry. *Characteristically American*. NY, 1949. p. 18–19; George F.
    Kennan. *American Diplomacy*. Chicago, 1984. passim.
61 John Aloysius Farrell. *Tip O'Neill*. Boston, 2001. p. 340; Jimmy Breslin. *How the
    Good Guys Finally Won*. NY, 1975. p. 16: "It was a shakedown. A plain old-fashioned
    goddamned shakedown."
62 Christopher Caldwell in: *New Republic*. Apr. 5, 1999. p. 15–16.
63 Bray Hammond. *Banks and Politics in America*. Princeton, NJ, 1957. p. 361.

Chapter 4

1   Ilya Ehrenburg in: *Harper's*. Dec. 1946. p. 565; John Keegan in: *American Heritage*.
    Feb.–Mar. 1996. p. 40; Paul Starr in: *New Republic*. June 21, 2004. p. 27.
2   Alexis de Tocqueville. *Democracy in America*. NY, 1945. v. 2, p. 10 (bk. 1, ch. 2);
    Edward Dicey. *Six Months in the Federal States*. London, 1863. v. 1, p. 305–306;
    Harold Nicolson. *Good Behavior*. NY, 1956. p. 17; Evelyn Waugh. *The Loved One*.
    Boston, 1948. p. 43, 53–54 (ch. 3).
3   Koenraad W. Swart in: *Journal of the History of Ideas*. v. 23 (Jan.–Mar. 1962).
    p. 84–5; G. K. Chesterton. *What I Saw in America*. NY, 1968. p. 169; Irving Kristol
    in: *Times Literary Supplement*. May 26, 2000. p. 15; Carl L. Becker. *Everyman His
    Own Historian*. NY, 1935. p. 6.
4   Edward C. Stewart, Milton J. Bennett. *American Cultural Patterns*. Yarmouth, ME,
    1991. p. 136; Clement Greenberg. *Collected Essays and Criticism*. Chicago, 1993.
    v. 3, p. 267: standardized manner and personality.
5   Alexis de Tocqueville. *Democracy in America*. NY, 1945. v. 1, p. 170 (ch. 8);
    André Maurois. *From My Journal*. NY, 1948. p. 171; James Bryce. *The American
    Commonwealth*. NY, 1893–94. v. 2, p. 824 (ch. 116: "The Uniformity of American
    Life").
6   Alexis de Tocqueville. *Journey to America*. Westport, CT, 1981. p. 356; John Keegan
    in: *American Heritage*. Feb.–Mar. 1996. p. 40.

7 Willa Cather quoted in: *New Republic*. Aug. 11 & 18, 1997. p. 20; S. Gorley Putt. *Cousins and Strangers*. Cambridge, MA, 1956. p. 50.

8 George Santayana. *Character and Opinion in the United States*. NY, 1921. p. 47 (ch. 2); Hector Saint-John de Crèvecoeur. *Letters from an American Farmer*. letter 3; John Jay in: *The Federalist*. no. 2.

9 Jonathan Kay in: *Commentary*. Feb. 2004. p. 69; Peter H. Schuck. *Diversity in America*. Cambridge, MA, 2003. p. 101.

10 Herbert J. Gans. *The Urban Villagers*. NY, 1982. p. 278; Jeremy Waldron in: *Times Literary Supplement*. Jan. 22, 1993. p. 11; K. Anthony Appiah in: *New York Review of Books*. Oct. 9, 1997. p. 31–32.

11 Fernando Diaz-Plaja. *The Spaniard and the Seven Deadly Sins*. NY, 1967. p. 77; Mark Abley in: *Times Literary Supplement*. Nov. 26, 1999. p. 8.

12 Dinesh D'Souza. *What's So Great About America*. Washington, DC, 2002. p. 33.

13 Todd Gitlin. *Twilight of Common Dreams*. NY, 1995. p. 44; Byron E. Shafer. *Is America Different?* Oxford, 1991. p. 7.

14 Richard Hofstadter in: *New York Times Book Review*. Feb. 27, 1955. p. 7; Dinesh D'Souza. *Illiberal Education*. NY, 1991. p. 230.

15 Mary Ellen Jones. *The American Frontier*. San Diego, CA, 1994. p. 11.

16 Alexander Mackay. *The Western World*. Philadelphia, 1849. v. 1, 213–14; J. B. Priestley. *Midnight on the Desert*. NY, 1937. p. 127; Daniel J. Boorstin. *The Genius of American Politics*. Chicago, 1953. p. 137–39; Louis Hartz. *The Liberal Tradition in America*. NY, 1955. p. 141; C. H. Bretherton quoted in: George Harmon Knoles. *The Jazz Age Revisited*. NY, 1968. p. 91: "the pie counter."

17 Stuart Miller. *Painted in Blood*. NY, 1987. p. 146; Marshall McLuhan in: *Horizon* (London). Oct. 1947. p. 132.

18 David J. Hoeveler. *Watch on the Right*. Madison, WI, 1991. p. 279; Alexander Star in: *New Republic*. Mar. 20, 1995. p. 38; *Economist*. June 3, 1995. p. 30.

19 Francis J. Grund. *Aristocracy in America*. NY, 1959. p. 272 (ch. 19).

20 George Grant. *Lament for a Nation*. Princeton, NJ, 1965. p. 64–65.

21 Alexis de Tocqueville. *Democracy in America*. NY, 1945. v. 2, p. 99 (bk. 2, ch. 2).

22 Tocqueville. *loc. cit.*; Max Weber. *From Max Weber*. NY, 1958. p. 149 ("Science as a Vocation").

23 Jacob Heilbrunn in: *New Republic*. Oct. 20, 1997. p. 17; Paul Gottfried, Thomas Fleming. *The Conservative Movement*. Boston, 1988. p. 66.

24 Thomas Frank. *What's the Matter with Kansas?* NY, 2004. p. 17; Rush Limbaugh quoted in: Thomas Frank. *One Market Under God*. NY, 2000. p. 43.

25 George Gilder. *Microcosm*. NY, 1989. p. 113, 352; Emma Lazarus. "The New Colossus." 1883.

26 George Santayana. *Character and Opinion in the United States*. NY, 1921. p. 170: "The luckless American who is born a conservative…"; Florence King in: *National Review*. Apr. 17, 2000. p. 56 (reprinted in her *Stet, Damnit!* NY, 2003. p. 352–54): an entertaining account of her futile search for an "elitist conservatism."

27 Adam Smith. *An Inquiry into the Nature and Causes of the Wealth of Nations*. bk. 5, pt. 3, article 3: "…two different schemes or systems of morality current at the same time…"; Richard Hildreth. *Theory of Politics*. NY, 1853. p. 262; George Combe. *Notes on the United States of North America*. Philadelphia, 1841. v. 2, p. 265–66.

28 George Santayana. *The Last Puritan*. NY, 1936. p. 387 (pt. 4, ch. 1): "…liberty is something aristocratic…in a pure democracy you must always do, and always think, what other people like."

29 Alexander Mackay. *The Western World*. Philadelphia, 1849. v. 1, p. 125; James Bryce. *The American Commonwealth*. NY, 1893–94. v. 2, p. 269 (ch. 78); James Bryce. *Modern Democracies*. NY, 1931. v. 2, p. 114–15 (ch. 44); David Riesman. *Individualism Reconsidered*. Glencoe, IL, 1954. p. 499; Clement Greenberg. *Collected Essays and Criticism*. Chicago, 1993. v. 3, p. 266.

30 Michael Lind. *The Next American Nation*. NY, 1995. p. 144.

31 Alexis de Tocqueville. *Democracy in America*. NY, 1945. v. 2, p. 229 (bk. 3, ch. 17).

32 Daniel W. Howe in: *Journal of American History*. v. 77 (Mar. 1991). p. 1222; Paul Boyer. *Urban Masses and Moral Order in America, 1820–1920*. Cambridge, MA, 1978. p. 59–60.

33 Francis Fukuyama. *The Great Disruption*. NY, 1999. p. 268, 270.

34 V. S. Pritchett. *Complete Collected Essays*. NY, 1991. p. 545: "Mark Twain: The American Puritan"; Thomas Hardy. *Jude the Obscure*. pt. 4, ch. 5: "All the respectable inhabitants and well-to-do fellow-natives of the town were against Phillotson to a man. But, somewhat to his surprise, some dozen champions rose up in his defense as from the ground."; Compare and contrast an English novel (*Tom Brown at Oxford* (1861) by Thomas Hughes) with an American one (*Stover at Yale* (1911) by Owen Johnson) in their respective treatments of sex with lower-class females as a temptation to the moral delinquency of college boys.

35 Alan Lomax. *The Folk Songs of North America in the English Language*. NY, 1960. p. xvii–xviii.

36 Francis J. Grund. *The Americans in Their Moral, Social, and Political Relations*. Boston, 1837. p. 37, 169–171.

37 Alexis de Tocqueville. *Democracy in America*. NY, 1945. v. 2, p. 236–37 (bk. 3, ch. 18); Edith Wharton. *The Custom of the Country*. NY, 1956. p. 206–207 (ch. 15).

38 Theodore Roszak. *The Making of a Counter Culture*. NY, 1969. p. 14–15.

39 *Economist*. Feb. 25, 2006. p. 42: "Puritans or Pornographers"; Gary Althen. *American Ways*. Yarmouth, ME, 1988. p. 15, 75.

40 Walter Cronkite quoted in: *Playboy*. June 1973. p. 26.

Chapter 5

1 Charles A. Murray. *Travels in North America During the Years 1834, 1835, 1836*. London, 1839. v. 1, p. 121 (ch. 7).

2 Carol Z. Stearns, Peter N. Stearns. *Anger*. Chicago, 1986. p. 129; Peter N. Stearns. *American Cool*. NY, 1994. Chapter title: "Impersonal, But Friendly."

3 Clifford Orwin in: *American Scholar*. Summer 1993. p. 427; Hervé Varenne. *Symbolizing America*. Lincoln, NE, 1986. p. 217.

4 Julián Marías. *America in the Fifties and Sixties*. University Park, PA, 1972. p. 229–230; Stuart Miller. *Painted in Blood*. NY, 1987. p. 230.

5 Edward C. Stewart, Milton J. Bennett. *American Cultural Patterns*. Yarmouth, ME, 1991. p. 101–102; Geoffrey Gorer. *The American People*. NY, 1964. p. 132.

6 George Gallup, Jr., Jim Castelli. *The People's Religion*. NY, 1989. p. 253; E. M. Forster. *Goldsworthy Lowes Dickinson*. NY, 1934. p. 132; Nelson W. Aldrich. *Old Money*. NY, 1988. p. 93.

7 Robert L. Woolfolk, Frank C. Richardson. *Stress, Sanity, and Survival*. NY, 1978. p. 68.

8 Edward C. Stewart, Milton J. Bennett. *American Cultural Patterns.* Yarmouth, ME, 1991. p. 108; Geoffrey Gorer. *The American People.* NY, 1964. p. 107–108; Karen Horney. *Neurosis and Human Growth.* NY, 1950. p. 227.

9 Stuart Miller. *Painted in Blood.* NY, 1987. p. 23; Rosellen Brown in: *New York Times Magazine.* May 6, 1990. p. 26.

10 John Harmon McElroy. *American Beliefs.* Chicago, 1999. p. 70; Peter Ustinov. *Quotable Ustinov.* Amherst, NY, 1995. p. 122.

11 Geoffrey Gorer. *The American People.* NY, 1964. p. 130; Alexis de Tocqueville. *Democracy in America.* NY, 1945. v. 2, p. 172 (bk. 3, ch. 3).

12 Geoffrey Gorer. *The American People.* NY, 1964. p. 133; Joanne B. Ciulla. *The Working Life.* NY, 2000. p. 124–25.

13 Benjamin Spock. *Baby and Child Care.* "Good Manners Come Naturally"; Courtney Rosen. *How to Do Just About Everything.* NY, 2000. p. 185; Charlene Mitchell, Thomas Burdick. *The Right Moves.* NY, 1985. p. 142–44.

14 Luc Sante in: *New York Times Magazine.* Oct. 17, 1999. p. 140.

15 Francis J. Grund. *Aristocracy in America.* NY, 1959. p. 151 (ch. 10); Richard F. Kuisel. *Seducing the French.* NY, 1993. p. 242; Henry James in: *Nation.* Oct. 3, 1878. p. 208; Margot Asquith. *My Impressions of America.* NY, 1922. p. 200–201.

16 Harold Laski. *The American Democracy.* NY, 1948. p. 16; Frances Trollope. *Domestic Manners of the Americans.* NY, 1949. p. 328 (ch. 29).

17 Jacques Barzun in: *Foreign Affairs.* v. 43 (Apr. 1965). p. 427; Denis Lacorne. *The Rise and Fall of Anti-Americanism.* NY, 1990. p. 238; William J. Lederer, Eugene Burdick. *The Ugly American.* NY, 1958. p. 114; Florence King in: *National Review.* July 29, 2002. p. 56.

18 Stuart Miller. *Painted in Blood.* NY, 1987. p. 43–44, 50–51; Whittaker Chambers. *Witness.* NY, 1952. p. 350: "Americans do not like irony"; Richard Critchfield. *An American Looks at Britain.* NY, 1990. p. 34; Simon Hoggart. *America: A User's Guide.* London, 1990. p. 77.

19 Adam Hodgson. *Letters from North America.* London, 1824. p. 32; Philip Guedalla. *Conquistador.* NY, 1928. p. 34; F. Scott Fitzgerald. *The Great Gatsby.* ch. 9; Johan Huizinga. *America.* NY, 1972. p. 180–81.

20 "The Wasp." *Spectator* (London). July 25, 1992. p. 21; James Bowman in: *Times Literary Supplement.* Aug. 28, 1992. p. 12; Daryl Michael Scott. *Contempt and Pity.* Chapel Hill, NC, 1997. p. 188.

21 Rochelle Gurstein. *The Repeal of Reticence.* NY, 1996. p. 77–80; J. A. (John Alfred) Spender. *Through English Eyes.* NY, 1928. p. 52; James Truslow Adams. *Our Business Civilization.* NY, 1929. p. 211–12; J. (John) Martin Evans. *America: The View from Europe.* San Francisco, 1976. p. 46.

22 Quotation from Kevin Baker in: *New York Times Book Review.* May 2, 1999. p. 23; Kurt Lewin. *Resolving Social Conflicts.* NY, 1948. p. 16; Peter Sacks in: *Nation.* May 5, 2003. p. 30.

23 Daniel Yankelovich. *Psychology Today.* Apr. 1981. p. 86.

24 Karen Horney. *The Neurotic Personality of Our Time.* NY, 1937.

25 Werner Sombart. *Why Is There No Socialism in the United States?* White Plains, NY, 1976. p. 39–40; George Packer in: *Harper's.* July 1998. p. 72; James Bryce. *The American Commonwealth.* NY, 1893–94. v. 2, p. 291 (ch. 80).

26 Paul Bourget. *Outre-Mer.* NY, 1895. p. 176; Hugo Münsterberg. *The Americans.* NY, 1904. p. 240–41, 252.

27 *American Economic Review.* v. 60 (May 1970). p. 480; Paul Goodman. *Toward a Christian Republic.* NY, 1988. p. 47; Paul E. Johnson. *A Shopkeeper's Millennium.* NY, 1978. p. 19.

28 Thomas C. Grattan. *Civilized America.* London, 1859. v. 2, p. 82; J. A. (John Alfred) Spender. *Through English Eyes.* NY, 1928. p. 317–18; Moisei Ostrogorski. *Democracy and the Party System in the United States.* NY, 1910. p. 411; Fredrika Bremer quoted in: Oscar Handlin. *This Was America.* Cambridge, MA, 1969. p. 230.

29 Alexis de Tocqueville. *Democracy in America.* NY, 1945. v. 1, p. 191 (ch. 12); Arthur M. Schlesinger, Sr. "Biography of a Nation of Joiners." *American Historical Review.* v. 50, no. 1 (Oct. 1944); Robert D. Putnam. *Bowling Alone.* NY, 2000; Alan Wolfe. *One Nation After All.* NY, 1998. p. 253, 257, 260, 262.

30 Thomas C. Grattan. *Civilized America.* London, 1859. v. 2, p. 82–83; William E. Channing. *The Works of William E. Channing, D.D.* Boston, 1877. p. 139.

31 Alexis de Tocqueville. *Journey to America.* Westport, CT, 1981. p. 39, 42–43; James Bryce. *The American Commonwealth.* NY, 1893–94. v. 2, p. 278 (ch. 79).

32 "Willst du nicht mein Bruder sein, dann hau' ich dir den Schädel ein!"

33 John Jay Chapman. *Causes and Consequences.* NY, 1898. p. 58; George Santayana. *The Last Puritan.* NY, 1936. p. 232 (pt. 2, ch. 18): "I suppose people aren't ashamed of doing or feeling anything, no matter what, if only they can do it together."; Alexis de Tocqueville. *Democracy in America.* NY, 1945. v. 2, p. 10 (bk. 1, ch. 2): "The same equality that renders him independent of each of his fellow citizens, taken severally, exposes him alone and unprotected to the influence of the greater number."

34 Alexis de Tocqueville. *Democracy in America.* NY, 1945. v. 1, p. 263–65 (ch. 15); George Combe. *Notes on the United States of North America.* Philadelphia, 1841. v. 2, p. 257–272.

35 Réne Rémond. *Les États-Unis devant l'opinion française, 1815–1852.* Paris, 1962. v. 2, p. 675.

36 Alexis de Tocqueville. *Democracy in America.* NY, 1945. v. 1, p. 263–65 (ch. 15); Alexis de Tocqueville. *Journey to America.* Westport, CT, 1981. p. 70.

37 Frances Anne Kemble. *Records of Later Life.* London, 1882. v. 1, p. 201; Frederick Marryat. *A Diary in America.* Edited by S. W. Jackman. NY, 1962. p. 295; Harriet Martineau. *Society in America.* NY, 1837. v. 2, p. 153–161; Francis J. Grund. *Aristocracy in America.* NY, 1959. p. 162 (ch. 10); George Combe. *Notes on the United States of North America.* Philadelphia, 1841. v. 2, p. 261.

38 Alexis de Tocqueville. *Democracy in America.* NY, 1945. v. 1, p. 260–61 (ch. 15): "When an individual or a party is wronged in the United States...."; John Fenimore Cooper. *The American Democrat.* Baltimore, MD, 1969. p. 197: "The man who resists the tyranny of a monarch...."; Francis J. Grund. *The Americans in Their Moral, Social, and Political Relations.* Boston, 1837. p. 18, 165; George Combe. *Notes on the United States of North America.* Philadelphia, 1841. v. 2, p. 261: "the Dandy Parson."

39 John Fenimore Cooper. *The American Democrat.* Baltimore, MD, 1969. p. 199–200; John Fenimore Cooper. *England, With Sketches of Society in the Metropolis.* London, 1837. p. 200; Nathaniel Hawthorne. *The Marble Faun.* ch. 12: "Rome is not like one of our New England villages...."; Samuel Longfellow. *The Life of Henry Wadsworth Longfellow.* Boston, 1886. v. 1, p. 267; Harriet Martineau. *Society in America.* NY, 1837. v. 2, p. 160.

40 Seymour Martin Lipset. *The First New Nation.* NY, 1967. ch. 3: "A Changing American Character?"; James Bryce. *The American Commonwealth.* NY, 1893–94. v. 2, p. 349–353 (ch. 85).

41 Van Wyck Brooks. *Sketches in Criticism.* London, 1934. p. 175; *New York Times.* Sept. 25, 1910. "Magazine Section." p. 4; Johan Huizinga. *America.* NY, 1972. p. 172; Arthur Ponsonby. *Casual Observations.* London, 1930. p. 86–87.

42 John Jay Chapman. *Causes and Consequences.* NY, 1898. p. 56; Loren Knox in: *Atlantic.* v. 104 (Dec. 1909). p. 823–24.

43 Mark Twain. *Following the Equator.* 1897. v. 1, ch. 20: "Pudd'nhead Wilson's New Calendar."

44 André Siegfried. *America Comes of Age.* NY, 1927. p. 168, 349–352; George Harmon Knoles. *The Jazz Age Revisited.* NY, 1968. passim; D. H. Lawrence. *Studies in Classic American Literature.* ch. 1: "This the land of the free!"

45 Jean-Paul Sartre. *Literary and Philosophical Essays.* NY, 1962. p. 108–109; Hannah Arendt. *Essays in Understanding.* NY, 1994. p. 424–25; Jean-Marie Domenach in: *Esprit.* Oct. 1960. p. 1523.

46 S. Gorley Putt. *Cousins and Strangers.* Cambridge, MA, 1956. p. 15; Herbert H. Hyman in: Daniel Bell. *The Radical Right.* NY, 1963. p. 239–250.

47 Peter Ustinov in: Art Buchwald. *Is It Safe to Drink the Water?* Cleveland, OH, 1962. p. 78; James Gilbert in: Rupert Wilkinson. *American Social Character.* NY, 1992. p. 66; Robin M. Williams. *American Society: A Sociological Interpretation.* NY, 1970. p. 484, n. 3.

48 Taki in: *Spectator* (London). July 9, 1994. p. 40; Peter L. Berger in: *Commentary.* June 1994. p. 26; Louis Menand in: *Times Literary Supplement.* Oct. 30, 1992. p. 4.

49 Quotation from: James Muirhead. *The Land of Contrasts.* London, 1900. p. 69; Esther B. Aresty. *The Best Behavior.* NY, 1970. p. 209, 214; Geoffrey Gorer. *The American People.* NY, 1964. p. 102.

50 Alexis de Tocqueville. *Journey to America.* Westport, CT, 1981. p. 45.

51 Harriet Martineau. *Society in America.* NY, 1837. v. 2, p. 158; David Riesman. *The Lonely Crowd.* New Haven, CT, 1950. ch. 4.

52 Alexis de Tocqueville. *Democracy in America.* NY, 1945. v. 2, p. 192 (bk. 3, ch. 8); Erik H. Erikson. *Childhood and Society.* NY, 1963. p. 318.

53 James Muirhead. *The Land of Contrasts.* London, 1900. p. 66.

54 Michael Moffatt. *Coming of Age in New Jersey.* New Brunswick, NJ, 1989. p. 42–44, 89, 166; Jeffrey Hammond. "Milton at the Bat." in: Bill Henderson, ed. *The Pushcart Prize 2001.* NY, 2001. p. 562–63.

55 Mark Edmundson in: *Harper's.* Sept. 1997. p. 42.

56 Steven Kelman. *Push Comes to Shove.* Boston, 1970. p. 166.

57 Louis Menand in: *Harper's.* Dec. 1991. p. 48, 52; Frederick Crews. *The Critics Bear It Away.* NY, 1992. p. xviii; David Brooks. "The Organization Kid." *Atlantic.* Apr. 2001.

58 George Santayana. *Character and Opinion in the United States.* NY, 1921. p. 169 (ch. 6); John Fenimore Cooper. *The American Democrat.* Baltimore, MD, 1969. p. 205–206; John Fenimore Cooper. *Gleanings in Europe.* NY, 1930. v. 2, p. 270 (ch. 18. "The Press"); John Fenimore Cooper. *England, With Sketches of Society in the Metropolis.* London, 1837. p. 194.

59 Royall Tyler. "The Contrast" (1787). in: Jeffrey H. Richards. *Early American Drama*. NY, 1997. p. 18, 24; Hilaire Belloc. *The Contrast*. NY, 1974 (originally published in 1924). p. 57, 61; J. B. Priestley. *Midnight on the Desert*. NY, 1937. p. 122.

60 Oliver Wendell Holmes, Jr. *The Occasional Speeches*. Cambridge, MA, 1962. p. 6–7; George Santayana. *Character and Opinion in the United States*. NY, 1921. p. 210–11 (ch. 7); George Santayana. *The Last Puritan*. NY, 1936. p. 126–27 (pt. 2, ch. 7): "…that herd-instinct, that sense that you must swim with the stream and do what is expected of you…there was no real choice open to you to live otherwise or to live better."

61 James Bryce. *Modern Democracies*. NY, 1931. v. 2, p. 121–22 (ch. 44); G. K. Chesterton. *What I Saw in America*. NY, 1968. p. 167; George Santayana. *Character and Opinion in the United States*. NY, 1921. p. 209 (ch. 7); James Bryce. *The American Commonwealth*. NY, 1893–94. v. 2, p. 353 (ch. 85); Jerry Farber. *The Student as Nigger*. NY, 1970. p. 94: "open-mouthed astonishment."

62 Quotations from: Mark Sullivan. *Our Times, 1900–1925*. NY, 1972. v. 5, p. 380; Michael McGerr. *A Fierce Discontent*. NY, 2003. p. 287, 291; David M. Kennedy. *Over Here*. NY, 1980. p. 60–61.

63 Herb Greer in: *Times Literary Supplement*. May 22, 1998. p. 17.

64 George Harmon Knoles. *The Jazz Age Revisited*. NY, 1968. p. 54; William E. Martin, Celia Burns Stendler. *Child Behavior and Development*. NY, 1959. p. 180–81; Paul Hollander. *Soviet and American Society*. NY, 1973. p. 137; Charles Lindholm and John A. Hall in: *Daedalus*. v. 126 (Spring 1977). p. 193; Jean-Paul Sartre. *Literary and Philosophical Essays*. NY, 1962. p. 104.

65 George Combe. *Notes on the United States of North America*. Philadelphia, 1841. v. 2, p. 265.

66 Stuart Miller. *Painted in Blood*. NY, 1987. p. 24; Edward C. Stewart, Milton J. Bennett. *American Cultural Patterns*. Yarmouth, ME, 1991. p. 97, 100, 103, 150; Diane R. Margolis. *The Managers*. NY, 1979. p. 240; Wilbert E. Moore. *The Conduct of the Corporation*. NY, 1962. p. 36–37.

67 Michèle Lamont. *Money, Morals, and Manners*. Chicago, 1992. p. 49–50; Gary Althen. *American Ways*. Yarmouth, ME, 1988. p. 24–25.

68 Whittaker Chambers. *Witness*. NY, 1952. p. 243; Gary Althen. *American Ways*. Yarmouth, ME, 1988. p. 107.

69 Edward C. Stewart, Milton J. Bennett. *American Cultural Patterns*. Yarmouth, ME, 1991. p. 139; Gary Althen. *American Ways*. Yarmouth, ME, 1988. p. 26; Dinesh D'Souza. *What's So Great About America*. Washington, DC, 2002. p. 31–32, 93–94.

70 Richard Pascale, Anthony Athos. *The Art of Japanese Management*. NY, 1981. p. 71–72; Stuart Miller. *Painted in Blood*. NY, 1987. p. 23; Michèle Lamont. *Money, Morals, and Manners*. Chicago, 1992. p. 92, 97.

71 Neil Chesanow. *The World-Class Executive*. NY, 1985. p. 13–14, 268.

72 Geoffrey Gorer. *The American People*. NY, 1964. p. 141; Edward C. Stewart, Milton J. Bennett. *American Cultural Patterns*. Yarmouth, ME, 1991. p. 106.

73 Daniel J. Boorstin. *The Decline of Radicalism*. NY, 1969. p. 50–51.

74 Joan Didion in: *New York Review of Books*. Sept. 24, 1992. p. 64: "this ungrounded quality"; Paul Hollander. *The Many Faces of Socialism*. New Brunswick, NJ, 1983. p. 309; Joseph Wood Krutch. *More Lives Than One*. NY, 1962. p. 105; Michael Lewis. *The New New Thing*. NY, 2000. p. 182.

75 James Muirhead. *The Land of Contrasts*. London, 1900. p. 91–92.

76 Neil Chesanow. *The World-Class Executive.* NY, 1985. p. 22, 25.

77 Alan Riding. *Distant Neighbors.* NY, 1985. p. 5; Neil Chesanow. *The World-Class Executive.* NY, 1985. p. 280; Edward C. Stewart, Milton J. Bennett. *American Cultural Patterns.* Yarmouth, ME, 1991. p. 106.

78 Michèle Lamont. *Money, Morals, and Manners.* Chicago, 1992. p. 49; Geoffrey Gorer. *The American People.* NY, 1964. p. 141–42.

79 Gary Althen. *American Ways.* Yarmouth, ME, 1988. p. 117; Charles Handy. *The Elephant and the Flea.* Boston, 2002. p. 60; Helen Caldicott. *A Desperate Passion.* NY, 1996. p. 85.

80 Stanley Hoffman. *Decline or Renewal.* NY, 1974. p. 121; Louis Ardagh. *France in the New Century.* London, 1999. p. 211.

81 Friedrich Nietzsche. *Also Sprach Zarathusta.* Prologue, 5; Willa Cather. *O Pioneers!* pt. 2, ch. 1: "…if a man is different…they put him in the asylum."

82 J. B. Priestley. *Midnight on the Desert.* NY, 1937. p. 123; Paul Hollander. *Soviet and American Society.* NY, 1973. p. 284–85; John Barron. *MiG Pilot.* NY, 1980. p. 165; Benjamin Wattenberg. *Values Matter Most.* NY, 1995. p. 199.

Chapter 6

1 George Santayana. *Character and Opinion in the United States.* NY, 1921. p. 196–97 (ch. 7); Hermann Keyserling. *America Set Free.* NY, 1929. p. 249–250; Alan Riding. *Distant Neighbors.* NY, 1985. p. 9–10; James Fallows in: *Times Literary Supplement.* Oct. 27, 1995. p. 7–8.

2 Felipe Fernández-Armesto. *The Americas.* NY, 2003. p. 196–97: "cloyingly gregarious, profoundly communitarian, boringly conformist"; J. B. Priestley. *Midnight on the Desert.* NY, 1937. p. 118; Roger Rosenblatt in: *Time.* Oct. 15, 1984. p. 116; Harry Stein in: *Esquire.* May 1985. p. 49–50; Francis Fukuyama. *Trust.* NY, 1995. p. 278.

3 John Masefield. "The Everlasting Mercy."

4 The anthropologist E. L. Cerroni-Long in: Philip R. DeVita, James D. Armstrong. *Distant Mirrors.* Belmont, CA, 1993. p. 91; Gary Althen. *American Ways.* Yarmouth, ME, 1988. p. 6; John A. Hall, Charles Lindholm. *Is America Breaking Apart?* Princeton, NJ, 1999. p. 150.

5 Ralph Waldo Emerson. "The American Scholar" and "Self-Reliance"; Richard Bach. *Jonathan Livingston Seagull* (1970) and the song "Rudolph the Red-Nosed Reindeer" (1939). The former was a best-seller; the latter has enjoyed perennial popularity.

6 Dwight D. Eisenhower in: *Vital Speeches.* June 15, 1949. p. 519: "…free individuals joined in a team…"

7 Ted Conover. *Newjack.* NY, 2000. p. 18–19, 54.

8 Robert B. Settle, Pamela L. Alreck. *Why They Buy.* NY, 1986. p. 230.

9 Henry Steele Commager. *Commager on Tocqueville.* Columbia, MO, 1993. p. 10, 26, 31–32.

10 Robin M. Williams. *American Society.* NY, 1970. p. 484: "external conformity"; Seymour Martin Lipset. *The First New Nation.* NY, 1967. p. 158: "inner autonomy."

11 George Santayana. *Character and Opinion in the United States.* NY, 1921. p. 209–210; André Siegfried. *America Comes of Age.* NY, 1927. p. 349; Daniel Bell. *The End of Ideology.* NY, 1962. p. 257–59: "Prophets of Play."

12 Leo Marx. *The Pilot and the Passenger.* NY, 1988. p. 343.

13 Mark Edmundson in: *Harper's*. Sept. 1997. p. 49; John R. Searle in: *Partisan Review*. v. 60, no. 4 (1993). p. 707; Frederick Barthelme, Steven Barthelme. *Double Down*. Boston, 1999. p. 104.

14 Theodore Sizer in: *Harper's*. Sept. 2001. p. 52.

15 Thomas Jefferson. Letter to John Adams. Jan. 11, 1816; Gordon S. Wood in: Robert H. Horwitz. *The Moral Foundations of the American Republic*. Charlottesville, VA, 1979. p. 125; George Sidney Camp. *Democracy*. NY, 1841. p. 199–205.

16 Henry C. Link. *The Return to Religion*. NY, 1936. p. 33; Henry C. Link. *The Rediscovery of Man*. NY, 1939. p. 60–61.

17 Henry C. Link. *The Way to Security*. NY, 1951. p. 39; *Rediscovery of Man*. p. 200.

18 *Return to Religion*. p. 101, 154; *Way to Security*. p. 41; *Rediscovery of Man*. p. 250.

19 *Rediscovery of Man*. p. 99, 174–75, 226.

20 *Way to Security*. p. 64, 153–54; *Return to Religion*. p. 126, 145; *Rediscovery of Man*. p. 95.

21 *Return to Religion*. p. 169–173, 179.

22 Richard Hofstadter. *Anti-Intellectualism in American Life*. NY, 1963. p. 269.

23 *Return to Religion*. p. 160; *Way to Security*. p. 150.

Chapter 7

1 Jack Beatty. *Colossus*. NY, 2001. p. 270, 272.

2 Irving Kristol. *Reflections of a Neoconservative*. NY, 1983. p. 204.

3 Gregg Easterbrook. *The Progress Paradox*. NY, 2003. p. 50–51, 266–68; Joel Bakan. *The Corporation: The Pathological Pursuit of Profit and Power*. NY, 2004. p. 56–57, 134–35.

4 David Montgomery. *Beyond Equality*. Urbana, IL, 1981. p. 205.

5 David A. Zonderman. *Aspirations and Anxieties*. NY, 1992. p. 115; Orestes Brownson. "The Laboring Classes." Joseph L. Blau, ed. *American Philosophical Addresses, 1700–1900*. NY, 1946. p. 185.

6 William M. Gouge. *A Short History of Paper Money and Banking in the United States*. Philadelphia, 1833. pt. 1, p. 42; Walter Austin. *William Austin*. Boston, 1925. p. 265: "Martha Gardner" (1837); Roger Ebert reviewing the movie "The Corporation" in: *Chicago Sun-Times*. July 16, 2004.

7 Daniel Webster. "Second Speech on the Sub-Treasury." Mar. 12–13, 1838; William Leggett. *A Collection of the Political Writings of William Leggett*. NY, 1840. v. 1, p. 143.

8 David L. Sills. *International Encyclopedia of Social Sciences*. NY, 1968. v. 3, p. 400.

9 George W. Perkins in: *North American Review*. v. 187 (1908). p. 397–98; John D. Rockefeller quoted in: Allan Nevins. *Study in Power*. NY, 1953. v. 1, p. 402.

10 Ron Chernow. *Titan*. NY, 1998. p. 253–58; David F. Hawke. *John D*. NY, 1980. ch. 36.

11 Daniel T. Rodgers. *The Work Ethic in Industrial America*. Chicago, 1978. p. 79: "A Message to Garcia"; Mark Pendergrast. *For God, Country, and Coca-Cola*. NY, 1993. p. 11.

12 Henry Seidel Canby. *The Age of Confidence*. NY, 1934. p. 239; Olivier Zunz. *Making America Corporate*. Chicago, 1990. p. 13–33.

13 David F. Hawke. *John D*. NY, 1980. p. 213; Ida M. Tarbell. *The History of the Standard Oil Company*. NY, 1904. v. 2, p. 110.

14 Ron Chernow. *Titan*. NY, 1998. p. 153–54, 263; David F. Hawke. *John D*. NY, 1980. p. 221.
15 Herbert Croly. *Marcus Alonzo Hanna*. NY, 1912. p. 405.
16 Eric Foner. *The Story of American Freedom*. NY, 1998. p. 125; Terence V. Powderly. *The Path I Trod*. NY, 1940. p. 268: "Abolish the Wage System."
17 Edwin L. Godkin in: *North American Review*. v. 105 (July 1867). p. 213.
18 Samuel Gompers in: *American Federationist*. v. 14 (Nov. 1907). p. 883; Robert Levering. *A Great Place to Work*. NY, 1988. p. 231; Charles Brown et al. *Employers Large and Small*. Cambridge, MA, 1990. p. 88–89.
19 John Mitchell. *Organized Labor*. Philadelphia, 1903. p. ix; *Harper's Weekly*. v. 48 (Jan. 2, 1904). p. 45; Jane Addams. *Newer Ideas of Peace*. NY, 1907. p. 146.
20 George Gunton in: *Chicago Conference on Trusts: Speeches, Debates, Resolutions*. Chicago, 1900 (reprinted 1973). p. 276–77.
21 Justice Peckham quoted in: Robert H. Bork. *The Antitrust Paradox*. NY, 1978. p. 25.
22 Grover Cleveland. "Fourth Annual Message to Congress." Dec. 7, 1896.
23 William T. Stead. *The Americanization of the World*. London, 1902. p. 145; Tony Allan Freyer. *Regulating Big Business*. Cambridge, UK, 1992. p. 47: "...only the Americans contended that the moral foundations of republican government itself were threatened."
24 Thomas R. Marshall quoted in: Richard Hofstadter. *The Age of Reform*. NY, 1955. p. 246; Richard Hofstadter. *The American Political Tradition*. NY, 1954. p. 230.
25 Woodrow Wilson. *The New Freedom*. NY, 1913. ch. 8 and 11.
26 Theodore Roosevelt in: Alfred Chandler. *Management, Past and Present*. Cincinnati, OH, 1996. p. 5–16; Theodore Roosevelt. *An Autobiography*. NY, 1920, c1913. p. 433.
27 Richard Hofstadter. *The Age of Reform*. NY, 1955. p. 243.
28 Richard Hofstadter. *The American Political Tradition*. NY, 1954. p. 206.
29 Lino A. Graglia in: *Public Interest*. Summer 1991. p. 53.
30 Thurman W. Arnold. *The Folklore of Capitalism*. New Haven, CT, 1964 (originally published in 1937). p. 218.
31 John Updike. *Self-Consciousness*. NY, 1989. p. 126.
32 Richard Hofstadter. *The American Political Tradition*. NY, 1954. p. v (Introduction, 1948); Richard Hofstadter in: *Newsweek*. July 6, 1970. p. 20.
33 Benita Eisler. *Private Lives*. NY, 1986. p. 306.
34 William H. Whyte in: Adam Smith. *The Roaring '80s*. NY, 1988. p. 62.
35 Peter Drucker. *The Concept of the Corporation*. NY, 1946. p. 5.
36 Hubert Horatio Humphrey quoted in: Michael J. Sandel. *Democracy's Discontent*. Cambridge, MA, 1996. p. 244.
37 Robert H. Bork. *The Antitrust Paradox*. NY, 1978. p. 5–6, 422.
38 John K. Galbraith. *American Capitalism*. Boston, 1956. p. 91; Lino A. Graglia in: *Public Interest*. Summer 1991. p. 64.
39 John K. Galbraith. *American Capitalism*. Boston, 1956. p. 48; John K. Galbraith. *Interviews with John Kenneth Galbraith*. Jackson, MS, 2004. p. 115: "How can an industry that brings so much intelligence to bear on the technical production and marketing aspects of its affairs be so bad in the case it makes for itself to the public?"
40 John K. Galbraith. *The New Industrial State*. Boston, 1972. p. 92–3; John K. Galbraith in: *Perspectives USA*. v. 13 (Autumn 1955). p. 69.

41 Rosabeth M. Kanter. *When Giants Learn to Dance*. NY, 1989. p. 17.

42 Joseph H. Boyett, Henry P. Conn. *Workplace 2000*. NY, 1991. p. 39.

43 Carmen Sirianni and Andrea Walsh in: Alan Wolfe. *America at Century's End*. Berkeley, CA, 1991. p. 426; Michael Ray in: *New Age Journal*. Feb. 1995. p. 57.

44 Tom Peters in: *New York Times Magazine*. Mar. 5, 2000. p. 83: "I want my company to be so attractive"; Barbara Ehrenreich. *Bait and Switch*. NY, 2005. p. 230–31: "passion"; Michael Lewis. *The Money Culture*. NY, 1991. p. 167: "the fire in your belly."

45 Thomas Frank. *What's the Matter With Kansas*. NY, 2004. p. 133–34; Thomas Frank. *One Market Under God*. NY, 2000. p. 173, 177, 184–85; David Brooks. *Bobos in Paradise*. NY, 2000. p. 111, 113.

46 David Brooks. *Bobos in Paradise*. NY, 2000. p. 133–34.

47 *New York Times Magazine*. Mar. 5, 2000. p. 68–69.

48 David Brooks. *Bobos in Paradise*. NY, 2000. p. 132–33.

49 Joseph Heller. *Something Happened*. NY, 1974. p. 13–59: This is a wild exaggeration (understandable from the author of *Catch-22*), but still only an exaggeration, of conditions in the pre-1980s office.

50 Jill Andresky Fraser. *White-Collar Sweatshop*. NY, 2001. passim; Jack Welch. *Jack*. NY, 2001. p. 158–161, 434; David Callahan in: *Nation*. Feb. 9, 2004. p. 15; Louis Uchitelle. *The Disposable American*. NY, 2006. p. 143.

51 Irving Kristol. *Two Cheers for Capitalism*. NY, 1978. p. 82, 117; Gregg Easterbrook. *The Progress Paradox*. NY, 2003. p. 268–69; *Fortune*. Apr. 28, 2003. p. 57.

52 Richard J. Murnane, Frank Levy. *Teaching the New Basic Skills*. NY, 1996. p. 31–33.

53 Aaron Bernstein in: *Business Week*. Dec. 1, 2003. p. 54–58; Paul Krugman in: *Nation*. Jan. 5, 2004.

54 Ralph Gardner. "Failing at Four." *New York*. Nov. 15, 1999.

55 David Brooks. *On Paradise Drive*. NY, 2004. p. 142.

56 Rachel Toor. *Admissions Confidential*. NY, 2001. p. 2–3, 124–25.

57 Ralph Gardner, Jr. "Give Me Harvard or Give Me Death." *New York*. Mar. 18, 1996; David Brooks. "The Organization Kid." *Atlantic*. Apr. 2001; David Brooks. *On Paradise Drive*. NY, 2004. p. 154–55.

58 Christopher Clausen in: *American Scholar*. Autumn 2004. p. 134.

59 Laura Kipnis in: *Harper's*. June 2005. p. 88: "available, cheaper"; Norman Mailer quoted by David Denby in: *New Yorker*. Apr. 20, 1998. p. 70: "gilt-edged peons."

60 David Brooks. "The Organization Kid." *Atlantic*. Apr. 2001. p. 41.

Chapter 8

1 William M. Gouge. *A Short History of Paper Money and Banking in the United States*. Philadelphia, 1833. pt. 1, p. 96.

2 Jane Walmsley. *Brit-Think, Ameri-Think*. NY, 1987. p. 97.

3 Geoffrey Gorer. *The American People*. NY, 1964. p. 159.

4 James Boswell. *Life of Samuel Johnson*. NY: Modern Library, n.d. p. 644 (May 1776): "the cry against the evil of luxury"; Benjamin Franklin (1784) quoted by Gordon S. Wood in: *New York Review of Books*. June 9, 1994. p. 49: "Is not the hope of one day being able to purchase and enjoy luxuries a great spur to labor and industry?"

5   Robert T. Kiyosaki. *Rich Dad, Poor Dad*. Paradise Valley, AZ, 1998. p. 156, 159, 164; Jacob M. Schlesinger in: *New York Times*. June 29, 1999. p. A6.

6   Royall Tyler. *The Contrast* (1787). Act 4, scene 2 in: Jeffrey H. Richards. *Early American Drama*. NY, 1997. p. 48; Thomas Jefferson. Letter to Madame de Corny. Apr. 2, 1790.

7   Esther B. Aresty. *The Best Behavior*. NY, 1970. p. 241; Raoul de Roussy de Sales. "Love in America." *Atlantic*. May 1938. p. 645–651; Blanche McCrary Boyd. *The Redneck Way of Knowledge*. NY, 1982. p. 83.

8   Thomas Paine. "Reflections on Unhappy Marriages" (1775).

9   Ralph Waldo Emerson. "Give All To Love" (1846); Leon R. Kass in: *Public Interest*. Winter 1997. p. 42.

10   Edmund Wilson in: *New Republic*. Oct. 26, 1938. p. 342–43: "the rights of the heart"; "Is the Freer Granting of Divorce an Evil?" *Papers and Proceedings [of the] American Sociological Society*. v. 3 (1908). p. 171.

11   Horace Taft quoted in: Arlene Skolnick. *Embattled Paradise*. NY, 1991. p. 44.

12   Hal D. Sears. *The Sex Radicals*. Lawrence, KS, 1977. p. 20; Michael McGerr. *A Fierce Discontent*. NY, 2003. p. 59; Charles Larsen. *The Good Fight*. Chicago, 1972. p. 175, 177.

13   Lawrence K. Frank. *Society as the Patient*. Port Washington, NY, 1969 (originally published in 1936). p. 7–8.

14   Ferdinand Lundberg, Marynia F. Franham. *Modern Woman, The Lost Sex*. NY, 1947. p. 364–65, 370–71; William H. Whyte. *The Organization Man*. NY, 1956. Appendix: "How to Cheat on Personality Tests."

15   "It's Smart to be Stupid." *Collier's*. Feb. 5, 1949. p. 21; Leo Gurko. *Heroes, Highbrows, and the Popular Mind*. NY, 1953. p. 54.

16   Benita Eisler. *Private Lives*. NY, 1986. p. 169–170; Ted Morgan. *On Becoming American*. Boston, 1978. p. 43.

17   John Steinbeck. *Travels with Charley*. NY, 1962. p. 128; Arthur M. Schlesinger, Jr., quoted in: Paul Leinberger, Bruce Tucker. *The New Individualism*. NY, 1991. p. 31; Osbert Lancaster quoted in: *Time*. May 5, 1958. p. 67.

18   Henry Fairlie. *The Spoiled Child of the Western World*. NY, 1976. p. 128; Irving Howe. *Steady Work*. NY, 1966. p. 334–35; Samuel Koenig. *Sociology: An Introduction to the Science of Society*. NY, 1963. p. 331: "the real problem."

19   Paul Tillich in: Keith Davis, William G. Scott. *Readings in Human Relations*. NY, 1959. p. 461.

20   Richard Hofstadter. "The Age of Rubbish." *Newsweek*. July 6, 1970. p. 23.

21   Tom Wolfe quoted in: Arlene Skolnick. *Embattled Paradise*. NY, 1991. p. 140.

22   David Halberstam. *The Fifties*. NY, 1993. p. 576.

23   Charles A. Reich. *The Greening of America*. NY, 1970. p. 356.

24   Blanche W. Cook quoted by Elizabeth Fox-Genovese in: *Times Literary Supplement*. May 21, 1993. p. 13.

25   John Bradshaw quoted in: Wendy Kaminer. *I'm Dysfunctional, You're Dysfunctional*. Reading, MA, 1992. p. 15; Sam Keen quoted in: *American Spectator*. Jan. 1992. p. 66.

26   Warren G. Bennis, Philip E. Slater. *The Temporary Society*. NY, 1968. p. 89.

27   David Brooks. *Bobos in Paradise*. NY, 2000. p. 238.

28   John J. DiIulio in: *Public Interest*. Winter 1995. p. 35; *Atlantic*. Dec. 2004. p. 70; Gertrude Himmelfarb in: *Public Interest*. Spring 1998. p. 10.

29   John B. Judis in: *New Republic*. Sept. 12, 1994. p. 23.

30 Ramesh Ponnuru in: *National Review*. Mar. 22, 1999. p. 41–43.

31 Sheldon Wolin in: Stephen Macedo. *Reassessing the Sixties*. NY, 1997. p. 136; Thomas Frank. *What's the Matter with Kansas*. NY, 2004. p. 121; Frank Rich. "Naked Capitalists." *New York Times Magazine*. May 20, 2001. p. 51 ff.

32 Katha Pollitt in: *Nation*. July 26 & Aug. 2, 1999. p. 10; Christopher Caldwell in: *New Republic*. Apr. 5, 1999. p. 15; Virginia I. Postrel in: *Reason*. Apr. 1997. p. 4.

33 Robert H. Bork. *Slouching Toward Gomorrah*. NY, 1996. p. 152.

34 Democratic Leadership Council. *Idea of the Week*. July 12, 2002; David Sirota in: *Nation*. Jan. 3, 2005. p. 19.

35 Christopher Caldwell in: *New Republic*. Apr. 5, 1999. p. 15.

36 David Brooks. *Bobos in Paradise*. NY, 2000. p. 84, 259; Dinesh D'Souza. *Letters to a Young Conservative*. NY, 2002. p. 214.

37 *National Review*. Mar. 16, 1992. p. 10; David Brooks. *Bobos in Paradise*. NY, 2000. p. 238.

38 Herbert Kohl. *The Discipline of Hope*. NY, 1998. p. 331.

39 David Brooks. *On Paradise Drive*. NY, 2004. p. 140.

40 David Brooks in: *Atlantic*. Jan. 2002. p. 21.

41 Joanne B. Ciulla. *The Working Life*. NY, 2000. p. 186; Kay S. Hymowitz. "Ecstatic Capitalism's Brave New Work Ethic." *City Journal*. v. 11 (Winter 2001); Michelle Cottle. "The Heart Beat." *New Republic Online* (www.tnr.com). Feb. 14, 2003.

42 Mark Lilla on Daniel Bell in: *New York Review of Books*. May 14, 1998. p. 7.

43 David Brooks. "Manly Upscale Proles." *New York Times*. Oct. 4, 2003; David Brooks in: *Atlantic*. Apr. 2001. p. 40.

Chapter 9

1 Tocqueville. *Democracy in America*. NY, 1945. v. 2, p. 164–65 (bk. 3, ch. 1).

2 William Hazlitt. "On the Feeling of Immortality in Youth" (1827); William Wordsworth. *The Prelude*. bk. 11, line 108.

3 Felix Markham. *Napoleon*. NY, 1963. p. 177.

4 David T. Courtwright. *Forces of Habit*. Cambridge, MA, 2001. p. 178.

5 E. M. Forster. *Two Cheers for Democracy*. "Mrs Miniver" (1939): "…the class which strangled the aristocracy in the Nineteenth Century, and has been haunted ever since by the ghost of its victim."

6 Anthony Trollope. *Doctor Thorne*. ch. 1.

7 Gustave Flaubert. Letter to George Sand. Oct. 7, 1871.

8 Thomas Jefferson quoted in: Henry Adams. *History of the United States of America During the Administrations of Thomas Jefferson*. v. 1, ch. 6.

9 Leon Trotsky. *Literature and Revolution*. Ann Arbor, MI, 1960. p. 256.

10 Andrew Hacker. *The End of the American Era*. NY, 1970. p. 152: "Where is Tom Joad today?"

11 Andrew Kenny in: *Spectator* (London). Sept. 5, 1987. p. 12.

12 Marvin Olasky. *The Tragedy of American Compassion*. Washington, DC, 1992. p. 125–26; a social worker quoted in: Christopher Lasch. *The New Radicalism in America, 1889–1963*. NY, 1965. p. 149.

13 *Time*. Jan. 6, 1941. p. 58 (reprinted in: Whittaker Chambers. *Ghosts on the Roof*. New Brunswick, NJ, 1996. p. 60).

14 Lionel Trilling. *The Last Decade*. NY, 1979. p. 140, 198; Morton Hunt. *The New Know-Nothings*. New Brunswick, NJ, 1999. p. ix–x.

15 Murray Kempton. *Part of Our Time*. NY, 1955. p. 139; Richard Hofstadter. *Anti-Intellectualism in American Life*. NY, 1963. p. 141, 292; Alistair Cooke. *A Generation on Trial*. NY, 1950; Whittaker Chambers. *Witness*. NY, 1952. p. 789; Irving Kristol in: *Commentary*. Mar. 1952. p. 229: "There is one thing that the American people know...."
16 Alberto Alesina, Rafael Di Tella, Robert MacCulloch. *Inequality and Happiness: Are Europeans and Americans Different*? National Bureau of Economic Research. NBER Working Paper, no. w8198. Apr., 2001: "a sub-group of rich leftists"; Whittaker Chambers. *Witness*. NY, 1952. p. 616: "In the United States, the working class are Democrats. The middle class are Republicans. The upper class are Communists."
17 Christopher Lasch. *The True and Only Heaven*. NY, 1991. p. 455–465; Barbara Ehrenreich. *Fear of Falling*. NY, 1989. p. 120.
18 Johann Wolfgang von Goethe. Letter to Charlotte von Stein. June 8, 1787.
19 David L. Kirp in: *Nation*. Apr. 21, 2003. p. 26.
20 J. Anthony Lukas in: *New Perspectives Quarterly*. Fall 1990. p. 39; J. Anthony Lukas. *Common Ground*. NY, 1985. p. 242.
21 *Newsweek*. Mar. 4, 1985. p. 25; Thomas J. Cottle. *Busing*. Boston, 1976. p. 45.
22 Jim Sleeper. *The Closest of Strangers*. NY, 1990. p. 122.
23 Fred Siegel in: *Times Literary Supplement*. Jan. 10, 1997. p. 9.
24 Stephan Thernstrom, Abigail Thernstrom. *America in Black and White*. NY, 1997. p. 437.
25 Conor Cruise O'Brien. *The Long Affair*. Chicago, 1996. p. 199.
26 Michael Moore in: *Nation*. Nov. 17, 1997. p. 18.
27 Irving Howe in: *New Republic*. Oct. 15, 1990. p. 47.
28 Geoffrey Gorer. *The American People*. NY, 1964. p. 159; George F. Will. *The Leveling Wind*. NY, 1994. p. 270.
29 Nathan Glazer. *We Are All Multiculturalists Now*. Cambridge, MA, 1997. p. 7.
30 Morton Kondracke in: *New Republic*. Sept. 21, 1992. p. 50.
31 *New York Times*. July 27, 2001. p. A18.
32 Judith Rich Harris. *The Nurture Assumption*. NY, 1998. p. 112, 140.
33 Gordon S. Wood in: *Times Literary Supplement*. Apr. 30, 1999. p. 34.
34 Brian Thomas Gallagher in: *Nation*. June 5, 2000. p. 36; Victor Davis Hanson. *Mexifornia*. San Francisco, CA, 2003. p. 139.
35 One example among many: Daniel Moran, Arthur Waldron. *The People in Arms*. Cambridge, UK, 2003. p. 261–62.
36 Irving Kristol in: *Times Literary Supplement*. May 26, 2000. p. 14.
37 As one anthropologist discovered (ch. 6, note 4).
38 Richard Bernstein. *Dictatorship of Virtue*. NY, 1994. p. 5–6; Dinesh D'Souza. *Letters to a Young Conservative*. NY, 2002. p. 46.
39 Mary C. Waters. *Ethnic Options*. Berkeley, CA, 1990. p. 151; Christopher Clausen in: *American Scholar*. Summer 1996. p. 383.
40 Margaret Talbot in: *New York Times Magazine*. Nov. 18, 2001. p. 23.
41 Rosalie Pedalino Porter. "Why Voters in Massachusetts Overturned Bilingual Education." *Atlantic Forum* (http://forum.theatlantic.com). Dec. 18, 2002.
42 Frederick R. Lynch. *The Diversity Machine*. NY, 1997. p. 359.
43 Charles Lane in: *New Republic*. Dec. 7, 1998. p. 4.
44 *Harper's*. Mar. 1991. p. 28.
45 *Utne Reader*. July–Aug. 1991. p. 54.

46 Tom Wolfe in: *Harper's*. June 2000. p. 80; Dinesh D'Souza. *Illiberal Education*. NY, 1991. p. 212.

47 David Gelernter in: *Commentary*. Mar. 1997. p. 34; Anthony Sampson. *Company Man*. NY, 1995. p. 195; Walter Olson. *The Excuse Factory*. NY, 1997. p. 75.

48 Eric Korn in: *Times Literary Supplement*. Nov. 30, 2001. p. 36: scrabble; *National Review*. July 15, 2002. p. 12: "sportslike"; *National Review*. June 16, 2003. p. 6: Smith College.

49 Philip Roth. *The Human Stain*. NY, 2000. p. 290.

50 Dinesh D'Souza. *Illiberal Education*. NY, 1991. p. 143; Glenn C. Loury in: *Public Interest*. Fall 1995. p. 99.

51 Dinesh D'Souza. *Illiberal Education*. NY, 1991. p. 9; Nat Hentoff. *Free Speech for Me, But Not for Thee*. NY, 1992. p. 156.

52 David English in: *Spectator* (London). Oct. 30, 1993. p. 7.

53 Michael Kelly in: *New Republic*. Dec. 9, 1996. p. 6; Hanna Rosin in: *New Republic*. Feb. 2, 1998. p. 16.

54 James B. Jacobs, Kimberly Potter. *Hate Crimes*. NY, 1998. p. 43; James Q. Wilson in: *National Review*. Sept. 11, 1999. p. 20.

55 Jeffrey Rosen in: *New Republic*. Dec. 9, 1996. p. 39–40; Jonathan Rauch in: *New Republic*. June 23, 1997. p. 26; Alan Wolfe in: *New Republic*. June 1, 1998. p. 40.

56 Eugene D. Genovese. *The Southern Tradition*. Cambridge, MA, 1994. p. 112–13; Shelby Steele. *A Dream Deferred*. NY, 1998. p. 83–84; John Leo in: *U. S. News & World Report*. Nov. 12, 1990. p. 25: Egyptologists.

57 Richard Bernstein in: *New Republic*. Aug. 2, 1993. p. 16.

58 James B. Jacobs, Kimberly Potter. *Hate Crimes*. NY, 1998. p. 50–57; Andrew Sullivan in: *New York Times Magazine*. Sept. 26, 1999. p. 112; Tammy Bruce. *The New Thought Police*. Roseville, CA, 2001. p. 41–42.

59 Linda Chavez in: *Mother Jones*. Sept.–Oct. 1997. p. 41.

60 Daniel J. Kevles in: *New York Times Book Review*. May 11, 2003. p. 18.

61 Christopher Clausen in: *American Scholar*. Summer 1996. p. 384.

62 Richard Rorty. *Achieving Our Country*. Cambridge, MA, 1998. p. 82.

63 Harvey Cox. "The Market as God." *Atlantic*. Mar. 1999. p. 18–23; Thomas Frank. Address to the Commonwealth Club of California (www.commonwealthclub.org). Nov. 16, 2000: "reverse-communism."

Chapter 10

1 Larry D. Nachman in: *Salmagundi*. Fall 1980–Winter 1981. p. 219; Morton Hunt. *The New Know-Nothings*. New Brunswick, NJ, 1999. p. 21.

2 Francis Wheen. *Idiot Proof*. NY, 2004. p. 201; William A. Henry. *In Defense of Elitism*. NY, 1994. p. 5; Russell Jacoby. *Dogmatic Wisdom*. NY, 1994. p. 170.

3 Susan Haack in: *Times Literary Supplement*. July 9, 1999. p. 12; James D. Guy quoted in: Alan Wolfe. *The Transformation of American Religion*. NY, 2003. p. 179; Barbara Ehrenreich in: *The Progressive*. v. 63, no. 3 (Mar. 1999). p. 17.

4 Bruce Robbins in: *Tikkun*. Sept.–Oct. 1996. p. 58.

5 David L. Kirp in: *Public Interest*. Summer 1991. p. 27; Erich Eichman in: *New Criterion*. v. 15 (Dec. 1996). p. 80.

6 Clark Kerr. *The Uses of the University*. Cambridge, MA, 2001 (5th ed.). p. 228.

7 Martin Bernal quoted by Molly Myerowitz Levine in: *American Historical Review*. v. 97, no. 2 (Apr. 1992). p. 458.

8   Lynne V. Cheney. *Telling the Truth*. NY, 1995. p. 139; Dinesh D'Souza. *Letters to a Young Conservative*. NY, 2002. p. 26.

9   Samuel Koenig. *Sociology: An Introduction to the Science of Man and Society*. NY, 1957. p. 330–31.

10 Robert R. Detlefsen in: *New Republic*. Apr. 10, 1989. p. 20; Morton Hunt. *The New Know-Nothings*. New Brunswick, NJ, 1999. p. 22–23, 43; Larry D. Nachman in: *Salmagundi*. Fall 1980–Winter 1981. p. 217.

11 Steven Pinker. *The Blank Slate*. NY, 2002. p. 121.

12 Morton Hunt. *The New Know-Nothings*. New Brunswick, NJ, 1999. p. 16, 44–45, 114; Frederick R. Lynch. *The Diversity Machine*. NY, 1997. p. 304.

13 Thomas Frank. *One Market Under God*. NY, 2000. p. 281.

14 Bruce Robbins in: *Tikkun*. Sept.–Oct. 1996. p. 58–59: "...what is really expressed by the angry tirades against cultural politics that have accompanied the Sokal affair" etc.

15 Clark Kerr. *The Uses of the University*. Cambridge, MA, 2001 (5th ed.). p. 217; Louis Menand. *The Future of Academic Freedom*. Chicago, 1996. p. 11.

16 David Brooks. *Bobos in Paradise*. NY, 2000. p. 51–52.

17 Mary F. Corey. *The World Through a Monocle: The New Yorker at Midcentury*. Cambridge, MA, 1999. ch. 6: "The Romance of the Other"; *New York Times*. Oct. 20, 1991. p. 36; David Brooks. *Bobos in Paradise*. NY, 2000. p. 221.

18 Thomas Frank in: *New York Times*. Nov. 5, 2004. p. A31; Thomas Frank. *What's the Matter with Kansas*. NY, 2004. p. 240–45.

19 William A. Galston in: *Public Interest*. Fall 2003. p. 100–104.

20 Vera Shlakman in: *Smith College Studies in History*. v. 20 (Oct. 1934–July 1935). p. 61; John Steinbeck. *America and Americans and Selected Nonfiction*. NY, 2002. p. 27; John Podhoretz in: *Policy Review*. Aug.–Sept. 2001. p. 90–93.

21 *National Review*. Mar. 11, 2002. p. 10; "Captain Outrageous: Ted Turner '60..." in: *Brown Alumni Magazine Online*. Mar.–Apr. 2002. (www.brownalumnimagazine.com/march/april-2002/captain-outrageous.html).

22 Adam Smith. *Theory of Moral Sentiments*. pt. 3, ch. 3.

23 Ralph Waldo Emerson. "Self-Reliance."

24 Ernest Hemingway. "The Earnest Liberal's Lament" (1921); Randall Jarrell. *Pictures from an Institution*. NY, 1968, c1954. p. 220 (ch. 5, pt. 9). On p. 59 (ch. 2, pt. 4), Jarrell's satire contains a precursor to the forbearing response of high-minded people when confronted by the terrorist attacks of September 11: "we ought to hear his side of the case."

25 *New York Times*. Nov. 30, 1969. section 4, p. 6.

26 Daniel Walker Howe's review of *The Market Revolution* by Charles Sellers in: Melvyn Stokes, Stephen Conway, eds. *The Market Revolution in America*. Charlottesville, VA, 1996. p. 260; Gordon S. Wood in: *New York Review of Books*. Mar. 29, 2001. p. 18; Alan Wolfe in: *New Republic*. Feb. 10, 2003. p. 25–32; Dinesh D'Souza. *Letters to a Young Conservative*. NY, 2002. p. 114.

27 Rochelle Gurstein. *The Repeal of Reticence*. NY, 1996. p. 6; Robert B. Edgerton. *Sick Societies*. NY, 1992. p. 8.

28 Sven-Eric Liedman. *The Postmodernist Critique of the Project of Enlightenment*. Amsterdam, 1997. p. 7–8.

29 Robert B. Edgerton. *Sick Societies*. NY, 1992. p. 10, 12; Raymond Tallis in: *Times Literary Supplement*. Aug. 16, 2002. p. 6; Lawrence H. Keeley. *War Before Civilization*. NY, 1996. p. 174.

30 Mark Edmundson in: *Harper's*. Sept. 1997. p. 42: "...the exigencies of capitalism lead to a reserve army of the unemployed and nearly inevitable misery"; Frank Lentricchia in: Alexander Star. *Quick Studies*. NY, 2002. p. 31–32.

31 A. S. Byatt in: *New York Review of Books*. Nov. 30, 2000. p. 53; Evelyn Toynton in: *Commentary*. June 1994. p. 61–62; Jeffrey Hammond. "Milton at the Bat." in: Bill Henderson. *The Pushcart Prize 2001 XXV*. NY, 2001. p. 548–564.

32 Lawrence W. Levine. *Highbrow, Lowbrow*. Cambridge, MA, 1988. p. 256; Charles Taylor quoted by Andy Lamey in: *Times Literary Supplement*. July 23, 1999. p. 14; Tony Tanner in: *Times Literary Supplement*. July 14–20, 1989. p. 768.

33 Robert P. Newman. *Enola Gay and the Court of History*. NY, 2004. p. 116.

34 Martin Harwit. *An Exhibit Denied*. NY, 1996. p. 189.

35 Roger Kimball, Hilton Kramer. *Lengthened Shadows*. San Francisco, 2004. p. 133; Chester E. Finn in: *Commentary*. Dec. 2002. p. 56.

36 Alexander Cockburn in: *Nation*. Feb. 21, 2005. p. 9.

37 Alfie Kohn. "Teaching About Sept. 11." *Rethinking Schools Online* (www.rethinkingschools.com). v. 16, no. 2 (Winter 2001–2002).

38 Michael Walzer in: *Dissent*. Spring 2002. p. 19–23.

39 Peggy Noonan. *Life, Liberty, and the Pursuit of Happiness*. NY, 1994. p. 52; Chester E. Finn. "Reforming Education." *American Experiment Quarterly*. v. 1, no. 1 (Spring 1998). Minneapolis, MN: Center of the American Experiment; *National Review*. Mar. 27, 2006. p. 8–9: a rather extreme example of pedagogical guilt.

40 Richard Bernstein. *Dictatorship of Virtue*. NY, 1994. p. 278.

41 Richard Rorty in: *London Review of Books*. Apr. 8, 1993. p. 3.

42 Charles Lemert. *Social Things*. Lanham, MD, 1997. p. 58.

43 *Detroit News*. Apr. 24, 1991; P. S. Mueller in: *Harper's*. Nov. 1998. p. 20.

44 David English in: *Spectator* (London). Oct. 30, 1993. p. 7.

45 *National Review*. Dec. 31, 1999. p. 8: Hawaiian monarch; Bill Clinton. Speech delivered at Georgetown University. Nov. 7, 2001: Jerusalem in 1099; Jacob B. Levy. "Without Apology." *TNR Online*. (https://ssl.tnr.com/p/docsub.mhtml?i=scholar&s=levy043004). April 30, 2004.

46 Dinesh D'Souza. *The End of Racism*. NY, 1995. p. 477; *Economist*. Aug. 6, 2005. p. 13, 21.

47 John Dovidio quoted by Robert R. Detlefsen in: *New Republic*. Apr. 10, 1989. p. 18; Ellis Cose in: *Newsweek*. Nov. 25, 1996. p. 54.

48 Quoted by Heather Mac Donald in: *New Republic*. July 5, 1993. p. 24.

49 Catharine MacKinnon quoted by Alex Kozinski in: *New York Times Book Review*. Nov. 2, 1997. p. 46; Daniel A. Farber, Suzanna Sherry. *Beyond All Reason*. NY, 1997. p. 31–32; Paul M. Sniderman, Thomas Piazz. *The Scar of Race*. Cambridge, MA, 1993. p. 68, 86, 174.

50 J. Anthony Lukas in: *New York Times Book Review*. Oct. 1, 1995. p. 10.

51 Daniel A. Farber, Suzanna Sherry. *Beyond All Reason*. NY, 1997. p. 182.

52 Heather Mac Donald. "A Cop's Life." *National Review Online* (www.nationalreview.com/comment/comment-mac-donald072302.asp). July 23, 2002; Andrew Sullivan in: *New York Times Magazine*. Sept. 26, 1999. p. 57; Dan Seligman in: *Forbes*. Dec. 15, 1997. p. 140.

53 Mario Cuomo in: Jim Sleeper. *The Closest of Strangers*. NY, 1990. p. 151.

54 Simon Blow in: *Spectator* (London). Jan. 11, 1997. p. 11; Bernard Goldberg. *Bias*. Washington, DC, 2002. p. 103–106.

55 Alfred Lubrano. *Limbo: Blue-Collar Roots, White-Collar Dreams*. Hoboken, NJ, 2004. p. 15, 126.

56 William H. McNeill in: *New York Review of Books*. May 23, 2002. p. 57; Phyllis Katz, Dalmas Taylor. *Eliminating Racism*. NY, 1988. p. 41.

57 Dominic Lawson in: *Spectator* (London). Nov. 19, 1994. p. 9.

58 Frank Lentricchia in: *London Review of Books*. Apr. 3, 1997. p. 10.

59 Michelle Cottle in: *New Republic*. May 7, 2001. p. 27: "America's preoccupying race trauma"; Heather Mac Donald. "Appeasing the Race Hustlers." *Weekly Standard*. v. 7, no. 31 (Apr. 22, 2002). p. 27–29; Heather Mac Donald. "When Cops Err." *City Journal* (www.city-journal.org/html/eon_01_29_04hm.html). Jan. 29, 2004.

60 James Traub in: *New Republic*. Jan. 27, 1997. p. 15; Heather Mac Donald. "N.Y. Press to NYPD: Drop Dead." *The American Enterprise*. v. 11, no. 6 (Sept. 2000). p. 16.

61 W. J. Weatherby. *James Baldwin, Artist on Fire*. NY, 1989. p. 204: "I met another bunch of masochists"; Horace Sheffield quoted in: Tamar Jacoby. *Someone Else's House*. NY, 1998. p. 244.

62 Tom Wolfe. *Radical Chic & Mau-Mauing the Flack Catchers*. NY, 1970. p. 8: "These [Black Panthers] are no civil-rights Negroes wearing gray suits three sizes too big…these are real men!"

63 Gregory Rodriguez in: *New York Times*. June 3, 2001. p. WK1; Heather Mac Donald. *Are Cops Racist?* Chicago, 2003.

64 Heather Mac Donald. "Appeasing the Race Hustlers." *Weekly Standard*. v. 7, no. 31 (Apr. 22, 2002): black Cincinnati businessman: "The civil rights leadership is killing us; it's absolutely killing us"; Gerald Early. *Lure and Loathing*. NY, 1993. p. 88: Washington, DC, resident: "I hate it when niggers fuck up the motherfucking public trust, then, when they get caught, pull out their civil rights credit card and charge racism."

65 George L. Kelling, Catherine M. Coles. *Fixing Broken Windows*. NY, 1996. p. 167–68; Jim Sleeper. *The Closest of Strangers*. NY, 1990. p. 83, 85; Larry Nachman in: *Salmagundi*. Spring-Summer 1993. p. 173–74.

66 Stephan Thernstrom in: *Commentary*. Dec. 1997. p. 30–31; Sharon M. Collins. *Black Corporate Executives*. Philadelphia, 1997. p. 140–41.

67 Roger Kimball, Hilton Kramer. *Lengthened Shadows*. San Francisco, 2004. p. 233–34; Peter H. Schuck. *Diversity in America*. Cambridge, MA, 2003. p. 182; Stephan Thernstrom, Abigail Thernstrom. *America in Black and White*. NY, 1997. p. 401–402.

68 Jonathan Kay in: *Commentary*. June 2003. p. 42–43.

69 Heather Mac Donald. "The Diversity Taboo." *Weekly Standard*. v. 9, no. 19 (Jan. 26, 2004). p. 10.

70 Timur Kuran. *Private Truths, Public Lies*. Cambridge, MA, 1995. p. 231; Tamar Jacoby in: *New Republic*. Oct. 17, 1994. p. 36; *New Republic*. Feb. 2, 1998. p. 8.

71 Peregrine Worsthorne in: *Spectator* (London). July 15, 1989. p. 7: "Write about it! You must be crazy. I can't even talk about it in public"; John Leo in: *U.S. News and World Report*. Feb. 16, 2004. p. 64.

72 Stephan Thernstrom, Abigail Thernstrom. *America in Black and White*. NY, 1997. p. 404; *U.S. News and World Report*. Feb. 13, 1995. p. 33.

73 Sam Fulwood. *Waking from the Dream*. NY, 1996. p. 120.

74 Jim Sleeper in: *New Republic*. June 28, 1993. p. 12; Nicolaus Mills. *Debating Affirmative Action*. NY, 1994. p. 316–17.

75 Nathan Glazer in: *New Republic*. Oct. 23, 1995. p. 43–45; Peter D. Salins. *Assimilation, American Style*. NY, 1997. p. 171.

76 Ellis Cose. *The Rage of a Privileged Class*. NY, 1995. p. 192; Dinesh D'Souza. *What's So Great About America*. Washington, DC, 2002. p. 101–102.

77 Thomas Sowell. *Black Rednecks and White Liberals*. San Francisco, 2005. p. 203–204, 243–44.

78 Nathan Glazer in: *New Republic*. Oct. 13 & 20, 2003. p. 46; Heather Mac Donald. "The SAT Comes Full Circle." *City Journal* (www.city-journal.org/html/eon_5_6_02hm.html). May 6, 2002: "the sky will fall."

79 Francis Fukuyama. *Trust*. NY, 1995. p. 415.

80 Gunnar Myrdal. *An American Dilemma*. NY, 1944. p. 961 (ch. 44); Lawrence W. Levine. *Black Culture and Black Consciousness*. NY, 1977. p. 417–18.

81 David K. Shipler. *A Country of Strangers*. NY, 1997. p. 438; George Davis, Glegg Watson. *Black Life in Corporate America*. NY, 1982. p. 111; Thomas Kochman in: Bernard R. Gifford. *Test Policy and Test Performance*. Boston, 1989. p. 281: blacks and whites at office meetings.

82 Lee Rainwater in: *Public Interest*. Summer 1967. p. 122; Lawrence M. Mead. *The New Politics of Poverty*. NY, 1992. p. 150; George Davis, Glegg Watson. *Black Life in Corporate America*. NY, 1982. p. 39–42, 95.

83 John McWhorter. *Winning the Race*. NY, 2005. p. 215–221.

84 Andrew Delbanco in: *New York Review of Books*. Feb. 27, 2003. p. 24.

85 Francis Fukuyama. *The End of History and the Last Man*. NY, 1993. p. xii.

86 Friedrich Nietzsche. *Thus Spoke Zarathustra*. part 1, "Of the New Idol." Although the subject of this discourse is the state, its observations could be applied, with certain modifications, to any modern corporate body; Friedrich Nietzsche. *The Genealogy of Morals*. essay 1, part 14: the dark factory.

Afterword

1 Johan Huizinga. *Erasmus and the Age of Reformation*. ch. 9. "The Praise of Folly."

2 John Gay. *The Beggar's Opera*. London, 1728. act 3, scene 16.

Conclusion

1 Allan Bloom. *The Closing of the American Mind*. NY, 1987. p. 25; Christina Hoff Summers in: *Public Interest*. Spring 1993. p. 4; Gertrude Himmelfarb. *One Nation, Two Cultures*. NY, 1999. p. 122–23.

2 David Brooks in: *Atlantic*. Apr. 2001. p. 53; Kenneth Keniston. *The Uncommitted*. NY, 1965. p. 373.

3 Jean Bethke Elshtain in: *New Republic*. Dec. 22, 1997. p. 11; Charles Moore in: *Spectator* (London). May 14, 1988. p. 7; Alan Wolfe. *One Nation After All*. NY, 1998. p. 54; Richard Hoggart in: *Times Literary Supplement*. June 23, 1995. p. 15; Diana Schaub in: *Public Interest*. Fall 1999. p. 20.

4 Rosabeth Moss Kanter quoted in: Kay S. Hymowitz. *Ready or Not*. NY, 1999. p. 212.

5 Christopher Lasch quoted in: David Elkind. *Ties That Stress*. Cambridge, MA, 1994. p. 57.

6 Laura Shapiro in: *New York Times Book Review*. Sept. 10, 1995. p. 15; Laura Kipnis in: *Harper's*. June 2005. p. 83; Sandra Tsing Loh in: *Atlantic*. May 2003. p. 119.

7 Arlie Russell Hochschild. *The Time Bind*. NY, 1997. p. 40–41, 200–201; Caitlin
   Flanagan in: *Atlantic*. Oct. 2002. p. 164–65: more time on the job rather than
   with their children.
8 Michael Maccoby. *The Gamesman*. NY, 1976. p. 193.
9 Carl Elliott. *Better Than Well*. NY, 2003. p. 47–50, 309.